Letters from Manchuria
The story of Marion Young,
missionary in Japanese occupied China.

edited by Neil T. Sinclair

Published by
Little Knoll Press
First published November 2016

ISBN No. 978-0-9935078-1-6

Copies of this book can be obtained
by emailing Jenny@LittleKnollPress.co.uk
online from www.LittleKnollBookshop.co.uk
and from UK bookshops

Printed in Great Britain by
Biddles Books Limited
Castle House, East Winch Road
Blackborough End, King's Lynn
Norfolk   PE32 1SF

DEDICATION

For Helen, without whose help this book would not have been possible, and in memory of Marion, Huei Chün, Ssu Wen and their colleagues in Manchuria. Also in appreciation of their successors who built on their achievements, and those who carry on this work in their communities in China today.

The author's royalties support the Amity Orphans Programme through the Friends of the Church in China.

iv

CONTENTS

FOREWORD
by the Right Hon. Douglas Alexander

I should, at the outset, declare an interest. My own grandparents, Hugh and Isobel Garven, spent the years covered by this fascinating book in Manchuria (in Moukden) where my grandfather taught physiology and pathology at Moukden Medical College and my grandmother raised their children. So it should be little surprise that I found the letters of Marion Young an engrossing account of a part of the world and a period of history of which many of us know too little.

Marion's upbringing – in a Presbyterian Manse – is another point of connection. For, while on my mother's side of the family I come from a line of medical doctors, on my father's side of the family they were Presbyterian Ministers. When I became a Cabinet Minister I felt a definite sense that while I'd become a Minister of sorts, in terms of my family heritage, it wasn't the real deal!

This personal family heritage I think helps me understand the deep sense of service that drove extraordinary women like Marion (for as this collection of letters attests, to just how many Missionaries were indeed women) to lives of work and witness in far off lands. These letters were nonetheless still a revelation – taking the reader back to a period before the connectivity we have come to expect today, to an era where a letter took six weeks or more to reach home whether by sea or by Siberian railway. From describing the rescue of an unfortunate neighbour from the bottom of a well, to the description of negotiating the daily risks of the Japanese occupation, this collection of letters demonstrates the physical courage and psychological resilience demanded by a Missionary life in Manchuria at that time.

The book first introduces the reader to Marion's early life in Ireland, setting the scene with accounts of her upbringing and her studies, for the life of service that she chose at such a young age. Next we are introduced to the hugely troubled region of Japanese occupied Manchuria in the 1930s with descriptions of the history, people, and the church of Manchuria during that decade.

The letters of Marion Young are set out chronologically with chapters following the years up until 1941, before Marion's life after China is narrated at the end of the collection. From her first letter on Christmas Eve 1935 (written from a train bound for Moukden,

Manchuria) to her last, (written on her return to the Manse back home in Clones, Co Monaghan) on 8th November 1941, we gain a unique and highly personal account of Missionary life.

One feature of the letters that strikes the reader is how genuinely international was the community of Missionaries in this troubled region. Irish, Scottish and English missionaries joined colleagues from Canada, Denmark and the United States. This internationalism was matched with ecumenicalism. Despite the perhaps inevitable description of a schism within a local Protestant church (!) it is clear that Missionaries and members of different Christian denominations worked – and socialised – well together during this time in Manchuria.

These letters reflect their times, and indeed the censorship that was part of these times. Of course there is the inevitable, if often veiled, references to the political events in Europe hurtling towards catastrophe. Marion describes the declaration of War in September 1939 as 'a nightmare you can't wake up from.' The following year the personal impact of that global conflict is already emerging when she writes to her parents, 'If it were not for the War I'd be making my plans more joyfully, who knows what 1940 will bring forth, either here or at home?'

In truth, however, these global events tend to be in the background rather than the foreground of these letters, up until the final months of Marion's adventure when she travels back to Ireland during the Second World War. The correspondence inevitably and touchingly reflects the flow of family news between Ireland and China, such as the death of Marion's grandmother and the acknowledgement of family birthdays, and Marion's first meeting with her future husband, Rymer Cayton.

The letters also contain very human nuggets of information that give you a sense of Marion's likes and dislikes at the time. In a letter in February 1937 we discover in a description of a bus journey that Marion 'cannot stand the smell of dried fish'. In a letter written the following year, we learn that Marion 'misses home bread and butter' badly! In contrast, her love of travel, and sheer delight at discovering new locations and meeting new people, shines through on page after page.

Marion clearly took her own studies seriously – not least the hard slog of learning Chinese – but these letters reveal a young woman with an admirable zest for life – always proper and sincere, but neither pious nor sanctimonious.

I was understandably fascinated to read in a letter of 31st July 1936 that Marion had just dined with my grandparents and their 'so good mannered' children! Yet it is perhaps more revealing of her reserved Presbyterian upbringing that on the same day she wrote to her mother that she had seen but not spoken to the well-known Olympic athlete, Eric Liddell (who was himself a Missionary in China with the London Missionary Society) because 'I am content with seeing famous people at a distance, I don't like to speak to them …'

The film *Chariots of Fire*, which told the story of Liddell's refusal to run on the Sabbath during the 1924 Olympics, has since highlighted the deep Christian commitment that led so many at the time into lives of missionary service. Despite this, all too often, missionary service during this period is viewed unsparingly through the lens of imperialism. Yet what emerges on these pages is the deep respect and indeed fascination with which Marion and so many of her colleagues regarded their Chinese students and the culture and civilisation of which they were part. What also emerges is also a moving and powerful account of one woman's deep and enduring Christian faith.

The compilation of these letters is a tribute to the interest and commitment of Marion's family. They have shone a light on an extraordinary life, and illuminated a record of service undertaken in a far away land at a time of trial and tribulation. My hope is that, as we move through what many now anticipate will be an 'Asian Century', many other readers will take the opportunity to learn about and be inspired by the missionary life of Marion Young in Manchuria all those decades ago.

Rt. Hon. Douglas Alexander
Senior Fellow, Harvard University,
Cambridge, Massachusetts.

PREFACE

The letters in this book were written to her family in Ireland by Marion Young during 1935 - 1941. Her mother happily kept all those to her parents and also gathered in some to other members of the family. They were later returned to Marion, who was then living in Bristol, and over the years she looked through some of them to remind her of her years in China. She also had many photographs she had taken in China, as the Irish Presbyterian Church Girls' Auxiliary, which had sponsored her as a missionary in Manchuria, had given Marion a camera for use there.

After Marion's death in 2000, the letters and photographs passed to Helen and I, her daughter and son-in-law, as the 'family historians'. When we began to look through them we realised the insight they gave to being a missionary in Manchuria and to life there in the late 1930s and felt they were worthy of publication.

Retirement gave the time to first sort out into date order the hundreds of letters, which had become jumbled up over several moves since they were received in Ireland. The contents of each letter were then summarised and the difficult decision taken about which of the many interesting passages should be included in this book. Once this had been done, Helen read out the selected passages which I typed into the computer. Helen's contribution in this and choosing the photographs from her mother's collection has been invaluable and this book is very much a joint venture.

During the period we have been working on the letters we have travelled to China three times and visited some of the places Marion wrote about and photographed. In 2005 a tour organised by the Railway Touring Company meant that we could see some of the historic sites in Peking and Shenyang which Marion mentioned, while the steam-hauled trains though the rather arid landscape of Inner Mongolia, with frozen rivers, recalled some of Marion's descriptions.

Our next visit in 2009 was with the Friends of the Church in China and was to provinces south of Manchuria, but the rural areas of Henan and Hunan still had something in common with the rural areas of the North East in the 1930s. In Henan we saw the work of Amity, the Chinese Christian organisation, in supporting orphans' education. This recalled Marion and other missionaries' support for orphans and we are contributing our royalties from this book to support the Amity Orphans Programme through the Friends of the Church in China.

Between our first two visits to China we became members of another organisation supporting work in China, particularly in Shenyang, – the Scottish Churches China Group. At their meetings we met Jean Doyle, who was one of the four 'dearest of children, all so good mannered but full of life' whom Marion wrote about when she had been invited to their parents', Dr and Mrs Garven's, holiday home in July 1936. Jean had known Rymer Cayton, who was a colleague of her father's in the Medical College there. This book tells the important part that Rymer was later to play in Marion's life.

We are grateful to the Rt. Hon. Douglas Alexander, the grandson of Hugh and Isobel Garven, and former Secretary of State for International Development, for writing the Foreword to this book.

We have found many links between Presbyterian Missions in China and people and places we know. One is through Sunderland where we live. It was here that the decision to start a mission in China was taken by the Synod of the Presbyterian Church of England in the original St George's Presbyterian Church building, 1847. William Burns, who had travelled down from Scotland to offer himself to the Synod as a missionary to China, was immediately ordained. He established first the English Presbyterian mission in South East China, and then in 1867, the Manchuria mission which was to became jointly run by the Irish and Scottish United Presbyterian Churches. The second St George's building in Sunderland is now Stockton Road United Reformed Church, to which we belong. This contains a memorial to Margaret Dryburgh, a notable English Presbyterian Church missionary in South East China and Singapore.

Our third time in China was in 2013 with the Scottish Churches China Group. This included a visit to the Shengjing Hospital, a vast modern building, which is the successor to the Moukden Mission Hospital. A statue to its missionary founder, Dugald Christie, had just been unveiled.

The highlight of all our visits to China was to travel in 2013 to Faku, where Marion had been based, in the company of Mark O'Neill, the grandson of her senior missionary colleague there, as we describe in the Introduction. We had been able to provide Mark with photographs for his biography of his grandfather, published a year earlier. We are grateful to Mark, both for making the Faku visit possible and for the help he has given us in the preparation of this book.

We would also like to thank Frances Corkey Thompson, daughter of Marion's friend and colleague, Colin Corkey. She has edited her father's letters, *Letters from China* (which formed the basis of a BBC documentary series) and has made many useful comments on the draft text of this book of Marion's letters. Frances has also allowed us to include in this book one of the poems from her Chinese collection, *Wild Gooseberries of Hailung*.

Several others have greatly helped us in preparing this book, especially Elizabeth Young, Marion's niece. Peter Crush has provided valuable information about Chinese railways and geographical names. We would also like to acknowledge the assistance provided by the staff of the libraries of the Presbyterian Historical Society of Ireland and of the Union Theological College of the Presbyterian Church in Ireland, as well as that of Professor Laurence Kirkpatrick of the College.

Our particular thanks go to our publisher, Jenny Knowles, who has provided us with much useful guidance and help in the preparation of *Letters from Manchuria*.

The majority of the photographs in this book were taken by Marion, or are from her collection. Others, as noted in the captions, were taken by Colin Corkey. The illustrations on pages 29, 58, 111 and 165 are by courtesy of the P.A. Crush Chinese Railway Collection and that on page 349 of Matthew Dryer.

Neil T. Sinclair

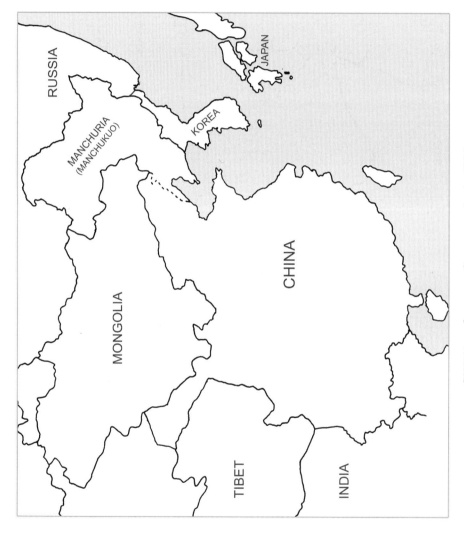

CHINA and surrounding countries in 1935.

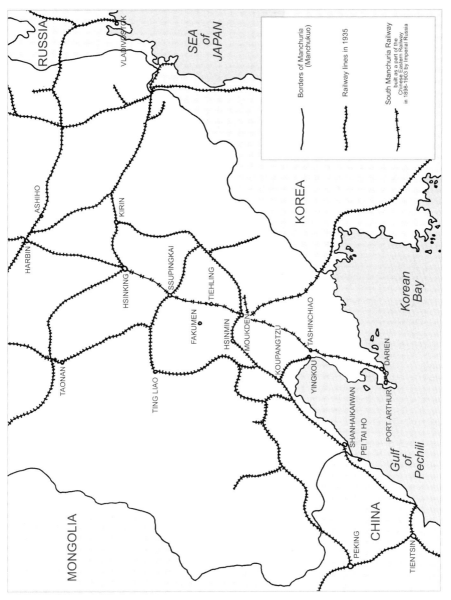

The area of north east China in which Marion worked.

Legend:
- Borders of Manchuria (Manchukuo)
- Railway lines in 1935
- South Manchuria Railway built as a part of the Chinese Eastern Railway in 1898-1903 by Imperial Russia

RUSSIA

SEA of JAPAN

VLADIVOSTOK

MONGOLIA

ASHIHO

HARBIN

KIRIN

HSINKING

SSUPINGKAI

TIEHLING

FAKUMEN

HSINMIN

MOUKDEN

TAONAN

TING LIAO

KOUPANGTZU

TASHINCHIAO

YINGKOU

SHANHAIKAIWAN

PEI TAI HO

PORT ARTHUR

DARIEN

KOREA

Korean Bay

Gulf of Pechili

PEKING

CHINA

TIENTSIN

Faku church in 1940.
Marion Young is sixth from the left in the front row. To her left are: Annie O'Neill,
Pastor Shang, the headmaster of the Church's Boys' School, and the Rev Frederick
O'Neil. This photograph was taken with the pupils and teachers of the Boys' School,
who are all in uniform as the Japanese required.
The lettering on the photograph says 'Farewell to Teacher Yang Muen'.

INTRODUCTION
In Marion's Footsteps

Our minibus sped up the dual carriage from Shenyang, the industrial capital of North East China, and past the wind turbines and the Ibis Hotel at the entrance to the town of Faku. This journey in October 2013 was very different from that Helen and I had read of in the letters of Marion Young, Helen's Mother, which were sent back home almost every week to her parents and other relatives when she was a Presbyterian Church in Ireland missionary in Faku from 1936 to 1941.

To reach Faku, Marion travelled by train from Moukden (the original name of Shenyang) to Tiehling, from where a crowded bus ran, provided the rain had not made the unsurfaced road impassable. In the winter, the trip could be quicker as the bus ran along the frozen river.

Inside Faku itself we initially saw nothing that Marion would have found familiar – there were broad streets and multi-storey flats with solar panels. Until that is we saw the cross on a stone building that was now almost surrounded by new houses; an advertising board for some under construction informed us (in English) that this was to be the 'Caesar Bay luxury complex'.

Faku Church in 2013.

1

The church, built in 1907, which must have been about the oldest surviving building in Faku, was instantly recognisable from the photographs we had looked at with Marion, which showed her as a young missionary with members the congregation. Alongside her in several of the photos were her senior colleague, the Rev Frederick O'Neill, and his wife Annie. Frederick served as the senior missionary in Faku for a remarkable 44 years, from 1898.

What made our journey to Faku even more meaningful were our companions – Mark O'Neill, the grandson of Frederick, his wife, Louise, and their friend, Helen Wu. Mark had recently written the biography of his grandfather, which told of the challenges he had to face during his years in Faku. These included having to flee during the Boxer Rebellion of 1900, when the most prominent Christian in Faku, Elder Xu, and Xu's son had been executed, the Japanese occupation of Manchuria in 1932, and finally his expulsion in 1942 after Japan entered the war against the Western Allies.

The end of the war in 1945 only brought temporary relief to the Christians in Faku, because in 1948 a new form of control appeared with the triumph of the Communist party. Any links with the former missionaries were lost and the town was closed to the outside world. It was only in 1986, that Mark, who was working for Reuters in Beijing, read in the *People's Daily* that Faku was one of 240 towns being opened to foreigners, and determined to make the visit. In spite of official unease, he made the journey and found his grandfather's church, which had been taken over by the government for a sports hall in the 1940s. Remarkably, in view of the strong discouragement of religion during the Cultural Revolution, he discovered there was still a 'Faku Protestant Association' meeting in the town.

Since 1986, Mark O'Neill had visited Faku twice again. In the visit in 2009 he had been accompanied by the Rev John Dunlop, a former Moderator of the Presbyterian Church in Ireland, and a television crew from BBC Northern Ireland who were making a programme about the Rev Colin Corkey who had been one of Marion's missionary colleagues. They found the church had been handed back to the congregation, who were busy working to make it suitable for worship again.

Before our visit in 2013, we were, however, by no means certain that we would find the church had survived. Four years earlier new houses were being built round it and indeed we discovered the adjacent Boys' School had been demolished.

Happily the church was still standing, and inside were several members of the congregation fitting polythene secondary glazing to keep the cold out during the winter months. We received a warm welcome from the members when Mark explained who we were, and they called up the minister, the Rev Yen Jingfen, who came to meet us.

Inside Faku Church: with members of the congregation around them, Mark stands in the centre at the back, Louise is to his right and in front, and the Rev Yen Jingfen, minister at Faku, and Helen and Neil are to his left. On the left of the wall can be seen part of the words 'The Glory of the Lord shall fill the whole earth', a copy of the original lettering placed there by Mark's grandfather.

We then travelled to the second, more modern, church in Faku, where the minister explained to us how there was an expanding congregation in the town. This meeting took place in the caretaker's home, one of the surviving traditional houses with a k'ang, which served as a heated bed and seat, in the main room. Adjacent to this was one of the last remaining narrow streets that Marion had commented on.

The Rev Yen Jingfen, along with Mark, Helen and Louise, in the caretaker's house. As usual with meetings in China, we were given tea to drink.

Our final visit in Faku was to the site of the Women's Compound, where Marion had lived and the school and hospital had been. While all these buildings had disappeared, the Girls' School had become the 'No. 1 Faku County Middle School'. We were greeted by pupils who were keen to try out the English language they were learning.

As we drove back to Faku, we reflected on the important links we had found with Marion's letters. It was not so much the surviving buildings, but the friendliness we had been received with by the church members and the school pupils. This welcome by the Chinese people shines through Marion's letters from the 1930s, as it did with our visit in 2013.

Marion and members of the Bible Class from the Girls' School in 1940, shortly before she left Faku.

Helen and pupils of the 'No. 1 Middle School of Faku County', the successor to the Girls' School. They are standing close to where the 1940 photo was taken.

On our first visit to China we had been, like Marion, to the Forbidden City and the Summer Palace in Beijing, and the Great Wall, as well as the Imperial Palace and the North Tombs in Shenyang. Outside these tourist areas, we had also visited Inner Mongolia. Here we saw sights that would have been familiar to Marion when she had been on her travels there with her evangelist colleagues, such as donkeys drawing carts and farmers working in the fields.

China is a rapidly changing country. Between our first visit in 2005 and our third in 2013 the number of cars on the roads in the towns and cities vastly increased at the expense of bicycles and scooters. We, like Marion, travelled on a sleeper train between Beijing and Shenyang, but now there are bullet trains between the two cities.

One of several steam hauled trains at Sanjuzi Junction conveying miners to work in 2005. A branch line from here now serves Faku, where coal mining developed in the second half of the 20th century.

In 2005 we had seen steam locomotives at work close to Faku and had travelled on the world's last regular steam hauled main line trains in Inner Mongolia. Now it is planned to extend the high speed trains into Inner Mongolia.

In the cities, shops and show rooms bear the name of Western luxury brands, such as Gucci and Rolls Royce. Even in Faku the names on several of the goods in the shops were familiar to us.

There is one area where China is not following the West, and that is that the number of Christians is increasing. We have attended church services with congregations far larger than any that is normal in Europe. This growth in Christianity would have gladdened Marion's heart.

CHAPTER 1
From Ireland to China

Marion's Childhood

Marion Cromie Young was born on 7th July 1911 in the manse of the Presbyterian Church of Ireland at Fourtowns, County Down, where her father, the Rev William Young, was the minister. He was the second generation of his family to be ordained, as his father was the Presbyterian minister of Millford, County Donegal.

After attending Campbell College, Queen's University, and the Church's 'Assembly College' in Belfast, William served first as an assistant minister, before being ordained as the minister of Fourtowns in May 1910. This appointment meant that he could now marry his fiancée, Marion Cromie, whom he had first met in Donegal in 1906 and become engaged to two years later.

His wife-to-be was the daughter of a prosperous farmer at Millvale, Rathfrilland, County Down. William later recalled that the driver who brought him up to Millvale for the wedding said, "You have the quare cheek coming about a house like this to look for a wife." ('Quare' is a rural Irish pronunciation of the word 'queer'.)

William Young and Marion Cromie, photographed at Millvale on their wedding day on 20th September 1910.

7

Marion was the oldest child of William and Marion Young; she was followed by three boys – Willie, Hugh and Frank – during the time they lived at Fourtowns. The family left there in 1917 when William became minister of Galway Presbyterian Church, where Cyril and Jim were born, and then in 1924, to Marion's joy, her two sisters – the twins Clara and Helen.

In Galway, Marion attended 'Galway Academy', which was a small Protestant private school for girls and young boys. One of her fellow pupils, Margaret Griffiths, was later to write about Marion in her unpublished memoirs:

> 'Marion was big and bonny with coal black hair which I envied ... she had a rosy round face, heavily freckled, blunt nose and wide grinning mouth; she was square and stocky and as hard as nails, with a strength of arm which could send me spinning if I chose to provoke her. In revenge we teased her and called her 'a big lump of an ugly bruiser', and I really believe we made her think she was plain; but the kind of good looks Marion had, came from good nature, and the good heart does not know how others see its goodness, so Marion never came to think she was anything better than free from deformity.'

In this photograph, probably taken at Galway Academy about 1919, Marion is standing second from the right. Her friend, Margaret Griffiths, is on the far left.

'Of course some people might say that whatever Marion was she became by force of circumstances. A girl who has a lengthening tail of younger brothers behind her is likely to have her failings continually pointed out with unkind accuracy, so she has no chance of being vain. She has to be tough as well. When she goes out to fetch Willie in for his tea and he shoots at her with his catapult instead of coming, she has to advance as if the sting of a pellet was no more than a fly alighting on her cheek. If Willie and his gang attack her in force and get her down, she must maintain an air of pleasant nonchalance while they twist her arm until a slight slackening of pressure gives her the chance to throw them off, knock their heads together and depart into the back yard cackling with scorn ... she must be bold and quick to rescue her juniors when they climb into dangerous places and cannot get down, when they set themselves on fire by smoking brown paper, or fall into the water tank.

Without the prestige of a parent, she has to keep them in a proper condition of humility and obedience; there is nothing for her to rely on but her own unaided prowess. In addition she must, of course, master the usual feminine arts; she must be able to mend clothes, buy dinners, and direct operations in the kitchen in a crisis. Marion had all this laid upon her, and she succeeded.'

The final paragraph of Margaret's writings about Marion as a girl read:

'... It was the good and simple spirit in her which made her so dear a friend to all who knew her. In her company, life seemed to be a straightforward matter, with the orderly gladness of a Bach chorale. She passed securely through chaos with serenity of heart. Fortified as she was by this serenity, it was fitting that she should become an adventurer.'

Margaret partly attributed the 'air of serene and confident strength which radiated from Marion' to the background of the Ulster farming stock of her mother's family. Another major influence was her parents' strong Christian beliefs.

Spires House, the Presbyterian manse in Galway, about 1920. A gate in the wall to the left of the tree led to a lane, at the end of which were outhouses and stables. On the other side of the lane was the walled kitchen garden.

Margaret Griffiths writes that:

> 'While the Reverend Young could be made to take his turn on the swing in the manse grounds with the children '... his coat tails fluttering in the wind and his long legs flourishing to heaven ... this was Mr Young's holiday mood; on Sunday morning we saw the other self, austere and commanding, in the pulpit, and knew that romp with us as he might he was no man to be trifled with. He had hero-worship in plenty from us all, and from Marion the most devoted and pugnacious loyalty.'

The Christian influence of Marion's home was a major reason for Marion deciding, before she was ten, what she wished to do in life, for as Margaret remembered:

> '... None of us had such clear ambitions. We were going to be film stars, actresses, spies, poets, university professors, dancers, doctors, duchesses, nurses decorated for gallantry in war, everything by starts and nothing long. Marion was going to be a missionary. It was not a day-dream, but an intention; she had no need for day-dreams.'

While Marion had a happy childhood in Galway and was bitterly disappointed when she had to leave, the city was affected by the political upheaval and armed conflict in Ireland in the early 1920s. The Black and Tans, a paramilitary force recruited by the British government mainly from demobilised soldiers in 1919 to try and maintain some control in Ireland, operated beyond any acceptable role of peace keeping, sometimes firing indiscriminately as their lorries passed through the streets of Galway. They were also almost certainly responsible for the murder of a popular pro-republican Catholic priest, Father Griffin, whose death horrified the Protestants of the town. It is noticeable that Marion used the code 'Black and Tans' for the Japanese occupiers of Manchuria, when she was writing home.

During this period the homes of some families who were known to have pro-British families were burnt down. On one occasion the horses from such a house were brought to the stables at the manse, which were otherwise unused.

The Anglo-Irish Treaty of 1921 did not end the violence, as conflict developed between forces supporting and opposed to the Treaty. In 1922, William Young, who was returning from Dublin where he had been attending a meeting of the Presbyterian Church Synod, found that his train home was terminated at Ballinasloe because of the danger it might be caught up in conflict between the two opposing armed groups hoping to control Galway. Anxious to return to his wife and family, he borrowed a bicycle from the local Presbyterian minister and was able to return to the manse – but only after the forces surrounding the city had slit open the heels of his shoes to make sure he was not carrying any messages for their opponents.

Being an Ulster Protestant family, the Youngs continued to feel that they were 'British' after the partition of Ireland into the Free State and Northern Ireland. In spite of the political divisions, however, they still also felt a strong allegiance to Ireland, as we find in the way Marion celebrated St Patrick's Day in Manchuria – and she certainly supported the Irish rugby team for the rest of her life!

In 1925, the Youngs left Galway when William was appointed minister of Clones and Ballyhobridge. He later wrote that this was for the sake of his children's education. Although Clones was in County Monaghan in the Irish Free State, it has been described as being very obviously an Ulster town, with large Presbyterian and Methodist churches. The Presbyterian Church had been responsible for the setting up of Clones High School, which became the main school for Protestants in the area. It was here that Marion completed her schooldays and where her siblings were educated before going to boarding school in Belfast.

Marion and William Young and family outside the Manse at Clones in 1926. Sitting on the back step are Willie and Marion, Cyril, Frank and Hugh are on the middle steps, and Helen, Jim and Clara on the bottom step.

The market town of Clones was a major agricultural centre. It had, however, suffered from the new border with Northern Ireland, which had led to the setting up of Customs posts and the loss of much of its hinterland in Fermanagh and Tyrone. William's other church in Ballyhobridge, although only a few miles from Clones, was in County Fermanagh.

Clones was also a major railway junction on the Great Northern Railway of Ireland, with through trains to Belfast and Dublin. Marion was later to compare their trains with those in Manchuria – and not always favourably!

Although she was sorry to leave Galway, Marion settled down happily in Clones. She was keen on sport, and played tennis and hockey. She accompanied her father on visits to members of his congregation and taught in the Sunday school. She also helped her mother keep the family in order and run the Manse. This adjoined the field where the Manse cow grazed, and Marion was involved in milking 'Branny' and churning the milk into butter, often with a book in hand.

During her holidays Marion went to stay with her mother's parents at their farm at Millvale, in County Down, within sight of the Mourne Mountains, or her father's parents at Millford, in Donegal. The green grass on the Mournes and the hills of Donegal would be recalled fondly when Marion was writing home from the more arid countryside of Manchuria.

Marion is seated second left in this photograph of the Clones Mixed Hockey Team. Hockey and tennis were the two sports which Marion particularly enjoyed and which she also played in China when possible.

From Student to Missionary

In 1929 Marion was admitted to Queen's University in Belfast, where she studied English, French and Latin for two years, but left before completing her degree course. She went instead to Millvale in Donegal to help look after her paternal grandmother. Her grandfather, the elder Rev William Young, died in December 1931 in his 51st year of ministry in Millvale. Clara, his wife, continued to live in the Manse with her daughter, Phyllis, until her death in October 1933.

Although there was a need for someone to help look after her grandmother, it seems surprising that Marion gave up her degree course. We do know that she did not particularly enjoy her time at university and she could have felt that a degree was irrelevant to her

13

aim to be a missionary, for which she would need to undertake other training.

Marion's childhood desire to become a missionary had certainly remained very much alive. She was an active member of the Presbyterian Church's Girls' Auxiliary. This had been set up to supplement the work of the Women's Association for Foreign Mission in the two countries in which the Irish Presbyterian Church was active – supporting women missionaries in China and India; it was recognised that they could carry out work among women there that male missionaries could not.

During 1933 Marion offered as, and was accepted as, a candidate for missionary work by the Women's Missionary Association. This was a major decision for her. It would mean that she would be thousands of miles away from home for five years before she could return on leave. She would be leaving behind those whom she was very close to – her parents, brothers and sisters, and her grandmother, Mary Cromie, who was now in her eighties.

Marion's maternal grandmother, Mary Cromie, who lived at Millvale Farm, in County Down, one of the family members to whom Marion wrote frequently from China.

In January 1934, Marion became a student for eighteen months at St Colm's, the Church of Scotland Women's Missionary College in Edinburgh, which the Irish Presbyterian Church also sent their missionaries to for training. The college syllabus included not only theology and worship, but also psychology and practical work. Marion particularly enjoyed the latter which included helping with the 'Lifeboys', the junior section of the Boys' Brigade, and visiting women, both at home and in hospital, and taking ward services there.

Marion, sitting on the far left of the front row,
and some of her fellow students at St Colm's.

The social life of the college students was something that Marion enjoyed. There was a certain amount of rivalry between the Scottish and Irish students over the international rugby matches which she referred to. She was nevertheless rather surprised to find that she had to speak about Ireland as a student from a 'foreign country'!

Marion hoped to be sent as a missionary to Manchuria in China, rather than India, the other country that the Irish Presbyterian Church had missions in. This wish was possibly influenced by the fact that her parents had considered going to China after their marriage.

In September 1934, a new student, Flora MacNaughtan, who had qualified as a doctor, arrived and Marion struck up a close friendship with her. Flora was the daughter of two missionaries in Manchuria, who were home in Edinburgh on furlough, and she was going out to serve in a missionary hospital there.

Mrs MacNaughtan arranged for Marion to attend a meeting of the Edinburgh 'Manchurian Group', an informal gathering of missionaries home on leave and retired missionaries. Marion wrote on 20th January 1935, '… they all came and spoke to me very kindly and friendly and said they envied my youth and wished me joy.' She commented particularly, 'Dr Christie (80 or over) was head of the big Hospital in Moukden. He's retired now of course, but is a very fresh looking wee man still. He has the courtly manners of the old Dr in Ramelton and he gave me a patriarchal blessing before he left.'

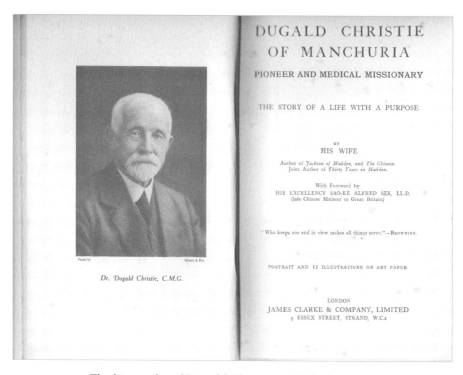

DUGALD CHRISTIE
OF MANCHURIA

PIONEER AND MEDICAL MISSIONARY

THE STORY OF A LIFE WITH A PURPOSE

BY
HIS WIFE

Author of *Jackson of Mukden*, and *The Chinese*.
Joint Author of *Thirty Years in Mukden*.

With Foreword by
HIS EXCELLENCY SAO-KE ALFRED SZE, LL.D.
(late Chinese Minister to Great Britain)

" Who keeps one end in view makes all things serve."—BROWNING.

PORTRAIT AND 12 ILLUSTRATIONS ON ART PAPER

LONDON
JAMES CLARKE & COMPANY, LIMITED
9 ESSEX STREET, STRAND, W.C.2

Dr. Dugald Christie, C.M.G.

The biography of Dugald Christie published in 1932.

At the beginning of February 1935, to her joy, Marion received a letter from the Secretary of the Women's Association for Foreign Mission to say that 'unless I do something DREADFUL she <u>thinks</u> they will appoint me to China all right! So I'm trying to be good in the meantime.' Needless to say the appointment to China was agreed and she was also chosen as the missionary to be sponsored by the Girls' Auxiliary. In May she received news that she would sail from Southampton on 18th October.

Marion completed her studies at St Colm's in June 1935. Apart from the academic study and the practical work, which Marion found valuable, she had met some of those who were to be her future colleagues in China, including Flora MacNaughtan and other Scottish students she mentions, such as Ella Gordon.

Having already received details of when she would be leaving Britain, Marion was introduced as a new missionary at the annual meeting of the Women's Missionary Association on 6 June 1935, which was being held in conjunction with the General Assembly of the

16

Presbyterian Church in Belfast. Marion's dedication service as a missionary took place in her father's church on 8th September.

The Northern Standard reported that:

> 'The evening service in Clones Presbyterian Church on last Sunday was reminiscent of the scene depicted in the Acts of the Apostles when Paul and Barnabas were separated and set apart as the first Christian missionaries. It was a service of dedication to overseas work of Miss Marion Young, eldest daughter of Rev William P. Young, the highly esteemed Minister of Clones Presbyterian Church.
>
> Everyone felt that the occasion was worthy of the presence of the Moderator of the General Assembly and accordingly the Right Rev Dr Moody was the preacher and conducted the service. The popularity of Miss Young and the visit of the head of the Presbyterian Church in Ireland brought together a very large congregation and the building was occupied to its utmost seating capacity ...'

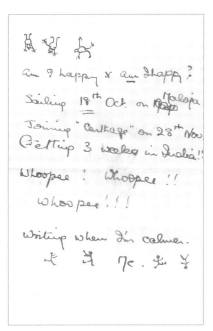

Postcard sent by Marion to her parents on 17th May 1935 about the confirmation of her voyage to China. The break of three weeks in India was to see the Rev Howard Cromie, her mother's brother, who was a missionary there.

17

Our New Missionaries

"*O COMPASS with Thy love*
The daily path they tread;
And may Thy light and truth
Upon their hearts be shed,
That, one in all things with Thy will,
Heaven's peace and joy their souls
may fill.

"Guard them from every harm
When dangers shall assail,
And teach them that Thy power
Can never, never fail;
We cannot with our loved ones be,
But trust them, Father, unto Thee."

MISS MARION YOUNG

MISS MARION YOUNG is going to Manchuria. She leaves on 18th October, and will break her journey at Bombay and spend three weeks in India visiting her uncle and other friends there. On 28th November she will join the s.s. "Carthage," on which Mrs. McCammon and her daughter are travelling to Dairen, and go with them to Manchuria, arriving about Christmas-time.

She is the daughter of Rev. W. P. and Mrs. Young, Clones, and it is not surprising that she should dedicate her many gifts to missionary service, since all her life she has lived in a home where the cause has been followed with interest and efforts made on its behalf to the point of sacrifice. She has spent a year and a half at the Women's Missionary College in Edinburgh in order to fit herself for evangelistic work when she goes to Manchuria. She has been a member of the G.A. for some years, and will be the Junior G.A. Missionary.

Miss Pearl Fullerton, B.A., comes from Mountjoy Congregation in Omagh Presbytery. She took her B.A. degree at Trinity College, Dublin, and for a time gave valuable assistance as a worker in the Victoria Homes for Children, Belfast. She also has had a year and a half at the Missionary College, and her training, and enthusiasm to make Christ known, promise to make her a useful and successful missionary.

MISS PEARL FULLERTON, B.A.

A page from the magazine of the Women's Association for Foreign Missions.

18

Later in September Marion attended a Girls' Auxiliary event when she recorded she met Dr F.W.S. and Mrs O'Neill who were home on furlough from Manchuria. In China they were to be significant figures in her life.

There was another Church event which Marion took part in before she left for China. This was the Missionary Rally in Belfast on 3rd October at which new missionaries were introduced by the Moderator and had to reply. This must have been a rather daunting experience for Marion. One of the prayers at the rally was by Dr O'Neil

The Young family photographed outside Clones Manse shortly before Marion left for China. In the back row are Willie, Hugh, Rev William and Mrs Marion Young, Frank, Marion and Cyril. Jim, Clara and Helen stand in the front.

The Voyage to China

In the middle of October Marion travelled to London, along with her parents and the twins, Clara and Helen, who had been allowed off school to see their sister off to China. They stayed with friends of her parents and did some sightseeing before Marion embarked on the P&O liner RMS *Maloja* which would take her to India on the first part of her journey to the Far East.

Marion wrote letters back to her parents, which were posted at the different ports she called in at. She commented on the different passengers she met, including Father Egan from Tipperary, who on seeing *The Spirit of Ireland* beside her, 'started to talk – what we haven't discussed! Politics religion, marriage of clergy etc. Etc. Etc. ... Neither of us gave in to the other on anything, but we parted good friends.' She later told of taking part in 'a grand Irish concert' with Father Egan and other priests, around a piano on the ship.

Marion (front left) with the other passengers from her table in the dining saloon in the Maloja.

The letters back home recounted of other passengers Marion met, including three tea planters who 'have been very nice to me – I've been circumspect Mother, 3 is a safe number!' They also told of her taking part in the games and sports on the ship and of a fancy dress ball in which she appeared as a gypsy.

On 7th November, the *Maloja* arrived in Bombay where Marion was met by her Uncle Howard, who was an Irish Presbyterian missionary in India. He was her mother's youngest brother and was only six years older than Marion. They then travelled by train, the *Kathiawan Express*, to Surat, where there was an Irish Presbyterian Mission, several of whose members she already knew.

Marion wrote enthusiastically about India as being: 'thrilling, entrancing, anything anyone ever said of it (but don't suppose I'm looking forward to China any the less). The women's stately walks, the children's bright faces and shy smiles, the interest the people take in us, the respectful cheery salaams from any Christians, the new smells, colours, noises, faces, buildings, the light on the river in the evening. ... the bells in the temple beside us when the priests are putting the monkey god to sleep ...'

Marion (left) in Surat with her uncle, the Rev Howard Cromie and, probably, one of Howard's missionary colleagues.

The Jain Temples at Palitana, in Gujarat. Marion wrote that they were 'beautiful and made of solid marble and there were thousands of pilgrims carrying offerings to lay before their special gods.'

From Surat, Marion visited the temples at Palitana, before going to stay with a friend in Ahmadabad, returning to Surat and then to Bombay. Here she joined the S.S. *Carthage*. This had brought Pearl

Fullerton, the other new woman Irish Presbyterian Missionary who was about to take up her post in India, and Miss Rogers and Mrs McCammon, who were both going to China. Miss Rogers was a former missionary and was going to visit the stations in Manchuria on behalf of the Women's Missionary committee, and Mrs McCammon was returning to join her husband in Manchuria.

Marion was able to go ashore at the ports which the *Carthage* called in at – Colombo, Penang, Singapore, Hong Kong, and Shanghai. The visit to Colombo proved to be a quiet day as Miss Rogers did not approve of sightseeing on the Sabbath, but a visit to a Missionary Home also provided a good opportunity to see the flora and fauna of Ceylon. At most of the other ports Marion was able to take advantage of the leaflets with tourist information and maps, which P&O provided. At Shanghai, however, nearly all the time was taken up with visiting the huge headquarters of the China Inland Mission. Mrs McCammon left the ship at Shanghai to travel north by train.

On leaving Shanghai there were only 20 passengers in 2nd class and eight in first, but Marion noted that the voyage 'still paid P&O because of the amount of mail and cargo'. She also remarked that the weather had turned very cold and the only opportunity for exercise was to walk up and down the deck, as games were now impossible. Some of Marion's time was taken up by filling in a huge collection of forms, which she and Miss Rogers had to complete before they could disembark in Kobe, Japan, – 'The Japs are filled with curiosity to find out all about everyone who lands.'

At Kobe they stayed for two days at a missionary hotel, 'Emmaus House', for American missionaries coming through the port. Marion wrote that 'it was surrounded by little squat houses with funny black curly tiles that sparkle all the time in sunlight and moonlight', and that the houses have wonderful flowers and plants in spite of the temperature. She also remarked that while most of the women wore traditional clothes, the men wore Western suits.

Marion and Miss Rogers completed the final part of their journey to China by the *Nekka Maru*, from Kobe, travelling first class. This was a new boat and Marion was very impressed by its facilities. She wrote home on 21st December, sitting on the glass enclosed verandah looking out on 'a perfectly glorious sunset' with '3 ranges of hills against it, each a different shade of blue, from mist to purple ...'

The OSK Line's Nekka Maru *was only a few months old when Marion travelled on it to Darien. The glass enclosed verandah where she wrote her letter can be seen.*

On 24th December the *Nekka Maru* arrived at Darien in Manchuria. It was on the train from there to Moukden that Marion wrote the first of hundreds of letters from China home to Ireland.

CHAPTER 2
Manchuria in the 1930s

This chapter describes briefly the Chinese and the Christian communities which Marion found when she arrived in December 1935. The geographical names used are those used by Marion in her letters. The modern names are given on page 35.

History

The term 'Manchuria' was used to describe the region of North East China where the Presbyterian Mission was based. As T. Ralph Morton, a former missionary, noted in his book *Today in Manchuria: the Young Church in Crisis* (1939), this was a foreign name and had no equivalent name in use by the Chinese, who instead referred to the region as 'The Three Eastern Provinces'. The region's capital was the City of Moukden, whose most notable building was the palace of the Manchu rulers who had moved south to Peking when they established the Quing Dynasty as rulers of the Chinese Empire in 1644.

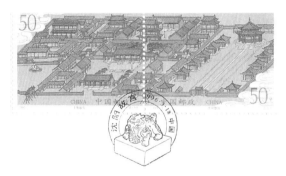

The Imperial Palace in Moukden shown on a Chinese stamp of 1996.

The history of North East China was greatly influenced by the fact that it lay close to the rival powers of Russia and Japan. As the power of the Quing Dynasty declined, Russia increased its influence in the area. In 1904-1905 the Russo-Japanese war broke out, and this resulted in Japan replacing Russia as the dominant power in the region. Areas such as the city of Harbin, nevertheless, still retained a Russian character with, during Marion's time there, around a third of its population being Russian.

In 1912, Pui Yi, the last Emperor of China, abdicated and a republic was declared. For many in the rural areas in China the nature of the government was, however, not a major issue, because power was exercised by the warlords and the robber and bandit gangs who, as Marion describes later, were still operating in the 1930s.

One of the important bandits, Zhang Zuolin, became the leading warlord in the region and was the ruler of Manchuria from 1916 until 1928, when he was killed by a Japanese bomb that was detonated under his train. Three years later, the Japanese exploded a further bomb on the railway (the 'Moukden Incident') and used this as a pretext to occupy Manchuria and establish their puppet state of Manchukuo. They installed Pui Yi as the Emperor of Manchukuo, but all control rested with the Japanese army. The Chinese magistrates were nominally in charge of towns like Faku, but the senior Japanese army officer was the real authority.

Stamp issued by the Manchukuoan government with the head of the Emperor Pui Yi, one way in which the Japanese tried to disguise the fact that Manchukuo was in fact their colony.

The People

The dominant people in the region had originally been the Manchus, but in the 18th century there was a significant influx of Han people from the south and by 1800 they formed the majority population in the towns. In October 1938 Marion noted that Faku was one of the towns that had been established by people from the south and that it differed from the Manchu cities, such as Peichen, having instead high city walls, pagodas, temples and carved gates to the old house.

Immigration from the south continued well into the 20th century. Ralph Morton estimated that in the late 1920s the influx was as much as 1,000,000 people a year. In April 1939, Marion wrote that the trains were packed with the poorest Chinese she had seen 'moving north in the spring now to open up new land'.

In addition to the Chinese, there were Mongol people in the far west of Manchuria which included parts of Inner Mongolia. There were also Russians and Japanese, who had moved into Manchuria as their countries exercised power, and Koreans who followed the Japanese after their takeover. One does not gain the impression from Marion's letters that there was any significant European (apart from Russian) or North American population in the North East China.

Mandarin was the language spoken in the region, as in much of China. In other Provinces of China there were exceptions, such as in Yunnan where the indigenous 'tribal' people, the Miao, Yao, Ko-p'u and others, had their own languages. In the Chinese languages, including Mandarin, the exact tone for a word was important because a slight variation could give an entirely different meaning, as Marion found out. Missionaries, and others arriving in China to work, were

sent to the Language School in Peking. Marion noticed that when she later visited her language teacher he was unhappy with her Manchurian provincial accent.

Marion and other foreign Chinese language students not only learned to speak and understand Mandarin, they also learned to read and write the Chinese characters. Mandarin is not a phonetic written language so every character has to be learnt by rote. Much Chinese writing was then done with a brush, a skill as hard for every child to learn as it was for the foreign adults.

Mother teaching her daughter to write the characters of the Chinese language.

The Region

Some notes, possibly written by one of the missionaries, which were among Marion's papers describe Manchuria as being an area of 360,000 square miles with a population of 20 million. The climate is also described as remarkable for its extreme coldness in the winter, being bracing in the south and bitter in the north where there could be 80 degrees of frost and the rivers were frozen for half the year. The heat during July and August was 'very great'.

The frozen Sungari River at Kirin in February 1937. The ice could be four feet thick.

The notes go on to record that the Sungari was the largest river in the area, 1,000 miles long, and that the plains of the river were rich in the productiveness of its soil. Millet was the staple crop of the area, although around Harbin wheat predominated. Soy beans were grown, and bean cake and bean oil were exported from Manchuria.

While the majority of Manchuria's population was dependant on agriculture, there was a limited amount of industry, such as coal mines, in the region. Once in control, the Japanese set about expanding the industry in their new colony and building, for instance, steelworks. There were

Tobacco sellers. Tobacco was one of the crops grown in region.

significant populations in Moukden and Harbin, and the Japanese were building a new capital at Hsinking, but most of the people lived in small towns or in the countryside.

Transport

Transport often figured in Marion's letters, both as she travelled between Faku and Moukden and then sometimes further afield when she visited the scattered churches in the country area beyond Faku.

Faku was some miles from the railway at Tiehling. When Mamie Johnston first came to take up her missionary post in Faku, in 1922, it took her two days, travelling in a 'Peking cart', a springless covered vehicle with broad wheels and drawn by mules. By the 1930s the Peking carts seem to have been replaced in towns by Russian droskeys. Marion usually travelled from Tiehling to Faku by the bus service that was then operating, although the buses would be cancelled when the unsurfaced roads became impassable after heavy rain in the autumn.

Winter brought some advantages as the bus could then travel along the frozen river and the journey was quicker.

Wang Ssu Wen, the Faku senior woman evangelist (far right), and colleagues, travelling out to the country in a cart with broad wheels for the poor roads.

There was at least one bus service from Faku further out into the countryside, but for most travel to the outlying areas the missionaries and evangelists had to walk, cycle or travel in a farm cart.

There was a good network of railways in Manchuria, the earliest parts of which reflected the struggle between Russia and Japan for dominance in the region. The Russians had built the Chinese Eastern Railway to link up with their railway system, but had to cede the section from Changchun (which they renamed Hsinking) to Port Arthur to the Japanese after the war of 1905. This became the 'South Manchuria Railway'. The remainder of the line later passed into Japanese control in 1935. There was an 'explosive' growth of railways in Manchuria, first by the Chinese during 1920 to 1930 and the by the Japanese in the years to 1938.

South from Moukden was the line to Peking, which was largely built with British finance and by British engineers. These engineers had been responsible for the development of Pei Tai Ho, served by a branch line, as a holiday resort popular with the Manchurian missionaries and during the almost unbearable heat of the summer.

As well as providing passenger services between the main centres of population in the region, a service which Marion took good advantage of, the railways provided essential transport for produce and other goods. Problems with supplies occurred when the Japanese commandeered the use of the railways for moving troops and military equipment. Some goods, particularly to places on the Sungari, were still moved by river transport.

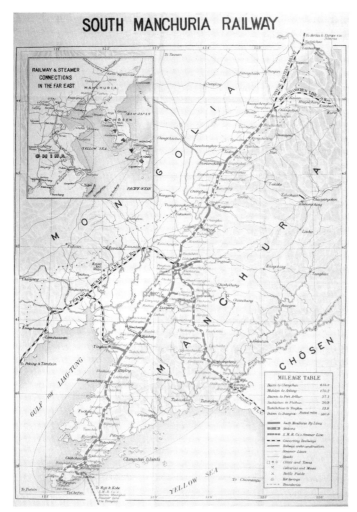

SOUTH MANCHURIA RAILWAY

Map of the South Manchuria Railway in 1917 showing several of the towns mentioned by Marion in her letters. The railway network in Manchuria had greatly expanded by the mid 1930s.

A station scene, probably between Moukden and Peking as the wagon on the right lettered 'P.N.' is from Pei-Ning Railway which linked both cites. The steel coal wagon on the right has the logo of the Kailan Mining Administration, which, along with its logo, still survives in 21st century China.

The Church in Manchuria

When Christianity came to the North East of China there were other well-established religions. In Faku there were Taoist Buddhist and Muslim communities. The main religious emphasis of many of the people living in the area seems from Marion's letters to have been the worship of household gods and ancestors, while prayers were also offered at outdoor shrines.

A street shrine at the base of a sacred tree in Tiehling, with women in prayer before it. The cloths on the walls are offerings.

Roman Catholic missionaries arrived in Manchuria in 1838. The Catholics had a cathedral in Moukden, as well as missions in other areas of the region, including Faku which was staffed by French Canadians.

The Presbyterian mission in Manchuria was initiated by William Burns, a Scots-born missionary of the Presbyterian Church of England. Burns, who had worked in China since 1847, moved north to Newchang, Manchuria, in 1867 and encouraged the Irish Presbyterian Church to establish a mission there. Sadly, he died before the first two Irish missionaries, Revd Hugh Waddell and Dr Joseph Hunter arrived in Newchang in 1869.

In 1873, the United Presbyterian Church of Scotland sent their first missionary to Manchuria, the Rev John Ross, who was later to translate the Bible into Korean. A division of the area where the Irish and Scottish Churches would work was agreed, and in 1891 they formed a single 'Manchuria Presbytery'. In 1896, the Danish Lutheran Church began work in the region in co-operation with the Presbyterian mission, and became formally linked with it in 1918. As Church union in Scotland progressed, the United Presbyterian Church became the United Free in 1903, and then in 1929 the United Free joined with the Church of Scotland.

The Canadian Presbyterian Church had its own mission in Manchuria from the 1920s and had links with the Irish and Scottish mission. There were also missionary stations of other denominations and several independent Chinese churches, some of which had been formed by secessions from the churches established by the missionaries.

For the first part of Marion's time in China there were 25 stations, each staffed by Irish, Scottish or Danish missionaries, but later the Scots and Irish worked together in each other's missions.

In addition to the mission stations, which had schools attached, the Irish and Scottish Presbyterians established a theological college for Chinese pastors in 1902, in the city of Moukden. A dispensary, which developed into a major hospital, was established in 1883 in Moukden by Dr Dugald Christie, who also founded a medical college, run by the Church of Scotland, in 1912. Several of the other stations also had hospitals. As well as providing services to the local people, the schools and hospitals were seen as ways in which the Chinese might become engaged with Christianity.

The hospital founded by Dugald Christie (whose bust is inset in the photograph) is the low building on the left and the medical college is the large building on the right.

The governing body of the Scottish Irish Presbyterians was the 'Manchuria Conference', to which all missionaries and their wives belonged. The Danish and Canadian missionaries in Manchuria also sent delegates to this. The Manchuria Conference met every January in Moukden after the separate Council Meetings of the Scottish and Irish missionaries.

Alongside this was the annual meeting of the Synod of Manchuria, which was held in July and was where the Chinese ministers and evangelists, who formed the majority of the Christian workers in Manchuria by the 1930s, met. Liu Chuen Yao was the first Chinese man to be ordained as a minister in 1896 and three years later he was elected Moderator of the Manchuria Presbytery. The Synod had several missionary members, but the Conference had no Chinese members.

There were many Chinese Christians by the beginning of the 20th century, and when the Boxer Rebellion against western influence in the country broke out in 1900, Christians were targeted. While some renounced their faith, 332 Christians were killed in Manchuria and the missionaries had to flee from their stations. A multi-national force crushed the uprising. . The Church recovered from the Boxer Rebellion and in 1908 there was a religious revival in Manchuria which spread from Korea.

A section of the plaque in the church at Faku commemorating the six Christians killed in the town during the Boxer rebellion.

The Synod of Manchuria became part of the 'Church of Christ', a union of several of the Protestant churches in China, which was formed in 1927. This connection was severed, however, when the Japanese created Manchukuo and ended many of the region's links with the rest of China. The Japanese were also suspicious of Churches, and Chinese Christians began to suffer for their faith.

The Synod was now subject to attendance by the police and discussion of any government order would have attracted repressive action. The Conference, being solely composed of Europeans, avoided this attention.

It was into this uneasy situation, caused by the Japanese occupation, that missionaries arriving newly in to Manchuria were plunged. No wonder that Marion shows in her first letters from Manchuria an element of what we today would call culture shock.

Marion's letters

The distance was great and the time it took for letters to get 'home' was often 6 weeks or more, but communication by post was both the vital link with family and the way to inform the people who supported the missionary work in 'far off lands'. When Marion arrived in China she was at last in the place that she had long dreamed of and her, often long, letters were full of the experiences she wanted to share. The main text of this book is comprised of extracts from these, which unless indicated otherwise, are complete paragraphs.

In some cases the punctuation has been altered, but otherwise the extracts are as Marion wrote them. She always used figures e.g. 5 rather than five, probably to save time in writing letters, often at the end of a very busy day. We have also left terms such as 'English' when it clear that Marion meant 'British'.

Marion wrote mostly to her family, whose names are listed below, along with their locations as in 1936:

Dad and Mother – the Rev William and Mrs Marion Young, who lived in Clones, County Monaghan.

Willie or **W.A.** – William, Marion's oldest brother, who was at the time a medical student at Queen's University, Belfast.

Hugh – Marion's second brother, who was at the time a theological student at Magee University College, Londonderry.

Frank – Marion's third brother, who was at Campbell College boarding school, Belfast.

Cyril – Marion's fourth brother, also at Campbell College boarding school, Belfast.

Jim, **Jim Bug** or **J.D** – Marion's youngest brother, James, also at Campbell College boarding school, Belfast.

Boys – the above four younger brothers.

The Twins – Marion's sisters, Clara and Helen, the youngest of her siblings, at school in Clones.

Grandma – Mrs Mary Cromie, mother of Mrs Young, who lived at Millvale Farm in County Down.

Place names in China, then and now

Some names of towns and cities, such as Faku, which Fakumen was usually shortened to, have kept their original names. The names of others have changed. The names used by Marion sometimes varied, as indeed did those on the maps of the time, particular as the name could be given in one word or two or three words.

Listed below are some of the geographical names used by Marion, alongside their present day names:

Ashiho – now Acheng

Chefoo – now Chify

Darien – now Dalian

Ern Niu So K'uo – now Erniusuokou

Great Stone Bridge Junction or Tashihchiao – now Dashiqiao

Haichneng – now Heishen

Hsinmin – now Xinbin

Hsinking or Xinming – now Changchun (name pre-Japanese occupation)

Kamping – now Kanping

Kirin – now Jilin

Ko Pang Tzu – now Goubangzi

Liao Yuan or Chung chia Tu'un – now Shuangliao

Moukden or Mukden – now Shenyang

Nanking – now Nanjing

Paimingcheng – now Baimingcheng

Pei Tai Ho – now Beidaihe

Peiping Pekin or Peking – now Beijing

Peichen or Kwangning – now Guangning

Shangaikwan – now Shanhaiguan

Sian – now Xian

Ssupingkai – now Siping

Sungarir River – now Songari River

Tawa – now Dawa

Tiang Liao – now Tongliao

Tiehling – now Tieling

Tientsin – now Tianjin

Tung Chiang K'ou – now Tongiangkou

Yinkow or Newchang – now Yingkou

CHAPTER 3
1935 and 1936

C/o Miss Hudson
West Moukden
In the train bound for Moukden
24th December 1935

To Dad and Mother

See my address – I can't imagine I'm here at last. Does it seem possible to you? We've know there was a place called Moukden for so long and in about 3 hours I going to see it.

I've just been thinking how easily the way has opened up before me, how happy this journey has been, how Clones folk with their kindness made my stay in India easy for my pocket and thinking how little I deserved it. Lots of other girls have fought their way out here ...

I've been realising too what home and all the kindly restraints of it have done for me and what too much liberty can do for people – I've met many folks since I left home who have missed that – and missed a lot.

I've found I've been respected because I was 'stiff' about certain things in the boat and wasn't liked any the less for it I think. I know I don't lack friends all the time and among the rowdy element too.

Well, all this isn't telling you what Manchuria is like, but I've just been sitting thinking about things and I thought I say thanks to you and Dad for what home has meant to me – love and happiness – the best place in the world and the place I've always been glad to come back to.

We landed at Darien this morning and Mr and Mrs McCammon and Margaret McKeown and her husband were there to meet us ...

Marion then says that there was no problem with the Japanese passport and customs staff, but they had to wait until her luggage came up from the bottom of the hold before they could catch the train to Moukden.

As we come up in the train I've been watching the country – it is all so different from anything I've ever seen. Brown and bare, the only spot of colour being snow and ice and now and then patches of pine or fir.

The hills are bare red-brown earth, what grass there is yellow and dry and short, and the fields have little in them but the still little stumps of the cut millet crop ...

I'm glad I'm here and not in India – the people I've had anything to do with are friendly and as easily amused as children. In shops and with porters and in restaurants I've liked what I've seen of them.

Marion recounted here the great fun they had had at the station with the staff, which had resulted in them being waved off on the train by 12 or 14 laughing porters.

On Christmas Day Marion attended the West Church in Moukden. Moukden had been the capital of Manchuria and the place where the Manchu rulers, who had in 1644 become emperors of all China, had their original palace. While Moukden, a large industrial city, was the biggest in Manchuria, the Japanese were establishing a new capital for Manchukuo at Hsinking.

The West Church photographed in 2013.

c/o Miss Hudson,
West Moukden
26th December 1935

To Dad

Marion described the Christmas Day service at West Church in Moukden:

… The church was beautifully decorated and there is a boy at the Theological College, an artist, who did some lovely panels in black and yellow of the Christmas story for the walls. The church was packed, the main body is bigger than ours by half the length and there is an annexe (that held 140 children when I was in again yesterday for another service of song). The children all sat on the floor round the pulpits, and the women and men sit separately. The greater part of the service was song, from the children, from the school girls, from the school boys, Theological boys, Theological girls, and the last two combined. All except the 'biddies' were part singing and I noticed especially in the school girls one fine alto. The combined effort of the Bible School (girls) and the Theologs *[male theological students]* was very fine indeed – unaccompanied too.

Marion then continued with what she had been doing on the 26th December:

Today has been a full one and isn't over yet. In the morning I sorted up some of my possessions and then walked to the Hong Kong & Shanghai Bank to open MY ACCOUNT – to find it closed on holiday. Moukden is a grubby place, the snow has been lying for a long time and is all covered with dust. The streets where there aren't many shops are just blank walls, for the people live in compounds and the only door is in the outside wall.

The streets are fairly whiffy in spots as a good deal of refuse is thrown out, and now and then you meet a dead dog lying around. The people are all muffled up – they look like Russians with their high fur hats – and often very dirty. They have quite cheery faces when they are talking, but very stolid – expressionless – when they aren't.

One of the droskey carriages, which the Russians introduced into Manchuria.

The traffic is mostly by horse, some donkey and a few motors – lots of bicycles. The Russians brought the 'droskeys' to China and they have remained, driven by grubby looking bandits with miserable scraggy grey horses. All this doesn't sound very cheerful – but I am interested, not doleful, over it all! The children are cheery little beggars and usually very fat and well coloured.

The following letter was written at the end of December 1935 by Marion to the Presbyterian Church of Ireland. To avoid the Japanese censors it was not posted, but given to one of the missionaries returning home on furlough. Furlough was leave for a year granted after the missionaries had completed five years in China, but it was not a holiday as they were expected to travel round their home country giving talks and helping to raise funds.

Marion refers to the arrest by the Japanese of many people, including 40 Christians, on 10th October:

… Things are none too good out here, although they are better now than before we arrived. Christians have been going through an awful time as you may know, but they have stood up to it wonderfully. The Japanese are really scared stiff of communism, and whether they do think some of the Christians are mixed up in it, or whether they are trying to get one back on the missionaries whom they hate, no one knows. The missionaries have such an influence with the Chinese that the Japs are afraid of them, and as they cannot touch the missionaries on account of British influence, they seize their friends.

One of the men who suffered most is Pastor Liu, who lives in this compound. He is one of the saints of the earth. They took him on some ridiculous charge, and he has been in prison for 73 days, just getting out on Xmas Eve. He was tortured terribly. It seems to take one right back to the Middle Ages just to hear of it. He had 8 different tortures and came through triumphantly. He had the water test, which is absolutely agony I believe – water is put under the skin and pumped in until one nearly goes mad. He had bamboo slips bound to his fingers and squeezed till the veins burst. There is no use telling you about them, it is all so beastly to think of anyone coming through such pain.

That was all bad enough, but I think he did not mind it so much as the cramped airless quarters. He was in a little room 12 feet x 6, with thirteen other men. They could not all lie down at once, and for the first month they never got a breath of fresh air. He says that for one half hour on sunny days a streak of sunlight came in, and he used to stand up and let it fall on his face while it lasted. They got only bread and water twice a day, and far too little. He was ravenous when he got out. But worst of all, they only got water once a week to wash in, and one basin for the whole room. To a sensitive man like the pastor it must have been appalling. He is a man you would like from the moment you saw him, straight-eyed, wise looking, with a humorous twinkle sometimes and such a bright peaceful look about him. He has not one resentful word to say now he has got out and he rejoices in the fact that God used his time there to convert 15 out of the fluctuating company. One man, a notorious robber, was chained next to him for some time. He wants to become a Christian when he is released.

There were about 70 Christians, men and women, taken at that time. Miss Hudson's No. 1 Biblewoman, a quiet wise girl, who never had anything to do with politics, was held for two months and her nerves are a wreck now.

One boy, a theological student, is insane after 4 days' torture, electricity played on the nerve centres, and is in the Asylum now. One or two are in hospital, and 7 or 8 are still in prison.

It is wonderful being here at this time. Who says Chinese simply become Christians because of what they can make out of it?

On Sunday December 28th, after all this time of horror, 73 men, women and children were baptised in West Moukden Church by Pastor Liu, as nice an answer to the Jap authorities as one could wish. We are all rejoicing in it.

The missionaries have all felt the strain terribly. Miss Hudson had to keep Mrs Liu and her family from going into despair, and hold the girls in the Bible School steady, for no one knew who would be taken next after the Biblewoman went.

There were several [Chinese] doctors taken from the hospital and tortured terribly. One has had to leave when he was released.

Dr Faulkner has lost her head doctor through it too, as he had to fly the country, and now they are threatening to take the Locum if he does not come back. They told some of the girls in the High School that if they did not find their brothers they were coming for them.

The missionaries are safe enough as yet, but it is just as bad seeing some of their Chinese friends taken as if it were some of themselves, and the strain is just as great.

This is not for publication, because all papers that come out are opened, and all letters that they suspect are copied, and it would all come back on the Chinese Christians.

Everyone that was released was told not to speak to the foreigner, or tell anything of what happened in prison. So they are very reluctant to give details. Mrs Liu says that the pastor has not told the half of what happened.

It is a time of great strain, but a time of great happiness too. Miss Hudson says it is just Acts *[of the Apostles]* over again, and the Church has hung together in a wonderful way, and encouraged the missionaries every way they could. She can't say enough about the way the girls in the Bible School stood up to it, and the lads out of the Theological Hall took the pastor's place in the Church. I have met several fine looking boys, with wise kindly faces.

Now don't be worrying about us – we are all safe still and our Father has us all in His Hand both here and in Ireland.

Although the Japanese claimed that those detained were involved in a Communist plot, a major reason for their resentment was the report of an international commission headed by Lord Lytton which criticised the Japanese takeover of Manchuria and concluded that Manchukuo was not an independent state. After it was presented to the League of Nations, Japan withdrew from the organisation in 1933.

The Japanese were angry about the fact that missionaries had helped the Chinese in collecting and submitting evidence to the Lytton Commission in 1932, and, while they could not target the Westerners, they could punish the Chinese whom they felt had been involved. The Rev Frederick O'Neill was known to have presented evidence. As Pastor Liu had previously worked with O'Neill in Faku, he would have been a prime suspect, which would explain his torture by the Japanese.

In his book Today in Manchuria, *published in 1939, Ralph Morton, a former Irish Presbyterian missionary, suggested that some of those arrested were under suspicion because they belonged to the One Cent Society whose members paid one cent a week for the school fees of an orphan boy. The Japanese, however, knew of a Communist society of that name in the South of China and believed the members of the Manchurian group must also be Communists.*

In the train for Pekin
3rd January 1936

To Mother

After the first two paragraphs of this letter Marion wrote 'the train was too shuggly so I had to stop' *and the letter was completed in Peking on the 5ᵗʰ. In the letter she wrote about what she had been doing before she joined the train. In Moukden she had quite a lot of entertainment, such as:*

... a big reception that Miss Hudson gave to which nearly all the missionaries came, Scotch and Irish, a luncheon party at the Stevenson's, a lunch at Mrs MacNaughtan's, tea at Dr and Mrs Garven's (Church of Scotland), a supper party at the Normal School with Irene *[Rutherford, an Irish missionary]* and her two Scotch colleagues and several guests, a night there with Irene and a view of the work in the East of Mukden, and then I started off for Hsinmin and two days with Dorothy *[Faulkner, an Irish medical missionary in Manchuria since 1927, who was in charge of the hospital in Hsinmin]*.

Hsinmin is a dreary looking spot at the first sight, it is all mud built and the country round about is a flat sandy desert. The soil is all full of sand and at certain times of the year when the sandstorms come it is just piled up against every bank and tree and wall. The sun is cheery however, and at the end of two days I began to think it could be quite attractive if you lived there – wide spaces have their own beauty and the evening lights are lovely.

While at Hsinmin, Marion attended a wedding with Dorothy Faulkner and Jenny Morton, wife of Ralph Morton who was the missionary there. Marion wrote that they were 'the only white people in a moderately large country town.'

The wedding ... was supposed to start at 8 o'clock (in the morning), but it isn't a Chinese virtue to be punctual so Dorothy warned me that we would have to wait a long time. The sun was up, but it was bitterly cold – the water in my room had ice on it in spite of the fact that a hot pipe runs through the wall. We went along to see the carriages start off for the bride from the bridegroom's house. The bride's carriage was curtained inside in red silk so that no one could see her and the outside was decorated with coloured paper of every possible shade. This was a Christian wedding remember, but old customs die hard and the customs of the country can't be changed all of a sudden without doing harm. The girl had possibly seen the boy once and had never talked alone to him. Her uncle had made the match and although the uncle has good position in a European firm in Peking and he dresses in

European clothes, he went through all the old formalities when he came to arrange the wedding with the bridegroom's go-between.

The carriages all set off, driven by villainous looking old men with fur caps pulled down over their ears and looking like pictures you see of Russian revolutionists wrapped up in their padded gowns. The bridesmaids, two Chinese girls in pretty dark green and dark blue silk gowns, came in the next carriage, and then the groomsmen with 'duncher' caps and European clothes and great scarves around their necks and chins. The 4th carriage had the two small train bearers and two little girls with baskets of coloured papers to scatter in front of the bride. While they were away for her we waited in the church and had plenty of folk to talk to – me complete with interpreter of course!

At 9.20 they arrived and the bride and groom came up the aisle arm in arm with all their attendants following. The bride is not supposed to look happy, so she came up with her head hanging and a very dejected look on her face. She had a beautiful deep red silk gown on and a pale pink veil – white isn't favoured as it is a mourning colour in China. The only things that spoilt it were the wreath of paper flowers and the bouquet with paper flowers – plus tinsel off Mrs Morton's Christmas tree. He wore English clothes and as he is dark and rather good looking he looked quite well. You know at home we think of Chinese as yellow, but I haven't seen any yellow ones yet! They are sallow skinned, but sometimes just about as brown as us when we are sun-tanned ...

But we are getting away from the wedding. The service proceeded in the usual way as at home, except that we had a band dispensing Chinese music, and that one small train bearer occasionally used the bride's veil as a hanky!

When it came to the ring the bride gave one too, but both placed their rings on the table in front of the pastor and a bridesmaid put on the groom's ring on the bride and the best man the bride's ring on the groom. It wasn't proper even then for him to touch her hand in public! Then they had to bow – 3 times to the pastor, 3 times to each other, 3 times to his mother, 3 times to hers, and at last to us in the church, and we had to rise and bow back. As they left the church they were pelted with confetti and dried peas. I was hit once or twice and I was sorry for them. I am sure they wished the peas had been boiled ones!

Photographs were taken and then we went to the bridegroom's

house before the feast began. We, Dorothy, Mrs Morton and myself, as the honoured guests, were taken into the inner room and there we had the privilege of seeing the bride change her frock! She got into a beautiful brown silk, a soft warm shade with little sprigs of pale pink on it and apple green piping around the neck, arms and hem. The trousers she wore underneath right down to the ankles were beautifully embroidered. If I had known a little Chinese I would have gone and examined them – they were gorgeous things with rich colours.

Then the feast began. We – Dorothy, Mrs Morton, the bride's mother, two other Chinese ladies and myself – sat at a little table at the top of the room. The innermost seat in a room, furthest from the door, is the most honourable and I was conducted to it as the new guest, but I bowed Mrs Morton into it and was told that I had done the right thing! The older you are, the most honourable and to be honoured.

On the menu were sea slugs, sharks fins, jelly fish, fat pork, chicken, rice in plenty, all sorts of strange vegetables, the homely cabbage, sweet potatoes – 12 or 14 dishes were on the table altogether and I had a scrap out of each I think. I ate with chopsticks too, to everyone's great amusement, but I managed to get enough into my mouth to do! The proper thing to do with the chicken bones by the way is to spit them onto the floor. I contented myself with shoving them off my plate onto the table – the Chinese table when a meal is over is a nasty looking mess. The other guests, I forgot to say, were all seated cross-legged on the k'ang by round little tables with short legs – we had chairs provided for our table. At one point the bride and groom came in and made their bows to us, but they, poor dears, weren't allowed to eat until everyone had been fed and then they would eat in different rooms, he in the men's, she in the women's.

How would you like to be married to a man you had probably never spoken to and of whom you certainly knew very little and to have to start life together and learn everything about each other after you were married? That is what living in a heathen country means for India – Africa – China, all marriages are arranged and it will take it several generations of Christianity to change it, even in Christian homes.

At Hsinmin station Marion joined three other women missionaries who were already on the train to Peking (also known as 'Pekin' and 'Peiping') where she was going to attend language school:

We travelled down to Pekin in comfort in a 2nd class sleeper – 3rds were all packed out – and arrived here yesterday (Sat) morning at 9.30. The train going out from Pekin on the same line was boarded by bandits some distance up the line and quite a number of people injured. However, the guard, there is always an armed guard on the trains now, chased them off and no one was very seriously hurt. It is exciting to have been as near things as that, but we were selfishly glad it didn't happen during the night instead of the day.

Pekin is a glorious place. I haven't seen much of it yet, but the streets are wide and the houses and shops all so interesting-looking that it is a pleasant change after Mukden. There is more colour about everything and there isn't the same grime in the air which makes Mukden so grubby.

From the beginning of January to the end of June Marion attended the College of Chinese Studies in Peking, learning both the spoken and written language. Her class included missionaries from New Zealand, Southern USA and England, and British Embassy staff who were being trained as interpreters. While there she had the opportunity to observe different aspects of life in the city, including the Temple Fair:

College of Chinese Studies
Peiping
24th January 1936

To Mother

The Temple Fair, which Marion attended in Peking.

… It is a fair held once a month on the Old Temple grounds just about five minutes' walk from here and I <u>did</u> wish you were here. It is extra-interesting as it is Chinese New Year this week, today is New Year's Day and a holiday, the biggest in the year for them. The fair spreads over a big piece of ground and all the colours of the rainbow light it up in paper lanterns – kites made like dragons, prawns, beasties of every kind – and ordinary ones like kites of course. All that action is interesting, but we dived through it and went to the curio part – you would have gone ramping raving mad, mother o' mine, if you could have seen those stalls. Great willow pattern plates about 9 ins in radius, apple green bowls and platters in heavy heavy stoneware with the pattern right in the article, not laid on – jade, porcelain of every weight from eggshell upwards – colours in dragons and phoenixes, flowers and strange beasties that just made you want to stand and gape for hours, brass ware, white brass, silver, pewter, jewels of every kind, pictures, tapestries, hard wood, black wood, great jars of some wonderful red brown stone shot with gold gleams that I just longed for – oh dear! Why can't we gather up all that beauty to enjoy all the time.

The brass shops are the loveliest places. I went to Brass Street and Embroidery Street with Flora yesterday. I wanted book ends and got nice ones that collapsed flat for packing ... The embroidery shops, especially where they sell old stuff, are just breath-taking – the blending of colours is an art they know from A to Z in China, and the hand done wall tapestries are enough to make anyone break the 10th commandment. 'Pekin stitch' is a lovely thing and later on when I can find out more about it I want to send a piece home.

The front of what this commercial photo describes as a 'sacrificial articles shop' in Peking.

It is great fun buying things here, in the Market and all the smaller shops you never think of paying the price asked. I bargained at the Temple Fair for a piece of matrix jade and got it for 80c when he asked $4.50 for it. You look over a thing and don't pick it up unless you are definitely interested. You only ask a price if you are really thinking of buying it and then put it down quietly and move away or make a loud disgusted noise if you are a rather low class China man or woman. The dealer trots after you and takes a dollar off, you take two or three off and if he immediately trots back and puts it down, you know it <u>is</u> worth more. Then it is up to you to raise your price or lose it. They often ask you to name your own price and if you do you have to take it – that is a binding law – if the dealer thinks it is worth its while. The chances are an unwary customer will offer more than it is worth and then of course he has you.

College of Chinese Studies
Peiping
6th February 1936

To Dad and Mother

We had a very exciting day on Tuesday. Sometime each term a crowd cuts classes for a day and goes off to see the Great Wall. The teachers don't mind as long as you get the new words up before you come to class next day. Our party was an American girl – a visitor, a Dr Stahl from California – a globe trotter, the three English Baptist boys from my class, an American nurse, Flora and myself. We got up at 6, breakfasted and got to the station shortly after 7 o'clock. We travelled 3rd and the whole journey only cost 3/6 including tips, donkey rides and everything.

The day was perfect, no wind and brilliant sunshine. The train was most amusing and everyone in our 'carriage' – a room with wooden benches seating about 20, had as much fun out of us as we had out of the journey. The train crawled along, went into sidings to let another pass, stopped at deserted stations for no apparent reasons and meandered backwards now and then. We bought peanuts, fruit and jondsas (meat and veg dumplings) at the stations and ate them Chinese fashion – out of our hands. Madge, one of the Baptists, got left behind when he was out looking for more peanuts once and he chased the train along the line, egged on by our howls of laughter, only to have to jump out of the way of the train when it started to back. Then, what made us laugh even more, the man wouldn't let him on again until we were back into the station, so Madge had to trot meekly back alongside!

The group from the Language School at the Great Wall.

Marion is seated in the back row between two of the Baptist missionaries. One of them, Bill Upchurch, who is to the right of Marion, wrote in his autobiography, A Prevailing Wind, *that among the other members of the class* were 'an Irish girl and a Scots lady doctor'. The *latter was Marion's friend from St Colm's, Flora MacNaughtan (seated in the centre of the front row).*

I'll have one or two snaps of the wall for my next letter I hope. It is a wonderful spot, started 200 or 300 years before Christ, the stones look as fresh as if they had been laid yesterday. Mongolia lies on one side of the part we were at, so just to see what it was like we went through one of the great gates, where the camels pass through on their way to Peking laden with wool and grain, and stood in Mongolia. We rode donkeys. I had a big black fellow as meek as Moses who trotted along at a great rate on the level spots and picked his steps amongst the rocks like a ballet dancer.

What a day! I won't forget that long wall winding like a snake over the bare brown hill with every gate guarded by a big fortress and every stone of it more than 2000 years old.

College of Chinese Studies
Peiping
20th February 1936

To Mother

Another week nearly past, it doesn't seem to have begun until it has ended, every day is so filled with things. The work has been piling on this week. We have started doing memory work and I have got all my characters written out on little cards to start memorising them too. The private teachers do that for a small amount – 1/- *[one shilling]* or so for the term's collection and then I am putting the pronunciation and meaning on the back. We have various stories to learn and every day or two we get a new proverb to learn. They are very concise and interesting and quite easy to remember. 'Dear is not always dear – cheap is not always cheap'. Another, that goes with a great swing is 'Live till you are old, study till you are old and there is still a fraction of learning unlearnt' in 13 Chinese sounds.

Our class had a test sprung on us today. One of the head teachers came in and started to ask us our memory work, up to date reading, and then talking. When the last named started the fun started too and I never had such a riotous exam! He said that he was going to be pupil and we the teachers, so we had to ask questions. He said he didn't understand and asked for questions to be repeated. He used all our old phrases, made all our pet mistakes and generally amused the class for half an hour – but got all he wanted from us by it! I don't think we disgraced ourselves and I said my story about dear little Meng Ke and my proverbs with only one prompt. It is funny being in the kindergarten again.

During the Easter holidays of the college, Marion was invited to stay at a Buddhist temple in the hills above Peking, by Kitty Cherry, an Irish teacher in the Anglican Mission School in the city. The previous month, Kitty had heard that there was an Irish girl in the Language School and asked Marion to tea, where they enjoyed talking about 'home'.

Wofussu (The Sleeping Buddha)
The Western Hills
13th April 1936

To Mother and Dad

I'm out at the Hills now, having arrived this morning at lunch time. The temples round here have always taken guests, people who come to inquire or to be instructed, and now they take ones of a different sort.

The Y.M.C.A. in Peking have taken over all the guest rooms here and make quite a good business of letting them out to people who want a short holiday in the summer. Miss Cherry rang me up and asked me to join her and a Dorothy Rotten (what a name!) for a few days during Easter week, so I joyfully agreed.

The Temple at Wofussu.

The Temple is a big one and all round the main courtyard are little courtyards, each with 2 guest houses in it. We are lucky to have one to ourselves, so we feel quite private. The house has a little green tile roof with a high ridge pole and funny little Peking dogs chasing each other down the steep edges of the roof. The windows opening into the courtyard are paper covered, but the two opening into the hillside are glass with curtains. Everything is very simple but clean. A stove, table and chairs, plus 3 beds are our furniture, stone floor and whitewashed walls. We take one Chinese meal a day provided by the kitchen here and for the rest I am cook. We have plenty of cold meat, bacon and eggs, so the 'cooking' isn't a big job.

Today has been glorious, almost too warm to walk. After lunch we lay on the slopes above the Temple and I confess I slept. After the sun went down a bit, about 3.30, we started on a steep climb which brought us to a glorious view of the plain lying to the north of the hills. The rice is just appearing now and the paddy fields covered with water were gleaming as the sun sank down behind the hills at our back. There was a purple rosy mist over everything and the walk back, first along the ridge of the two hills and then down easy slopes was glorious ...

It is very interesting staying here for the temple life goes on just the same. Black-robed priests wander round the big courtyard in a meditative way. Some wear a girdle which I think must denote a higher rank. One rather nice faced one stopped today to ask me if I wasn't afraid of the cold. I was sitting on stone steps and he looked quite pleased and amused at my halting Chinese.

Every 3 hours a great gong rings and they all flock into the temple and chant continuously to the sound of a small bell and a drum which rumbles quickly and quietly through it all. I expect it will be quite awesome to hear at night. At present I think they are saying good night to the Buddha, for they are slowly beating a drum and a bamboo instrument. Miss Cherry says they keep it up for ages and the man beats it until he is in a sort of trance. It is well we have had a lot of exercise today – I could sleep if they beat it outside my window. Isn't it strange hearing about all this in Ireland? It is funny to think of it in the home setting, but here it is interesting, exciting, strange – but not frightening …

Marion added that the next day they had been invited to visit an Anglican mission.

14th April … Another day of this grand holiday over – I feel this is going to be a short snippet for I have been energetic today. We started off this morning at 8.30 with two donkeys complete with donkey boy. It was a glorious morning, sun well up and a nice little breeze that just kept us cool. We had to tuck into a steep slope at once that took nearly an hour to climb, but once on top the view was glorious. We climbed over three ridges, each higher than the last. We stopped to see a mummy in a Temple (- only it was really a daddy) and then dipped down into a lovely valley – Ba Ta Chu – to the mission house. The Mummy Temple, Tien Tai San, is a lovely little spot, the cleanest I've seen with beautiful paintings of the Goddess of Mercy on the walls. In this part of the world instead of sainting a monk or priest or holy man

they preserve him. When he dies they put him in a box for a couple of years and if he doesn't decompose, a sign of extreme holiness (!), they cover him over with gold paint and put him in his pet temple ...

Marion wrote on the back of this photograph that it showed 'a strange old bridge with no seeming reason, which we came across in a valley in the Hills. It may have been a protection in the old days to the temple below, but there was very little else to keep folks out of that valley.'

We had two donkeys, as I said, Miss Rotten took one and rode it a lot, but Cherry and I only mounted for the fun now and then. It was a glorious feeling to be able to march along, flinging your feet out in front of you. There is very little green out yet – only willows and of course, firs, but the cherry blossoms were all shades from deep deep pink-purple to white, scattered everywhere on the brown hills.

We took 4 hours hard-going to get there, but lunch and a cheery chat with 5 Britishers set us on our feet and we started off home again in good heart, this time mostly by the road. I got on the donkey quite a lot for gallops and I learnt all the proper noises to the donkey boy's great delight. You can't drive these beasties, you have to talk to them as I found before long. The noises are all strange, but the funniest of all is the one to make them go, 'Drrrrrrk!' very brisk and sharp.

Marion photographed this funeral of a rich man outside the College of Chinese Studies.

The cart, horse, car and servants were made of paper, which would be burnt, to ascend to the 'other world' where they would be transformed into real items and people to serve the deceased.

College of Chinese Studies
Peiping
10th May 1936

To Dad and Mother

Did anyone ever tell me China was cold? Here it is May 10th. I am clad in a voile dress and have both windows wide open and I am still 'presbyterianing' gently. Our flat roofs have all got top hats on in the shape of straw matting about 8ft above roof level, because the top floor rooms would be ovens otherwise. Our windows have eyebrows so that we can pull them down outside and keep the room nice and cool; they are big rolls of straw matting, but I haven't experimented with mine yet.

Yesterday was stifling because it was both hot and dusty. Some of us had arranged to cycle round the Beihai, taking sandwiches with us and have a sort of tea supper 5ish on the lake. The minute we started off the dust began to rise and by the time we got there we were beautiful Red Indians between heat and dust, but as we hoped there wasn't so much dust on the lake and we reclined there and watched the yellow haze settle over Peking.

Marion sent the next letter to her brother Cyril, a pupil at Campbell College boarding school in Belfast, to wish him a happy birthday. She had been in bed for several days with mumps.

College of Chinese Studies
Peiping
23rd June 1936

To Cyril

I suppose you may have heard I had the mumps. Today is my first day out of prison and it feels good to be able to roam about again. My dear little face was bigger than ever – but I really was very lucky, because I only had it slightly on one side and the swelling went down in 5 days and the pain is all gone. It has held up my work by a week, but has done no other damage. I hope to go down to the seaside town, where we work for the summer, next Monday and get started again with my teacher there.

I'll write my name at the end of the letter for your sole delectation, but I warn you it is very badly written compared with the beautiful Chinese characters that my teachers write. My name is 'Yang Mu Eu' (French eu). 'Yang' means 'a poplar tree'. 'Mu' means to 'seek earnestly for', 'Eu' is 'grace' – 'Heavenly Wisdom'. Chinese call your surname first and then your Christian name, so here I am

'Young Marion'.

College of Chinese Studies
Peking
26ᵗʰ June 1936

To Dad and Mother

I've finished packing practically, *[Marion was about to leave for Pei Tai Ho]* the stuff for Manchuria is awaiting the American Express Company to collect it tomorrow morning for transhipment and my trunk for PTH has only odds and ends to go into it. I don't know whether I told you I had bought a camphor chest – a big one. It is about 2½ft wide by 2½ deep by 3½ long, and very nicely carved with chrysanthemums. Miss McMordie *[a former Manchurian missionary who had returned to Ireland after her retirement]* gave me money to buy one, but I added to it and got it here instead of Hong Kong, as she suggested. It will be grand to keep all my woollens in – a moth would faint within 5 yards of it and it wouldn't live a moment inside it! It is really a decoration to any room and will look well in my house – when

I have one! I only paid about £1 – 18/- for it complete with a ½ sliding top (Alice Gleystein who went with me suggested this, as she said it saved lifting the top out every time time you wanted anything and was grand to keep winter gloves in) and my Chinese name.

The camphor chest which Marion bought in Peking.

20 Tung Po Lie
East Cliff
Pei Tai Ho
Hopei
30ᵗʰ June 1936

To Dad and Mother

Pei Tai Ho was a popular seaside holiday resort for Western diplomats, businessmen, missionaries and their families in north China. Here they could avoid some of the high temperatures and the dust of the Chinese summer. It had been established in the 1890s by

engineers building the railway from Peking to Moukden. The house Marion initially stayed in was rented by the Language School for their students:

The house is near the sea – across a 'garden' – rough grass down to the beach – 3 minutes' walk and we dress and undress at the house which is great comfort. The sea hasn't the kick to it the Atlantic has, but it is good nevertheless and I've had 3 bathes in 2 days. Aren't you all grinding your teeth?!

Marion's photographs of the house at 20, Tung Po Lie (left) and her fellow Language College students and teachers in front of the grass shades of the house (right).

We have 4 bedrooms, each with a little porch opening out of it with a whole wall open – no glass, only a grass shade to pull down if the sun is too hot. There are a table and chairs there and we work with our teachers and study or write as I am doing now, a big comfortable living room and a veranda across the front and one side of the house. The bathroom arrangements are primitive, but who minds beside the sea? And at any rate we have a little room to wash in off each bedroom, not like home rooms which just have a basin in the bedroom itself.

We get up at 6, breakfast at 6.30, work begins about 7.15 when the teachers arrive and ends at 12. We have a break of 15 mins at 9.30 when the teachers drink tea. The poor dears must suffer here only getting it once in the morning, because they take it between every class in school I think! Two hours work in the afternoon or evening and the rest of the day is ours. The trouble is we have to go to bed shortly after 9. We get so sleepy if we don't and the sea air and bathing kills any desire for late nights,

There lots of houses built by missions and owned privately by missionaries round here, and this is called the 'proper' end of P.T.H.

The other end is gov. and civil people with a lot of white Russians where the mode of dressing is rather extreme and the social life goes hot and strong. We have a gorgeous beach, very sandy and lovely shells.

Marion recorded that she bought this lacquer plate from a travelling salesman in Pei Tai Ho in 1936.

20 Tung Po Lie
31st July 1936

On Sunday night, the Garvens, a very nice couple whom I met in Moukden, invited me over to supper. They are Scotch, he is a Dr and they have 4 of the dearest children, all so good mannered, but full of life. Mrs Brown also S.M. *[Scottish missionary]* was there with her sister who has been on a world trip with her husband. She *[Mrs Brown]* and her husband are Drs in Tiehling.

Mrs B. Thrilled me – she is pretty in a dignified way, wore her clothes well and her accent – everything that was refined and nice. Is there anything better than a refined Scottish accent spoken by a lady with a lovely voice?

20 Tung Po Lie
East Cliff
Pei Tai Ho
Hopei
31st July 1936

To Dad and Mother

Marion had just completed her Chinese language exam and went over to see Flora's parents, the MacNaughtans, whom she had met in Edinburgh when she and Flora had been students at St Colm's. The Rev MacNaughtan had been a Scottish missionary in Manchuria since 1898. Five years later he married Isabel Philip, who had gone to China as an Irish Presbyterian missionary and had served in Faku.

56

Marion then was about to move over to stay with the MacNaughtans at their house, also in the East Cliff area. Her comments about her exam turned out to be justified, as she did well in both her language and written exams.

Whoopee! Am I on my head or my feet?? My exam is over today and my holiday has started. I did better than I had hoped, because I honestly didn't think it was possible to cover the course in a month – I started on the 1st and took my exam on the 31st. Tsssst – whizz! That's me, that was. Kuang gave me a thorough exam too, far more so than either of the other two I've had and I knew my material, though of course I can't tell about the tones – every now and then he gave an encouraging grunt when I hit one well and I just hope all the spots when he didn't grunt weren't wrong! I still have writing to do on Wednesday next, but it is rather fun and I quite look forward to it.

Flora *[Marion's friend from St Colm's]* comes tonight at 12 *[arriving from Ashiho]* and I move over tomorrow, another Whoopee! It will be grand to be with home folks again ...

And mother dear who do you think I saw – Eric Liddell (I think that name is spelt right – the Olympic runner.) He is in the L.M.S. *[London Missionary Society]* in Tientsin and is here on holiday. Mrs Mac*[Naughten]* knows him and she was going to introduce me, but I am content with seeing famous people at a distance, I don't like to speak to them – so I refused the introduction. I knew how interested you would be though.

Eric Liddell, later to become well-known through the film Chariots of Fire, was a hero to many because in the 1924 Olympics he had refused to compete in the heats for the 100 metres on a Sunday, because of his Christian beliefs; he then won the 400 metres for which he had only recently started training. In 1925 Liddell became a missionary in China.

One of the beaches at Pei Tai Ho.

There is glorious lightning tonight – sheet lightning, which Dr Fulton says plays on the hills most of the summer and doesn't mean a storm in the offing. The other night I had the most exciting bathe I ever had in my life. It was new moon and we decided to bathe about nine o'clock. When I got down I could see sparkles all along the edge of the water and thought it was just the moonlight – and then found it was phosphorescence. When we went in and drew our hand along, it raise sparkles like fire crackers and when you swam the light just streamed out from your hand like a great blaze of light. When we got out you just rubbed your hand along your suit and got a sparkle all along. What a thrill! I've often read of it, but never hoped to see it.

C/o Miss I. Stokes
Irish Presbyterian Mission
Hsinking
3rd September 1936

It had been intended that Marion would go to her mission station at Faku at the beginning of September. This was changed because Mamie Johnston, the senior woman missionary in Faku, was to take a Bible School in Hsinking and Marion first went there. In the letter Marion gives descriptions of both Hsinking and Pei Tai Ho. 'The Diamond' was the square in Clones.

Well here I am in Hsinking – arrived last night on the Asia, the most luxurious train I have ever been in, streamlined, grey and silver. I travelled 3rd, as well fitted out as our 1sts at home in Ireland, efficiently attended by neat pleasant-faced little Japanese train boys.

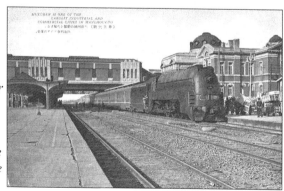

The South Manchuria Railway's streamlined Asia Express, shown on this postcard at Moukden where Marion joined the train for her journey to Hsinking. The Japanese-built train linked Darien, the port for arrivals from Japan, and Hsinking, the new capital of the puppet state of Manchukuo.

It was almost as bad as my first train journey in China. I was just as tongue tied again because none of them spoke Chinese or English that I could find. A business man beside me finally said, "Speak little English," so he told me what information I wanted about when we arrived. Mamie, Ivy and Mrs Johnston were at the station to meet me and we drove down through wide (as wide as The Diamond) well-kept streets with the evening sun shining through the trees that line the pavements. The church and three mission houses are in the one compound, a tennis court too, but what else I don't know yet.

What a holiday I've had! Every day was almost perfect. I only wished you were all here to knock out the 'almost', but I was glad too when it came to packing and getting back to Chinese again. I shouldn't like to have enough money not to have to work – I sympathise with G.B. Shaw's plea for pity for the idle rich.

P.T.H. couldn't be bettered for scenery, trees, mountains, a river and the sea. Sandy roads, no cars allowed – no trippers, everyone the same class and meeting without any feeling of superiority or inferiority, good Chinese servants – pity anyone who has to go home and settle down with our British species – little trouble housekeeping because the cook prefers to do it himself, and the sea water so warm that you can float in it for hours and never feel chilled. Where our house was you overlooked a little valley which gradually rose to sand dunes and then across the plains to the hills. The sea formed the diameter to the semicircle we saw and trees behind us shut out the view towards Rocky Point. The sunset hour was the most glorious every day, the sea touched with pastel shades, the hills outlined in gold and purple, and the final glory of the peak behind which the sun was setting.

The fields are green now and evening saw the driving in of herds of white goats by small ragged goat boys, scampering along with small rods in their hands. Galian, the corn crop *[most probably sorghum]*, 8 to 12ft high is ripening into russet red all through the fields. It will get brown soon, but just now it is at its best.

Mamie tells me autumn in Manchuria can't be beaten – and I think I believe her, except by autumn in Ireland. The greenest thing I've seen yet is myself, the sun doesn't give anything much chance to stay the fresh green of the trees and grass we get at home, but it is acceptable when compared with brown sandy earth.

While in Pei Tai Ho, Marion ran a cookery class for the children of missionaries. All the children were American, apart from Maureen McCammon (Irish), to the right of Marion, and Elizabeth Brown (Scottish), at her feet.

Irish Presbyterian Mission
Hsinking
8th September 1936

To Dad and Mother

Hsinking (or Xinmin) meant 'the new capital' The Japanese had established their capital for Manchukuo in the town formerly known at Changchun. The buildings that were being constructed included a palace for Pui Yi, the last Emperor of China, who had been deposed in 1912, but whom the Japanese had installed as the Emperor of their conquered territory.

We took a droskey and went towards the Japanese town where building is going on rapidly and efficiently. Three years ago the ground on which a town the size of Portadown is now built, was either rough country or else had rough little Chinese shacks on it. Now it is a big modern town, business flats, banks, shops, suburban villas – street after street of the type of house you see on the outskirts of any big town at home – and some of them architecturally were beautiful looking.

I saw the ground which is to be the new palace, a huge winding lake is in the process of construction, with a hill forming a stand in the middle. I saw the site for the Altar of Heaven where the 'Son of Heaven' will offer sacrifice for his people once a year – and in the distance the hills, 5 miles away, which form the municipal boundary for this new metropolis. The ministry of this and that, the barracks, the new town parks, everything looks so solid and prosperous looking that my adjectives were all used up before I got far. I am not writing this for possible readers *[Japanese censors]* – I really mean it, although

60

there is a good deal unsaid – I am afraid my rebel blood boils as at the hated Sassenach *[Japanese]* betimes.

C/o Miss I. Stokes
Irish Presbyterian Mission
Hsinking
23rd September 1936

To Grandma

Included here are family references, which Marion also makes in most of her letters to Ireland.

I was sorry to hear in Mother's letter this week that you hadn't been so well. I hope long before   it reached me that you were feeling quite fit again. You have to take care of yourself Grandma dear – think of the rest of us and don't be rash if you aren't feeling too well. I'll be hearing in next week's letter I'm sure, and I hope it will be good news. You had some of the boys *[Marion's brothers]* along for holidays I expect – I wonder if you see the change in them after almost a year. I just had photos of them all in last week's letter – Hugh in his clericals! and the twins looking as big as myself – they are going to be better looking than their big sister, bless 'em.

One year has made such a difference in our family – Hugh preaching, Frank at college *[Magee College in Londonderry where he was studying divinity]* – Cyril and Jim at Campbell *[College, a boarding school in Belfast]*, the twins ready for *[Clones]* High School and myself at the other end of the earth. I'm sorry I'm missing these years at home as the boys grow up – but I'm not sorry I came out here, if you see the difference!

It has been a great year – I have seen and done more in it than any year of my life before and I've enjoyed it all. I'm just ready to take a new step now – I go to Fakumen to settle down to language study in a country station. I've seen every sort of station now, visiting an industrial town – Moukden, a country town – Hsinmin, a river port – Kirin, the capital – Hsinking, and now I am going to a village 20 miles from the railway. We can get there by bus now when the roads are hardening for the winter, but in summer they are mud tracks which you have to travel over either by cart or by foot.

Mamie Johnston will be the only other white person there until the O'Neills come back in August *[Rev Dr Frederick O'Neill, the senior missionary in Fakumen, and his wife Annie were away in Ireland as Frederick was serving as the Moderator of the Presbyterian Church there during 1936-1937.]*, but I fancy that when they come I will be moved to another station to start my own work – presumably having enough Chinese imbibed to be able to talk fluently!

There are 2 girls in this house besides Mamie and myself – Dr Dorothy Faulkner and the nurse, Ivy Stokes. The next house has Mr and Mrs Johnston and their 2 children and the next Mr and Mrs Harold Corkey and their new baby – Caroline. The Corkeys have come up to take over from Johnstons when they go on furlough. The new baby is a dear little thing, fine and healthy looking – her mother is an American, whom Harold met at Language School, you know.

Harold's cousin, Colin Corkey, has arrived here. I fancy you never met him although he is one of the boys who camped with Uncle Howard in Donegal. You may know Vernon, his older brother, also a minister. Colin is a nice lad, full of fun, fair and stocky, rather like Billy Boyd *[a young Irish Presbyterian minister]* in general appearance, with Bill's nonsense but without his rowdiness. *[Colin Corkey's father, like Marion's, was also an Irish Presbyterian minister and Colin himself had just been ordained as a minister before coming to serve as a missionary.]*

Isn't it grand about Miss Elizabeth Gibson? I was pleased as punch to hear about it in August *[the recent birth of Marion's cousin, baptised Elizabeth Marion]* – I had just hoped I might have had a namesake for my birthday, but it hadn't the discrimination to choose an important date like the 7th July *[Marion's birthday]*.

Colin's sense of fun was shown in his 'lifelike representation of a big grey ape being watched by some children at the zoo' *in charades which Marion also took part in. She feared Colin's performance might have caused* 'the sudden death from too much laughing' *of some of the older missionaries who were watching.*

Heaps of love to yourself and take good care of yourself – <u>you belong to us</u>! If the Hill folk of Rockmount *[other members of the Cromie family]* are round give them my love. I'm sure all my small cousins will be grown out of all knowledge before I see them again.

This photo taken by Marion in Hsinking, shows her companions on a picnic. From left to right are Colin Corkey, Harold Corkey, Dorothy ('Wiggie') Faulkner and Ivy Stokes.

C/o Miss I. Stokes
Irish Presbyterian Mission
Hsinking
24th September 1936

To Frank

Marion sent this letter to her brother with a birthday present. While at Hsinking she had gone to the Irish Presbyterian Mission in Kirin with Ivy Stokes, as had Colin Corkey.

You'll see I've been having an exciting month travelling round, from my letter home this week. Kirin is a lovely place with hills and water, I'd love to work there. Hugh met Colin Corkey at the B.A. camp and I had such a thrill seeing Jim's old mug and Hugh's in a photo of the camp that Colin had. *[The B.A., whose camp in Donegal Colin had been at along with Marion's brothers, was the Irish Presbyterian Boys' Auxiliary, the equivalent of the Girls' Auxiliary which was sponsoring Marion.]*

This photograph taken at Kirin, with Colin Corkey in the right foreground, shows the Sungari River with a soldier from the fort watching a junk loading cargo. The furthest boat is piled with flour.

I told about some of the things I did, but here is another incident I didn't mention. A huge gunpowder factory was on the other side of the river from Kirin in the old days and it blew up – leaving 2 men alive out of all the workers. That was in Dr Gregg's day and he packed his bag and waded and swam across the river the moment he heard the explosion to see what he could do to help. Colin and I decided to explore this place, so we crossed in a ferry and then had a look at the small cliff that rose above us from the river bank. It looked climbable, so I started up first.

I told Colin he could catch me if I fell – and he did! I was up a bit when I discovered the rain had loosened all the shale and down I began to come. I was shooting for the bank and was due to go into the water, when Colin put his walking stick into the slope to steady himself and caught me when I went past! We tried another place, but the same thing happened, so we just had to go the long and prosaic road round the hill and up.

While Marion wrote about her adventurous climb to her brother, she did not mention it to her parents. Neither did Colin Corkey in his letters home. However, Frank mentioned it to his brother, Hugh, who told in turn Colin's brother, Peter, and the tale, now of Colin 'saving Marion's life', reached the Rev and Mrs Corkey! In reply to their query about it, Colin wrote that 'had it not been for me Marion would have fallen at least three feet into the Sungari mud.'

I.P. Mission
Fakumen
4ᵗʰ Oct 1936

To Dad and Mother

Marion had arrived in Faku the day before, travelling by train from Liaoyang to Moukden and then, with Mamie Johnston, to Tiehling. She then travelled onto Fakumen. The journey from Tiehling was by bus. When Mamie first travelled to Faku it had been by Peking cart.

Fakumen, often shortened to Faku, was described in 1925 by Frederick O'Neill in his book, The Quest for God in China, *as 'a busy market-town in Manchuria, pleasantly situated between low hills away from the track of the railways'. He continued that attached to the town* of Fakumen was 'a diocese 13,000 square miles in extent, with a Chinese population roughly estimated at 500,000, much the same as the population of British Columbia. The Christian community is under the charge of five Chinese ordained ministers, placed in different stations of the diocese, and supported by the congregations which 'called' them; in addition, there is a staff of evangelists whose salaries at present are mainly derived from Mission funds distributed through the Chinese Church of the Synod of Manchuria. Christian work in Fakumen includes a Girls' School, a Boys' School (having a Middle School department), Kindergarten, Women's Bible Training School, and Women's Hospital.'

The Boys' School was in the O'Neills' compound, the remainder of the buildings were in the compound occupied by Mamie and Marion.

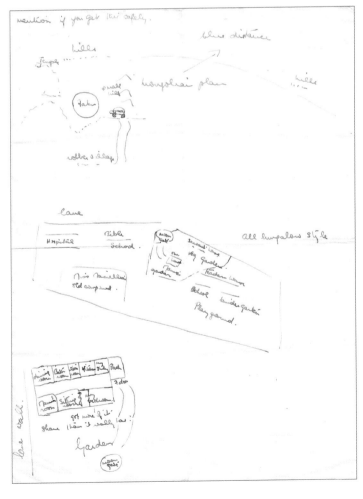

This page from Marion's letter of 4th October shows the countryside around Faku and the layout of the compound in Faku where Marion and Mamie lived. Marion notes in her letter, 'mention if you get this' suggesting that she thought the Japanese censors would remove the page from the letter.

The route to Faku seems different from later journeys as this is the only one that mentions a ferry:

We had a 2 hour run by train through country all full of crops ready for harvesting – it was interesting to notice the kaolien *[possibly the same crop as galian mentioned in her letter of 3 September]* cut 200 yards back from the railway – to make bandit raids less likely. (We always travel with a train guard by the way, and usually a bus guard.) At Tiehling we went to an inn and there got the bus for Faku. We sat on a weighing machine for half an hour before it came and were the centre of a good deal of attraction. They've seen foreigners before of course, but they are still interested to see one close up. Our bus wasn't laden fortunately, comfortable seating even with the luggage all piled up in the centre – an absolute death trap if anything were to happen, for there is only one door and a rail across the window which prevents anyone getting out!

It was an interesting journey – we went through country all gold and red in the afternoon sun, dry rice, millet and kaolien – emerald green in great patches of winter cabbage and silvery grey in a tree like willows, some of it in crops and some in rolling hills like the downs I remember crossing with Dad in the motor bike in Tyrone.

We came to a ferry and got out of our bus to cross the river and board another bus that was waiting for us. The boat was already fairly crowded and when we got in, it sank nearly to water level. A couple of fat pigs were decanted, then a bicycle and its protesting owner, a couple of market baskets and the farmers appended, and still it looked dangerous. Finally, after much cursing and protesting, as many of the folk who weren't going to the bus were persuaded to get out as would rise the boat 2 ins from the water and we started across. I concocted suitable obituary notices as we went.

Having arrived safely, we were drawn up to a mud bank, a crumbly mud bank, elevation 80 degrees, and told to disembark. Several old grandmothers displayed considerable agility and I watched one man jump out with a huge suitcase in one hand and a bundle in the other, balance precariously for a minute and land safely. Finally, when the crowd was well thinned, several of the oldest and ourselves being left, they decided they could run us down to a more comfortable landing stage and we stepped off in elegance and safety.

The rest of the journey was enlivened with boo-peep with a sweet little Japanese baby who never once cried in a 3 hour noisy, bumpy journey, and watching, fascinated by a old grandma who was getting more and more bus sick but refused to let go her own to the end.

Finally, after climbing and climbing up into the hills, we reached a plateau and from there looked down into the Mongolian plane on one side and Faku in a valley on the other. It was 4.00 o'clock on a perfect October day, warmer than at home, with the softness of autumn sun over everything and the evening smoke of Faku in a blue mist as the fires were stoked up for the supper.

We went inside the city walls through narrow winding streets, with mud walls on either side, to the inn yard and there we found the servants waiting to carry our luggage. We walked along dirty streets, still muddy and soft after rain the week before – and wound round corner after corner – evil spirits can't come round corners, so the village streets are never more than 20 yards straight I believe.

This photograph taken in Faku in 2013, shows one of the few surviving muddy streets, similar to those described by Marion.

The compound that Mamie lives in is something like the sketch as far as I can remember after one day's reconnoitre of the church, Boys' School and the pastor's house. We are in another compound about ten minutes' walk away or less. (The O'Neills' house is in a compound adjoining this one.) Mamie's wee house is very comfortable, designed by herself and supervised by her too in the building. The garden is rather barren – it is going to be ploughed up this winter to see if that will help it for next year.

The sitting room looks across a little hedge to the playground and you see the kindergarten children always hopping about playing hopscotch, tig or on the big six-seater swings. We have a dog – 'Abraham' because he came from a far country, contracted I'm afraid to 'Abie' ... a most affectionate cheery beastie, about Mattha's size [a

67

reference to the family dog in Clones], but with smooth hair instead of rough. I'll send you a photo some time, a dog is great company in the house and I'm glad to find one here.

Abie, Mamie's and Marion's dog.

My room is about the size of the spare room, cream and blue. Mamie has just had it done up for me and it looks very fresh. There is a blue bed, a blue chest of drawers with a mirror on top, a hanging corner cupboard with blue and cream front, and a varnished floor. When I have my nice camphor chest, a small bookcase which I'll get made here and my Peking rug down, I'll be in luxury!

Monday

I've brought my bike here – it is coming by freight and should be along soon. It will be a quick way to get about town and the roads outside the town are really very good. The bus route on Saturday was on clay roads and the surface is fine as long as there is no rain. In the winter they freeze 6 or 8 feet deep and a Crossley lorry could make no impression on them.

The place I have marked 'Robber Village' is a spot about 6 miles away which Mamie pointed out as we came along, but Faku has a very sufficient guard so it isn't likely to be attacked, it is only lonely houses and people passing along the roads who are occasionally robbed. (I'm not going to go cycling in that direction Mother!)

Mamie and I spent 2 hours this morning trying to get my Residency Cert. We had to report at the local police office and then go to a central one where time means nothing – or perhaps a show of authority. Every foreigner has to get a certificate, first for three months, extended later to six months, and then to a year, after which I believe you extend it every year. It feels like a prisoner out on good behaviour leave having to report to the Police Office – they keep track of all the undesirable characters! The highest authorities are not native of course and an interpreter doubled the length of time we had to spend ...

We are going round now to pay a ceremonial visit on the Catholic mission – French Canadian – I'll be interested to see how much French I've forgotten! Mamie is good friends with one of them and a lot of mail has come here by mistake during her month away, which they will have expected, poor things. I've been eating some lovely black grapes every morning, which came as a present from them – what would some of the good Christian supporters of our mission in Belfast say to that?

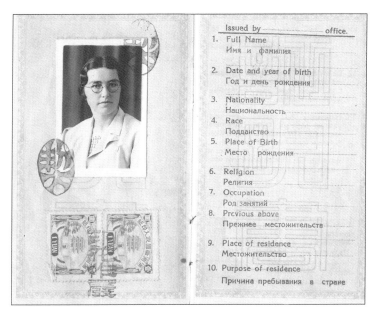

Pages from Marion's Residency Certificate.

The clouds are slowly disappearing – sure sign winter is setting in. We'll have brazen blue skies for many a month except when it greys over for snow – the wee white clouds of April are very joyfully greeted.

On Sunday morning I was at a service here of about 200 – 'feast days' – Xmas and Easter – or such, might see 600 or 700 in from the country villages. The Boys' School marched into their seats, then the kindergarten and the Girls' School, all very neat in school uniform. The elders sat towards the front, men to one side and women to the other and the general congregation filled up the back of the church. I was introduced at one point and had to go up to the platform below the pulpit to make my bow. My name is 'Yang' and the word for foreigner is the same, so he made a pun on my name, which was a great joke and means that no one will forget it!

8th October 1936

To the Twins

... The cook (a man) has his wife and children living in a house outside the back garden and they have a dear wee fat baby, six months old. It made friends with me in no time and I was nursing it today for a while. It has very fat cheeks and wee brown eyes that look almost black and a funny wee gurgle of a laugh. I am going to try and get a snap of it someday laughing, to send to you.

The cook's wife and her 'dear wee fat baby'.

Wee girls don't get names here, because Chinese think girls aren't very important. It is only in Christian homes that they are given a name. They call them things like 'No 1' or 'No 3', wherever they come in the family, and 'Wee bit of Iron', 'Wee Rabbit', 'Wee Button', 'Wee divided head' (because they wear 2 plaits sticking up sometimes). 'Wee mistake' – because they wanted a son, or 'A son's coming' – don't look at this wee thing – there'll be a son along soon.

How would you like names like that!

Fakumen
11th October 1936

To Dad and Mother

I got Mamie in a story telling mood last night and I wish I could give you half of them – with her touches.

She came here to be with Miss MacWilliams just at my stage *[in experience]*, and one night shortly after her coming they heard a great row coming from the school. It was about 8 o'clock on a dark winter's night and the school bell and all the school band was being sounded for all they were worth. "O dear," said Miss Mac casually – "It's those robbers again and I suppose we'd better go across – here dear, you take this" and she handed Mamie a stick out of the hall stand. So Mamie trotted across after Miss Mac with the stick in her hand wondering how you set about hitting a robber – and wondered still more when she saw there were 6 to be hit! However, whether the robbers thought they were the beginning of the rush or whether their chivalrous instincts made it impossible for them to hit foreign women, no one knows, but they fled.

After that a guard was asked for from the town authorities and one was posted in the lane outside the wall. It was reported that 13 men were in the compound round one of the buildings, so while Miss Mac led the attack of the servants, Mamie scooted over to the wall and looked for the guard. There he was leaning peaceably against the far wall.

"There are men in the compound," Mamie hissed.

"I know that."

"Well, why don't you come on?"

"There are 13 men there, I saw them go in – I am only one – What's to do?"

Thereafter they provided their own guard in the compound and got new 20 foot walls built with strong gates.

Stories of the taking of the place before Manchukuo came into being: The magistrate was sent a note asking, would he welcome the oncoming forces, J. *[Japanese]* – nothing else to do. But a bandit chief, head probably of a crowd of the disbanded soldiers, got wind of their coming via a very strategic point in the hills and attacked them. The townspeople heard firing, realised what had had happened and thought they would be wiped out in retaliation. Mr O'Neill legged round with the pastor to the Yamen – (offices where all business for town is done, Town Hall), and when the forces did arrive helped to make peace, translating in French and the other tongue.

Mamie and Mrs O'Neill in the meanwhile were left in the house alone and they decided they would go across the road and see if the schoolgirls were frightened by the firing. Just as they got into the middle of the road crossing from O'Neills' compound to ours, round the corner of the wall and in through the open gate 20 yards away swept the soldiers with fixed bayonets legging it for the Town Hall.

The servants in O'Neills' compound, hearing the row and thinking the others were safely in the house, slammed the compound gates – and the two women were locked out. They had just the same protection that our road gate would give if the railings were a high wall, but they shrank in against it and watched the squad hare past.

Peace was made, but the gates were knocked down, part of the city wall damaged and the electric wiring – live wire – snipped in several places. The moment the fêting of the new forces was over and they had withdrawn, O'Neill and the pastor were elected unofficial heads for the town and O'Neill immediately ordered the defence of the city against robbers. It was just about done and a levy of some men from every house in town finished, when about 6,000 men swept down round the place. Things were ready for them and Faku withstood a siege of about 6 weeks. Shells were used and old cannon balls and our property came in for a good deal of the shots as it is almost beside the wall. Mamie actually had bullets pass through things she was carrying and whiz near her – and this all sounding so story-bookish happened about five years ago in this very spot.

About 14th October

19th September 1936 was the date when the next letter was begun, but in a later letter Marion says that the majority was written about 14th October 1936. It was posted on board a ship to avoid being censored by the Japanese authorities; they would not have searched any Europeans before they boarded.

To Dad

Marion writes about the problems Christians were encountering under the occupation:

I think that this is a safe general area – the unpleasantness is not anti-Christian, but it is anti-intelligentsia and the Church is a menace because it makes people think ...

The authorities have just been trying to spread terror so that they have everyone under their thumb. Church and Govt institutions are both under suspicion because the authorities think that any group of people who gather together are sure to discuss present conditions unfavourably – and engender a spirit anti-Manchukuo, and may be they have reason enough.

The campaign goes on through little pinpricks that keep everyone on the qui vive. Sometimes it is through a letter sent from some unsuspecting friend 'within the wall' – all letters from South are sure to have something Communistic in them the Japs think – and off the poor person goes to prison 'to have their thoughts examined' – in ways better not thought on.

All our parsons and school teachers are in rather nerve racking positions because they are all helping to mould the thought of Manchukuo, so every letter and paper they get, every book they have in their house, is examined and no one knows what will be pounced on as evidence that they are anti-Manchukuo. One poor lad had a newspaper sent from Nanking to him up here and in it was some unfavourable comment on the Japs in the south and he hasn't been heard of since he went into prison three months ago.

We are in no actual danger ourselves but just live in a state of cold fear when a rush is on, not knowing what good friend will disappear next. It is only one here and there who are in amongst our people, but the strain is there. And what is even worse is that there is no certainty of any kind of justice or reprieve. If anyone sends in a piece of false evidence or any letter making a charge, however untrue, the law here is that you are guilty until proved innocent.

Marion then wrote that the pastor, the leading elder and the Boys' School headmaster (both called Shang) had been arrested:
... All the week they sat, never lay, in a little room with prisoners who had been tortured, and once a day got a bowl of the food they give the animals here – all carefully calculated to break a man's nerve ...

The pastor and the elder were released, but the headmaster, Mr Shang, was sent to be imprisoned in Tiehling, the Japanese headquarters for the area.

The authorities, Japanese and Korean, are paid a very small wage and get a bonus on convicted prisoners or collected evidence, so you get the worse type of ignorant cruel beasts who are on the make all the while ...

Here, those in authority are fairly kindly disposed to us, except the two head yins, a Jap called 'Pig's Mouth' by his Chinese confederates, and a Korean. One boy in their office, a Mohammaden, has allowed his wife to come to meetings and is himself a frequent church goer ...

Don't worry about us personally – the Church needs our prayers and those brave Chinese who are taking leading parts and not flinching. The 27th Ps. is in our thoughts and is our comfort at the moment.

The 27th Psalm begins: 'The Lord is my light and my salvation; whom shall I fear? The Lord is the strength of my life; of whom shall I be afraid? ...'

I.P. Mission
Fakumen
18th October 1936

To Mother and Dad

R.H. Boyd, the Convenor of the Irish Presbyterian Church's Foreign Mission Committee, and his wife, Annie, had arrived in Faku during their visit to mission stations in Manchuria.

Harvest Thanksgiving in the church at Faku. The lettering over the altar reads 'The Glory of God shall fill the whole earth'.

Today is Harvest Thanksgiving and the sermon is to be given by R.H. and interpreted by Mamie. We will have Harvest Songs by the schoolchildren and all the place is decorated with veg, flowers and grain – I'm looking forward to seeing it, because Mamie has been away and it has all fallen on the Bible School people and Elders of the Kirk. In the old days people also gave clothes and any gift that they liked to have sold, putting the price on themselves. If their gift wasn't bought, they bought it back themselves – a good idea for the Elephant Stall in a Sale of Work (?!). One Harvest Thanksgiving day Mamie went down early to find a pair of Mr O'Neill's inside pants decorating the front of the reading desk – a place of honour for the 'Moshih's' garment – however intimate they may be. Needless to say Mamie put them somewhere less before the public eye!

I.P. Mission
Fakumen
20th October 1936

Letter from Annie Boyd to Marion's mother, which was enclosed with Marion's letter of 18th October:

We have got this length in our travels and are having a lovely time with Mamie Johnston and Marion. I thought you and her father would like to know how well she is looking – just blooming and so cheery and full of life and enjoyment. We left Moukden on Saturday morning with Mamie as guide. Everywhere was covered in a blanket of snow. We arrived here after a long journey, delayed on account of the snow and thaw, and found Marion at the door of their nice G.A. house to welcome us. She had a lovely fire to greet us and while we warmed our feet a good cup of tea was brought in. Marion had on a pretty soft warm cream frock with white frills at her neck and cuffs, and looked so bonny and happy. She was delighted to get talking English after having had several days without companionship. It did us both good to see her and we feel you can be easy in your minds as to the climate of Manchuria suiting her!

Mrs Boyd has a flower pinned on by Shu Hang, a 12 year old girl 'dressed up' in Western clothes, after the new Girls' School dormitory had been officially opened.

She is evidently getting on well with the language. We've had several walks through the fields with her and she has chatted with the Manchurian folk – and translated for our benefit what they are saying. She could not have a better chance than here. Mamie is extremely good at Chinese and there is plenty of opportunity for Marion to air it.

I.P. Mission
Fakumen
29th October 1936

To Mother and Dad

I've promised you a letter for a long time telling you about our household arrangements, so as this is your letter here goes. I've sent you a snap of the house already I think and explained how it lies. It is very cosy, prepared both for heat and cold. In the hot weather all the windows and outside doors have wire windows and doors to keep out the flies and let in all the air – you'll see our windows can be thrown wide open in summer and our sitting room has most of the front wall window. Each room has a stove in the winter and the grate in the sitting room is a grand one, it throws the heat half way across the room. In the winter double windows are put on and all pasted round with paper and cotton wool. But above each is a fanlight opening upwards which lets in air without draught. Carpets only go down in the winter and small mats on varnished floors take their place in summer.

We have no flower garden this year but the O'Neills' has supplied us well since I came and we have taken some of their potted plants over to save them ...

Mamie normally has the one boy who does everything – not always easy to get a cook who will do coolie, but he is a Christian and Mamie has had him since he was about 17. At present we have a coolie part time to do grates, shoes, carry water etc. He is O'Neills' and is really doing watchman for their house but the arrangement in Faku is when one is at home on furlough the watchman is taken on by the other and his ordinary wage made up in that way between. It saves them looking for a job for the year elsewhere.

We get our stores from Moukden in bulk – milk and butter is tinned. At present we are getting frozen Russian butter, not tinned, and it is better. Meat, veg and fruit we get here. There are lots more veg here than at home. I can't think of any of our home ones – apart from red turnips – we haven't got, even artichokes and asparagus. There are several different sorts of cabbage and other white vegetables, and little white bean sprouts (that look like maggots! but taste good). At present our fruit is apples (awfully good red ones) and persimmons – soft and sweet. Fruit is a bit expensive in Faku because of carriage, but a lot cheaper than at home. I've had pomegranate, rather a disappointing fruit, all little seeds packed tightly together and each is covered with a pink skin which is just full of water ... There are good grapefruit at another time of the year and plenty of pears and grapes.

Marion writes about the cook: Yu Shih Fu – 'Fish' as he is called by us ('Yu' being 'Fish') is a grand cook just to be a country boy. He has a wonderful way with remains ...

She continued that: ... Fish, wife, his mother and 2 small children live in a two roomed house across the yard. Mrs Fish is a <u>very</u> pretty little thing with lovely smooth white skin, very clear skinned for a Chinese – I have a good photo of her, I am getting copies and will send one soon. A very happy family – the old lady is a good Christian and very fond of Mrs Fish.

A couple of facts about the mother-hood of Manchuria. If a girl is born there is no rest for the mother – the next one is usually along inside the next year. But if a son is born she can heave a sigh of relief and have a couple of years respite. I know one family where there are three girls inside the same number of years – and now a son at last has appeared. In farming families it is quite usual to marry a son to a girl several years older than him – they want a 'good strong girl' about the place. The other day there was a wedding here of a lad of 14 to a girl of 17 (heathen) – pretty awful isn't it? – and that is normal in heathen families.

Marion also describes the changes that had taken place in society in China: ... it is only in the country stations (like Faku) that a man doesn't speak to women in the street I think. In the old days – only 12 years ago when Mamie came out, if Miss McWilliams took Mamie and Rachel *[Irwin, who was then in charge of the hospital]* out in the street they walked in single file and never opened their mouths except when they were in shops!

I.P. Mission
Fakumen
29ᵗʰ October 1936

To J.D. *(Jim)*

You probably get all my letters eventually, so you've heard where I am and all about the place. Did you see a photo yet of two little boys taken beside a wall? One is smiling and the other serious. The one who is smiling is Ping An (Little Peace) and the other is En Fu (Happy Grace). Ping An is our cook's son and a cheery wee imp. He used to smile at me from a distance, but he is quite friendly now.

I work in a bright window and they can see me from outside. The two of them creep round and look in from a distance and the quickest way to scatter them is to look up and wave to them – they flee like two little fat bundles with feet stuck on the bottom. Then they come creeping back along the hedge and when they come to the end of it, nearly stand on their heads to see my window under it. They are both about 3 years old and the greatest of friends. En Fu still runs with a shriek of "Ping An! To lie la" (Ping An she's coming) when I heave in sight.

En Fu and Ping An in the photo referred to in the letter to Jim.

Yesterday, Ping An stopped beside me – very conscious of the admiring gaze En Fu round the corner of the house – and said, "Huh! Ta po mi" (Huh! he's afraid of you), but when I said, "Oh why?" his courage left him and he fled too!

Ping An decided to go to school this year, so a pencil was bought for him and off he went to kindergarten. He was in about 5 minutes when the organ started for a song and at the first toot with one bellow of fear Ping An rose and fled. He's never been back since and they are waiting until he is a bit bigger.

I.P. Mission
Fakumen
1st November 1936

To Dad and Mother

Let me introduce myself – I'm sending my card! Everyone has them here – I expect to get one handed to me by our cook soon – and we folks find them useful, because every call we have from the Town Hall commences with the question, 'What is your name -?' I think nearly every 'Bobby' will have been in soon to find it out either in English or Chinese. Yesterday they thought of another one and came up to ask us it in Japanese!! ... Mine is 'Malinyan Yang' I believe ...

10th November 1936

To Dad

This was another letter which was to be posted on board ship by a missionary returning home to avoid being read by the Japanese censors. It was added to over a period of several months and probably not sent back until a missionary was leaving in March 1937. The extracts written during November are included here. Marion takes up the story of Mr Shang, the headmaster of the Boys' School, who, as she had related in her previous letter of about 14th October, had been imprisoned by the Japanese.

... we were having constant visits from the army on one pretext or another and men were dropping in to school to say to the girls, "You won't see Mr Shang again – he's gone all right." – this to see what the girls' reaction was. It got so much on our nerves that the barking of Abie – he hates soldiers – made us jump and speeded up our hearts about twenty beats!

Finally Mamie got tired of doing nothing except keep her temper and be heavily polite to these ill-mannered beggars, so she decided to do some sleuthing. The head interpreter in Tiehling has a Christian wife and as they used to be in Fakumen, Mamie knew them well (Shang by this time had been sent to Tiehling). Mamie departed as unostentatiously as she could for the bus one evening – and didn't report to our police box that she was leaving town! – and when she got into the bus it was to find that there were several police officers in the bus too! They didn't know of course that she hadn't reported, but one followed her when she got out. If she was seen going to the interpreter's house it might mean bad trouble for him of course so she had to shake off Mr Spy. She got into a rickshaw and said clearly for his benefit, "The station," then when she got to the shops she stopped at one to buy fruit as the gent behind her heard. He went on expecting her at the station I suppose, and M. paid off her man and departed to Mrs Hsing's by a back way.

The news she got was that he was probably dead as there had been a wholesale execution a day or two before of about twenty men – some they had tried and some shot off hand. Well you can imagine M.'s feelings with that news to bring back to his wife and brother. Mrs Hsing's husband was away on some job in the country, so she slipped out to see Hsieh the interpreter, who works under Hsing to get details. The news she brought back was amazing – a mass execution had been ordered and Shang had been put on the list, but through some mistake he had been taken off with another bunch of men (who had been released by the military authorities) and sent to the ordinary police for trial or imprisonment. Mrs Hsing promised to get Hsieh's help in the matter and Mamie went off to tell the Moukden folk what was happening.

Mamie had worked in Faku since 1925 and was Marion's senior colleague in 1936. As the account of the journey to Tiehling indicates, she was a determined person. The letter also shows that Mamie was very tactful in dealing with the Japanese. Marion admired the work Mamie did and the good relations she established with the local people in Faku. Mamie occasionally clashed with some of the other missionaries, but she and Marion got on well

Mamie Johnston and one of the schoolgirls in Faku.

with each other and remained friends until Mamie's death fifty years later.

The next day an amusing thing happened. Mamie had left Moukden on a very early train and had had no breakfast (here I had a better say in extenuation of her hostess that M. had slipped out about six without any previous warning to the lady!) When she got back to Tiehling and did some more business with Mrs Hsing, she was ravenous and stopped on the way to the bus to buy some very ordinary-looking Chinese bread. She had noticed a little Jap snooping round, so she went in to the park with her bread to see what he would do. Sure enough he appeared and in a minute or two she heard him say to a man who was sweeping up leaves, "Do you think that foreigner is English?" The Chinese evidently took into consideration her hungry munching of the bread, because his reply was, "No. English have more money than that."! She got home safely without any trouble, the man on the gate was a Chinese she knew and he didn't ask her any questions. But in the meanwhile a comic touch had been added – the day M. left, a little soldier had come into the school and amongst other things had said to the headmistress, who is just a girl, "If Miss J. *[Mamie Johnston]* goes away anywhere you are to come and tell us – we are going to limit her movements." Fortunately she didn't know that M. was gone or she might have given herself away as she is a bit nervous.

In the meanwhile, we haven't heard of Shang being tortured, but he is pretty sure of being beaten and this long continued imprisonment doesn't look too hopeful for his getting out. One thing we have heard, but we don't know how much to believe, is that he is now in a room with a stove in it and that he is getting three meals a day. If he is, he will probably be freed. They treat folk a bit more kindly before freeing them, to give the marks of beating or torture a chance to clear up – isn't it a bright thought?

While Shang was being held in Tiehling, Marion wrote that in the Boys' School the Japanese authorities had been carrying out 'one inspection after another for treasonable literature and it is all very wearing, because we don't always know what is treasonable and what is not.'

They also turned their attention to the Girls' School:

... another deputation arrived to go through the school – and it being the Sabbath, Mamie has just been over to say that the room is cold and when they have finished will they come over and have a cup of tea in her 'poor miserable cottage'.

They came, they saw and we (or rather M.) conquered. There is one thing that Eastern courtesy hasn't bettered yet and that is a bit of Irish blarney. When I saw them come back from the school with M. my heart stood still, for they had half a dozen books and this after the searching that had been done. However, we never even saw the books – for a while – and treated the Korean and Chinese who were searching as our honoured guests.

I searched anxiously for all scraps of information in the back of my mind on etiquette and Mamie told me afterwards I acquitted myself quite well. I presented the teacup held in both hands with my head meekly bowed and he bowing twice took it in both his. I offered everything three times to his polite refusals, Mamie murmuring at his sixth helping of cake that he was eating nothing ... and all the while she was keeping up a flow of complimentary small chat that was painful on my face muscles, but later I found the reason of this distortion of the truth. One book they had found was a testimony of Chang Kai Shek's as to 'why I am a Christian' – with photo and all complete and it was very <u>bad</u>.

When the noises which the gentlemen were omitting signified repletion – not mere politeness – Mamie began the offensive. She was very sorry about these books because she had lost face over them badly. There was no real headmistress this term so the books were really her fault – she was only a foreigner with little learning and in going through the books she must not have seen these – she was a timid woman without courage and she was glad it was two gentlemen of education and understanding like themselves who had been sent to the school – if it had been a boor of a man she could not have discussed things with him (the Korean who is in charge can't write and is known as the biggest boor in the office). At this point he got all fatherly and began to explain she needn't worry as the books weren't dangerous, but they had to bring some away to show that they had done their job properly.

M. said that there was one she wasn't happy about, the Chang Kai Shek one – "Oh that was alright, they understood that it was only a religious book – in that case when they had put it in their list of prescribed books they would burn it." "Well if they were going to burn it there was no time like the present," quoth M. rapidly ... and 'the gentlemen had been so kind that she couldn't think of bothering them further and she would just do it now,' and suiting the action to the word, she picked it off the mantelpiece and thrust it into the middle of a good roaring fire. The men's faces were a study! It had all been done in the best Chinese tradition however, and no one had lost any face. So they probably went away without any ill feeling and a new respect for foreigner's ways. It was as much as I could to restrain a cheer when I saw the book go into the fire (which would not have been in the best Chinese tradition). It afforded M. and myself a good laugh afterwards.

Later in the letter, in a section dated 26th November, Marion tells of Mr Shang's eventual fate.

Hsieh the interpreter in Tiehling: ... in order to find out what the Jap in charge meant to do with Shang in the end, went to a cabaret where he knew he was going and accidental-done-a-purpose ran into him. He then proceeded to make him drunk and asked about his opinion of Shang; "Oh he hasn't proper thoughts 'off with his head'." Hsieh asked if there was any definite evidence – "No, but he's not a good man, he'll have to go."

So when a few days later Shang was due for final trial by this man, the interpreter left his name off the sheet. He was tried by another and decenter Jap – and he's home ... I don't have to dilate on our feelings or the prayers that have gone up from everyone here. We feel now that all this trouble is over for a while. As long as there was a teacher in prison, the whole Church was implicated and there would be constant searching for all concerned. We are vindicated now with the three men out without a stain on their character.

The other day the head of the govt. school met the pastor in the street and stopped to speak to him "You Christians are wonderful! If one of my teachers had been taken there wouldn't have been a boy or a teacher in the school the next day, but here you are carrying on as if nothing had happened." And that is what I have been feeling ever since this has started – we missionaries are safe enough, but the Chinese have no other court of appeal, yet there is no panicking and no hysteria. Everything goes on as quietly as ever, and attendances at church or prayer meetings don't suffer. It is good to have been here.

Marion also revealed in the form of comic play on a sheet accompanying the letter that two Japanese officers had called to sell pills 'to cure sore head, cure sore mouth, cure sore throat, cure sore chest, cure sore belly ...' *Mamie and Marion bought a couple of bottles and then collapsed hysterically after their guests left. Marion's concluding line read,* 'Oh! Oh! To think of a captain in the British Army selling pills!'

Faku
24th November 1936

To Mother and Dad

In this letter Marion refers to the Taoist priest as 'Mamie's friend'. The relations of the missionaries with other religions, the Muslims and Buddhists, as well as the Taoists in Faku, seem to have been good.

Since I started wearing my Chinese gown outdoors I've had a bit of fun – Mamie's fair hair marks her as a foreigner at once, but it is only when I am walking that anyone behind would know that I am foreign. Several people in church last Sunday asked who I was, because it is only the old people who sit in the front seat where Mamie and I usually are, even the girl who is head mistress in the Girls' School and sees me every day didn't know me.

Then on Sunday afternoon Mamie and I went for a walk to a Taoist Temple on a hill near here where the old priest is rather a friend of hers. It is a lovely little place, very clean and with a glorious view of Faku in the valley and the hills all around. He was introduced to me as a newly come 'Yang chiaoshih' and he looked at me several times in a puzzled way and then said, "She isn't of our people then?" I felt highly complimented.

A Taoist Priest photographed by Colin Corkey.

Faku
19th December 1936

To Mother and Dad and all the rest of yous

The reference in the second paragraph is to the 'Xian Incident' involving Zhang Xueliang ('the general'). He had succeeded his father Zhang Zuolin as warlord of Manchuria, and then, after the Japanese takeover, had moved south to be one of the generals supporting the Kuomintang government of Chiang Kai Shek ('C.K.S.'). Chiang was involved in a civil war against the Communist forces under Mao Ze Dong. Zhang Xueliang felt, however, that it was necessary to end the civil war and have a united front against the Japanese, and in December 1936 he and another general kidnapped and imprisoned Chiang in Xian and only released him when he agreed to form the united front. Zhang accompanied Chiang to Peking, but was then placed under house arrest. These events took place on 25th December, so the news Marion was hearing was anticipating correctly the outcome and Chiang did indeed turn out to be a 'double crosser'.

Mamie came back the other day from a visit in a Chinese house with a great mouthful. She's told me how the Chinese count the remotest step

-by-marriage relation as a 'cousin' or 'uncle' or such, and I hardly believed her. Here's someone who was counted as a close relation however – 'My grandfather's concubine's stepbrother's wife's sister' – and all that a Chinese would think about in a little matter of a relationship like that is whether she is of the same generation as himself or not. Is she a cousin or an aunt? As Mamie said airily, "Oh – that was someone mentioned in passing in the conversation and everyone in the room understood the exact relationship, except myself."

We haven't seen any papers lately, but we have heard that things are happening down south which don't look so good. C.K.S. is a double crosser and if the general is really in his hands as we hear, there's a black future in a land not far from here ...

We were thankful to be in Moukden the time the business about the King came to a head *[the abdication of Edward VIII]*. We had heard rumours in the Chinese rags and none too savoury ones, so we were longing to hear the truth. Everyone was just living from one BBC announcement to the next – Hong Kong relays very clearly for us and there are several radio sets amongst the mission. We heard Edward's and the Queen's speech repeated for the *Empire Broadcast* by gramophone and we heard Baldwin's to Parliament the same day as he gave it.

We were interested to find that German, French, etc. in Moukden thought it was only because she was a commoner and an American that Mrs Simpson was being turned down. The moral side of it *[being a divorcee]* never seemed to strike them. And of course the fact that the people, through Parliament, could dictate to the King struck the Eastern mind dumb with amazement – (he isn't a god in England!) "Can he not do what he wants?"!! was one astounded question I heard.

Faku
25th December 1936

To Mother and Dad

The events which Marion described in this letter took place in the O'Neills' compound, which was some distance from that of Mamie and Marion. Gow was acting as caretaker while the O'Neills were in Ireland. Ivy Stokes, an Irish missionary nurse, was staying in Faku.

Haven't I said, "Come to Faku and see life?!" – hear me say it again – this Christmas has been the most interesting and exciting of any I've ever had – now I didn't say 'happy' – don't misunderstand me! ... the films aren't in with it.

Christmas morning – grey, dank at 10 to 5 – I shot up in bed, wakened, I was sure by running feet outside my window' .... Nothing more happened and I was just dozing off when I heard Fish dash in through the back door and down to Mamie's room. I was out before he had her door opened and heard him say, "Gow's wife is in the well" – I nabbed my flash light and rope which I had brought for skipping, and Fish disappeared. I had bought about 30ft of rope in a hank – couldn't get less, and thought it would come in useful for roping my boxes later – thank goodness! There wasn't as much anywhere about the 2 compounds.

Mamie and I pulled on knickers and Chinese gowns over our nightdresses and fled across to the other compound. The rest is a muddled picture of nightmare and comic effects (- yes indeed!). She had fallen into a well – must be over 100ft deep – 40 before you reach water and they had thrown down the bucket to her. We heard her groaning and moaning – the mother-in-law, husband and Fish were shouting encouragements to her – I suddenly realised someone would have to go down to her – the husband was too big for the well mouth – sick feeling in my middle as I decided it must be me - but it wasn't! Thanks be – Fish was busy getting off his gown, tying a board to the rope end, sat on it, twisted it round his shoulders, between his legs, around his waist and then we started to let him down – flash failed, candle brought, went out – Mamie and I trying to hold the girl up on well rope – Fish shouted he had her and then we started to haul – what a haul! Ivy was there by that time and she, Mamie and I hauled the weil rope; two men hauled Fish's rope – wet rope, hands blistering – God's will, make the old rope hold! – what a weight, ice slipping under our feet –hey Ivy keep back – you'll be in on top of them! they're up – Hey! Stop hauling! One man at the end of Fish's rope trying to haul both through the wee hole at once – Fish shoves her up – then is nearly drowned himself when some fool empties the whole bucket full of water on top of his face – Girl into the house – back to ours in the darkness for blankets and hot bottles, knocking up the hospital for the nurses and the drawing breaths of relief sitting round a stove in one of our bedrooms trying to sort out what happened.

86

She – Gow's wife – is only a youngster – 18, and got very sick in the middle of the night – the mother-in-law, a decent old soul really, got sick of her groans and moans and told Gow to hit her – he didn't, but said he'd go over to the hospital for medicine – he started out and the mother-in-law said something crossly and the girl, hysterical between pain and bad temper, screamed she was going to kill herself, lifted up her son under her arm and made for the well – fortunately she dropped the kid at the well mouth and jumped in herself. It is quite a small hole, a round lid on the top – Gow had just got his big compound gate open, heard the yells and came racing back – she had decided she preferred to live – Gow dropped the bucket down and got her hauled up a bit, but she dropped back – the mother-in-law held the wheel so that the rope was long enough just to keep her out of the water and Gow ran for help. It must have taken him several minutes to get anyone knocked up to open our compound gates, several more to run a 4 minute walk across our compound and get Fish knocked up – think what water 40 feet down Christmas day here must feel like! The girl must have been 15 minutes in the water in all – and she's alive and well.

I don't know how the ropes held – mine was only a fairly thick skipping rope, and the well rope has been three years in and out of water and lying in the sun. I won't forget the honour of having them almost up and wondering what under the sun we could get if either rope went and they fell in again. The comic moments – I said there were some, were provided by the mother-in-law – the moment Mamie and I appeared, "The chiaoshihs are here, what are you making that noise about?" went down the well to encourage her. Then, on a fresh outburst of howls, "What! Still shouting! Look at all the trouble you've made, getting the chiaoshihs out of their beds on a cold winter morning." Fish tackling the job of getting himself ready for going down as if he were used to doing it once a week at least – hat and gown off, another small bit of rope tied into mine – that was another of my horrors, I'd seen the knot tied and I couldn't remember whether it was near his end of the rope or ours – fortunately, we got past it in the first few feet of pulling. Then when he hauled out of the well and the cold air hit him, capering like a mountain goat and asking for his own home shouting, "Ooo! Cold! Cold!" with thirty feet of rope trailing behind him. And the final reaction as I saw Gow passing my window an hour later with the water for breakfast – thank goodness it wasn't our well she went into!

Mamie Johnston, in her account in her memoir, I Remember it Well, *recounts a detail which Marion did not want to worry her family with:* 'Where we had been cut or scratched, the blood had frozen as it flowed, so we appeared to have short strands of red wool sprouting from arms and hands and feet.'

In a second Christmas Day letter addressed only to her mother, Marion added: Thought there was no use adding the details in a letter for general family consumption – but the 'illness' the young wife was suffering from was a baby! Mamie had been telling me about 2 months ago that the first child the girl had – when she was 15, they had had a terrific time with her, 2 days labour up here and then 30 hours by cart to Tiehling where Dr Brown saved both of them by some miracle. She suffered appallingly and the thought of going through it again must have been driving her crazy ...

After we had hauled her out of the well and had left her in the hands of the nurses from the hospital, I again said, "Well, if the baby lives after that, it will be a wonder!"... But during breakfast the cook said, "Did you know a daughter was born to Gow's wife half an hour after you got her out of the well?" ... We heard afterwards the girl hadn't even warmed up before the child was born – just over 8 months old. New way of having twilight sleep – freeze the patient stiff! Both mother and baby in excellent health thank you!!

They hadn't expected the child and I suppose even the mother herself didn't realise what the pain meant when she got ill in the night. Gow is a decent big country lad, very shy and quiet, we like him as a servant. I was congratulating him and he said a most un-Chinese thing – "No matter about the baby – you saved my wife and that is what matters – whether it lived or died wasn't so important." The child is the important person in China – Gow is the one Christian member of the house – so you see it tells.

Faku
30th December 1936

To Grandma

We had a very happy Christmas here, we had a nurse, Ivy Stokes, as a visitor for 10 days. It sounds lonely I know, just 3 girls 100 miles from the nearest foreigner, but somehow I never think of that now, the Chinese are friends of ours (in a way that I don't believe the Indians can be to missionaries there) and I never feel any great need for other foreigners. The Chinese are like ourselves in a good many ways, the same sort of thing amuses them, they are a Northern people, hard-working and keen on education. I don't say I would like to stay here all my life and never see a foreigner! But a trip to Moukden once every 6 weeks is all we need to keep us happy and the rest of the time we are busy with our work and never have time to think long – or at least we don't let ourselves!.

The tongue is still slow in getting loosened! Chinese, I've been relieved to know, takes 5 years to soak into even the clever brains that come out in the consular service, so I've given myself until then before I despair. The first year exam is over, whoopee! We have a nice way here of going up when we are ready and just asking one of the examiners in Moukden to take us, we don't have any special date of taking as long as we don't run over our year. We don't have marks either, the examiner warns us if we have only scraped through, that we'll have to put more work into it for next year – but Dr Inglis said I had done well, so I came home rejoicing.

I've been going round today giving out picture texts that Mrs O'Neill sent for some old wifies, her special friends. I had to find the texts in their Bibles and leave them well marked so that they could look them up again. All Chinese have their walls papered with white paper or newspaper, but Mrs O'Neill must have given one old lady her wallpaper for lo and behold when I looked round the place was covered with pages out of *Punch*! It is well she couldn't understand the jokes, they mightn't have suited her sense of the proprieties.

While most of the letters Marion sent were on plain paper, some, such as this, had printed designs at the top.

89

CHAPTER 4
1937

The beginning of January 1937 found Marion in Moukden for the annual meeting of the missionaries, the Manchurian Mission Conference. In a letter of 7th January she told of the preparations she had been involved in, including spending 'mortal hours' with four 12 to 14 year olds, washing and counting crockery that had been left in a dirty attic since the previous meeting a year before. The meeting included business sessions and Bible Study groups.

c/o Miss Hodgkis
Moukden
18th January 1937

To Dad and Mother

Marion was staying in the house of the Secretary of the YWCA in Moukden. She had been given the job of editing the Irish missionaries' reports (anything from two to six pages long) to 'produce an interesting and comprehensive report for home consumption'. *However, there was still time for relaxation with a rather fierce game of hockey and some skating.*

On Sat we had a fast and furious game of hockey – Dr Brown got his lip split. Two sticks were broken – I got the knee the size of a small pillow and one of the Chinese Drs got a terrific wallop on the back of the head from one of the broken sticks when it was in flight. Dr Brown's accident was really no one's fault – he was scrumming and someone swung a stick too high – the sticks which broke had already been mended and my knee is almost better – with more recklessness than sense I got in front of a ball driven at full speed by one of our strong men – but I stopped a certain goal and nearly got hugged by a Chinese Dr, he was so delighted about it! Mrs Brown massaged it later on and bound it up, and it is as right as can be today.

I went out with the 'Brownies', Helen, Elizabeth and Alexander, on Saturday morn to skate, and being clad in a high necked blue jumper and no hat on, I was presented to our great amusement – with a

½ ticket at the skating rink – China hasn't aged me any. I can stay on my feet – I haven't had a tumble yet, but I am far from graceful and I feel such an inferiority complex creeping over me when I watch the Chinese. The rink is just a big bit of the river railed off and swept and well kept. There is an outside circle where only racers go and then the centre is for figure skating and beginners. Some of the boys, clad in close fitting tights with hands clasped behind their backs or else folded nonchalantly across their breast, go round the outside circle like blue and green streaks. Inside they perform the most amazing acrobatics, waltzing, figure 3 and 8s, jumping distances or heights, stopping suddenly, + springing right round on their toes – while I, like a snail (much less gracefully), creep unhappily round the edge clinging to lampposts conveniently placed at intervals.

Emily Brown and her three children, Helen, Alexander and Elizabeth – 'the Brownies' with whom Marion went skating in Moukden. Marion had met the Browns in Pei Tai Ho in 1936.

The photograph above was taken in Tiehling where James Brown was in charge of the Scottish Mission Hospital, and Emily Brown, also a doctor, was responsible for work with women patients. Because she was married, however, she, like all missionary wives never appeared in the list of missionaries.

Today a Chinese boy out of the hospital dispensary came up and spoke to me in English of a sort, a nice lad and a graaand skater – I was only sorry it wasn't just the proper thing to do or I would have asked for his hand to cling to and asked him to coach me, he could skate in any position I think.

Any students who can speak English just love to speak to us – they get such 'face' before the other lads and it gives them quite a kick to speak to a foreign woman I expect – they are always so courteous that no one could object in the slightest.

I hope I'll get skating every day this week before I go back to Faku, because before I am up in Moukden again I fancy the ice will be gone The children here do enjoy it, the place was crowded with school boys and girls today and of course the foreign children home on holiday still are revelling in it. Chefoo *[school]* gives two months at Christmas and in the summer, because the roads are frozen enough for country children to get back to the mission stations by cart, some can't get *[here]* at all in the summer and have to holiday at Chefoo beach which isn't a very good spot I believe.

After being educated at home by their mother until the age of 12, the Brown children attended the boarding school run by the China Inland Mission at Chefoo on the northern shore of the Shandong peninsula.

c/o MacNaughtan
Moukden
24th January 1937

To Dad and Mother

Marion had now moved to stay with the MacNaughtans for a few days. Their daughter, Marion's friend, Flora, was in Ashiho where she was in charge of the woman's hospital.

I hope you haven't had large gaps in the mail lately, but I am afraid from newspaper reports that my last two weeks letters are still lying in the north waiting for a train to go on in. You may have seen from the newspapers that the Siberian train hasn't been coming into Manchuria owing to a dispute with the authorities, the reason given is brutal treatment of Soviet employees by Japanese at one of the border stations – and I wudna wonder ...

Mrs Mac says to tell you – Mother – that there will be someone in China for the next four years who can spank me, she thought it might relieve your mind to know. She was marking the linen handkerchiefs with Chinese ink and vinegar (a mixture that is supposed to be indelible) – well it wasn't working, the linen didn't seem to take it. At last I hit on the reason why – they were decent Presbyterian hankies from the North of Ireland and objected to any work being done on the

92

Sabbath. Whereupon, Mrs Mac rose in wrath and skelped me ...

26th January

Marion continues her letter after a couple of days.

Marion took this photograph of children skating – in a less busy place than Moukden.

Mamie and I go off this afternoon by bus direct to Faku – over the river on the ice, that will be a new experience. This bus only runs in Jan, or Dec and Jan, when the ice is firmest. It was lovely to watch the traffic going along the ice when I was over in East Moukden – all the Scotch Mission property is on the banks of the river there – old pictures of Holland came back to my mind. Children played on it all the time, men carrying bundles of firewood on the end of a long pole over their shoulders, or baskets of farm produce or hens, these people trot along with a short hopping step, donkeys with bundles – boys on skates with their school books under their arm – it made a very lively road and a sparkling one when the sun was shining.

Moukden
26th January 1937

Letter from Mrs MacNaughtan to Mrs Young

Marion sits beside me writing home, so I'm scribbling a note to go with it. She's a dear and everyone likes her, just the sort of girl to get on here. She looks happy and sees the fun in every situation – as you know – that's a priceless gift for the foreign field! Her language is getting on well. You may be easy in your mind about her, for she has many friends and many homes are open to her when she wants a change.

Fakumen
28th January 1937

Letter from Mamie Johnston to Mrs Young.

The letter thanks Marion's mother for sending her two 'beautiful hankies', and continues: Marion and I just returned here on Tuesday last. It's good to get home again in spite of Moukden luxuries. And I am enjoying having Marion for company – she is so amused at things that have become ordinary to me, that I seem to see them afresh, or with eyes ten years younger. She is so much the making of a good missionary that it will be a real calamity if she gets married ... However, Fakumen is as exclusive as a nunnery, so she's all right in the meantime!

Fakumen
31st January 1937

To Dad and Mother

Wang Huei Chün, the Headmistress of the Girls' School, who impressed Marion and Mamie when she came to take up her appointment in 1937.

We have a very nice lassie, the new Girls' headmistress, staying in the house for 4 days before school opens. Mamie asked her to come down early and get things talked over and fixed up before opening day. She is a minister's daughter and sister, and the general knowledge that lassie has, filled Mamie and myself with delight after the usual conversation of the average well-educated person here. Name 'Wang' – she is healthy looking, long, well-shaped capable hands and two short pigtails just reaching her shoulders. That is the way a good many girls wear their hair and it makes 20 year olds look absurdly young. This girl is 23 and she knows a thing or two about running a school. Mamie took her round the buildings and she started planning out everything as if she were a bride going into a new house – she has all sorts of interesting plans for the school programme, both religious and secular – a most refreshingly constructive person after the girl Mamie had to work with last time ...

31st January 1937

To Mother

In addition to her usual letter home Marion also sent a separate letter to her mother as it was to be 'all about clothes'. *She did, however, write about other topics in it:*

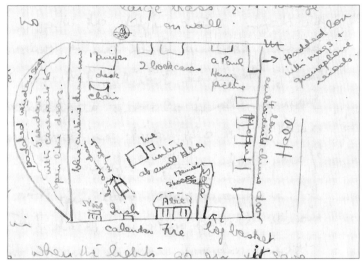

The plan of Marion and Mamie's sitting room.

I'm sitting in our sitting room – I'll give you the shape of it I think. That room looks a bit more spacious than it is, but there is comfortable room with no feeling of crowding – Mamie prefers sofa, I, large chair. She puts the sofa there to help break any draught from the door. Abie occupies most of a very pretty, hand-worked wool rug. The curtains are soft blue silk and look especially lovely in the firelight. We pull them across when the lights go on and it saves having little adjustable curtains on each of the little windows. There are several more pictures than I have put in – but these are the ones I like best. The Paul Henry has lovely green fields and trees, water and a white clouded summer sky. It takes me home in a minute. I like China, and never feel particularly 'strange' in it – as far as the country goes, but it hasn't many half tones like Ireland – every season comes loudly – no wee green sprouts slowly coming out on hedges – they pop and burst at once, no first snowdrops, no wee pink rose buds, they are born roses I think! Bluebells in the wood on Monaghan estate and on the banks around the lake, primroses in under the overhanging hedges in the Lagan lane, smell of fresh cut hay, the Mournes with gorse blazing gold, the smoke lying over Milford in a hollow on a summer evening seen from Allan's lane – the scent of the garden in the evening – these are all the things I see, but I don't sit and weep over them – I can remember them completely enough in a bus here – to cut out completely the spits and smells around me. They are the things that are Ireland for me, and the smell of the peat fires is never in the air anywhere else.

In this letter Marion was referring to the various parts of Ireland she knew well – first to Clones in County Monaghan, where she had lived with her parents, then to County Down, where the Mournes could be seen from her maternal grandparents' farm, and finally to Milford, in Donegal, where had stayed with paternal grandparents.

Faku
2nd February 1937

A continuation of the letter begun on 10th November 1936, to be sent back with missionaries returning to Ireland as the information was too sensitive to be seen by the Japanese censor.

It is a long time since I wrote anything in this epistle – but things have been quiet and there hasn't been anything worth the writing. Did I tell you that the schools all have to teach Japanese now? In some way it was intimated that a Jap in the school was necessary. That of course was to have a spy on the spot, and one on the school board too where we spend a good deal of time thinking out ways to circumvent their rules and regulations! Mamie was just beginning to cast about to find a friendly person amongst them, who would only report things that she actually heard or saw and not invent them, when Chu the Korean got in before us and sent someone to suggest his wife to Mamie. Of course we couldn't refuse, so she is now installed on the board of teachers. As a matter of fact, as far as Mamie can see she could be a lot worse, for she is only a country woman not overly clever, inclined to be friendly

96

and quiet going, so we hope nothing more will turn up for a while to disturb us. Mamie made her toe the line early – she hadn't been long accepted when a notice came that all the teachers in the town were to attend a Jap class during the holiday for a fortnight. Some of our teachers don't belong to this district at all and one comes from a place two days journey away, so Mamie wasn't going to keep the poor lass here and only give her a week's holiday before starting a five month term. She turned out a fairly good crowd, then she remembered Mrs Chu! She was on the staff so she should go – and she did – and we hoped Chu had cold meals for the fortnight, for they had to attend six hours a day. Chu couldn't say no because the order came from his office, and besides Mamie was so polite when she went to see her, she could take no offence.

Just a few days ago before school opened all the teachers in the schools in Faku were called up before the head of the Education Office and told where they could get off and what they were to do. Each school has a photograph of the Emperor – the poor wee creature – and at all special meetings the school had to bow to him. One of the dictums of the education man was that the head master or mistress was in charge of the photo and that he or she had to sleep on the school premises to take care of His Majesty – and TO COMMIT SUICIDE IF ANYTHING HAPPENED TO THE PHOTOGRAPHS – that just as calmly as if he were saying you must report if to the police at once.

The Emperor referred to was Pui Yi, whom the Japanese had installed as their puppet 'Head of State' in Manchukuo.

This photograph, taken by Marion at Kirin in September 1936, of school children 'celebrating' the date of the Japanese recognition of Manchukuo, is an example of how the authorities used school pupils for their political ends.

Things are quite quiet now, and we have no feeling of suspense, one of the unpleasanter men in the head office has been moved and the new one was very polite when Mamie and I went in the other day to see about an extension of my residency cert. You will be glad to know that my republican principles have not been noticed and I have been elevated to a six months certificate. *[A reference to Marion's home being in the Irish Republic, although she had in fact a British passport.]*

Well I hope there will be nothing more to add to this before it goes. Mamie goes to Moukden soon and I send it with her to go with some of the folk who go home soon.

Faku
4th February 1937

To Dad

Any one at home who thinks mission work consists in going out and stopping at villages to preach and then moving on again, would get their eyes opened out here! I've just seen another little bit of unexpected work that I will have in my future, and at the present very nebulous, station. The Girls' School has a good many boarders and there are stoves in each room, as well as the kitchen fires to be provided for each winter at Chinese New Year, the time all the farmers sell their produce. We use a good deal of coal of course, but some of the cooking and lighting of the stoves is done with millet stalk. Fish goes out into the street and bargains with men, then they come to the school and Mamie sees to the unloading of the bundles. Fish has agreed to pay so much for a cart of say, 150 bundles, taking the man's word for it. Then the carter starts unloading here and shouts each number as he throws it out. The count goes like this 25, 26, 27, (drops a bundle) 29, 30 – "Oh no, you don't." Mamie joins in, "28, 29." The man grins and takes the count again. I'm sorry most of this goes on while I am at 'school' in the morning, so I've only seen a little of it. Yesterday I watched her standing like Joseph in the middle of a crowd of hairy old carters, dispensing jokes, reproofs and money with equal rapidity.

7th February

I had hoped to see home mail today, we often get it on Sunday, but I suppose the rush of Chinese New Year has put things back. It falls on the 11th February this year and there is as big a fuss and bustle here as round about Christmas at home, and everyone is on holiday. The narrow streets in Faku are crowded with country people in to buy and sell – or I should say sell and buy, because they have to get some money to spend on feast meals. I told you before that the Chinese rarely have meat – the poorer ones I mean – and that is the greater part of the population. But they make up for abstinence at the New Year. Mamie says that in having a New Year feast for any of the folks here she has to order 3½ lbs per head! And that sort of feeding goes on for several days before and after New Year's Day.

A fish hawker.

The frozen fish is being hawked about by men with baskets and this week when I was in town I saw a fish shop on the pavement! – or what passes for one. The fish was arranged in high piles according to size, some fish about 9ins long, some 3 feet, stacked across each other, with a dirty old man squatting beside them, scuffling and spitting all around him – it was a cold day. I said something – "My goodness! have a look at our fish shop," to Mamie, to which she replied, "It probably is our fish shop and very useful too, it is always fresh."!!! I feel rather off fish just now.

Today was the 1st Sunday for the school kids after Christmas holidays – and many colds continued with a north wind that would freeze you to the back bone, produced three rows of sniffling, snorting wee boys and girls in the Primary seats in front of me. They kicked up such a row that I couldn't hear the pastor at all in the 1st prayer! They usually stay all the service, except once a month when they have their own special one, but today Mamie signed to the teachers to take them out before the sermon and I had great difficulty in keeping my face straight when I saw the wee boys receive the news. They are the same the world over! They looked at each other sideways, grinning from ear to ear as they tried to suppress it as they fled out into the aisle to march out, but they couldn't manage it and their eyes were still sparkling and their faces alive with mischief as they went. The girls have more sense of the proprieties, but I saw nudges passed along from elbow to elbow!

Faku
13th February 1937

To Dad and Mother

Kitty Cherry, Marion's friend and fellow-Irishwoman from Peking, had come to stay in Faku:

Kitty Cherry took these photographs in Kirin in February 1937, just before she paid a visit to Marion in Faku. They show wood being transported, horses resting after moving wood and a view showing the Kirin hills in the background. There was clearly snow in Kirin at this time, unlike Tiehling which was further south.

She *[Kitty]* was up staying in Kirin with the Sloans for a few days and then came here for the inside of a week. I went up to Tiehling on Monday to meet her, as the bus place is a bit awkward to find here, and had a very comfortable run up in a new bus – as nice as anything at home, upholstered seats, polished handrails, windows that opened downwards so that you can have air without draft – and curtains – the latter I saw used as a hanky and a towel when an orange was finished! Kitty's train was early, so we had to put in two hours or more in town. I had brought lunch and we took it out to the hill outside the town and got a spot in the sun to lie and laze in. It is cold, but as long as there is no wind and the sun is shining on you it is very pleasant. Kitty was commenting on how miserable a picnic in Feb would be at home, one thing of course is that the ground is as dry here as can be.

The journey home was not the best part of the day, however. It was a day or two before New Year and everyone was coming home. Kitty got wedged in the back seat between two men laden with bundles, who spread themselves all over her. I sat down on the floor at her feet – and the aisle was very narrow! I can stand putting up with sitting up on the floor (some feat). I can stand having old men sitting on my knees, as one poor old lad did for quite a while when he got knocked off his feet as he was getting out of the bus. I can accept being stood on, and having cigarette ash from the six smokers round about sprinkled over me. I can stand the smell of garlic, wafted strongly on the breeze from one sleeper who was hanging over me and whom I had to prop up every now and then – but I cannot stand the smell of dried fish ... and there was a large and bulgy bundle wrapped in sacking on someone's knee just on a level with my nose ... quite the worst experience of smells I have had in a fairly varied acquaintanceship with smells, my dears. I was rapidly becoming unconscious, when the old lad aforesaid nearly brought disaster on himself by landing on my tummy. He left the end of a case vacated however and with much expenditure of will power, mind conquered matter and I reached the case without – er – further incident. There was an open window near and a cool breeze fanned my beaded brow, and in a minute or two I was able to do the honours of the country to my hitherto ignored guest. Aye, we sit convenient in a Chinese bus.

Marion started a second letter on 13th February:

One of the leading merchants in the town asked us to eat at one o'clock, at which time Mamie, Miss Jang, Miss Lung and I went. We reached the shop to find our host, various men relatives, and a child or two sitting round the stove in the back of the shop, eating melon seeds and drinking tea. This man lives in the shop often, and does not always go home, so we were invited there instead of to his house.

We sat down on the k'ang and were given handfuls of melon seed and tea. I was sitting listening to as much of the conversation as I could understand, and solemnly cracking melon seeds, spitting them out on the floor with the best of them – I reached my host's foot in a sitting spit once – one has to do something to cheer oneself up in a strange land, don't look so shocked Mother. I was badly tempted to get the giggles a couple of times this afternoon and once was when I stopped and listened to the crack – crack—spit, spit, of about eight or nine politely conversing leaders of the Church. Before I go further I had better point out the uniqueness of this meal. There were women asked by men, there were men sitting talking to women and accepting their pronouncements as sense and worth the listening to, and these men and women sat down together to eat. Then, apart from us there were some of the shop assistants at the table and the shopkeeper would not usually sit with any underling. But this house is Christian.

After about half an hour of nuts and tea and conversation, we went to another room to eat, a big round table with Mamie and myself in the upper seats. The cold dishes were served first and very good too – there were six – cold meats in sauces, a sort of salad with bean sprouts, cold strips of sort of egg omelette, pickled cabbage, liver and garlic. We made inroads on these before anything else appeared, then the hot dishes came – there were twenty in all – and that does not count the six or eight plates of a species of saltless bun with bean sauce in the middle, that were emptied, and all the little dishes of sauces and pickles that strewed the table! The one that I remembered best was an extremely good fish covered with sweet sauce, a piece of boiled pork, so tender that it was falling to pieces, but with all the flavour intact. Soups and soups and more soups, with all the vegetables that could be put in and egg forby. A soup that was really baked custard with tree fungus in sauce on top. Little balls of meat in thick gravy. There were lots more, but they were swimming in a sea of steam before I had satisfied the courtesies!

I can manage my chopsticks now without causing too much comment, but at a feast like today's where there is a little more ceremony than I am used to, I have my bad moments. The worst is when each new dish comes in and the host waves each of the honoured guests to it before anyone starts on it. Then the whole table watches while I tremblingly put out my chopsticks and try to wrest a piece of fish out of its side or negotiate a slippery piece of vegetable across a large expanse of table to my bowl. It isn't done to move the bowl near you, so you can imagine the state of the table before the meal is far gone.

Our host is a proper merchant, the sort one sees in books, very fat, very shrewd, very kindly, with a nimble tongue, wears a round hat with a little button on top and fills my heart with joy every time I see him, because he looks exactly the kind of Chinese I have read of and imagined.

There were several high spots for me in the meal. One was when I was beginning to feel that another bite would do the trick (but everyone else looked like beginning the meal, so I did not dare stop) and the table was a hazy swimming mass of soups, bits of dropped vegetables and meat. I noticed a steam rising above my host's head in a sun beam. I traced to its source, thinking it was a new dish, but found to my joy that it was his nice, large, completely bald pate that was steaming and that it was glistening with the nicest crown of sparkling dew drops – when we eat in China we put some force into it! Then I spat out my fish bones with the greatest aplomb upon the floor, it was quite a new experience. I had never had the courage to do it before.

And at the end I was given a cup of hot water – to drink I thought, until I heard a strange sound and there was every one solemnly sitting making the most wonderful noise as they washed out their mouths and it spat it on the floor. I had been glad to see that water and there wasn't much left, but I found enough in the bottom to make a good gurgle and quite a respectable splash. We were finished and we rose straight from the table and left, waddling home.

Faku
14th February 1937

On 2nd February Marion had said in the letter to be sent home by returning missionaries to avoid the Japanese censor, that she hoped that there would be nothing more to add before it went off. It turned out there was ...

I was a bit quick in saying that everything was quiet again, hardly had I put your letter into the envelope when news came of another arrest. I think I mentioned Fang, an elder who was in danger from a man called Ding, in the middle of the last spasm. He was accused of selling guns and a day or two before New Year (Chinese) he was arrested in his shop. Jap soldiers came down when the shop was packed with New Year shoppers and would have roped him up to pull him through the streets if the man in charge of him, a Chinese interpreter who has always been very courteous to us, had not insisted on his being left free.

He was put in the prison here late in the afternoon, in a room with three robbers who had been taken a few days before and left without any food. Then his adventures started. The robbers were led out to a room outside to wash, a soldier with a gun keeping guard. One asked to go outside and the door was left open between their room and the guard room. There were three soldiers in it, one standing beside another prisoner who was washing, one asleep and the other cleaning kit. When the third robber came back, the other two were near the door, tipped him the wink and they rushed the guard room. One snatched the gun from their guard and held up the room while the others got their fetters off. I don't know how they managed that, because they were chained hand and foot, but they did, and dashed out through the compound gate which was not locked. They knocked down the sleepy sentry, but he managed to get his gun up and got one through the head. Thank goodness he was killed at once, poor beggar. The other two escaped and probably got help for there is no word of them since.

All this was the best thing that could have happened from Fang's point of view. The place was so disturbed and the folk in charge so busy trying to save their own bacon that they had not time for Fang. It was Saturday when he was taken, no work is done on Sunday in Jap offices so he was free until Monday. He remarked since he got out that it was one of God's way of giving him a rest, that he had been very tired with the New Year rush and his arms were sore with lifting boxes down, so he slept all Sunday!

In the ordinary way he would have been kept here and tortured to find out where the guns were and then sent to Tiehling for trial, this procedure lengthened by the fact that it was New Year and no one bothering much about the work. The escape of the robbers brought the Head Bug down from Tiehling to investigate the business and Fang came to light long before he might have. He was also helped by our old enemy Chu, who has become quite friendly lately. If he is a beast, he is a just beast and seems to have decided that the Christian church is not guilty of treason against the state until it is proved. He put in a good word for Fang, gave the two Japs some drink and they mellowed enough to say that they would take Fang up to Tiehling and investigate. They had a very small car and were standing by it when Fang came waddling along, he is a huge and most respectable old josser, so they started to laugh when they saw the prisoner. He was told to get in and sit in the middle of the back seat to balance the car, but that did not appeal to his sense of the proprieties and he said, 'Oh no, he would sit on the floor if the Japs sat on the seat.' He must have made good progress on his way, he had a shrewd and amusing tongue and the Japs spoke the language, for when they reached Tiehling and were getting out of the car someone asked who Fang was and the Head replies with a laugh, "Oh, this is a friend of ours." His case was taken up at once and he was treated with the utmost courtesy, given a chair and told finally who his accuser was. Fang said they were not enemies and he had not seen him for some time, so we still suspect that Ding or some of his minions are at the root of this, because the unfortunate accuser has a brother a robber.

The next day Fang was sent home, the man even asking if he had money with him for the bus! He also told him that if any interpreter or spy tried to tell him that he had used his influence to help him (Fang) out of this trouble and demand money for it, that he was to be reported. This looks like new days for us.

Before Christmas and just after the last trouble, a Christian Jap going up to Hsinking to take up office gave Tiehling the once over on his way and gave the folks in authority there a going over for the way things had been going on in the name of justice. A new lot of men have come in since, both here and at Tiehling. We have got rid of Pig's Mouth, God help the place that has got him, and the new man in that office has been very polite to us when we went to the office for my extended residency cert. Also, to our great joy, now that the two men who searched our house have left the town, an apology was tendered one day for it by two men who came to say that they had heard this had been done, and OF COURSE they knew it was quite against the law!

However, we feel that things are settled for another while – until this lot of men get a move – and the new lot have to satisfy themselves that we are not deliberate and treacherous enemies of the state.

We had a school inspection the other day, just to see that we had started everything according to regulations. The magistrate, the head of the Education Office, a Jap and an interpreter. They were all very friendly. The magistrate is a friend of Mamie's and he helped all he could. The Jap could speak a little Chinese and understood quite a lot, so when he went away from our house his refrain all the time in the teachers' room was that Mamie's language was so good! It was he who asked if I was Mamie's wee servant girl, as reported some time ago! They were amazed at the neat rooms and the quiet polite teachers. When they hear what our school grant was, they asked, "Per month?" and looked so astonished when Mamie said, "Per year." The magistrate said to the head teacher that our premises were the neatest in the town and that he did not know how it was done on the grant we had. Even if that was only politeness, it indicated a friendliness that cheered the teachers very much.

The above letter was typewritten. Added in pencil below was the following message. (The Stevies were the Stevensons who were returning to Ireland on furlough):

I had so hoped to get the letter off with the Stevies, who go in March, but we have no excuse to go to Moukden this month and I can't spare the time for a holiday again, so I'm not sure when I will go now. However, I am going to round it off in hopes that there will be nothing more to report.

Faku
27th February 1937

To the Twins

The letter was sent to Helen and Clara to give them good wishes on their 13th birthday. A card and present of socks had already been posted.

I was glad to have your letter Helen with Mother's last – boys-o-boys your writing is improving – you'll soon be as good as me! You asked if nurses always wear trousers like the Chinese one I sent you. In the winter they wear them down to their ankles and tied tight; in the summer they wear them about half down their legs and white stockings underneath.

I said I would keep this letter over until after I had been out to see the lantern festival. I had hoped I should see a dragon to tell you about, but they were not out when we were in town. I saw one, one day, a small one about 6 or 7 feet long that some wee boys had made, green and black circles with a wide and ferocious mouth. They usually put a lantern in the mouth and the wee boys walk, making legs for it.

It was a full moon night ... The streets were crowded and all the shops still open. Each door had lanterns on the outside, some very big and very pretty. They were painted with flowers and fish and fruit, or a Chinese scene, and we moved along slowly looking at everything. There was music in some of the shops – some had gramophones and some had men playing. I used to think Chinese music awful – and still

106

do if it is too near – but it is a very good rhythm and makes you want to snap your fingers in time to it.

Faku
13th March

To Dad and Mother

In this letter Marion explains how there were two Protestant churches in Faku:

It isn't only at home that there are splits in the church because a few folk think themselves better than their brethren draw their skirts aside and form a group of their own. A few years ago there was a bad split here after the present pastor *[Shang]* came – he is a fine man, a scholar and yet not above the heads of the people – but he didn't preach hellfire enough for the man Evangelist and the Bible Woman who were here then. They did all they could to get him to resign and then they called a Church Meeting off their own bat – even telling a good many of the old women, who didn't understand what it was all about, that it was a meeting to ask the Bible Woman to stay on because she was thinking of leaving and that they were just to vote when they saw his hand go up. (Well!)

However, Mamie went and made her protest, and took the two leading elders with her, who rose and left with her. When she finished speaking, the back of that meeting was broken. Eventually about 20 people, one family of 8 women and 1 man being part of it, left and set up a Church on their own.

The Evangelist Wang agreed to go away south if they gave him his travelling expenses for himself and family – and the Bible Woman. The money was raised and he gave it over to the newly-formed church, saying that it was given to him and he could do what he liked with it. Eventually they raised the price again and bought them tickets and they went off to Yinkow, which place receives all malcontents with open arms – and incidentally trains a good many of the malcontents who go out to trouble the Church. The Evangelist was married and his friendship with the Bible Woman was a great scandal here because he was never out of her house, they called themselves 'Ling hsin ti peng yu', 'Spirit-friends' 'Soulmates'!

By the way, here the Evangelist once preached on 'O thou man of God, there is death in the pot'. O'Neill, Mamie, Pastor and co. being the death – and he, by inference, the man of God who could cure it. 'S wonderful what spiritual pride can do.

The account of the split is totally at variance with that by Minister Hu Changyu in his history of the Faku Church quoted in Mark O'Neill's biography of his grandfather. Hu Changyu claimed the split was as a result of a difference of opinion between Frederick O'Neill and two very popular preachers – Wang Shangling, the Evangelists referred to in Marion's letter, and Yao Zhihui. Frederick used the excuse to dismiss the two because of lack of funds. Hu Changyu wrote that when Wang went to discuss the stopping of his wages Dr O'Neill 'impolitely' expelled him from his house which caused anger among many of the church members. The breakaway church was then set up and eventually grew to more than 150 members. They re-joined the parent church after Frederick left in 1942.

Hu Changyu, while expressing a high esteem for Dr O'Neill felt that the split was as a result of the latter's arrogance because foreigners considered themselves 'first class citizens'. It must be said that the extreme behaviour attributed to the Irishman seems at variance with what else we know of him and there must have been some truth in Marion's account. Difference over theology could well have been a factor and accounts for some of the tensions between the official and the house churches in China in the 21st Century. Whatever the correctness of the two accounts, that attributed to Hu Changyu does show there could be tensions between the missionaries and the Chinese Church in the 1930s.

The reference to Yinkow training 'a good many of the malcontents' refers to the Bible School set up there by the McCammons independently of the Missionaries' Conference and the Chinese Synod. It became the principal centre of conservative theology. While Marion got on well personally with the McCammons, she, like many of her colleagues, felt that they went their own way irrespective of the views of the other missionaries.

Marion then changed the subject:

I was in the kitchen a few moments ago giving Fish the recipe for salad dressing and when I had finished I began to laboriously explain the

108

ingredients of salad because I didn't know the name. Fish listened to the bitter end and then remarked, "We call that sal-lad"!! I could have popped with wrath that he hadn't mentioned it earlier. You never know when they use the foreign word and when not – if there are Chinese sounds something the same they make a stab at it. "Bu-ding", "ka fa le" you may recognise as 'pudding' and 'cornflour', and "ca ki" are 'cakes'. On the other hand cloves are 'fragrant nails', 'huang tinga', which is a pretty name I think.

'Fish' the cook stands on the right of this photo. He was so called because the Yu of his name (Yu Shih Fu meant Fish).

He is wearing a hat he was proud of, but which Marion considered made him look like a bandit.

On the left is Kao Kuei I, the houseboy who was employed by Mamie and Marion in the autumn of 1937.

Faku,
19th March 1937

To Dad and Mother

Marion explains how she and Mamie had celebrated Ireland's National Saint's Day on the 17th:

The top of the morning to you – Long Live Ireland! Mamie and I celebrated St Patrick's Day the best way we could. I began it by singing 'The Wearing of the Green' outside her door in the early dawn (well – er – round about 7) – I couldn't remember 'The Dear Little Shamrock', and then when I got to the table I found she had cut paper shamrocks out and had a map of Ireland in green paper on the wall (It was a bit thin about the middle, but she said it was because there was a large bit of Clones missing – the beggar!).

We were busy the rest of the morning, but in the afternoon attended a Welcome Meeting, play and concert given for the headmistress and a new teacher. After that Mamie and I had planned the day for ourselves.

109

We went down along the bank of a wee stream where the ice was just melting and we could hear the tinkle of the water underneath and there we gathered armfuls of pussy willows, some out and some just coming. We put them on the bookcase, the mantelpiece and the floor and then we got into our party frocks, got some Irish books out and *[gramophone records of]* John McCormack singing 'Mother Ireland' – 'The Rose of Tralee' – 'The Road to the Rosses' – 'The Irish Emigrant', and settled down to enjoy the evening by ourselves.

Mamie had thrown out large hints to the teachers and the Bible Woman, for they usually drop in for shorter or longer periods in the evening, but the Bible Woman didn't take 'em and in she came. We talked for a while, but we wanted to read aloud and couldn't with any courtesy while she was there, so at last I struck on a plan. They sit quite happily through jazz or light music, but opera chases them. I was afraid it wasn't going to work – it took four Mischa Elman and Chaliapin to move her, and Chaliapin at his deepest and most passionate is enough to give me the dreeps.

Then having bowed her out, we came back rejoicing to our books – F.W. Marshall's *Ballads and Verses from Tyron* and Moira O'Neill's *Songs of the Glens of Antrim* – and lastly and most rib-stretchingly, Somerville and Ross's *Lisheen Races* ...

Dad was enquiring tenderly about my acquaintanceship with the flea family in my bus trips. I've never met one and my average allowance on the Crumlin Road trams *[in Belfast]* was one per week. The coy who run these buses are up and coming – the buses are kept very clean and the conductor and driver have snappy looking uniforms, a blend of Western and Chinese. The Japanese trains couldn't be cleaner, 3rd class is as good as our Irish 2nds *[Irish trains still had 2nd class compartments as well as 1st and 3rd]* and a boy comes round brushing up about every hour and in the summer sprinkles disinfectant as he goes.

The Japanese consider us rather dirty as a matter of fact – the better class amongst them seem to wash most of the time. They carry their sponge bags with them on the train run – a 2 hour journey would probably have 2 washes. Of course, country China is not like that! Mamie says she is crawling when she comes back from a tour, but I happen to have struck lucky so far.

110

This photograph from the South Manchurian Railway's Fifth Report on Progress in Manchuria in 1936, *probably shows one of the Company's buses. While Marion wrote favourably about the buses between Tiehling and Faku, the road, which was sometimes closed as a result of the weather, was very different from the well-constructed 'New Highway' shown in this photograph.*

A General Direction Bus and a New Highway in Manchoukuo

Yesterday I wrote my first letter in Chinese – over a whole page – imagine that – boy! What a job it was trying to express myself consecutively as well as making sure I had collected the proper number of strokes. It was to my ex-teacher and was not written with the courteous polish of a proper Chinese letter – I haven't learnt how to do that and never will. The missionaries rarely write their own letters – it takes far, far too long and a Chinese man or woman could polish off in 10 minutes what it would take us 2 hours to do. Mamie's are all done by the Bible Woman.

Scotch Mission Hospital,
Tiehling
7th April 1937

To Dad and Mother

In a previous letter Marion told her parents she had contracted flu when in Moukden and had spent several days in bed at the MacNaughtan's. She had set off by train at the start of her journey back to Faku, but had been delayed in Tiehling, the nearest railway station, as detailed below. A note alongside the address read, 'No I'm not ill.'

As you will see by the address – I haven't got back to Faku yet. I'll hardly have the face to take a summer holiday after this! But it is the country, not inclination, which is prolonging this holiday. I came up on Friday (2nd) only to find that the bus was off and would be for a few days as the thaw had melted the road badly. I knew the Browns were due back here last week to start work again in their hospital here after doing six months relief work in Moukden Medical College, so I came round hoping to find them, but they were not coming up until Saturday evening, so back I had to go to Moukden. I got some hockey in, so I didn't altogether regret the delay! Then I came up here with the Browns and I think the road looks hopeful for going tomorrow. I toyed with the idea of going by droskey, but if the road were really bad I might have to spend the night in a Chinese inn by the way, and although Mamie has told me they are very decent people, I don't relish the thought with my smattering of Chinese. The Browns wouldn't let me go anyway, so don't worry! ...

I think I have also spoken about Kathleen Whitehead – an English girl who came out to run a small school for a year for the community children until she could get married to Lionel Ford, a curate in Peking. She was also here for the weekend, as Lionel, who was in Moukden for the Easter services and had to go on to Harbin for a weekend, had promised to come and spend a couple of days with the Browns during his visit.

The Anglican Church in Moukden had no rector and, in a spirit of ecumenical cooperation, was kept open by the services being taken by Church of Scotland missionaries. On special occasions an Anglican curate, such as Lionel, was sent up from Peking to Moukden.

He arrived here on Monday, to be greeted by the glad news which had come in his absence, from the Bishop that they could get married at the end of June, instead of waiting until the November of 1938 as was the Bish's first pronouncement. Well, was he glad or was he glad?? and were they interested in other people or were they not!? It is rather distracting to have one's most pithy remarks on the political situation in Europe broken into by Lionel putting his head on Kathleen's shoulder and breathing 'daaarling' into her shell pink ear. However, I finally took refuge in my bedroom when the Browns weren't there to support me and they (strangely enough) never seemed to miss me. Bless them! Who wouldn't be slightly overcome by having their wedding advanced by 18 months? But I have come to the conclusion that the English are more demonstrative than the Scotch or Irish – in public, though I suppose it is hardly fair to judge by one specimen under the microscope.

Before I left Moukden I got a couple of parcels sewn up and

addressed. Mrs MacNaughtan's outside man was to post them for me on Monday. The contents are – silk for Willie and Hugh's dressing gowns, a dress length for a summer frock for you, 8 yards for Miss Galway which I thought would make a coat and frock, and two pieces for the twins. One is 6 yards of dark rose waste silk *[lower grade material]* and I hoped might do for a couple of cotton frocks. It may not wash well, so don't trim with white and don't dry in the sun – but I have had quite good wear out of a navy blue in the same material which I made for wear in the house in the autumn ...

I don't want any money for the things, except the boys' dressing gowns. I hope you won't think them dear (£1 13s), but they will be made of material not easily bought in Manchuria now – real old Chinese silk with the old patterns. The shops we bought them in said they had very little sale for these now when Mrs Mac said something about their cheapness ... Mrs Mac and I had quite a lot searching before we could get anything that would do – these are what they call 'old' colours and were colours and material only worn by officials and very well-to-do folk – none of which exist in the same way now. Lots of stuff we were shown they said they would never replace. Cheap Japanese silk floods the place and you could see the difference at a glance ...

Your frock material by the way, Mother, comes from Calcutta. There are two Indian silk shops in Moukden with pretty things. I buy British when I can, but of course it isn't in the same street as the good Chinese stuff. Later I'd like to send a dressing gown length for Frank, but the bank balance is reduced at the moment and I thought I'd try perhaps in the autumn if there is any money left after my summer holidays.

I'm longing to get home to mail. There will be about 3 weeks' letters waiting for me – it seems ages since I read your last letters.

Faku,
11th April 1937

To Dad and Mother and all of yous

You'll see by my address that I have got back to work at last – I came on Friday by bus. I had to plan something definite on Thursday as the Browns were going to Moukden to give lectures in a course they are giving in the Medical College there. There was no word of a bus and the gateman said he could arrange with a good man who had an extra special horse (for this part of the world) and that I would likely do the trip in six hours. I was quite keen, for the weather had suddenly got warm and I could have walked all the hills, of which there are a good many.

However, after I had planned to start at 7 o'clock, a phone message came saying that I would get a bus at 10 o'clock on Thursday morning. I felt really cross with the good friend who had phoned! I dandered around at 9.30, thinking that as it was the first bus for a fortnight there would be a crush – the driver of the afternoon bus, Ma, was there and he greeted me with the wild waving of his arms and the news that the bus was just leaving. The conductor yelled at the office for my ticket, Ma heaved my luggage in and put me in a comfortable front seat, and with several bows and my warm thanks to them both, the bus forthwith shot off.

I don't know why it went so early. The few Chinese in it also thought it was timed for 10 and several expected friends to join them. I was in luck. I knew Ma's name and used it with the respectful equivalent of Mr the last time I was in the office, so were friends from that date! Names seem to mean more here than at home.

It was a glorious day, the sun is quite warm now, and although the buds are not burst yet, they are just coming out of the dark sheaths and there is the sort of a green haze over the trees in the distance – can you image a country completely without green? and what a joy it is to see the first blades of grass. Baby hares were lolloping about and the birds are beginning to discuss nests with great fervour. Men are out in the fields spreading manure – a pleasant sight – in the distance! I saw a V of wild duck coming west with us – about 20 of them.

Have you read any stories of dust storms in this part of the world? I have read about them in one of the French Cable books, but now I know what they are like. We never had one in Peking at all, at all. If I mentioned dust it really was only a skiff of street dust stirred up by east winds. This was dust sand, and preserve us from it again for a while. It started after breakfast and lasted until 6 o'clock without 'letting up'. The wind was hot and there was no air to breathe outside and inside was almost as bad. We have double windows and they are pasted round with paper inside but we keep an 'eye lid' open above (I

mean we have no paper on it) and the dust poured in round it –
although it is so tight, it is hard to open at times.

I had such a headache with the dry air that I could neither read nor
write, so I took to sewing and had to keep a duster beside me to keep
the machine and table clean. After the 3rd dust of the room in the
morning, I gave it up and Mamie said I'd soon get used to the taste of
it!

I'm glad there has been a lot of snow this winter. I hate to think
what spring must be like after a dry winter. The sand was piled up
against everything 2 and 3 inches deep outside.

Faku
7th May 1937

To Dad and Mother

*Marion begins this letter with explanation as to why two of the Irish
Presbyterian missionaries had chosen to be married by the Bishop at
the Anglican Cathedral in Shanghai:*

The reason of Betty Gallagher and Howard Hills being married by a
Bishop in Shanghai will probably not be understood by the folks at
home who may not approve of it! The Cathedral in Shanghai is the
only piece of 'England' that we have nearer than Hong Kong, and
saves all the fuss of two marriages, one by the clergy and one by the
consul *[in Moukden]*. Quite a number of our folk have been married
there I believe. On the other hand, several have gone off on their
honeymoon without being legally married, because they couldn't get
the consul's good offices at that time. The last two weddings have
been like that and there were a lot of jokes about it amongst their
colleagues.

This week has been very busy and has just flown through. I've
had my nose close to my books, and any spare minutes I've been in the
garden. The things we planted are all springing up – the lily-of-the-
valley has the sheath well shoved up, a week's sun should see the
flowers out. I'm longing to see the first bunch picked. The growth here
is amazing – we had the young trees and plants in only a fortnight
when the buds formed on them, and the leaves are just coming out now
in less than 3 weeks. You can see the young flowers grow! But that

means of course that they are all over the sooner.

I told you we proposed making a lawn, didn't I? You can imagine the labour that means. Take a weedy piece of your front field as an example. We dug up the old grass last winter. Now we are digging it all over again and taking every piece of the old grass and weed out of it – four of us this afternoon working steadily for 2½ hours only did a piece about 18ft long x 5 wide, and it will all need to be done about twice over again and then rolled and re-rolled and made perfectly level. It will be glorious to have a lawn if it turns out well. The two servants came out to help when Mamie and I started today. "What are you going to put in? Cabbages?" said Fish, with a gleam in his eye! "Grass?? Grass!!!" and they both digested that for several moments of shocked silence. "What sort of grass?" – "Oh just grass – but finer than any here." – "Oh!" – silence and then a few deep sighs. "It will waste a lot of time," was Fish's only protest as he relinquished his dream of great rows of cabbage all down our front.

(Left) The bungalow, funded by the Girls' Auxiliary, photographed in 1937.
In front is the area which was to be laid out as a lawn, much to the disgust of
Fish, the cook. (Right) A close-up of Marion, Mamie and Abie the dog in front
of the bungalow.

Today has been like an April day at home – rain clouds chasing across, white wind-blown clouds all the time, gleams of deep blue sky, sunshine and shadow. Cherry blossom against the blue and white, the slim apricots with snow white blossom against a sunlit brown mud wall – it was a delight to be outside all afternoon. The lilac is just coming out and the pear blossom will be here in a week. The spring is a bit later than usual this year. It is very warm in May usually, but today is just as cool as an April day at home – I'm glad of it, it keeps the great heat off the longer.

116

Sunday Morn

I've just been round 'the estate' with Miss Wang *[Huei Chün, the headmistress]* looking at the cherry and apricot blossom and picking a big bowl full of violets. It is a sunny morning – chillish – because it is only 9 o'clock sun time, 10 by Japanese time – which is also Manchurian official time.

Faku,
16th May 1937

To Mother and Dad

I'm just back from Church now and am waiting to be called to Miss Wang's *[Ssu Wen the Evangelist]* for dinner. I've had 3 Chinese meals this week and thoroughly enjoyed each one of them. One, I'm afraid I asked to be invited to! The 'background' of any of the meals that I have ever been

Wang Huei Chün photographed under a cherry tree on the Sunday morning walk she had with Marion.

asked to has either been rice or flat pancakes with which you parcel up the meat and vegetables. The usual food that the folks eat is another grain (that we haven't at home) called 'shu me' (so me) *[a type of millet]* and I had never had it, so I asked Miss Wang if she would give it to me some day. It was very good, like flake meal porridge without salt in flavour, but with a grain slightly bigger than barley – I could imagine you could get very tired of it eventually.

I'll start my news from last Monday when I got the prayer meeting over quite intelligibly (Mamie tells me). I never imagined I could be so nervous – I never got off to sleep the whole of the night before and whenever I dozed I had a nightmare! However, by morning I was 'nerve proof' and I got up without a quaver. I'm relieved to know now that with preparation I can be perfectly clear, as I know a few of the missionaries who have quite a good command of the language cannot speak clearly from some fault of annunciation or accent. Mamie gave me a good crit afterwards and I think she isn't the sort to let mistakes pass – she is on the Language Committee and is supposed to keep us young 'uns up to scratch.

Ping An *[the cook's son]* has a new suit – like the big boys' *[school]* uniform, grey cotton made like a soldier's uniform with brass buttons. He was very pleased with himself and came strutting across the compound, with the pride of a whole regiment of soldiers, to show it to us. I nipped in and got my camera and got back in time to snap him as he showed Mamie how the trousers stay up.

Ping An showing Mamie how his trousers stayed up.

On Friday I had one of the most interesting and enjoyable days I've had since I came here. Miss Chang's *[the Drill Teacher at the Girls' School]* home is in the village about 4 miles from here and she asked Miss Wang and myself to come with her as she wanted to see them that day. We started out about 8 o'clock so as to get there before the heat came ...

After a while, we left the road and took to a field path which led us by a willow line stream to the village of Wei chia lo. We turned into the first compound in a short street – at Miss Chang's call of "Look

after the dog," (a necessary warning where dogs are bred as watch dogs) the family came pouring out to greet us. I got some of the folk disentangled eventually, but I never discovered how many people were living under the one roof.

Standing in this photograph at Wei chia lo are Miss Chang with, to her left her, brother, his son, wife and a daughter-in-law. In front are her mother and her brother's three youngest children and a daughter-in-law of her brother. Marion wrote that the old lady wasn't blind 'that's Chinese politeness. Don't laugh in a photograph'.

118

There was the 80 year old mother, a cheery faced old lady, very clean, with a surprising lot of grizzled hair, good hearing and sight just beginning to go a bit. She complained that she was getting old for she couldn't do what she did last year – walk in and out of Faku in the one day – not a bad step for an 80 year old! There was honourable Big One – the eldest son (Miss Chang's brother) – and his wife. I made out one son, two daughters-in-law and 3 smaller children from his family. Then, an unmarried son came from the fields and, with him, one uncle, I believe, with his offspring – some married and some not – in another room in the house. I should think that there were at least 16 people in a 2 roomed house, each room about twice the size of our drawing room.

Scotch Mission
Ashiho
Sunday 30th May 1937

To Dad and Mother

Marion had left Faku the previous Monday and travelled by bus to Tiehling, where she caught the train to the Irish Presbyterian Mission at Hsinking where her friend Dorothy (Wiggie) Faulkner was in charge of the mission hospital, Agnes Gardiner was a nurse who worked closely with Dorothy, and the Rev Harry Johnson was the missionary.

I started off for Faku last Monday. Had lunch and spent the afternoon with the Browns in Tiehling. Caught the express for Hsinking and arrived with Wiggie about 10 o'clock. I had sent her a card saying that I hoped to be there on Monday night but I'd find my way from the station as I didn't know what trains there were. I saw the house looked dark as I came up, a sudden thought 'Were they out in the country?' gave me a stagger. However, when I got round the side of the house I saw the hall light on and went in and called out, "Wiggie." Harry Johnson appeared at the end of the hall with a startled look on his face. "Hello! Where did you appear from? Are you come for a visit? – now isn't that awkward. Here I am alone ..." were the answers I got. His wife had gone home and I thought Wiggie and Agnes Gardiner had gone out to a village. Then one by one round the doorpost appeared, one on top of each other, Wiggie's face – Agnes' face – Austin Fulton's face, and all with a grin from ear to ear. The beggars had concocted it as they heard me arrive. Austin is taking over Harry's work when he goes home and had been up seeing what had to be done. We had a riotous night and talked until next day - it was one ish when we girls went to bed, the men, respecting the proprieties, had gone over to Harry's house earlier.

One of the subjects under discussion was Harry's furlough of course and he was sorry he was going to be home before the 12th July. He said he was afraid to leave the quiet shelter of Manchuria to face the dangers of Christian Belfast around the 12th [the day that the victory of the Protestant William of Orange was celebrated by the Orange Order].

Wiggie you know has looked after the sister of the Emperor *[Pui Yi , the puppet Emperor of Manchukuo]* and seems to be quite a friend of the family's now. She has had tea there several afternoons and is expecting to have the lady herself and a small daughter for a visit one day soon. We move in high society, don't we?

The next day Marion travelled on to Harbin, the most Russian of the Manchurian towns and cities, where she met her friend, Flora MacNaughtan. They stayed at the Grand Hotel for two nights at a cost 4/- each per night. They then moved on to Ashiho, where Flora was responsible for the hospital at the Scottish Mission.

I arrived in Harbin on Tuesday night – a most exciting spot. Very cosmopolitan, all well kept, wide streets, good shops, bright lights. Lots of Russians, small British and Continental community, lots of up and coming Chinese and Japanese business people. Unfortunately, the Russian crowd there is very immoral or is it unmoral? They haven't had much chance, poor beggars, to know much, if any, other world than that of the flesh – and the Chinese and Japanese there have no high opinion of foreign morals. Quiet little girls like Flora and myself have to conduct ourselves very circumspectly.

Grand Hotel
Harbin
6th June 1937

To Dad and Mother

120

Take a look at my address – I should really have gone downstairs and used some hotel paper to write to you – but take my word for it I am here. And this is the place I hope to be in a year or two when I'm coming home via Siberia. Toora la!

I am alone in Harbin. Flora has just deserted me. But I have my ticket bought for Tiehling and I'm only waiting an hour for the south-bound train. I am going to be 11 hours on the train – what a thought! – stay the night with the Browns and go on Faku in the morning. I had really meant to get back on Thursday, but a bad case came in *[to the hospital in Ashiho]* and Flora had to operate, and then our train did not leave in time yesterday to get the night train which I had planned. It was 2 hours late in coming in. Held up by robbers we heard, but I suspect that was only a rumour. Going back on the same route our train guard of soldiers did not look any more numerous than usual and they all had bunches of wild flowers. Two had baskets of wild lily-of the-valley, which they sat and held as they sang some very sweet minor melodies – Japanese of course, so I can't tell you whether they were drinking choruses or dirges.

This time, as we are old friends of the management *[of the Grand Hotel]* we only paid $1.75, about 1/9 each, for our bedroom for the night and we got a bed sitting room with writing desk and water laid on for that.

Did I tell you anything about the Russian food you can get here? I am glad I don't live here – it is too good! Their soups are meals in themselves. I have had 'borsch' twice – cabbage soup – but it hadn't only cabbage in it – potato, a green vegetable, white cabbage and sour cream with enough meat for a meal for two! Scrummy! Then I sampled sauerkraut. I'm sure you've seen it mentioned in German books – pickled cabbage. It is salt cabbage, and mine was fried with onions and served with wild duck. As I say, I'm glad I don't live here! The Russians are very good with animals and they have hundreds of fat, sleek cows, which provide the foreigners in all this district with milk and butter and cream – all very cheap.

Their horses are a joy to see after the poor starved beasties in Moukden – their example has set a standard for the Chinese here and you see well-groomed little Chinese horses in the droskeys.

All the well-doing Russian businesses in Harbin are gradually having one Japanese or more inserted in the staff, often in a place of authority. One big place, a store – everything from groceries to ironmongery, to Paris models – was beginning to go down a bit, so my bank(!) bought it up and it is an extremely healthy concern, with a lot of British goods in it. We do most of our shopping there – by 'we' I mean the mission folk here.

The next paragraph refers to the Rev Daniel Robertson, a Church of Scotland missionary in Manchuria since 1890, and his wife.

The Robertsons go home to retire this month. They came to Ashiho in 1897 and just had their furniture bought and their little house fixed, when everything was lost at the Boxer rising. They escaped by foot across country to Harbin, and when things were quiet came back again. A couple more years' peace and the Russo-Japanese war was on top of them, and so on it went. Mr Robertson says it has been a series of major operations, alternating with minor ones, for his 40 years here; but he has a good steady church to answer for his work from what I saw of it.

Faku,
9th June 1937

To Mother and Dad

In this letter Marion describes the two day sports meeting for all the schools in the Faku district.

It is a tremendous affair. There are several big schools in the town, government ones, with 700 or 500 at them. Our Boys' School has under 400 I believe. Then about 1,000 children were in from the village schools round about, so that in all Mamie and I counted that there must be over 3,000 children alone there.

The meeting is held in a huge 'campus' belonging to a govt. school. It was built and endowed by the kind benefactor of electric light – General Yang (Faku man) who was one of the last Governor's *[Zhang Zuolin's]* big men. You can imagine the size of it when 3,000 children didn't fill more than ½ the actual sports ground and there must have been 2,000 parents or visitors seated or standing around it.

The Fire Brigade was also there, I forgot to say. Positively gorgeous. I'd love to have a fire for them to put out. They looked as if they had stepped out of a book of old Japanese history. They have helmets with long flaps that hang all over their shoulders (vide King Arthur's knights). Their tunic is red and black with painted patterns on it, tight breeks and knee boots. They only need a horse and spear to complete the picture. I did long for a movie camera when they came in on the run.

Sunday

To continue the story of the sports. The 2nd day was the one that interested us most because the girls' school was to give a physical display and the kindergarten had been asked for an item for the 1st time. There is no other kindergarten, so when our wee scraps came in to the field, the judges and high-heid uns all came down from their perches and hunkered down in a wide circle to see everything.

News was only sent to the school a week before the show, asking if they could produce something, so Mamie had a brainstorm, and then with 5 days of practising, children had to face that audience. We had a great rush getting costumes ready,

The kindergarten team in action at the sports day.

but all hands on deck did it. Mamie played suitable music on a small hand organ and the dance-cum-tableau began. 14 little flowers, green frocks, plus big petals stiff with starch sitting up round their faces, came on. They were 'planted' with brown caps with buds on their heads. Then 4 winds came on and danced softly round them, and raindrops sprinkled them and a big sun came out and shone solemnly on each of them, and finally they opened their eyes, pulled off the buds and slowly rose to their feet. Butterflies came and danced round them, and finally there was a dance for everyone together. It was really very sweet and most unusual – everyone was tremendously interested – they'd never seen anything like it before. The magistrate was so moved by it that he immediately sent off and ordered a fan for each child – there were 25 – and the kids were 'thrilled to bits'.

The winning team.

c/o Mrs MacNaughtan
Moukden
20th June 1937

To Dad and Mother

Whoopee! I've got my *[Chinese language]* exam – and more than that – a good crit. I came in on Thursday to find Dr Inglis *[the missionary who was the senior examiner]* laid low with dysentery, but he deputed Mr MacNaughtan to do the deed – and begorra! he took his duties seriously. Last time (with less work of course) Dr Inglis gave me an hour and a half's exam – less than 3 hours would have done this time. Mr Mac gave me 6 hours! – not all at one sitting! But it was worth it. He gave me quite a lot of pointers and corrected several of my weak points, but told me that I "spoke clearly and distinctly, had a good sense of tone and rhythm and showed promise of being a good Chinese speaker." He would not have told me any of that unless he meant it – he is an Oxford Grouper and believes in Absolute Honesty! *[The Oxford Group was an influential Christian movement in the 1930s. It later became known as Moral Rearmament]*

It was a tremendous relief to hear his considered opinion, because now at the end of 18 months it is clear whether you are going to be a success at the language or not – I know I'll never have the same ease or fluency as a few of the folks, like Mamie, who have a genius for language, but to know that I will be understood easily if I prepare well has lifted my heart high. He also said I wrote rather well – had quite a sense of the balance of the character – which was pleasing hearing, but less important.

Faku
23rd June 1937

To All-of-Yous

The Chinese language has two main pitfalls for the beginner. You may use the wrong tone and make a bad howler – or you may hear a wrong tone and get a message all mixed up. One day the Head Mistress and I were out for a walk and came on a field of young green sprouts. She asked, "What is that I wonder?" I suggested grain and when we looked at it sure enough it was. As we turned away she remarked in thoughtful tones, "Wo i wei shih t,sung." ... *[Marion then explained the different meaning of i and wei.]* So instead of hearing, "I thought it was onions," I heard, "I honourable one am an onion." I repeated it wonderingly after her and when it sank in what I had said, I thought I was going to have to carry her home. It sounds almost worse in Chinese, because you would never even in joke refer to yourself as honourable, you only say, "ta' i' wei." – "he honourable one," and you use an even politer phrase when talking to a person – "You honourable ancient one."

The problems the Chinese language could cause are also mentioned in the following letter.

Faku
4th July 1937

To Mother and Dad

The short term Bible School ended yesterday, Sat, and Mamie is drawing a breath of relief today. There were about 80 women at it and 65 sat the exam. They learn an amazing lot in a fortnight – one old woman of 60 (they look much older at 60 than they do at 70 at home) who couldn't read a character 5 years ago, now can

Mrs Li (on the left above) was the 78 year old who received her diploma after attending the Bible School for five years. She had bound feet and was wearing tiny shoes similar to those brought back by Marion from Manchuria, (see photo to the left).

read very well and knows great pieces of the Bible off by heart. One old lady of 78 finished her 5 year course (of a fortnight each year and 5 exams passed) and got her 'graduating certificate' – how's that for perseverance?

125

I have taken notes, as Mamie has told me the crack this week and I want her to sit down and write it up for *Women's Work* some day before the freshness is off it. You will probably see some of the stories then, but here they are – the Chinese for 'Tarsus' is 'Ta Shu' (Da Soo) and the Chinese for a big tree is the same sound and tone with different characters. When Mamie was examining orally one of the old women who could not write, she was informed of the startling fact that Paul was born on the top of a big tree!

Then two different ways of looking at a rainy day. One morning, while the *[Bible]* School was on, a short shower of rain fell and some of the older women were not in time for morning prayers. The elder taking prayers that morning said something to the effect – "Father thou has answered the prayers of the farmers for rain and we are glad to see it for their sake – although it is not quite suitable for us and as thou canst see has prevented some from coming this morning." Just a gentle hint of reproof! Then on Sat when we had the closing ceremony and the giving out of certificates it came down in buckets. We had had glorious weather all the fortnight – too warm indeed at times – but one of our old saints, a Mrs Wang, arrived early and twinkled up at Mamie, "Indeed the good God doesn't treat anyone unfairly. We have had grand weather all the meetings, but the farmers are all wanting rain and now he has sent it on a day when he knows none of us would stay away anyway. We all want our certificates!"

The School is held for 1) old women who have not learnt to read and write and who have been too busy rearing a family to be able to come much to church. 2) Young wives who are enquirers and who have married into Christian homes or whose husbands are away in a job some place else. 3) Girls who are engaged to Christian boys and need further teaching 'in the doctrine'...

I love old women's faces here, such wisdom and peace in them – those who have never had Christianity to help them have often reached some sort of philosophy of life which gives them a firm standing. The face of Mrs Wang (above) radiates peace and happiness and she has the most twinkly humorous eyes I have seen for a long time. She is not one of the species of saints who would produce martyrs – 'The martyrs were those who lived with the saints' – but I think she must be one of the best evangelists – unpaid – about the place. She has to work for her living – most old people have children or relatives to support them, but hers are too poor. So she sews on Chinese buttons for gowns made in a tailor's shop, getting one copper for each garment. The most she could make in a day would be 4 or 5 coppers – about 7/10 of a penny, and she willingly forgoes that to come to the Bible School and any special Church meetings. She 'graduated' this year and although she couldn't read a character 5 years ago, she can read well and is able to repeat lots like Psalms 23, 121, Corinthians 13, John 14, and so on.

We had a Mohammaden at the *[Bible School Graduation]* ceremony – a headmaster from one of the biggest schools in the town. I think he likes us because he gets straight talk and fair dealing from us – we like him for his good character and fine reputation for straightness in the town. He had expressed his interest and Mamie suggested that he might come along and see this *[ceremony]*, thinking that he would drop in for friendliness sake before the end – but no, he came early – before the meeting opened and saw it out to the last gasp – made a very good speech and seemed very interested in it all.

The last paragraph of the letter underlines again the good relations that existed between the different religions in Faku and presumably in other Christian mission stations in Manchuria. This is something which is not always apparent in histories of the missionary movement.

Moukden
14th July 1937

To Mother and Dad

Marion was in Moukden attending the Assembly of the Synod of Manchuria (the Chinese Church). In her letter she referred to clashes between Chinese and Japanese forces near Peking.

The situation south of us is nasty at the moment. If you look at the map you will see that Pei Tai Ho *[where Marion was about to go]* is out of the danger zone, but the trains are cut off at the moment and there are a number of our people there already – mostly women and children – the husbands had to wait here for the Summer meetings. We can't see what is ahead. Things may settle down with apologies from the Chinese for the Japanese attack, but I fancy that if the blow up doesn't come now, it will soon – even the Chinese cannot swallow insults for ever. The wording of our local rag has caused many sardonic grins –

'there is no doubt that the incident is a case of premeditated anti-Japanese armed resistance by China'. Set against that is the fact that in South Manchuria a fortnight ago there were agents going round discovering what accommodation the schools and inns could offer as military hospitals.

The last sentence implies that Japanese were planning confrontation before the clashes took place. They did indeed start full-scale warfare between China and Japan, which lasted until 1945.

Faku
20th July 1937

To Dad and Mother

Whoooopeeee!!!!! There are four foreigners in our compound, it looks positively crowded. Mamie and I came back on Sat. and the O'Neills came on Mon. (yesterday), it is grand to have them here. My relief is as much for Mamie as anything else, she couldn't have stood it much longer, I think. She goes off tomorrow on her hols and I will see her off with a thankful heart; she has had a lot of strain to bear this half year. She is taking six weeks hols, I think, but I think she will do nothing but sleep for the first week or more ...

The Rev Frederick and Mrs Annie O'Neill had been away from Faku for two years because of Dr O'Neill's Moderatorship of the Presbyterian Church in Ireland in 1936-1937. While Harold Corkey, another missionary, had covered for him in the first year, Mamie had to deal with his responsibilities in Faku, in addition to her own work, in the second year.

Faku
21st July 1937

To Frank

In this letter Marion contrasts the servants which the missionaries had in China, with the situation in Ireland where a maid would normally the only domestic help.

Thanks for your long letter, you wrote it just after the spring-cleaning had got under way, and you were feeling that your idea of heaven would be a well-padded and cushioned chair. I know exactly what you mean, I was in the middle of doing the O'Neills' house when your letter came and two years of no house cleaning is a bad preparation for that! We are spoiled here for servants of the usual sort at home. The Stevensons, for instance, who have gone home on furlough, when out here had a cook, a boy to wait at table, a coolie to do the dirty work, probably a gardener, and an amah for the two children. Now when she is on holiday, mark you, she has not even a servant of any sort. That was when she wrote last, I hope by this time they have found someone.

That probably sounds terrible to have so many servants, but that is only in the city; in the country we manage along with two, or where there are children, three, counting an amah. The servants have a sort of caste of their own, the cook buys the food fresh every day and cooks it, but he has no time to do rooms, the house boy would not touch the coolie's work for anything and so on. They eat in their own houses when they have given us our meals and the middle of the day is too hot to do anything, so it makes their working day short. Apart from that, they hate to see the mistress doing any of their work, they instantly think their work has not been well done and they lose 'face' in front of the other servants.

Faku
25th July 1937

To Mother and Dad, my sweatiest

(Hic) I beg your pardon, it is the typewriter, it is feeling the heat. You know the delicate lady who reproved her son for saying, "O, you are hot, Mother you are all sweating." "My dear, only animals sweat, gentlemen perspire, ladies are flushed when it is hot." Well they never heard that out here, we all sweat something awful. But Mrs O'Neill tells me that this week and next are the hottest of the summer usually, so that is not too deadly.

... you were having a little *[rain]* when you wrote – we could do with your surplus. The farmers are beginning to get worried here, the summer rains have not come and if they delay much longer they will either lose their crops through drought or through too much rain when the grain is beginning to ripen. Last year saw a flood here and the farmers are just hanging on until this year's crops are ready. Most of the country districts to the north are only eating once or twice a day and they are working from 4 or 5 in the morning until dark at 9 or so. One bad harvest spells famine for many here where there is never any margin from one year to another.

47 Ying Chiao Lu
East Cliff
Pei Tai Ho Beach
N. China
30th July 1937

To Dad and Mother

In this letter Marion refers to the consequences of the outbreak of hostilities between the Japanese and Chinese forces.

I hope you have not been getting worried these last few days over the new state of affairs, I'm sure it has not been pleasant reading for you. Things don't touch us – physically I mean – but of course we are very worried about the country. This is not going to blow over in a week or two and the thought of the loss of human life and the misery it will bring the farmer folk in the areas of war is never away from us.

I won't comment on the news for obvious reasons *[possible censorship]* and anyway it will be stale before you get it. Most of the Manchurian missionaries are down here. We got *[here]* without any trouble – getting back may be the only difficulty, but there is a pleasing assortment of gun boats here *[presumably to evacuate nationals of different counties if necessary]* and all the Embassy and Legation are here as being the safest place in N. China. The war may move south and we are in a corner here completely out of the direct line in any case.

The place it touched us most was over the Chefoo children *[children who would be returning from the China Inland Mission School to the south by sea]*. About 16 to 18 of the Manchurian children were to arrive today. Mr McCammon and a couple of mothers had gone to bring the party. We do not fear for their safety, but they may have to be taken on up north and landed at Newchang *[on the coast of Manchuria]* and so on down here by rail.

I am sure it sounds daft that we should be down here, but the summer would be insupportable in Manchuria without a breath of cool sea air. The children too would feel the loss of the holiday badly and tummy troubles are the housekeeper's great fear in the hot weather. We know as long as we get down here we will be alright, because for one thing no country wants to lose England's friendship in this part of the world by wanton bombing – not that we even contemplated that!

Pei Tai Ho
N. China
3rd August 1937

To Dad and Mother

We are leading a vegetable existence these days – bathing, eating, bathing, sleeping, reading, eating, sleeping has been about our programme. Today we played our first game of tennis and had 3 good sets, and tomorrow we must acknowledge our part in society and go out to see some folks. I am spending the day about 4 miles away in the opposite end of P.T.H. with Mamie. She is looking lots better already and is full of energy. She said she slept and ate for the first 4 days and didn't even go down to the beach 50 yards away to bathe.

A joke on me. A man appeared at the door with frogs to sell – bare pink things, revolting looking and Mrs Mac*[Naughtan]* asked me if I should like one for supper. She still chortles over my expression of utter loathing. The same day was Gleysteens' party – and we had frogs' legs for supper ... I ate mine, I was well brought up and don't make a fuss, but it was only the thought of Mrs Mac's joy when I would tell her that carried me through. The Chinese eat them and quite a number of the missionaries like them I believe. *[The Rev Gleeysteen was an American minister in Peking whom Marion had met when a student at the Language School.]*

Did I tell you anything about my visit to Miss Wang's *[Huei Chün the headmistress]* in Haicheng *[before Marion came down to Pei Tai Ho].*

... I arrived about 6 in the evening on one of the hottest days of the summer and was met by Miss Wang and a nephew about Jim's age. We drove in a horse carriage to their home, which is in the same compound as the church. The church is a new one with nice wood and colouring in it. The Wang's flowers and shrubs were pretty and well kept, their little thatched house very like a house at home, with pretty curtains and big flowered wallpaper. The old pastor and his wife, his son the present pastor, his wife and son and the two girls when they are on holiday, all live in the one house, but they have separate rooms and a main room for meals.

I had the bed to myself, but the girls and the old mother slept on the k'ang on the other side of the room. Everything was spotless and there were no more flies than in our house at Faku. The food was my only trouble. I had been eating very little in the heat and breakfast especially was a trial! Cold potatoes, rice, salted vegetables, cold minced mutton with a sauce I don't like – and boiled cucumber (horrible mash!). It was too hot to eat, but the Chinese get round huge meals and I had to do my best or have them flutter round with suggestions of things I might like better – I felt such a pest. I normally like their food and the Wangs' was extra good, fresh and clean, but even in Faku I couldn't have faced foreign food in quantities.

Marion, like Mamie, had several Chinese friends. She struck up a particular friendship with the headmistress, probably because they were of the same age, whereas Marion's other colleagues, both Irish and Chinese, in Faku tended to be older. The Wangs were also a ministerial family, like the Youngs. This was the first of several times Marion visited the Wangs. It seems that such a degree of social contact between European and Chinese church workers was relatively unusual. Pei Tai Ho was a contrast with the visit to the Wangs, as the gathering there was only for Europeans.

Pei Tai Ho
22nd August 1937

To Dad and Mother

One of the highlights *[of the holiday]* was a wonderful midnight bathe we had a few nights ago. Warm, full tide and glorious moon ... Colin Corkey and friends of his from Language School came over and joined Flora, Elizabeth *[MacNaughtan who was visiting from Britain]* and myself, and we came out of the water about 12 o' clock! When you are in the water your body is outlined in phosphorescence. It was no use for any of the boys to try to swim under water to duck any of us - we saw him long before he reached us!

The photograph below is of the Manchurian missionaries taken by Jim Brown after a tea party at the MacNaughtans' house on 19th August 1937. Marion wrote that they were a 'jolly crowd and good fun'.

a.Flora MacNaughtan b.William Sloan c.James Inglis d.James Findlay
e.Agnes Black f.Isobel MacNaughtan g.Mrs McCammon h.Mrs Davidson
i.William MacNaughtan j. (-)
k.Emily Brown l.Mrs Sloan m.Ella Gordon n.Mrs Findlay o.David Davidson
p.Mamie Johnston q.Mrs Johnston r.Catherine Hodgkiss s.Flora Fulton
t.Mrs McNair u.Elizabeth MacNaughtan v. (-)
w.James McNair? x.Ted Johnston b1.James McCammon c1.Austin Fulton
y.Dr Cowan z.Colin Corkey a1.Marion

The holidays at Pei Tai Ho (and the entertainment they organised for themselves at the January conference) gave the missionaries an opportunity to relax away from the pressures they were under for the rest of the year. They had the opportunity to let their hair down more than they would have either at their mission stations or indeed back home, where one feels that mixed midnight bathing would not have generally been approved. When Colin Corkey wrote to his parents, who were probably stricter than Marion's, he mentioned the phosphorescence of the sea when bathing, but not swimming underwater trying to 'duck' the girls!

Moukden
2nd September 1937

To Dad and Mother

Back again in Manchuria where one feels away from the seat of war and the news is so censored that it isn't worth reading anyway. We had an uneventful journey up, we expected worse as the line has been all out of order between floods and troop trains and some of the others took 28 or 30 hours for an 8 hour journey in the express. We left P.T.H. at 3 in the afternoon and got in about 5.30 to Moukden the next morning. We could not get sleepers so those who could sleep curled up, curled, and those who couldn't, sat up, poor dears. I have the acquired the Oriental habit of curling up on a seat that holds two, put my head on my purse and coat and sleep fairly peaceably. Flora and I got quite a lot that night, but Mr and Mrs Mac and Elizabeth only dozed, sagging on each other. Yesterday we slept for a good part of the day and did our unpacking and sorting of clean and dirty clothes.

The next few days are filled up with engagements and shopping. We have 3 dinner parties and one here in the *[MacNaughtans']* house, tennis and a lunch tomorrow at Rachael's *[an Irish missionary doctor who had been in charge of the Faku women's hospital from 1926 to 1929 and who had married a Scottish missionary, George Taylor]*. I have a long list of shopping to do for the O'Neills and our own house and I want to order a cardigan in the Blind School *[part of the Presbyterian Mission]* for the winter. Mamie is due up from P.T.H. on Saturday and I think we'll go back to Faku on Monday. It will be nice to get back to work again, one month's holiday is about as much as I can stand. I hope to try and finish my *[language]* exam in October, but there seems quite a lot to do in a month now I look at it.

One of the things that has been interesting us since our return is a new evidence of the cleanliness of the Japanese. I am going to send you a photograph if I can get one. Believe it or not, the horses have all got buckets tied under their tails. True, I am George Washington's twin sister. Oh dear have we laffed or have we laffed?

Faku
14th September 1937

To Mother

I'm hard at study again *[for the Chinese language exam]*. I think I may get finished before the end of October. It will be grand to have it done, but this pleasant life of study without much responsibility is hard to leave. I'll be given definite work at the January meeting I expect, if not before. This is not for repetition. I may be left with Mamie or she may be moved some place else. A lot of people feel that she should not be left alone in the house again. It is lonely even if there are other people in the Station. There are too many like that – Dorothy Crawford, Ruth Dickson, Lilias Dodds (for 6 months before furlough) and Mamie. It is dull eating alone and when something interesting or amusing pops up you can't be bothered trotting across to the other house *[of the male missionary]* to tell about it. However, another year with these 3 new folk should help out. 8 new folk altogether from our Church is good going. I wish a few more young ministers would come. F.W.S. *[O'Neill]* has probably sown some seed there.

Colin *[Corkey]* is going to be good stuff I think ... Tom Blakeley is doing very fine work with the young men in Kirin, he certainly has found his place there.

Well – must stop, grand to have a gossip with you now and then, Ma dear!

Faku
19th September 1937

To Dad

In this letter Marion tells of the O'Neills recounting some of the dramatic events that had taken place during their time in Faku. The Rev Frederick O'Neill, from Belfast, had arrived in the town in 1898, the first missionary to be based there. Two years later he had to flee during the Boxer Rebellion in which many Chinese Christians were killed, six in Faku. After the suppression of the rebellion Frederick returned to Faku and founded schools and a hospital in addition to the church. In 1903, Annie Wilson, the daughter of a minster, whom Frederick had known in Belfast, travelled to China to marry him in Shanghai Cathedral. Because she was a married woman, she was never classified as a missionary, but carried out many church duties in Faku.

Both Frederick and Annie O'Neill were to play an important part in Marion's life in the remainder of the time she was in Faku. Frederick was a major figure in the Presbyterian Mission in Manchuria. His work and the books he wrote show that he had an empathy and respect for the Chinese, which was perhaps not shown by all missionaries in that country. This letter also shows that Frederick had a balanced view of Japanese because of his experience of the period before the Meiji emperor in 1912, after which the government was hijacked by a minority of xenophobic militarists.

Annie and Frederick O'Neill.

Frederick could be a controversial figure – and indeed he sometimes seemed to like stirring up controversy. Marion had initially some doubts about him, partly through the comments of other missionaries. There was some concern that he could be too confrontational with the Japanese and in a letter of 3rd December 1936, she had written that she had heard that he was 'quite willing to suffer death for an ideal, but I am afraid it is a place where you have to consider others.' [i.e. Chinese colleagues] As Marion got to know Frederick she

136

came to admire and respect him.

Annie and Marion developed a close friendship, probably in part because Marion was young enough to be Annie's daughter. Sadness about her own children was undoubtedly a feature of Annie's life. Two sons had died in Faku, while her surviving three sons were being educated in Ireland. Now that the O'Neills had returned to Manchuria, after their furlough and then Frederick's year as Moderator of the Presbyterian Church in Ireland, they would not see their children again for five years.

Mamie was away for a couple of nights meeting Mary Hamill *[a new missionary who had just arrived in China from Ireland]* and bringing her back here, so I had the house to myself. I got in some good long hours of uninterrupted study and then had the O'Neills over for supper one night. Which night proved a wildly interesting one for me. I sat almost frozen stiff with interest, feeling that I was hearing things that had happened in another world and not in the very compound in which I was sitting.

It was the tale of the Russo-Japanese war of '04 when the O'Neills stayed here, and for a time Mrs O'Neill was the only white woman of her class in all S. Manchuria. I heard of the gay life in Faku when it was the headquarters of the Russian army. Handsome Cossack officers who bowed to 90 degrees and kissed one's hands in greeting (oh, isn't Faku dull now?), officers' wives, tennis parties, Mrs O'Neill a sweet young bride of 6 months. Then the clever, decisive drive of the Japanese through Korea; the battle of Port Arthur and Moukden; the gallant, steady stand of the Russian army along the railway, protecting the retreat of all the stores, guns, camp equipment and followers to the North. The slow retreat and constant skirmishes, until at Hsinking a truce was called and some sort of peace made. The interregnum of terror when roving bands of 'soldiers' were free to loot the country. The arrival of 3 whites, exhausted and famished, to Faku, where the O'Neills rescued them and set them on their way. They were an Italian, an Englishman and a Swede, all representatives of tobacco and wine companies who had been supplying the Russians, now they had to run too and got lost and knew practically no Chinese. They slept and ate, slept and ate until they were fit to go ahead, and then got safely off to China. The Englishman was Cecil Meers who bought Manchurian ponies for Scott's expedition *[to the Antarctic]*.

Then the coming of the Japanese under General Nogi, who is one of the best beloved of men amongst the present generation of Japanese. F.W.S. *[O'Neill]* had a great admiration for his ability, education and sense of duty to his Emperor. The story of his death is interesting. He hated the new Japan which was growing up and when he heard his Emperor was dying he decided there was nothing else to live for, so he prepared to go along and serve his Emperor in the next world. He put on his war paint and sitting on the floor of his room in the usual contemplative attitude, he drove a dagger through his heart. And so died.

But to go back – he was so well liked in Japan that they decided to collect amongst the people for an army band for him, and a very good one was got together and trained by a German. When Faku was Headquarters *[for the Japanese forces]* the band was here and one evening the O'Neills were asked round to hear it. As a courtesy, Irish airs were played – doesn't it sound like the Tower of Babel? A Japanese band playing, under German instruction, Irish airs in a Chinese compound to a mixed audience of French, German, Italians, Chinese and British.

The French came to be here in this way. I don't know whether it is so now, but it appears that in the old days when a war was on, any countries who approved of one side sent military attaches to be at the Army Headquarters, so there were American, Continental and British officers here, as well as journalists – from all countries. The O'Neills made friends with Frazer, then *The Times* correspondent, now in Peking. Wasn't this village back-in-the-sticks an exciting place then? Pity there were no other ladies except Mrs O'Neill to entertain the officers ...

... I find it hard to live down my Black North Presbyterian reactions – we have an empty cross behind the pulpit here (I say, "Thanks to be in a country where the cross does not mean Popery," but sometimes look on it with the eyes of some awful ancestor of an Orangeman. Mother, don't deny that skeleton in your cupboard – there must have been an Orangeman somewhere!) and more is made of Easter and the Church festivals. I enjoy them all and yet every now and then I have to pause to remind myself that they are Christian and not the projection of the Catholic Church!

'Black North' refers to the Royal Black Institution which consisted of members of the Orange Order.

138

Faku
26th September 1937

To Dad and Mother

Yesterday was the Girls' School picnic and some of the Bible School folk came with us too, under Miss Wang's *[Huei Chün's]* leadership. The kids were wild to go and although it looked darkish, they decreed go – and we went. Everyone brings their own food to a picnic here, (there are no elaborate buns and tea for kids here!) and afterwards there is a specially large meal prepared for them. The place we went to was more than 5 miles away and by the time they climbed over banks and ran into every field where they saw flowers, they must have walked nearer 8! We had over 70 children, but they were very good and didn't play us many pranks.

We were about 2 miles on the road when a good smart shower fell and everyone got well damp. We got to a village where a girl had a relation and she ran on to see her. Out came Ma in law and two daughters to insist that we go in and shelter, so in we went – 70 children odd, 10 Bible School, 4 teachers and Mary and myself. It was a huge space and we squatted on warm k'angs, while some of the wetter children dried out their gowns before the fire. We got tea and then on we started again.

The place we were making for was called the Snake Mountain and the Snake Mountain Village was at the foot of it. Then the rain started again and we were received by the Yang family, relative of the General Yang who gave Faku its electric light. There were 3 branches of the family in the one compound and we divided up into the various rooms – all the teachers going to the head of the family for tea. Such hospitality! The 1st house in the other village wanted to yoke up a couple of carts to take the smaller children home – this one offered to keep us for the night. There was not much good food in the house they said, but there was enough meal to keep us going for a day or two!

When the rain cleared we went to visit *[General]* Yang's grave. I took a couple of snaps, but I don't know how the mizzle will affect them, and then the children decreed that we going to visit the Snake Temple on the top of the hill. It was the cave there that drew them! Up we went and the rain stopped, so we sat under a rock and ate our lunches. The view was well worth it – I was glad the children had wanted it, and Mary got a glimpse of well-to-do farming country and well laid out farm houses.

A peanut seller outside General Yang's grave. Marion took the photo during a visit by the Church's Boys' School, in 1938.

Marion's companions having lunch in the shelter of the rock on Snake Mountain. On the left is Mary Hamill, recently arrived from Ireland, Wang Huei Chün, the headmistress of the Girls' School, is in the centre, and Wang Ssu Wen on the right.

We went back to Yangs' and had a very cheery ½ hour with all the ladies of the house. They were very amused to find that the two Miss Wangs, Mary and I were not married – no village girl of our age could <u>not</u> be married. They thought we were 'fat and beautiful', our eyes and skin were not bad – my hair was just right if I would oil it and take any tendency to wave out of it, but Mary should use something to darken her hair. I managed to chat fairly easily with them, they spoke clearly and did not use dialect as some of the villagers I have come across, so I felt I was coming on. They were very well-to-do farming folk and had a nice, prosperous, well-kept yard and house.

Faku
3rd October 1937

To All – of – yous

Yesterday I went out with Miss Wang *[Ssu Wen]* and Mrs O'Neill to the women in their homes for the first time, and was greatly interested. They do this every morning and there is a lot of good work done that way. The women, especially if they cannot read much, or none, do not follow the service in church. They are still plodding away in the first few verses when the reading is over and if it is a hymn they do not know, they give up the struggle. They need very simple, short preaching surrounding a story or with plenty of illustration, but it is a big Church with a lot of well-read folk and all the two schools, so they are not catered for often. They like coming, and do so faithfully, but most of them get their teaching in their homes.

We went first to a good old Christian woman, Mrs Wang, she immediately went out and raked in all the women in the compound, non-Christians and inquirers, and we had six in a room as big as my wee bedroom over the hall ... and our three selves. We read over a new hymn, Miss Wang explained it, and then we sang it over and over until they could make some sort of a shot at it. Then we had a few old favourites, and even some who could not read knew the words. Miss Wang spoke about the blind man outside Jericho, and had them making comments and answering questions in no time. It is that way they really learn. Mrs O'Neill led in prayer and we said the Lord's Prayer and we went on to the next compound. There was a lot of talk first of course and we heard the family affairs of most of them, but it is possible to go to five or six homes in a morning, taking it in turn to speak and lead. Sometimes it is not so elaborate a service as that. Perhaps an old woman can't take in much and you only give her a golden text and go over and over it again, leaving her a card or marking it in her Bible so that one of the family can read it to her. They always like a hymn and manage to pick up the words not so badly.

The first part of the letter was typewritten. There was also a handwritten P.S. – after attending 'a long and rather boring (to me) committee meeting':

Here's a story I remembered during the committee. There had been an old woman preparing for baptism with the Bible Woman, and although she simply couldn't learn the simplest thing she seemed so keen for baptism that after a year's hard work they sent her to the pastor for examination. He started to ask her questions and she said, "You needn't ask me anything Pastor, I can't remember a thing, my head won't hold anything." "Well, why do you want to be baptised?" "Well, you see it's this way – my old companion (old pal – i.e. husband) was a Christian and I never ceased teasing and nagging at him about it all the time he was alive. He's dead now and he has gone to heaven I'm sure for he was good, and I don't want to be separated from him afterwards so I want to join the Church too."

The pastor thought this was hardly grounds enough for baptism, but at last he said if she promised to take down the gods and come regularly to church and see that all her daughters-in-law and the families had a chance to hear the gospel, he would do it. She is a good old soul – does it all regularly and I don't know whether all, but pretty nearly all, are Christians now. She regiments them well!

In a letter written to her grandmother two days later, Marion again emphasises the significance of the senior woman in a family becoming a member of the Church:

If you get the old lady of the house out here it often means that you get the whole house for she orders all their business, often she is rather an old autocrat! and sees that the young people, sons and sons' wives all go the meetings and have a chance to become enquirers if they are interested.

Faku
6th October 1937

To Br *[brother]* William

Your letters always shed a bright light over my days – this was no exception – thanks for the stories. *The Humorist*, etc. arrived a day or two ago. You can't imagine the anxious care they are to me in case some of the teachers or Fish should see them. The shipwrecked ladies who seem to jump into the sea clad in neat fitting snugglies and high heeled shoes, or the chorus girls would be so much more shocking to them than the *La Vie Parisienne* would be to a Scotch elder. They never have used the human body for drawing at all. Their people are a face, hands and clothes. However, continue to send them – I reported some good jokes in a letter home out of them.

Faku
17th October 1937

To Dad and Mother

There is always great interest in the fact that I belong to such a 'proper' big family, and the possession of 5 brothers casts a radiance round me, you did yourselves and me great honour in having five sons, O respected Parents, "Ay – ya five honourable sons your stern Father and loving Mother have much happiness!" I found out to my great joy the other day that is the right way to talk to a person about their parents. Yen Fu, that is you fierce Dad, and Tz'u Mu, tender Mother. I also gleaned a bit of Confucian ethics that seem quite good. 'Tsun chun, ch'in shang, kung yu ti mu.' Which is a neat and comprehensive way of saying, 'Honour the King, love your superiors, respect your friends and live peaceably with your relatives.'

Marion tells how the head girl at the Girls' School, Chang Te En, who had an artificial leather leg, was able to go on a picnic.

I might have told you before about a thing we call a 'perambulator' that people use on the motor road for carrying their goods for sale from place to place. When the roads were being fixed under the new authorities a rule was made that only vehicles with pneumatic tyres could travel on the motor roads, all others such as carts had to keep to the old roads, the 'cart' roads which run alongside the present ones. They are awful usually, with ruts that even the Black and Tans with their Crossleys could not have bettered *[the Black and Tans, the anti-insurgency force set up by the British government during the Irish War of Independence used heavy Crossley tenders which caused severe damage to the Irish roads. Marion had seen such damage around Galway]*. So the Chinese, with their eye on the main chance, got these machines made with bicycle wheels. They are very simple, a platform set between the wheels, but swung so you can tip the seat up or down as you like. The handle is like a huge pram wheel, easy to push if it is packed with a good balance, but mighty heavy on the arms if it is not. Well, we borrowed one of these things putting some cushions on it, perched Miss Chang on it and started off. The girls were rather ashamed of pushing it through the town because we did attract rather a lot of attention I must admit! So we let them start off another way and two followed us to help when we got out of the town.

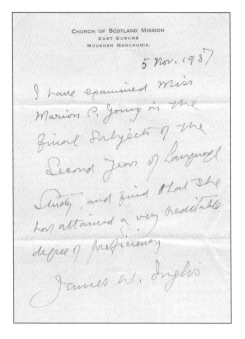

CHURCH OF SCOTLAND MISSION
EAST SUBURB
MOUKDEN MANCHURIA.

This letter from Chief Examiner, the Revd Dr James Inglis, shows that Marion performed very well in the second of her 1937 language examinations. Another part of the exam had been Marion taking a service in Faku (as detailed below).

Faku
12ᵗʰ November 1937

To Mrs Young from F.W.S. O'Neill

Marion may have told you about my share in her Language Examination. I just wished to add a few words from my side. The Morning Prayers in the Women's Bible School, which she conducted as part of her test, gave me an opportunity to listen carefully to her accent and tones and general manner of speech. If she sent you a copy of my brief report you would have gathered my opinion. It is a pleasure to listen to Marion's Chinese. Not only has she put steady work into this difficult task, but she has natural aptitude for the sounds. You have every reason to be proud of your daughter's attainment in her language studies.

Along with her other qualifications of character, temperament and devotion to our Lord, she has now this essential preparation of vernacular speech for the fine career that lies ahead. Marion is very popular out here.

Faku
20ᵗʰ November 1937

To the 'Fambly'

It's Christmas weather as ever was, snow without and a roaring fire within. Yesterday morning I found ice on the water jug and my face cloth as hard as a board. It will be too bad if I waken up some morning and find my breath frozen in a straight line shooting up to the roof. We are not usually as Spartan as this, but with Mamie away I didn't bother putting up the stoves. They are ugly big things and we have them up long enough, i' faith, before the spring thaw comes.

I'm living in our sitting room and it would be sheer extravagance to have stoves going in the studies. Fish served me my meals on a small table beside the fire and there I am, as cosy as a bug in a rug. I'm going to have my bath in the kitchen tonight! Fish was greatly concerned when I told him to heat water for a bath. "The stove isn't up in the bathroom. What will you do – you'll be frozen?" I assured him I wouldn't, but he came in later beaming to say that he could pin the ironing sheets over the kitchen window and I could have my bath there. So I graciously consented. But it will be just too bad if a thumb tack comes out of that sheet.

In the letter Marion enclosed a copy of the Treaty of Nanking, made after the First Opium War.

I am enclosing a copy of a 'Treaty' made by G.B. and China in 1843. Read it and see how G.B. made a proud nation eat dust. We have not much to argue against some of the happenings of today in the face of that, except that it is a century later. But Japan is many centuries younger than us in 'civilisation' I suppose one could say ...

When you think that the existing opinion of the English in China at that time was something like what we would have of the natives of a South Sea Island or the head hunters of Borneo, you can imagine that a 'Treaty' like that would not go far to fill her Britannic Majesty's pious hope that 'this should put an end to the misunderstandings and consequent hostilities which have arisen between the two countries.' Oh! We were an arrogant, overbearing nation in our days of expansion, and we are mighty shocked and disgusted at other nations growing up a century later than we did. Still, Rule Britannia!

Faku
30th November 1937

To Mother

I have an announcement to make – I am going out on my first country tour the day after tomorrow, December 2nd-16th (D.V.). My toes are wriggling with excitement at the thought. As I have told you, Mamie and Miss Wang were out this last fortnight to villages in the north – this time they are going to the west. They arrived home yesterday and are taking a couple of days' before they start out again. I had hoped that I might manage to slim off a bit – I put on a couple of lbs with all the sitting over my study this autumn, but they are back looking fatter and healthier than when they started!

Wang Ssu Wen, the Bible Woman and Senior Chinese Woman Evangelist in Faku, whom Marion accompanied on her journeys to the outlying villages. She had trained at the Nanking Theological College, as in 1920 the Faku College did not accept women. Miss Wang had been Principal of the Moukden Girls' School before Mamie Johnston asked her to come to Faku. She worked closely with Marion.

This signed photograph ('Sincerely Yours Wang Ssu Wen') was given to Marion when she left Faku in 1941. She used it in an article she wrote about her friend in the Irish Missionary Magazine Woman's Work *in 1942.*

Mamie, having a better digestion than a good many folk – me excluded! – never takes any foreign food with her. Some of the missionaries can't do with Chinese food – Dr O'Neill for instance – and they have to take a cook and their food with them. It looks rather elaborate and fussy, but poor Dr O'N when he goes to one Chinese feast – out of politeness – had to fast for several days afterwards. He'd have a sad time on a tour.

The Chinese in the winter only eat two meals a day, so you have to learn to 'pack'. Mamie says after the first couple of days you get quite used to it. We take our own thin cotton mattress and one big 'bei', a thing made with a coloured top and a white lining packed with cotton wool. I have 5lbs of cotton wool in mine! When you have that rolled round you like a bag, on top of a hot k'ang you sleep as cosy as a proverbial bug.

The area around Fakumen in which Marion travelled to lead Bible Schools during 1937 – 1940.

Faku
1st December 1937

To Mother and Dad

I wish you could see our luggage – Miss Wang has just been in sorting it out for us and even W.A. *[her brother William]* couldn't pack better! For the 3 of us there are only 2 bundles and one small hand case (2x1½ ft). The bundles contain all our bedding, one or two extra garments (linen) and our books. The case *[contains]* our wash things and oddments. Oh I nearly forgot the most important thing, a red enamel basin with roses in the bottom – our face basin. A 'wash face basin' accompanies the Chinese wherever they go and it is always filled with things and tied up in a gay piece of cotton. We have ours packed full of eats for me. A little coffee, sugar, tin of milk, butter, a large loaf and some fruit. I won't starve, Mother!

By the way, would you consider 4 pieces of Sunlight *[soap]* (each 2 blocks) not a rather ample amount per month for the washing of 2 people's clothes? And that doesn't count woollen undies or stockings. We don't give Fish any washing powder, but he uses that much Sunlight per month on a very small weekly washing. I said something today about it when I was doing accounts. He probably uses it for scrubbing, which he isn't supposed to. Mamie was away all October and he used 4 pieces too, which put me onto it.

Faku
Written at intervals – posted 5th December 1937 (by Mrs O'Neill)

To Dad and Mother, Boys and Twins

This letter also sent Christmas greetings to the family.

I was reading about Dad's visit to the Enniskillen church, this morning before going to our service. It is good to hear of such a crowd of young people. Looking over our church here, the Girls' and Boys' School and the Bible School must contribute 400-500 and the rest of the congregation is pretty small.

The women are much more in numbers than the men, because they can leave their homes but the men can't always leave their work. If a merchant is a Christian he closes his shop on Sunday – a really big sacrifice in this country – and his apprentices can come to church, but any Christian in a non-Christian's employ of course cannot. He has to depend on the evening prayer meetings in the chapel, or any odd moments he can drop into the Street Chapel for the preaching that goes on a couple of times during the day. A number of the men whom I know of are working hard to put by enough money to start on their own – so that they can have Sunday free. It is a hard struggle for some of them.

The next (very long) letter was written, in the form of a diary, over a period of several days as Marion, Mamie and Wang Ssu Wen travelled round the outlying churches in Faku County and Inner Mongolia. It was posted after Marion's return to Faku.

Wu Tai Tzu
3rd December 1937

To Dad and Mother

I'm sitting on a nice warm spot on a k'ang, warming up and listening to a sizzling next door that betokens the cooking of dumplings full of pork and vegetable. We had 'breakfast' at 10 o'clock and it is now nearly 4.30, so I'm ready for them. We started out yesterday morning in a droskey – I'm sorry I didn't get Mamie to take a snap of us departing – the north wind was particularly wicked that day and I had on 8 layers plus 2 pairs of stockings, lined boots, gloves, hat and scarf – the scarf you may know Mother, the big wide wool one that someone gave you the time there was a 'wee one' on your knee in the sidecar of the motorbike.

Our bedding was in the bottom of the droskey, so we stretched Mamie's mattress over the seat and luggage and sat on it. Then we had a big skin rug, which Miss Wang uses to spread under her mattress, wrapped round us – we looked as if we were starting for the North Pole! Mamie had had to go off suddenly to Moukden on business – of which more anon – so Miss Wang and I started out to the 1st two churches, at the 2nd of which we hope Mamie will join us before we leave. I'm quite glad to start out without her, because I have to talk Chinese all the time and it is all to the good.

We rolled along merrily for about 7 miles and then suddenly came to a broken down bridge. A steep bank took us down into a field and our charioteer was gaily starting down it, when we said we would get out. It was well we did, because the weight of the carriage came down on the wooden beam on which the swivel is fixed ... and it cracked across. If we had been in it, it would probably have been broken. The driver of the Clare Express couldn't have been more nonchalant! *[A reference to the popular song by Percy French 'Are you right there Michael?' which parodied a journey on the West Clare Railway.]* "It will do fine – now where did I put that piece of string?" and out of his pocket he hauled a fine piece of rope and tied it up! Fortunately, we had only 2 more miles to go and the road was good – but every time we hit a bump I expected to hear a horrid crack and feel us plunging down on the springs.

When we got here we went to the 'Manse'. The 'Church' is about the size of our Sunday School room at home and the 'Manse' two rooms the size of your vestry! There is one other room, but the young evangelist and his wife have no children so it does them. The one room has a k'ang about 6 feet deep on which we eat, sit and sleep. It is warm and comfortable to sit on, but the room itself is cold. They do know how to save, do the Chinese.

4th December 1937

We live in the evangelist's wee room. He sleeps in a house nearby and he comes back in the morning to eat and stay here all day. It means we have practically no privacy – but we are glad to have the place to ourselves at night from 9 to 8 in the morning.

The church I should think is a pretty good example of a country one, so I'll tell you about it and be done with it. The room is just like a small barn at home, whitewashed walls, beams in the roof – mud-brick floor, wooden forms with no backs, a tiny platform and book rest. The walls are decorated here and there with long strips of pink or green paper with texts written in good characters – if it is the evangelist laddie, he has a good hand to write, and on either side of the platform are the Beatitudes and the Creed. There would be about 20 – 30 attenders at Sunday worship – most of them baptised. There are actually 60 people on the list of those baptised in this Church in 5 years – so you can imagine what a shifting population a Chinese Church is – that is one of the big problems discussed every year at Synod. At the 2 evening meetings we had 60 to 100. There is a good Church here – fine deacons, which make all the difference and they have some very fine looking men amongst them ... good simple kindly faces – farming folk ...

"When we've eaten food we'll be ready," *[for the first morning meeting]* said Miss Wang – that was 10.30. "I'll say 10.30," says he *[the evangelist]*, "but you can go out and visit some of the people for an hour. If I say 10.30, they'll come after 11.30." As a matter of fact we started at 1! But you realise 'time was made for slaves' when you come here.

150

One of the houses we visited ... a well-to-do farming family *[had]* 14 grown-ups and 16 children. A very happy house to go into – we only saw one half of it – 4 husbands, their wives, and some of their children. The wives were busy preparing food and one husband was making bread – the men usually cook well. Our 'cook' is Deacon Chu (Ju) and he produces well-cooked simple food. The only thing I've found to tackle yet is 'dufu', a preparation made from beans. It is dried crushed beans squashed together until caked, smoked, put by for some months and then chopped into cubes or long strips as a soup basis or vegetable. Mamie says she likes it, I suppose it is an acquired taste.

Tuan Shan Tzu (Round Hill Village)
4th December 1937

We had a very pleasant journey today in our donkey cart. Chu Deacon's son, aged 14, was our driver and proud of himself he was! He came in last night after the meeting with a grin from ear to ear on his round freckled face, to tell us that he was going to drive us. He looked very much like a small edition of Jim trying not to show his delight because it wasn't quite dignified enough! A decent big lad of about 20 came with us to see we didn't fall down a bank or anything – and to be company for the small driver on the way back.

Mr Li, the evangelist, and the deacons who came to see Marion and Miss Wang off from Wu Tai Tzu.

The deacons all gathered to see us off and escorted us to the edge of the town. As we left I took a snap of them, I hope it comes out. Miss Wang and I walked most of the way as it was warmer and the lads chatted and joked with us and the passers-by – a most enjoyable journey.

I was glad to have the walk. I expect I walked 7-8 miles, as I haven't had enough exercise lately.

When we got here we found the church and manse was one! It isn't a good thing at all and when this man leaves it will probably be stipulated that the church remains church only. The room that they had for living in is far too small – only 4 people could sleep on the k'ang and there are 8 people (6 children). It suits us alright, because Miss Wang and I have the small room, all private like – and what is even better, we prepare our own food. The Lis (evangelist and wife) were to give us food, so we said we'd not bother them – they have 2 big stoves and we prepare our food in one. We had a nice mixture of Chinese and foreign food today, rice in which I put butter and salt, while Miss Wang put in dried fish and peanut! Followed up by bread and butter, coffee and apples. T'were good! – especially the coffee.

6th December 1937

Mamie arrived yesterday, so our family is complete. She came the 27 miles by open horse carriage so she was pretty frozen when she arrived. She came in during the service in the morning and slipped into the k'ang quietly. After the service, when the evangelist was announcing the evening service he said that "in the evening we will meet again at 7 o'clock for another meeting, and now that Miss Johnston has come, it won't half be a meeting!" He has a way of his own of announcing guests. He said about Miss Wang and myself – of me – that I looked like a Chinese and dressed like a Chinese, still I was from the West and they hadn't come to the meeting either to look at me or to listen to Miss Wang's eloquence, but to hear the word preached!

We have been out this morning going round the Christian houses – that is houses of people who have been baptised or are registered as preparing for baptism, there are plenty more enquirers not registered yet because they have not asked for baptism. There were about 12 or 13 homes in all, 6 belonging to the 1 family! The latter – Chu by name – until 2 years ago were one family of over 70 people and every day they ate together! Now they have divided up, but they all live in a cluster of families together and all of the houses have Christians amongst them.

One whole house are Church members. There was a boy of that

152

family went to our Church School once and he and his father were the only 2 Christians of the 70. They had a bad time under the tongues of the folk – especially the women – but they must have borne good witness judging from the results. We visited all the homes and told them we were going to hold worship in the old house, so when we got there we had quite a small congregation to meet us.

Another woman, Li, a deaconess in the Church here, told us it through her son, only a lad at school, that she became a Christian. She had been an ardent Buddhist, but he kept telling her about Christianity and she finally got interested and then baptised.

7th December 1937
Ma Tzu Pow (Hempstead Village)

We started off this morning from Tuan Shan Tzu after the deacons had gathered for a short prayer meeting. There was a flurry of snow just as we started, but it cleared up and was a lovely day with very little wind all the rest of the way. The cart we had was a 3 horse big farm cart and we layered it with mattresses so it was quite comfortable.

We'd been asked by a woman who was in at the meetings to stop in at her house on the way. She is a Shantung woman – lots of them come up from the south – or did – as colonists and decent folk they are – strong farming people, good stock. They lived in a little village a little off the main road and had a big household with 2 sons, their wives and children as well as smaller sisters and brothers. We got there about midday and the word must have gone round that we had come for the folks came crowding in. There were about a dozen men and 20 or more women and lots of children, all very interested in the foreigners ...

We spent about an hour there and after we had satisfied everyone as to family, age, country, and comments had been made on Mamie's Chinese and mine – Miss Wang in one corner, Mamie in another, and Mr Li the evangelist from the Tuan Shan Tzu Church (who was leaving us this length) all started preaching to small groups ... They would have kept us all day if we would have stayed, but we had to come on here for an evening meeting. The village they live in is far away from any church and it is not often young Li (again another [of the same name]!) can get from Ma Tzu Pow to them, so it was rather wonderful to find a small community of alive and missionary-minded Christians.

Coming here I experienced for the first time what it is like to ride over frozen drills in a wooden cart. Every bump shook you from toe nails to hair roots and your innards felt as if they were slowly disintegrating. The horses were trotting and I didn't like to yell out that I'd get off, as the carter seemed to be bearing it with the greatest equanimity. Mamie and Miss Wang were walking at the time and we had missed the path, hence the sudden excursion over the field. We took it in turn to ride and walk for both warmth and quickness.

The country we passed through was interesting, well wooded – which is rare round Faku – and the hills were near and glorious with the changing colours between sand and purple and the shadows of gullies emphasising the bareness of their outline. We passed out of Moukden Province and went into Inner Mongolia on our way. Part of that country had been robber country in the old days. Tuan Shan Tzu evidently had to provide hospitality for them pretty often. The Japanese did as the Romans did with obstreperous bits of Europe – made a wilderness and called it peace. They compelled the people to knock down their houses in all the small hamlets and to move into bigger centres where they could have police to see the people's behaviour. We passed long stretches of land where there were no houses – only the foundations of the houses standing about a foot high. It meant the robbers had nowhere to go in that district and either had to settle down and be peaceable citizens or run the risk of being hounded down by the Japanese army.

There are great stretches of the western Faku district that is very poor land – all full of soda. Here and there you saw it exuding from the earth like snow in the distance. They can only grow very poor hemp and a little poor millet in their sort of earth – nothing else grows. The water is bitter and hard – when we washed our hands there was a thick scum formed and we did not try to wash hankies or anything. The water here is beautifully soft and we are going to have a clothes wash this morning.

The country we are in now nominally belongs to Manchuria, but I fancy the Japanese have not penetrated very much this length, it is a pretty free land. The villages still have their big walls and fortresses at each corners, big strongly made gates, and possess guns and old cannon, I hear. There are lots of Chinese with strains of Mongol in

154

them, light brown eyes and brownish hair. They are a wilder, more uncivilised crowd than the last Church – the Church people themselves are all right, but we had a big crowd in last night attracted only by the foreigners and they wouldn't answer or respond much to questions, or request to repeat things, they just stared and stared, shrinking back a bit if we went near them. It was strange to find that after the friendly curiosity of the folk in the last village.

The church is a most attractive little place – the nicest we have been in yet and all due to the young evangelist here. There was no evangelist in Ma Tzu Pow for a good many years, they only had a visit from the Tuan Shan Tzu evangelist and the property had got into bad disrepair – no paper on the walls or ceiling, pigs food and grain in the 'manse'. The church had a k'ang for the women and it was used as a store room for the old caretaker – the whole place was a mess and no one's fault really.

The evangelist, Li, who is here now, is only 19 or 20, finished school last year and came here straight to take over this dead Church. The usual plan for anyone who wants to enter our Church as pastor is 1) Matriculate highest standard at Secondary School, 2) 1 year under the pastor's direction in the central station, 3) A year in an out station alone, 4) 2 years in Junior Theological *[College]* in Moukden, 5) 2 years in practice work either as a 'curate' in town or in charge of an outstation, 6) 3 years in Senior Theological *[College]*, 7) 1 year as a licentiate   and after that a 'pastor' Church can call them as a pastor. And then, after all that, they get the princely salary of £27 a year with a manse.

Marion then recounted how Evangelist Li, who had been a pupil at the Church School in Faku, had changed the Church in Ma Tzu Pow 'amazingly'. The church and manse had been refurbished and 'The people here are all very fond of him and he evidently knows them all well'.

11th December 1937
Fang Chiu Tun (The Village of the House of Fang)

Marion and her colleagues had arrived in this village the day before. Marion had nicknamed the Evangelist Feng 'Father William II' after the character in Alice in Wonderland.

I've chortled to myself all morning at him. He roars and scolds a la Father William, keeps on picking on his wife, pulling our legs – but all with the greatest good heart and the most un-Chinese lack of courtesy. I don't mean that he is rude, but he doesn't treat us to the ceremonial politeness usually given to the chiaoshih. His wife is the just the kindliest, most hard working old wifie, and real good stuff. He has been an evangelist in our Church for 34 years and he has always been chased round to all the churches that had been dying off, or to ones that had been without an evangelist, for some years as a sort of spiritual Eno's Salts. Now he has been here for quite a time and the people are

Evangelist Feng (Father William ll) and his wife.

so fond of him that they won't let him go – they put on a sprint and managed to raise enough money to have a claim on him if the Presbytery wanted to shift him.

We live in the same room as him, about the size of the dining room – they have the one k'ang and we the other. If we hadn't much privacy in other places, we have none here! The dressing and undressing and washing is all done in public. Yet it isn't polite of us to show ourselves unless we are clothed from neck to toe. We undress under our gowns and then get under the bedclothes and get into our pyjamas – in the morning before it is too light we get into all but our gowns and wash that way – it is all very much community life. Some of the women evangelists prefer not to share the family life, but I am glad Mamie does it, it's lots more fun! – especially in this house, with all the crack there is with Father William II.

The Church here is quite a big one and quite long established. Also there is a small Church School with about 50 pupils – it all makes for a more intelligent, well-educated congregation. In Ma Tzu Pow, the crowd of children were like wild wee Red Indians with no idea of discipline at all. (I'm probably maligning the Red Indians – but the whoops and disorderliness of the boys was something awful.)

14th December 1937
Erh Niu So K'ou (The Village of the Mouth of Two Cows)

Yesterday morning Father William II, us, a cart with a mule and two donkeys and a carter started out for 'ere ... Father William walked with me a bit and we cracked away with more freedom than I have ever talked with an old man here. He and his wife are both unusually free and easy for old Chinese. They can be very courteous if they need to be, but they received us as members of the family.

This place is summat different. The people about here are very poor anyway, and last year when the land was all flooded they suffered terribly. There were a great many, Christians included, who packed and moved further north, so the Church is only a skeleton now. There are 3 Christian families in this village and a number in small villages within 5 miles roundabout. The evangelist is only a young lad who wants to enter the Theological College. He has not done up to matric *[ulation]* standard, so he is studying and working at the same time. The people are poor and scattered so it can't be easy to have meetings, but I think his work is well reported on in Presbytery. The church is in a small room with a k'ang for the women, and his room is the one off that. But the folk round here are poor and can't afford much firing, so now he lives in the church and that heating does for all.

15th December 1937

The 5 Churches we have been round have been quite different in spirit and general personnel. The 1st, Wu Tai Tzu, had had a number of warm-hearted Christians who used to come into the Church in Faku most Sundays to the service there – men and women walking the 8 miles in, or taking a cart, staying for the whole two services and then doing the 8 miles back. When there were enough of them to have an evangelist, they set up their wee church and the young man there is in charge, with visits from the pastor or the foreigners. The lad in charge now is only 21, Wang by name, he finished in one school in Faku a year ago and went straight there – he should really have had a year under the pastor as curate, but it couldn't be managed. He is making quite a good job of it, but he is married, he didn't belong to a Christian home, and that isn't much help to a lad that age – it seems to stunt their initiative!

The next place has quite a good church – Tuan Shan Tzu – but the evangelist is a problem. He is one of the leftovers from the old days, when the foreign pastor going round had no other choice than to put one of the best Christians in a small group of Christians, in charge, and he became a sort of paid evangelist – without training. The man Li is a bit of a weakling and he married a wife who was just the wrong person for him, a forceful character with a real bad tongue in her head and a wonderful gift for making trouble – also a spender. Dr O'Neill, some of the Christians and the Presbytery, each have paid his debts over several times, but it is useless. She is a slattern and the church premises are all of a mess – and yet it is a big step to deprive a man of his place as evangelist. The Christians there are strong, there is a good Church and the work goes on, but he can't be much of an example as a leader to the eyes of the non-Christians.

It was good to go on to Ma Tzu Pow, the 3rd and perhaps most difficult Church, and find a fine Christian lad of 20 in charge. Mamie called him 'Young Timothy'. His name is Li Hsiang Ying and I expect he will make a name for himself when he has been through Theological *[training]* – he is on fire for the Church. The Christians there are few, but there are more enquirers now and the Church folk themselves had wakened up a bit to do some missionary work on their own. He paints and writes Chinese characters beautifully and his English writing is good too. He only had a year and a half's English, two 50 minutes periods per week, but what was taught him must have stuck because he talked and read a bit with me.

We went on to Father William's Church then, Feng and Mrs Feng I've told you of. The Church is pretty big, about 20 to 25 homes and all well behaved and responsive during the services. This place is rather different – more of the same uncivilised crowd that Li Hsiang Ying has to work with. The Church folk are few and far, as I've said, and the village people are very unresponsive and dull. They come to the meetings, but only here and there – apart from the Christians of course – do you see any evidence of intelligence. (Peu) Bun is the evangelist, not yet gone to Theolog*[ical college]*, a good laddie, but not much experience yet.

We've had rather fun with the police here. When they found that we were not agitators or enemies of Manchukuo, they became quite friendly and normal. They are all under 30 and some not long out of school. We have had 6 at the meetings and they have come out of interest – not to spy – because one visit is really all that is required. One has been coming to our services for some time here and last night has signed as one enquirer. Another head-laddie talked to Mamie – he is interested, but afraid of his place – he works under the eye of Alex *[the Japanese]*. The enquirer is just an ordinary Bobbie. We are giving the former a Bible and hoping he may find it worth the step necessary. Last night one arrived and found Bun trying to restrain the village boys in the church yard. We let in all the boys who want to come, once the Church folk and older people have seats. The police laddie offered his services to Bun and when Miss Wang went out to tell them to come – she found Bun had gone into the church and the police was standing at the church gate cursing the children up and down in good ringing tones. She said it wasn't the best advertisement for a Christian service she had heard!! So she sent him in to get a seat and coped with the kids herself.

17th December 1937
Faku

Back again to find a graaand mail, lots of *[Christmas]* presents, letters and cards. Two long letters from you – but I'm not going to answer them now – I'll keep that for next week's letter – this *[letter]* is already the size of a parcel! I'm scribbling this on my knee as I invigilate an exam in the Girls' School. They are all very well behaved and very much on their honour. Q.U.B. *[Queen's University Belfast]* examinees could take any example from them!

Yesterday we walked about 12 miles *[from Erh Niu So K'ou]* to a town *[Kamping, the head town of the village's Province]* where we could get a bus, and a cold walk it was. About 6 or 7 miles of it was along a bare flat plane and 3 or 4 of it not far from a series of frozen lakes – Brrrrh! I wouldn't like to go on North Pole exploration. Mamie took her gloves off to tie a knot in our baggage and got so cold that we lit a wee fire to warm her up – she was tired too of course. None of the rest of us got frozen and I kept warm by taking a run to myself now and then.

When we got to the bus station we found a cold room and 2 hours to wait. We were just thinking of going out to find a Chinese restaurant when 2 angels of mercy appeared. Old Father William had come on to this town the day we left his place and he saw two girls, women's nurses, one an ex-student of our Hospital, and told them what day we would be along. They took us to their nice wee room in the street nearby, where they had cakes and tea and nuts and a warm stove for us. We had a glorious time warming up and started off very comfortably on the bus journey.

Bun, the evangelist from Erh Niu, So K'ou, the carter's young brother, Mamie, Miss Wang and the carter on the journey to Kamping.

We had a bus, a small, well-upholstered one for 12 people, all to ourselves – Bun the evangelist was with us too and two jolly soldier lads for escort. They chatted with us all the way, and were better educated and had more general knowledge than most.

I've been busy all morning getting the house ready for our visitors, we are to have Mrs Brown and the 2 girls, and the O'Neills, Dr Brown and Alexander. Did I tell you that we are having a new pastor ordained on Sunday – Pastor Shang *[previously in charge of the Faku Church]* is to take over the position of Headmaster of the Boys' School. The Browns and Harold Corkey are coming to the service and several Chinese pastors. We are most excited at the thought of visitors!

Faku
23rd December 1937

At home we used to think that we were pretty busy in Christmas week, didn't we? ... well, let me tell you that we could run rings round you here! Brrrrrrr! When I think of being responsible for the working out of a rush like this, it makes my hair curl. We had an extra rush of course, with the ordination and visitors, but even without them we would have been busy. The Browns left on Tuesday morning and since then we have had the preparation classes for the would-be-baptised, the exam for them, the rest of the school exams left over from last week, which need a foreign invigilator, the Bible School party and concert, the School Concert, for the programme and outfit of which Mamie and I are mainly responsible. Tomorrow the Kindergarten Christmas tree, the School, repeat concert for all the high-heid-yins and headmasters of the town, and a dinner for them prepared and served by the girls should take up most of the day.

We have still to parcel up and deliver all our presents to the various good friends here who have been in and out all week. We have 6 presents already, and several boxes of fruit! All the time this week we have had people in to say Happy Christmas, and once or twice I could have wished they did not stay too long. I spoiled a making of fudge today chatting to one elder's wife! I am making up boxes of sweets to give some folk like the Browns and I have covered several old boxes quite successfully and stuck a picture on the front.

The weekend with the visitors was good fun and a pleasantly Christmassy feeling to have children in the house. The Browns are a delightful family, Helen, age 15, Elizabeth 13, Alexander 11, and Dr and Mrs – Emily to me now. The O'Neills took the two men folk and we the three women, five in our house was not a squash, but we would not be able to live like that for long! We had the Brown family for dinner the night they came and the next two nights were both at the O'Neills', on Sunday for a service after supper and on Monday for a party. That latter was grand fun. I fixed a series of competitions and then afterwards we played 'Up Jenkins' *[a game in which players concealed a small coin in their hands]* and blow ball and the like. It was real rowdy and a good time was had by all. The O'Neills, especially Mrs, were just delighted to have young folk in their house again. She has spoken about how much she enjoyed the whole night several times since.

The Ordination on Sunday last was a most interesting and impressive service. We had a packed church. There must have been about 800 there and some of the men had to stand at the back. The new man had never seen the church before and I think that he was very surprised at the numbers. He comes from a small, but very alive, new mission centre in Harry Johnston's district, where he was serving his last year after finishing his full theological course. It must be a heartening thing for a young man to see such a church full of young people in his first charge.

Pastor Liu of West Moukden, whose name you will know as one of those who have witnessed to their faith *[as detailed by Marion in her letter written at the end of December 1935]*, was the Pastor here before Shang, and he was asked here to take part in the service. Chuang, our Dr Watson, Chin, from the Scotch mission station of Kaiyuan, clerk of Fa-Kai Presbytery, and four other pastors, as well as a good number of elders and evangelists from our Faku out-stations – a goodly crowd.

The three men who led the service, four I should say, were exceptional men. Chuang and Liu are both fine men, you know their history. Chuang, the older man, as a result of his visit to Alex's country house *[torture in a Japanese prison]* shown in the slight shake of the head which he cannot control when he is sitting still, but it is not noticeable when he is speaking. Our wee man *[Shang]* you know of – I have a real affection and tremendous respect for him. Chin is a very fine young fellow, one of the big men in the Assembly although only over thirty, and a man for whom the foreigners all have a great respect was also in Alex's care *[see letter of 14th October 1936]* ... so you see the stuff there is in our Church, refined gold. I felt tremendously moved to see them all together and to hear the fine service they took, reverently, thoughtfully, earnestly and very humbly. The new man we have, T'ai, looks a good lad, very sensitive face, and if you will pardon the word ... cultured. The Chinese do not show emotion easily and I was very surprised to notice how much he was moved by his Ordination. It is good to feel that if ever we foreigners had to leave the country, that the Church could never die with men like that to lead it and they are only representative of a great number. I am looking forward to going back to the Chinese Assembly next year now that I can understand a little more, for I enjoyed it even with what I knew last year.

Marion's comments that 'if ever we foreigners had to leave the Country, the Church could never die with men like that to lead it,' *turned out to be very prophetic.*

CHAPTER 5
1938

Shen Yang Sanatorium
Pei Ling
Moukden
5th January 1938

To Dad and Mother

Marion had come to Moukden for the Missionaries' Annual Conference. She was writing from the Sanatorium, where their retreat was being held.

The San*[atorium]* is run by the 'Seventh Day Adventists', quite a well-to-do mission, though not a large one, (American) in Manchuria. They have a beautiful big San, which was partly built by a present from Chiang Hsueh Liang, the last General in Manchuria. It is beside the North Tombs (Pei Ling) where the first Emperor of the Ching Dynasty *[Abahai]* was buried – a beautiful pine forest and a lovely site on a slight slope.

The North Tomb.

We paid about 3/6d each per day and were most comfortable and well fed. We didn't know what the vegetarian diet would be like as no one had stayed there, but it was scrummy and most varied. They gave us tea, coffee, salt and jam, all things they don't use, and besides that we had huge quantities of the best sweet milk I have tasted since I left home. We had rather close quarters – 4 in a room, but it was all in the fun of the fair.

Our retreat was divided into an hour for personal devotions, morning prayers together, plus 2 hours' study in groups – in the morning, lunch, time for rest or walks, tea, 2 hours study, supper, evening meeting together.

Sunday

Marion had come over with Mamie for lunch at the MacNaughtans'. Marion was now a member of the Locations Committee. This made recommendations on where missionaries would be stationed in the following year to the governing Irish Council.

You may be pleased to know that my appointment *[as the senior woman missionary in Faku in succession to Mamie]* is settled and passed by Irish Council. Mamie is going to Peichen (or Kwangning) pronounced Beijun. I'm glad I'll have another year, with the comfortable feeling of being among people I know and especially that I will be working with Mrs O'Neill. I'll (perhaps!) feel more confident about starting work in a new station at the end of my 3rd year. This appointment holds, I fancy, for a year still, although it is said I'm to go to Kirin when Mamie is released from Peichen. That won't be until November I think and there is no use my moving until after the January meeting, because all meetings, Bible School and so on stop for Christmas until the end of Jan. But that is looking far ahead.

I was interested to see that you had spotted the likeness between Irish and Chinese in your reading of Liu Yu Tang's book, Dad. Tis true. I've noticed it in a lot of ways, but one most noticeable is their sense of courtesy which will let them tell as many lies as they like rather than embarrass or annoy a person. Do you know the story of the two Irishmen at a crossroads who were asked by a hiker how far it was to the next village. "Three miles," replied one. "What did you tell him that for?" asked the other when the hiker had gone, "Don't you know it's five at least?" "I do of course, but he looked that tired, the creature, I couldn't dishearten him." I've told that story to a most sympathetic and amused Chinese – he <u>quite</u> understood: An Englishman possibly might not see the point of that.

Great Stone Bridge Junction on the way to Yingkou
18th January 1938

To Dad and Mother

This was a junction for Yingkou on the railway between Moukden and Darien. Marion was on her way to Yingkou to stay with the McCammons, at the Irish Mission Station there.

I've half an hour at this junction I think, so I am going to start this week's letter, for the last two have been badly skimped. I've come down this length in the second fastest express in the East – the *Hato*, (the *Asia*, Harbin – Darien, is the fastest). I've been out watching it go on to Darien … I love seeing an Empress *[steam locomotive]* come in or start, it looks so powerful and moves so slowly. The *Hato* is one of these blunt nosed, streamlined trains without any excrescences anywhere. Today we are having the first big snow of the season and the undercarriage is all coated with snow and blobs of ice. It looks quite a Siberian picture.

One of the South Manchuria Railway's streamlined locomotives which Marion admired.

We had a really Christmassy world this morning, deep snow, trees all laden down and the men out on the streets sweeping as hard as they could – but unable to keep up with the fall. The Moukden streets are tarmacadam and get horribly slippery in snow or frost. I'm sorry for the horses and the rickshaw pullers.

Flora and Ella Gordon (my fellow sufferer under Dr Garvin's dieting at St Colm's *[the training college for women missionaries in Edinburgh]* went back to Ashiho *[from Moukden to Harbin]* last night on the *Asia*; it left at 12 midnight – heathenish hour! But it was rather fun going out on the snowy streets in the moonlight with them. Flora has been reappointed – temporarily – to Ashiho, and her people *[her parents, Rev and Mrs MacNaughtan, who worked in Moukden]* are rather disappointed. This is probably their last 5 years here and Flora is just as far away from them as she could be on the mission field. They can't run up for the weekends, it takes about 24 hours to get there and is too expensive. They are both busy people and can't often afford a week off, and Flora still less so, with all the hospital work and the administration of it on their hands.

The train is signalled to go, so I'd better stop, for when it is moving my writing will be even worse than it is at the moment – which is saying some!

Faku
30th January 1938

To Dad and Mother – and Fambley

I got back from Yinghou to Moukden last Saturday – 22nd, went to St Barnabas, the Anglican church, in the morning (Sun) and to the missionaries' service in the evening. Came on to Tiehling, Monday, and to Faku, Tuesday. Mamie and the O'Neills were back on Monday, but they stayed the weekend in Tiehling and I couldn't get a convenient train to catch up with them.

This week has been busy – Mamie had to get all her books ready to hand over to me, a 'book of words', written out for my perusal, about various things I ought to do and who I could get help from. Then she had to pack all she wanted for Peichen, what she needed for her holiday in Peking and put some of her things out of our way for the year. I helped with packing and she got away on Friday. She is staying the weekend in Moukden and then starting off with Jean Laurie, whom she has to take to the P.U.M.C. *[Peking Union Medical College]* in Peking, to see whether the Drs can do anything for her there or whether she will have to go home.

The account books, 3 large ones and 4 small, are my nightmare – ah weel, perhaps it will teach me to be systematic with my own – perhaps!

I've grand folk here to work with and the O'Neills are my props.

School doesn't open until the 12th Feb and the Bible School the 28th so the compound is very quiet, but Wang Ssu Wen, chiaoshih *[the last word meaning evangelist]*, is back and Wang Huei Chün, headmistress, will be here in a week.

In the next paragraph Marion refers to the women's hospital in Faku, which had only very limited services as, although it had a dispenser and midwives, it had no qualified medical staff based there for several years.

A piece of news, which you are to keep under your bonnets until it is made official – there are hopes of opening Faku hospital in the early summer. A Dr Ch'ang (a woman) has been asked to take it over, affiliated to Tiehling, which will mean a weekly visit from Dr and Mrs Brown or their Chinese man Dr. It isn't settled – there are several

166

things still unsettled. She hasn't seen the hospital yet! – it hasn't had a Dr for 6 or 8 years. She is working in a Scotch Mission hospital until Dr Anne Allen comes back from furlough in April and takes her appointment from the April Exec., and none of this business has gone through either Irish or Scotch Exec., here or at home.

However, here's to hoping! It would be nice to have a Brown popping in weekly or fortnightly. <u>And</u> it is very decent of them to say they will do it, because they are very busy indeed and their work is expanding. Dr Brown said it was because he read Dr Ida Mitchell's Life recently and couldn't bear to think that all those hopes and visions would come to nothing so he offered to do this. *[Dr Ida Mitchell had established the women's hospital in Faku in 1909, but had died of diphtheria there in 1917. Frederick O'Neill had edited the biography,* Dr. Isabel Mitchell of Manchuria, *published by James Clarke & Co, London (1918), which had inspired Dr Brown to help fully reopen the hospital.]*

Faku
31ˢᵗ January 1938

To Grandma

Marion began with concerns about her grandmother who had been admitted to a nursing home. Later in the letter she wrote about the decision that she should remain in Faku.

I'm very glad to be left here. It is a very friendly place and I have a number of fine Chinese colleagues to work with. Wang Ssu Wen, the woman evangelist, a girl of 33, is a graduate of a theological college in Nanking. She has been here for nearly 6 years and has the work and the personnel of the district at her finger tips. Chang Te Eu, a girl who was brought up by Dr Margaret McNeill

*Chang Te Eu,
the Bible School Head.*

[an Irish medical missionary in China from 1899 to 1927], is the head of the Bible School. She is a fine steady lass and very clever. My best friends are all here in the compound with me and I haven't far to go when I want to have a crack with them. The O'Neills are only 3 minutes away, in a compound across the road, and Mrs O'Neill takes responsibility for the greater part of the women's evangelistic work in the town, so I'll have plenty of help.

This week is the Chinese New Year holiday, today is the 1st day of their new year and the row that they made last night seeing the New Year in would have made you fancy there was an air raid on. They had fire crackers and bands out the great part of the night, and today at intervals, when they are not eating, the children are still out letting off crackers.

Eating however is the big part of the next few days' programme – they put more meat by in the 5 or 6 days than they would normally eat in a half year. That is honest, no exaggeration. They can make meat balls, which are considered a high delicacy, out of 2 ozs of meat and a lot of vegetable – enough for 4 or 5 people – but at New Year 2-3lbs is the allowance per meal per person. In some houses the feasting goes on for 5, in some 10, days.

Today all the men folk go round paying visits and drink tea or wine and smoke in each house. They do that for 3 days and then it is the women's turn, and if you are out in the street you meet a gay crowd of them moving round together in their best clothes with a paper flower or ornament stuck in their sleek black hair.

No work at all is done for the 1st week of the New Year, except a sketchy tidying of the house and the preparation of meals. It isn't 'lucky' to sew in the 1st week, but I haven't found out why. The Christians of the 2nd generation know practically nothing of other religions or customs. They have not the same curiosity to know as we have, and rather pull their skirts aside for fear of getting involved in superstitious practices, so I haven't been able to get much information from Miss Wang. I'll have to find a new convert for that I think.

We let the servants off as soon as breakfast was over today and I went to the O'Neills' for lunch and asked them in for supper. I must go and prepare it soon, and if you would like to know the menu I am going to lay before the ex-Moderatorial nose, it is onion omelette and chips – a very vulgar high tea.

168

The trouble is I hear Fish (the cook) in the kitchen at the moment, though he got orders not to come back to the house today. He 'loses face' if I do his work for him and I've only managed to get cooking twice – when he was away in his home village for 2 days and once he was ill a day. If I start anything he comes popping in, out of his own house across the compound, and takes it out of my hands.

In the letter of 30th January to her parents, Marion hopes that she gets an invite to a traditional meal as 'I'm quite pining for Chinese food again after none for six weeks or more!' The missionaries normally ate European meals in their own houses and at their meetings.

Faku
2nd February 1938

To Mother

This letter begins by referring to the fact that one of Marion's brothers, Cyril, was keen to become a missionary in India, possibly influenced by the Rev John Davey, a family friend who was a missionary there.

Don't you let John go smooching round our boys grabbing them for India – Cyril wants to go there so he can talk to him as much as he likes, but if anyone else is abroad, China has just as much need as India. Tell him from me to shoo off and expand his energies on some other family or I'll have a word to say to him next time I pay India a visit.

In the next paragraph Marion expressed the wish that she would be able to help her parents with the education of the twins in the future. Clara and Helen were about to become boarders at Victoria College, in Belfast.

... I'll see what I can put by, it should have begun at Christmas, but the result of my exam wasn't in until after the *[salary]* cheque had gone out. *[Marion's salary was presumably being increased now she had passed her Chinese language exam.]*

The trouble is we missionaries seem to have to shoulder the deficit on our work quite a lot in our stations. I don't know what it is like in other places, but Mamie certainly does it here. The School for instance had gathered a debit of almost $400 (about £24) in the last few years, which Mamie had taken over. When she was leaving this time she let $200 go down the spout, she said call it a 'private sub', and I took over the rest upon my body. Well, if this is a bumper year I may get some paid back, but it looks like being the reverse, said she optimistically. Church School revenues have only 2 sources, grants paid through our Education Board of money which comes from home, and fees. The govt. schools have govt. grants and fees.

Mamie and Marion with the pupils of the Girls' and Infants' School, in 1938 on a visit Mamie was making back to Faku.

From this year onward, the authorities are making a great song about providing the populace with very cheap education – they tax more, give the schools higher grants and reduce the fees to a settled standard. Well, we can't raise the grant, just at the moment anyway and unless we have a good many more pupils, we will have very small fees. However that is all my moan – the school fills a position in our Church that no govt. school could, and as long as it is kept going that is the big thing.

A night or two ago, I was very interested to hear Dr O'Neill starting to talk about a Stanley Wright who had made a big name for himself in the Customs in China. It was the one you know of course – he was evidently very keen to get the Chinese worked up into high positions and often went against the policy of the service in taking a Chinese assistant instead of a young Englishman straight out from the

170

Customs College at home. He seems to have been rather high-handed, again the authority sort of officer for any English man to manage – the sort F.W.S. thoroughly approves of.

Mrs O'Neill is a dear, she is an interminable talker – (as he is!). Honestly, I sometimes go over to tell her something and come away in despair, leaving it to tell another time if it isn't too important!! If I don't feel tired it is great crack to spend an evening with them listening to two streams of conversation, but when I am sleepy it drives me craaazy! She has got a touch of laryngitis at the moment and I told her that a day without talking was the best cure! She said she couldn't, unless she locked herself in her bedroom. She is a great family person and I hear of everyone to the remotest cousins' children by their first names, but she also asks about all the boys and what they are doing, by their names too, so I forgive her!

Last night we were talking about the loneliness of these little groups of independent missionaries who come out from America on their own. She said they had come on one house on their way up the Yangtze, a man and wife and child, who had no neighbours and were out on their own. "I think they must have had a cow," she suddenly remarked. "I remember we had fresh milk with our Shredded Wheat that night," This on her honeymoon! I was gurgling so much inside I nearly choked into my tea. Her whole conversation is dotted over with sudden joyful remarks like that. I don't know what sort of a mind or memory she has! But it is not a small one, whatever it is – she has read and thought widely and can give her opinion on most subjects.

[Marion had received her hoped-for invitation to a Chinese New Year meal, but now had some reservations about this.] Oh dear, I'm going to a Chinese feast in an elder's house in half an hour and I hate the thought, not of the food, but of the conversation. It isn't as bad as it used to be, however, I know most of the folk fairly well now; one or two of the men talk so fast that my mind goes a blank the minute they start, but Mamie says she only makes a guess at what they say, so I don't feel so bad!

What time of the year could you take up a few daffodil and snowdrop bulbs and send them to me? And what time should I pot them? Do you think I could manage to have them out here in early spring? I'm just longing to see some again. I wish, I wish, I wish I'd written about them in time for this spring. People here only seem to grow the white Japanese hyacinth, which are pretty but they have too sweet-heavy a scent to be a proper spring flower. I expect the snowdrops will be pushing up by the time you get this. We have gorgeous flowers, great masses of them when they do come, but there is none of the long slow coming of spring as at home. Everything seems to burst at once. Of course it is all the more wonderful when it does come here because can you believe it? Just now there isn't one green thing outside of any sort – grass, weed or leaf, everything grey-sand coloured. I can remember the thrill I had last year of picking my first blade of green grass, beside a wall with a Southern aspect.

Faku
Undated, but in same envelope as letter of 6th February 1938

To Mother

In this letter Marion writes about increasing the amount she sends home now the twins are going to boarding school:

... I think I can manage another £15 per annum. That is £5 for the first three quarters but in this quarter when they take about £12 off for my pension it leaves me a bit thin – especially coming after holidays! If I were living here all the time, didn't go on holidays or jaunts to Moukden I could live on very little, about £80-90 would cover food, servants, house and small ones! But with a couple of orphans (I must take a photo of my 2 girls and send them to you sometime), subs for this and that, holidays, travelling expenses and the mission expenditure exceeding the income and me paying the balance *[as outlined in the letter of 2nd February]* – wot with one thing and another, another £50-£60 a year just about makes life comfortable.

Faku
5th March 1938

To Dad and Mother

I'm quite busy, but not overwhelmingly so. I still have to spend ages in preparation for my class plus PM *[Prayer Meeting]*, but it doesn't take days now as it did at first – only hours! I'm also reading 4 days in the week with my *[language]* teacher. I've started the Sacred Edicts of

K'ang Hsi *[the fourth Emperor of the Quing dynasty]*, edited and enlarged, thank goodness, by his son and again by an official (Wang yu p'u, if you want to know, Salt Commissioner in Shensi around 1724) into something understandable by the ordinary people. K'ang Hsi wrote the 'wen'iest wenli', classical of the most classical and says in 7 words what Wang yu p'u, bless 'is heart, says in several pages. It is quite interesting, but awful tosh. I wonder if the writer really believed all he said. It is all about duteousness and subordination to all seniors in family and outside and your duty to the Clan.

'There is an ill-bred expression: such a man will say 'I do wish to be filial, but alas my parents do not love me.' He is unaware however that sons ought not to discuss rights and wrongs with their parents. Parents are like heaven ... The Ancients said 'Under heaven there are no parents in the wrong.' D'ye hear that Paw and Maw?

This week I have to take FWS's English Class in the Boys' School for him – 35 boys, I'm not looking forward to it eagerly – my Chinese is possibly better than their English, but that isn't saying much. He is going into Moukden for meetings.

The following week I hope to go in for a few days shopping and bring Mary Hamill back with me. Language School breaks up on March 18th and she will come up a day or two later I expect. *[Mary was the new junior woman missionary in Faku in succession to Marion.]* I'm looking forward to the trip in. In the old days *[before there were buses from Faku]* when you thought twice about going to Moukden I suppose you just resigned yourself to 6 months or so without seeing any other foreigners, I'm glad I was born in 1911!

Probably the spring is in my blood too – I don't like these days when there is just enough smell of growth in the air to whet your appetite but no signs of it anywhere. The rooks are building their nests but there isn't a green blade of grass visible – another month to wait.

Faku
12th March 1938

To Paw and Maw

I'm feeling more at my ease in the homes now. I go to a few alone and teach, read, sing and pray without too much preparation beforehand.

The singing is about the worst. One house I was in a day or two ago nearly had me in fits. A woman of over 50 and her daughter-in-law, one on each side of me. The daughter-in-law had a rough idea of the tune, but she sang in about 4 keys per verse. The old lady had <u>no</u> idea of the tune, but warbled very loudly and very happily into the other ear. And there was I in the middle, not very good at holding a tune at the best of times, doing my valiant worst.

Fish was away for 4 days this week and I kept house myself. I ate dinner with Mrs O'Neill, the Dr was taking meetings in Moukden, and cooked breakfast and supper myself – that was easy – an egg in some form and fruit! It was quite fun to be doing rooms and stoves again. Fish was very keen to get someone in and probably I made him rush back far sooner than he wanted to, poor man – but I didn't want to be bothered with someone I didn't know. I <u>did</u> allow him to ask the O'Neills' boy to carry the water for me – I didn't see myself with a carrier's pole over my shoulder, trip-trotting with their funny short little run across the compound every morning when the schoolchildren were all about.

Faku
5th March 1938

To Dad and Mother

I'm just one ecstatic sniff – not at the violet unfortunately, but at the moss. It arrived yesterday – <u>15</u> days. I haven't had anything as quickly for a long time. The violets, poor dears, were very dead. The water had rotted them, but there were a couple of green leaves and the moss to make it worth the sending, bless your thought for me, Mother o' mine. Mrs O'Neill and I sniffed and squeaked over it. The mail came in late last night (Sunday) when I was over at their house for supper. Also I found a bug, a little grey wormy looking object, and looking fondly at it said, "Bless its heart, it's Irish." Dr O'Neill came over and looking at it solemnly through his spectacles, said, "One cannot say it is beautiful, but it is Irish, so we must look at it with eyes of love!"

I put the moss round the roots of one of the plants in our sitting room here – and gave Mrs O'Neill some. It is so green and fresh – and scented – wet lanes and the smell of peat, the soggy wet days in spring, when there is growth in the air – oh it is good to have it!

I thought I'd better introduce Fish to it, in case he thought some strange weed had grown around the geranium in the night. There is no real moss here (Miss Wang thought it was seaweed when I showed it to her) so it all comes under the name of 'tsao' – weed or grass. "It came from Ireland yesterday," I said, "but I'm afraid it won't grow." "Oh? Weeds? (reflectively) What does it do?" "It grows amongst the grass and over the stones in Ireland." "Has it a flower?" "No." Sniffs – "It hasn't a fragrant scent." Bless his heart, he doesn't know. "It is green," I offered him feebly. "You are not to forget to water it when I am away," and we left it at that. "To spend money sending a <u>weed</u> out here ... well of all the – well it bates me ..." bewilderment fairly bristled out of Fish's neck as he turned away.

Faku
2nd April 1938

To Mother and Dad

Dad asked about my mail, all the letters are coming promptly and the seals are not tampered with.

The frostbite is a thing of the past. I was sore while it lasted, but once it started to peel, the pain went. I've learnt what <u>not</u> to do now. Experience dearly bought, says Mother darkly.

Mary *[Hamill]* is going to do quite well with her Chinese I think, she has more courage about talking it that I had when I came up here and she entertained the pastor's wife for one hour this morning when I was at a meeting!

Yesterday we were entertaining two officials, one Chinese and one Japanese, for about 40 minutes. And I felt so thrilled afterwards when I thought of my speechlessness a year before. They came to enquire about Mary and I felt a bit nervous when I saw them come in, but they were so polite and began by laying their hats and swords aside, so I picked up courage and we really had a very friendly chat. We fed 'em tea and cake, the ingredients of the cake being a great source of interest. The Chinese translated for the Japanese (a pleasant faced young laddie), but he understood a little because I said when we first came we were ashamed to speak, afraid of making mistakes, and he laughed and said he was the same. The Chinese has already asked about the Kindergarten for his little girl next year and asked us to visit

175

their home if I have time. It is such a pleasure to deal with them when they are courteous – when I think of the boorishness poor Mamie had to put up with 18 months ago, I wonder how she kept her poise and went on being pointedly polite to them.

This photograph, taken by Colin Corkey, shows a shepherd in his fleece-lined coat outside Faku.

Today Mary and I had a great walk. We took some sandwiches and fruit and went over the hills in a wide circle, cutting over from the old cart road to Tiehling into the new motor road. It took us 3 hours hard walking and the view was simply glorious. We could see 30 miles to the Tiehling hills, and 50 or more, I should think, into the Mongolian plains – it just fades into distance – there are no hills to meet the horizon – and then away south towards Hsinmin, though of course it wasn't visible. Both of us are quite sunburnt after it, my nose will be a shining light before tomorrow.

Mary and I came from Moukden on Tuesday and called in at the Browns for several hours on the way. We had quite an exciting day. The train was 1½ hours late in the morning, an almost unheard of thing on the South Manchurian Railway – I'd back it for punctuality v. The Great Northern *[of Ireland Railway]*! We stood the whole way to Tiehling in a 2nd class carriage – it was <u>crammed</u>.

Then the Tiehling-Faku bus started out with 26 people, seating room 18! Plus lots of luggage. I had a cheery Japanese official beside me who apologised for squashing me, and as the road was bad we spent our time picking ourselves off each other's laps so to speak, or our parcels off each other's feet. The road <u>was</u> <u>awful</u>. The rain the week before had left huge soft patches which had hardened into ruts and holes, reminiscent of the Connemara roads after the Black and Tan boys. 5 times, all the people near the door got out to lighten the load and the driver, having backed, took a running leap and careered over bad patches. We held our breath and our false teeth and prayed for sailors on a night like this.

176

Wot a journey! We were 2½ rather than 1½ hours on the road.

There was a French nun, seated beside a huge fat official. I was sorry for her when the bus rolled. I think she must have felt like a very small worm under a huge steamroller. She took refuge at last in her rosary.

Faku
10th April 1938

To Dad and Mother

... the W.M.A. *[Women's Missionary Association]* wired £200 to us, the decent souls!, for the hospital here. The Exec. Meeting was somewhere about the beginning of this month I think, so we thought nothing could be done about it till then, and after that we only thought of a letter – not a wire. That makes things easier for the O'Neills, because they were shouldering the financial side for the time being, although it is a W.M.A. hospital and by rights I should have been doing it.

Thanks to them, now the work can get well ahead before Dr Ch'ang is expected at the end of this month or the beginning of next. It is all public property now and the appointment approved by everyone, so we can cheer loudly over it ... I thought you would be delighted to hear of Dr Ida Mitchell's hospital being opened again.

We've had a sad house in O'Neills' compound this week – their cook's little 2-month-old daughter died. They already had 2 sons and were <u>so</u> pleased this one was a girl. I was very touched by poor Chao's grief over her death – gone are all the ideas that Chinese men only want sons. Chao has looked as if his whole family was dead all week and even yet I sometimes see him with his eyes all swollen up with crying. Poor soul – if the Dr had been here the baby might have lived. Miss Ch'ang couldn't cope with the trouble and she thought a Dr might have saved it. Their wee girl was born about the same time as Fish's baby boy – the latter is doing well and looks a healthy wee scrap, though small.

Quoting from R.H. Boyd *[the Irish Presbyterian Church Foreign Mission Convenor, whom Marion had met when he was visiting China in 1936]* in a letter of yours, Dad, you say evidently the schools aren't on as low a level as he thought. Well I don't know what he thought, but they are low! Definitely. The average girl of 16 or 17 here under this system will know less of <u>educational</u> subjects than most country children of 12 in a good National School at home. They may possibly know more of housekeeping than our girls – which is after all what the powers that be are aiming at. Educated women make for more thought and free speech, more emancipation generally. Here the women are to be good wives – that is enough.

For 14 year olds in our Irish High School, imagine 4 periods of English and 4 of maths a week, practically no history or geography and 12 hours <u>Irish</u> – 23 *[hours of]* manual labour or housekeeping. *[This is a coded reference to the education in Manchuria: Irish = Japanese.]* That is about our mark here in the Primary School. I'm not sure how the Middle School goes – that would take them up to the standard required for nursing or entering teacher training, but I fancy there is even more stress laid on the housekeeping, etc. I think all the drill, manual labour, i.e. making paths and growing vegetables etc., cleaning up compound and school premises, cooking and sewing, are splendid, but a little education is also needful if you aren't going to turn out girls useful for little else but feeding and clothing a family and without two thoughts to rub together.

Faku
16th April 1938

To Dad and Mother

As I remarked before, spring is here. The small boys of Manchuria are no different from those of Ireland. Our compound has been filled with squeaks and groans of the dying all morning – willow whistles of every key have been made and they started their chorus at 7 o'clock this morning.

Also, I see they are our willows they have been using! But knowing the irresistible qualities of a nice smooth green willow twig myself, I haven't been too fierce yet. I think I'll have to put a word in Miss Wang's ear though. The willows are a hedge in our garden, which runs from the big compound gate along the path to the school, and are just in easy reach of a small boy's arm.

Faku
21st April 1938

To Mother

I've been meaning to write to the *[Clones]* W.A. *[Women's Missionary Association]* and the G.A. *[Girls Auxiliary]* for a long time, but never got it done. This was really written with the W.A. in

mind, but you might read it to the girls too. I'll write another later for them, I hope! It takes such a time to do it – I've been writing steadily at this for 2½ hours and it isn't half of what I wanted to say – and it doesn't read easily to me – I'm sorry! ...

I suppose you show them some of my photos? If you haven't shown them the one of Wang Huei Chün our headmistress, I wish you would. She is a most interesting girl, she and I are really good friends. There is one nice one I took of her at the school door and another of her under a tree in blossom in our compound.

Wang Huei Chün outside the Girls' School door.

Faku
21st April 1938

To Clones Friends

The letter which was enclosed with the letter to her Mother gave a detailed description of Marion's work and also of life in Faku:

The people in Fakumen have not very many wealthy families amongst them, so the houses we visit are just the ordinary type of Chinese house without any of the Western 'comforts' which the richer homes sometimes have. It is only a pretty rich family which has more than 2 rooms ...

When you go into a Chinese compound you shout out first, "Look after the dog!" – if you don't you may be sorry for yourself! They keep rather fierce brutes who are good watch dogs and more than one of our missionaries has been severely bitten. When someone comes out to look after the dog, you step in through the big 10 foot iron studded gates and look round a wide yard.

There are homes around each side of the gate, usually two or three houses up each side and one along the top. Outside each door is a pile of millet stalk, which they use for cooking – they never use coal in their cooking stoves – several big earthen crocks about 4 feet high in which they have cabbage pickled in autumn for use in the winter. In the spring and summer that pickle smells to the high heaven, just like hens' food gone sour at home.

You stop outside the door and call out, "Is the honourable Wang family at home?" – and usually my foreign tongue betrays me and they are able to call out to me to come in. You step into the 'kitchen', perhaps shared by 4 families – a small place with a stove with one big iron pot, like a wash boiler, in which they do all their cooking. The roof is strung with dried vegetables or cakes of dried beans which they use for making a special kind of sauce. Vegetables are in every corner and all their simple cooking utensils are hung on the walls. In the non-Christian houses, a picture of the kitchen god and his wife hang above the stove with a little ledge in front where they burn incense or just put a little food out for him to eat.

Inside non-Christian houses Marion would have seen a family altar (left) and pictures such as that of the God of Wine (right). This print was brought back from China by Marion. It and several others are now in the British Museum's collection.

Then you turn to the right or left and lift a curtain hanging over the doorway and you are in someone's 'house'. Usually a room about the size our church school room (in Clones), most of which is taken up with two mud platforms (k'angs) running the length of the room and about 7 or 8 feet deep. The 6 or 7 feet of floor space left has a big trunk or two, or a cupboard, with all their possession packed inside it. They too live and eat on the k'angs. The women sit cross-legged, sewing or nursing their babies and the children play on them when it is too cold for them to be outside. A family I know of – 4 children, father, mother and grandmother, live on a k'ang 12 feet by 8, yet the place always looks quite tidy and not too crowded. They are content with far fewer possessions than we have. The clothes are usually kept in the big trunks, they don't hang a lot of things round the walls – except calendars and photos of the family who have gone away to jobs in other places. I often wonder how our servants ever get used to looking after the hundred and one things which we find necessary for our existence!

For instance, take our table laid for dinner – cloth, napkins, mats for the dishes, knife and fork, and spoon and fork, each in their particular place – glass for water, salt and peppers, each put just so! Compare a Chinese table. A bowl, saucer and pair of chopsticks for each person and you are done. No cloth and no trimmings. The first time a Chinese 'boy' sees a foreign table he must feel a bit dizzy remembering where everything must go.

Part of my work is to go out every morning to some of the homes to teach the women, and it is tremendously interesting though I still feel so useless with my stuttering language. Some of the homes we visit have Christians of long standing, perhaps old women who cannot read much and who like weekly visits from us to read and explain a little of the Bible to them or to hold a short worship for their family – that is what the Chinese call a service – 'to do worship'. Some other homes have people preparing for baptism and I have the greatest admiration for some of the women I know of over 50 who are learning to read for the first time.

The Girls' School is a great training ground for our young folk – a good many of the children are not Christians when they come, or perhaps they were too big for infant baptism when their parents were baptised. But last year we were delighted when every one of the 24 girls in the graduating class asked to join the preparation class for baptism. The teachers are all splendid Christian girls and they set a fine example to the pupils. The headmistress *[Wang Huei Chün]*, a girl of 25, is the daughter of a pastor, who lived through the Boxer rebellion (in 1900) and whose brother is the pastor in her father's old Church.

We had a great Easter Service on Sunday. There must have been about 500 to 550 people in the church, of which about 300 would be young people from the Girls' and Boys' Schools and the Bible School. The church looked like our own does at Harvest Thanksgiving! It was a praise service, with Easter hymns from the Boys' School, the Girls' School – these sung in 4 parts – the Bible School and 12 small scraps of under 8 years old from the Kindergarten.

It was good to be there and to see with what joy and understanding the people heard the story of Easter morning. Easter means far more to them than Christmas does, I think. I found in the homes that the women had been reading the story of Christ's death that week and some spoke of it with such wonder that showed they knew the life that Christ's death had given to them.

To see the difference in the homes when even one member is a Christian is proof enough – if I needed any before – that it is worth our while to come out here and that it is worth your while to make it possible for us to come. I hope you feel that too.

Faku
22nd April 1938

To Dad and Mother

[On Easter Sunday afternoon] we had – to me – a very unusual service. Every Easter Sunday they have a service in the graveyard. It was a most impressive and moving one. We gathered about 150-200 strong round the Boxer martyr's grave, an elder, Hsiu (I think), who was beheaded, the pastor's little son's grave and a pupil's father, and many others were nearby, and there, as never before, I knew 'we sorrow not even as others which have no hope'. It was a service of hope and faith and rejoicing, and the hymns we sang were 'Blest be the everlasting God', 'There is a better world they say', and ones of promise like that.

It was a lovely sunny evening as we walked out to the hillside,

182

and a great many of the boys and girls from the school came out too. As the service was almost finished, a rattle of thunder came and rain clouds gathered, but we got home without getting wet. The next day an old lady who is one of our finest Christians, said to Mrs O'Neill, "God must have been pleased with us at the grave yard yesterday." "Why do you say that?" asked Mrs O'Neill. "Didn't he speak to us when it thundered?" she asked – and she looked so happy about it, Mrs O'Neill could say nothing. He had spoken to old Mrs Wang anyway.

Did I ever tell you about a reforestation scheme that had been started some years before 'the change of affairs'. The schools had a fixed day in the year when they all turned out and a planted a tree per pupil – (Labour Day in America, I believe). Well in the old days the kids went out, and scraped a wee hole and popped the tree in any way – and most of them died.

Give the present authorities a pat for organisation. They send out workmen to dig big enough holes first, and then there is a meeting and all the schools turn out and plant their trees. This time there were about 3,000 children (from Faku alone!) who planted trees on a hill not far from us, in nice straight lines just like a row of soldiers on parade. If they all grow it should make quite a nice wood later.

I've invited Mrs Wang, Huei Chün's Mother (who is on a visit here), Huei Chün and Mrs O'Neill over for a Chinese meal this evening and the house is simply whiffing! Fish doesn't often make Chinese food and he is thrilled with the idea – he started preparing last night! and has had a chicken stewing in a bowl since 9 o'clock this morning.

This is my 4th Chinese meal this week, so I think I'll call a halt for a while happily. I like it now and then, but it is sleepy food for us foreigners and when I've had a meal about 3 in the afternoon I'm useless for the rest of the day.

Fakumen
25th April 1938

To Dad

We have just seen in the papers that visas have been refused for the via Siberia route for a few weeks ... They have been constructing a new line with a wider gauge, I heard a year ago – so perhaps this is the changeover. If you should come short of letters soon, you will know what has happened. None of our missionaries are travelling until June I think, so it will be in running order by then.

The railway north of Hsinking, which the Manchukuoan authorities had taken over in 1935, was in fact being narrowed by the Japanese, from the Russian gauge of 5'0" to the standard gauge of 4'8½" which was in use elsewhere in Manchuria.

Fakumen
27th April 1938

To Grandma

Marion started the letter by referring to the forthcoming wedding of her Uncle Howard (missionary in India) to Nora Gregg-Wilson.

While on the subject of weddings, I'll tell you about a conversation I had with a woman here the other day. She asked me how many of my brothers 'completed the home', i.e. were married, and was very surprised to hear that none had. She asked why and I explained our customs to her, putting it to her on a ground she might understand that if a boy and girl of 16 had a child it wasn't usually a very healthy one – which she admitted, 'they were sometimes hard to rear'. But she said, "We've a household of 8 people and I just had to have some help, so I married my son (a boy of 16 at school). She has to make shoes for every one of the children – a pair a month! The cotton ones they make don't last much longer. Also, they make nearly all their own clothes in the house. It would be only a pretty well-to-do household who could afford a tailor. Hence one of the reasons for getting a daughter-in-law into the house quickly.

The other is of course, that they want to see their grandsons. Once a grandson is born, the grandfather and grandmother can sit back and know that the ancestor worship will go on for another couple of generations. Yesterday I was speaking to a grandmother of 38! Her son had a son when he was 18. You often find grandparents younger than 38 and great grandparents of round about 50! So you see, your grandchildren haven't treated you at all well, Grandma!

Faku
30th April 1938

To Dad and Mother

[Yesterday] all the morning the wind had been rising and a regular dust storm was blowing when the time for the *[netball]* game came.

[After the game finished] the wind was getting worse and worse and I was glad when ... I could get in for a cup of tea. I had just taken about half a cup, when I looked out of the window as a particularly strong gust came – in time to see the thin iron roof of the Bible School rise straight up in the air, fall in two pieces and come crashing to the ground.

I leaped for the back door, yelling for Fish – and ropes – and got up to where the roof was, followed by Fish (he can move in emergencies, bless the man) before it did much damage. Every gust was lifting it nearer our compound wall (mud) and I was afraid if it came a crack against it, that it would do bad damage. Fish and I had a rope over it and tied to the roots of 2 convenient trees before anyone else in the compound appeared, and then we all got to it and with ropes and big stones got it weighed down.

The work had to be done under a constant rain of mud and dust from the flat roof (the roof is rafters, matting, 6 inches mud, papers, thin tin) and our eyes were nearly blinded. The Bible School is two buildings – one is the Classroom and Prayer room, the other is dorms and offices. The latter was intact so far, but there was an ominous rattle about it so we leapt to save it. There were 4 men, Huei Chün, Miss Wang *[evangelist]* and myself, as well as a good many B.S. *[Bible School]* students, so we got ropes right over the roof in 4 places and then started to hand up big flat stones which were there for some building which was done recently.

It took nearly 3 hours to get everything looking sort of safe and during that time I saw our garden wall (a pretty decorative thing made chiefly of holes) collapse on the windward side, and Fish's wife came to tell us the coal house had collapsed. The roof had come off it in one whole piece and one wall had caved in. The Bible School had kept me so busy that I think nothing, but the sight of our own bungalow caving in would have excited me by that time. The iron had twisted as it fell and it looked like the wreck of an aeroplane – and I hated the thought of the money that would have to be spent on getting it on again. However, everyone said it was the builder's fault (they were put on new last year) and he admitted to it himself, so we are pay only costs – the men's work and whatever new iron is needed to replace too badly broken bits. Nothing is to go to the man himself – so that's not so bad.

I'm glad I'm strong – it has been useful several times in emergencies since I came here. I held down that roof yesterday with Fish when it was 'bucking' under me like something possessed, and in ordinary moments I wouldn't have been capable of putting out so much force at all ...

We've had nearly as bad a blow today as we had yesterday – and I've been told we'll have just such another tomorrow – cheerful prospect. I know why R.L.S. *[Robert Louis Stevenson]* said there would be a high wind in his Hell. I'd say a hot dusty one!

Faku
8th May 1938

To Dad and Mother

Mary and I have been moving in high circles this week. The head of the Police Dept, a Japanese – Mr Big Stone (sounds like an Indian chief), came and made a personal (very) call on us last Monday. He was there for information and got it. What school and college did we go to? What did we do immediately after leaving coll? What we did since landing here? He wrote a personal description of us and demanded 2 photos each. He is new – our last friend left a month ago – and new to the job I think too, so he is extra thorough. He was very friendly and polite, however, and the interpreter is a decent laddie (sometimes they are rather warts, their position gives them a swelled head).

Then, when he had business over he sat down for a chat – "Weren't we lonely here with only 4 foreigners?", "How often did we get home – weren't we ever homesick?", "Why were we not married? Did our Church not allow it?" I said we could marry if we wanted to, our Church didn't manage that for us ...

Then, the next day Mary and I had to go to the Police Office to 'invite' a Residence Cert for her. You don't go and 'buy it' or ask for it

– you 'invite' it in polite tones, as it is given to you by the government. I was the 1st one Mr Big Stone had filled out I think, anyway he took 1 hour 20 minutes over less than ½ hour's work.

The interpreter laddie got worried about our wasting so much of our valuable time sitting in the office so he went off and got a Japanese lesson book with Chinese sentences – all good idiomatic everyday speech in it, and asked if we could read it. We sat happily with him having an hour's Chinese and think that he was quite pleased to act as teacher!

While we were there, 2 of the Japanese got very interested in the subject of our hair and discussed it for a long time. When I said there was golden hair, they laughed, but when I said 'red' they simply gaped – I think they pictured bright scarlet!

Marion had recently attended a wedding at the church in Faku:

The man who was a young widower – 24 or thereabouts – good Christian, does what he can for the Church, he is 2nd in command in the Telegraph Office. He was marrying a girl who is not baptised, but who last winter asked if she might come into the Bible School, as her sister was a baptised Christian, and wanted to 'study the doctrine'. Her home is 60 miles away and she couldn't get in all winter, owing to home affairs, however she says he wants to come in now in the next term and her husband says he is going to send her here to study.

He is an only son, mother dead and father too old to face the long journey, so he had no relatives here. Her mother was the only one who could come into Faku – so it would have been a small wedding if the Church had not rallied round. He went to T'ai and asked if any of us would care to come to the church for the service, and when

The wedding attended by Marion in Faku. On the back of the photograph she wrote that 'the old mother behind wouldn't come into the picture.'

we heard how friendless they were, we started inviting our people. About 100 went to the church at 7 o'clock on Thursday morning, and 40–50 were guests of his at a restaurant for breakfast. He was very pleasant and grateful to everyone and the Chinese head of his office went round to thank T'ai for the way in which the Church people had supported him – I was very struck at all the gratitude for what seemed just part of our Church life.

Faku
10th May 1938

To Grandma

Marion had just heard from home that, after an operation, it was clear that her Grandma was terminally ill.

I was terribly sorry to hear that you had to have an operation after all. Willie wrote to me just after he had been in to see you. He said that though you were naturally weak, you were bright and cheery ... Mother told me that they hope to let you back to Millvale soon – that's good, I know you'd rather be at home than in Belfast. *[Millvale was the Cromie family farm in County Down, with a view of the Mourne Mountains.]*

Yesterday I was just longing to be back where I could see the Mournes again. I was looking at a soft range of hills very like the Mournes in outline, but they had no gorse on them and I knew the whole continent of Asia lay between them and the sea. Hills and a wet day (!) always make me think of home ...

We don't get much rain here – a little in the spring and usually some in July and August, but from September - March you won't see a drop of it. Uncle Howard *[from his experience as a missionary in India]* can tell you what a good smell there is when everything is wet instead of dry and dusty. We don't often have thunder and lightning here, except in August and then it can be daily.

I'm enclosing a card painted by an old cook of Miss McWilliams *[a former missionary in Faku]* – the two scenes on it are quite good – I got them this morning and thought this might interest you. The two in front are a blind man and his helper crossing a small stream. The blind beggars here all have a small assistant who walks in front holding onto

a stick which the blind man has in his hand. The blind men nearly always play a mournful minor ditty on a flute and most of them are fortune tellers.

The picture on the other side is of an old wifie sitting on the k'ang smoking a pipe – see the length of it! Their hair isn't usually in such a large bun, but most of the older folk wear it perched right on top like that, with a flower or a gay pin stuck into the side of the bun. The windows are paper, but they are quite bright – the paper is oiled, stiff paper – like very strong butter paper. So many of the old women when we go in to visit them are sitting cross-legged just like that, puffing away. They sometimes ask if we smoke, and if we said we did we would be presented at once with the one the old lady was smoking!

I hope you are feeling lots better when you read this in the good spring weather I'm hearing so much about. Take care of yourself Grandma dear, you are precious to a lot of folks.

Faku
22ⁿᵈ May 1938

To Mother and Dad

Last Sunday, 15ᵗʰ, the heavens opened and our compound was like a lake very soon. There had been rain all night, but a good many of the children came to Sunday school, getting there just before the downpour came. It was quite impossible to go to church – the Chinese wear cloth shoes and they couldn't have sat in wet clothes for a service

– so we arranged a service in our compound rapidly, and Wang Huei Chün led it. We had over 120 – children, Bible School, hospital and our servants and families.

The hospital is getting into shape now and there are a few people in, the outpatient department is growing. We are waiting until a few alterations are made before we have the opening meeting and welcome to the doctor. One disappointment this week was over a man who came in to stop opium. There is a family, Han, who are rotten with it.

The oldest and second sons both smoke, the wife of the second, and the son and daughter-in-law of the first. Only the wife of the oldest, a staunch wee woman and a good Christian, has prevented the family being ruined long ago. She got the son and daughter-in-law off to Yingk'ou with Mamie's help last year, and both took the hospital treatment and then went into Cammy's *[Rev. McCammon's]* Bible School. Both are quite cured and are very fervent evangelical Church members now – but they are still in Yingkhou and I hope will stay there another few years till the roots get a bit deeper.

The second son, called Han (= '2'), came in to break off the habit this week and he has been a failure as far as we can see. Since he was 12 he has been completely ungovernable. His father died when he was young and he did whatever he liked ever since. I don't blame his poor wife for taking to opium. He took in a woman of no savoury reputation, into his house a fortnight after they were married. His wife is of a good family and has a very sensitive 'well-bred' face. She must have had a bitter time, poor soul. He came in, got two jabs of the needle and refused any more – he was too sick and couldn't stick it out. He said he would break it off himself and actually stayed on for two days, but yesterday he packed up and left. We've prayed over him for months and Mrs O'Neill and the Pastor have talked to him till they are tired – now we are afraid that he will never give it up after this failure. Poor Dr Ch'ang was very downcast over her first opium case, but two more have come in and are getting along very well.

Moukden
5ᵗʰ June 1938

To Dad and Mother

Marion had accompanied Hessie Stewart, a relatively new missionary who had been staying in Faku and had been feeling ill, to Moukden to see one of the doctors there.

You asked about sending money directly to me for mission work. I think our Treasurer winks at money in small sums direct from friends or Churches that have a special interest in the missionary, but would not like it made a regular thing. The money sent to Jean or the G.A. *[Girls Auxiliary]* Office is all pooled of course. I should be glad if you could send me a small sum now and then as you feel the *[Clones]* G.A. can spare it. We sometimes have cases of special need and it is hard to have to refuse.

The O'Neills have used all the money they got given to themselves as Christmas presents, or money given for their own use before leaving home *[Ireland]*, for putting several people into our own, or Tiehling, hospital. I have the full charge of one orphan girl, over $100 a year at school, and have taken on an evangelist's sister for this half year. I don't know whether she is worth the cost of primary schooling. I want to see first, and if she isn't we'll have to think of something else for her to do. Any time you send me money just pay it into the H&S *[Hong Kong & Shanghai]* Bank in London and tell me when you have done it! I just get a note from them once a year.

Have you seen any articles on communism in China recently? I have seen a few – and they are interesting. Japan is just forcing communism on China – it is spreading far more rapidly this year than ever before. A modified type, but of that ilk. There is country not far from Peking where no official of the new provisional Government can do anything. If he is content to be a figurehead, he can live, if he makes a nuisance of himself, he dies. Many of the officials just have their food money as salary, i.e. about 6/- a month, and the communities live on very Spartan lines. Women are also mobilised. Things don't seem too well in the Far South all the same.

Faku
12ᵗʰ June 1938

To Dad and Mother

Sorry to see that you had been worried over incidents on the Russian - Man*[churian]* border. Ever since I came out here there have been small incidents, but there is no danger of trouble here unless Russia gets aggressive. Japan is on the defensive up there, she can't take on war on 2 fronts and will be content to sit still up there until things are quiet down south.

Don't worry about us – if trouble comes the consul will shoot us out of the country as fast he knows how, I'm sure. I heard this discussed when I came out – we knew J.*[apan]* was preparing for something at that time, but didn't know whether it was the north or south.

I'm sending you some snaps, some are quite good, others not just so. I told you I was using F.W.S.'s old camera, didn't I? Good clear results in some. The small snaps are Mary's taking. Most are explained on the back. You don't still think I'm like a Chinese, do you?!

Marion 'plodding up the gulley'.

The two Mary took are good to give you an idea of the country. The one of me plodding up the gulley looks out over Faku to the hills beyond. The whole country is broken up in deep gullies as you will see in the land below the carter, sandy and red soil. (note civilisation in the lorry wheels on the cart). The road I am walking up is the old road to Tiehling, compare the surface with the one the carter is on which is the new one. The country beyond the carter looks grim, but the colours on it are wonderful, red and sand, mauve and blue, and now in the spring the green patches all over it are all the more vivid for their background.

Oh dear! I hate creepy crawly bugs and they are getting really numerous now. One thousand-legs got out of bed with me the other morning, it hit the floor just about the same time as I did and moved more quickly. I examine my night dress carefully every night now. I'd hate to find out one had got in before me.

Fakumen
15th June 1938

To Grandma

You are holding a royal court with all the visitors who are dropping in to see you – it is easy for folks with cars to drop in like that – out here, where distances are great and all village visiting done by cart, it is an occasion when some of the family set off to visit relatives or friends. The women always have a flower tucked into their neat, shiny black hair, everyone has new clean gowns and the cart usually has a few baskets and bags of vegetables to give the friends. I saw a cart start off today and thought how happy they all looked – it is nice to be in a place where you don't hear the roar of motor traffic and are only in danger of being run down by a farm cart! I feel a complete country cousin when I go into Moukden – I look both ways, twice, before I cross the road – I don't know what I'll do when I have to face Donegal Place *[in Belfast]*!

I'm afraid my 'missionary work' as yet seems to consist in office work – details of 'running' the station – all of them such small things that I get impatient at times. And yet, if I were to tackle much teaching, my language is a horrible stutter. I still enjoy the street visiting, although I have not been out all this week. We have a Short Term Bible School for the women soon ... and I have been busy with our Chinese woman evangelist preparing the work for it.

The children are always a delight, they are so friendly and sweet. One day recently it was pouring rain and I found a wee scrap of about 8, wet through coming to school. I took her in, took off her gown and while it was drying gave her a sweet to eat. After a while I saw it was still in her hand. I thought she was just being polite and had not dared to eat in my presence, so I told her to eat it up. She looked at me for a minute and then she whispered, "I have a smaller brother at home." "Do you want to bring it home to him?" – "Yes" – so I gave her another and she ate it happily. I thought that aged 8 I should hardly have been so unselfish – I'm sure it would have gone straight into my mouth without any thought of brother William!

We have had quite an unusual lot of rain this spring – and everything is coming on in the garden like a house afire – including the weeds! We are eating our own strawberries and lettuce. Tomato plants, potatoes, onions, cabbage of several sorts, a couple of Chinese vegetables like varieties of white turnip, leeks and celery, are all up 6 to 12 inches (according to the nature of the vegetable!) and looking very healthy. Our strawberry plants were new last year, so we are having gorgeous fat fruit this year – I want to see if I can bottle a few for winter deserts when we have visitors. There are no glass houses needed here for fruit like that – they ripen while you watch them.

Faku
17th June 1938

To Dad and Mother

Your tale of the spread you had at Henry's one day made my mouth water! We do miss home bread and butter badly here. Imagine that we are still using butter that I bought in Moukden on March 28th – now June 17th! I brought it home and put it in salted water – very heavy brine. It is still eatable, but I am glad to think it will be finished soon! It isn't rancid, just not fresh! Then a couple of tins will carry us on to July meetings, and a couple of lbs will be carried back from Moukden and I hope will do us till the August holidays start.

We are all right in the winter, the summer is the problem for butter. The O'Neills' pit is quite cool and keeps things pretty fresh. All the mission houses have ice chests in places where ice is sold, but there is none here.

Marion was used to plenty of butter at home. She made butter by churning the milk from the manse cow when she was in Clones.

Faku
2nd July 1938

To Dad and Mother

We've been tearing about this week at a terrific speed, and the scribble at the moment is due to my hand shaking from nerves! I'm going out to meet Mrs Brown in half an hour, then have to go to a funeral service in an elder's house, and after that, 12.30ish we have our Hospital Opening. I haven't anything to do with it, but I am as nervous as a cat about it, because we have invited a lot of the town officials, both Manchurian and Japanese.

F.W.S. is chairman and he hasn't a blessed thing prepared yet – he says the hospital has the programme, and they say he has – my hair is curling with rage and nerves, so I left him to come over here and work it off writing to you. It will probably all go off like clockwork – indeed none of the officials may come - ! but F.W.S. is so darn casual at times that you don't know where you are.

3rd July

We had a rather successful day yesterday, an unexpected crowd of the big wigs turned up and not only went to the hospital, but saw all around the Girls' School and then asked if they might see the foreigners' houses. About 18 crowded into our wee house! The great point of interest was our open grate. A couple of them had been here before and they explained how the smoke all went up the chimney and the heat all came into the room, they pondered over it for a quite a while ... then Fish did showman for our kitchen stoves and oven with gusto, as he happened to be making jam at the time they had a chance of seeing him at work.

Every room in our house has books, a good many are Mamie's, but Mary and I have added our quota too. The head of the Education and another man were talking in my study and one remarked to the other, "Western girls truly have a different position from ours. That two girls as young as they are should have education and status such as they have – ! a house like this and all these books! – why, here the Magistrate could not have a quarter of their books." Huei Chün reported this to me. These are all well-educated men of the old regime and it must be like being without food and water to them to have to live in this bookless Manchukuo *[presumably because the Japanese did not wish the Chinese to have books printed before their conquest of Manchuria].*

About the actual opening ceremony ... it wasn't an 'opening' because F.W.S., as chairman, stressed the fact that the hospital had never been shut – this was just a meeting to introduce the Dr to the town. The nurses all looked so nice in their white caps and aprons – there are 7 midwifery students and 4 actual hospital nurses, so it looked a big show for such a small hospital! ...

Dr Ch'ang (front right), Miss Ch'ang head of the dispensary (in the dark uniform) and nurses and midwifery students at the hospital ceremony.

Emily Brown and their Chinese Dr, Dr Gow, came from Tiehling and are staying over the weekend. I thought was very nice of them to spare two people – Dr Gow was really on holiday, and as there were a couple of bad cases in *[the Tiehling hospital]*, Jim *[Brown]* packed Emily off to do the speaking. She did it beautifully too – good clear Chinese and she looked so sweet herself as she spoke. There were 3 women who spoke – Emily, Miss Ch'ang of the hospital (who was in charge of the dispensary) and Dr Ch'ang. Dr Ch'ang doesn't shine in public – though she is a clever and most dependable person, but the other two caught the attention of the officials' eye. They rarely hear women speaking, but both did so well it was an added piece of education for them I should think!

c/o Mrs Miskelly
Moukden
9th July 1938

To Dad and Mother

Marion was attending the Assembly of the Manchurian Church, along with Dr O'Neill and Pastor Tai from Faku. The initial meetings were in the form of a 'retreat'. She gave details of the timetable during the day, and then:

8 - 9.30 evening meeting addressed by a Japanese pastor of the Japanese Presbyterian Church. He was at New College, Edinburgh, for 2 years and also studied theology in Germany – his English is splendid and very clear. Mr MacNaughtan translates into Chinese. It is quite a

strenuous day – especially for the likes of me, who has to concentrate all the time to get the meaning of the *[Chinese]* language before starting to think of the subject matter!

On Monday - Wednesday there are business meetings. These are getting smaller and less important, because with 'Black and Tans' *[Japanese spies]* there to listen in, naught of great import can be discussed.

You know 7.7.37 was the Lukuo Chiao Bridge incident outside Peking. I have reason to remember my birthday last year – the start of all this horror and misery. Poor China has had many a disaster before, but nothing to equal this, war, flood and cholera – and famine to come now that all this year's crops are ruined. It seems impossible to take it in, we are now near to it and yet little touched by it. Except that the price of living is going up.

This year the government decreed that the 7th of July should be a day of remembrance, celebration of the beginning of the war. We were very glad that in Moukden the Christian schools were allowed to go to church to hold this. It was quite a simple thing, held in the compound as the church couldn't hold students and Assembly delegates. We had the National Anthem, 2 minutes silent prayer – for the wounded and bereaved, and peace – a hymn for our country and benediction. There were several things that made Oi smile – wish I could tell you, but I dare not. *[The last remark and the coded reference 'Black and Tans' were because the letter could be opened by the Japanese censor.]*

The weekend before they came to Moukden:

Tai went up to Tiehling on Saturday to take the Sunday service, meaning to come back on the early morning bus – but it rained and there was no bus. So little Marion, lightly as a hippopotamus, leaped into the breach to take his house class on James that day, with less than an hour to prepare in. They listened with every symptom of intelligence and interest. I hope they took in a little.

But what pleased me most was one service I took in which I gave a 20 minutes talk and never looked at my notes once, I didn't even stick to the way I had prepared it, made it more chatty and colloquial and managed not to make any bad blunders, according to Miss Wang who promised faithfully to report any howlers. It was the lst time I felt at ease with the language. I had it well prepared of course – but I'd never before been able to break away from the actual words I had prepared. Time I had got to that stage though, after 2½ years it's naught to boast about.

The photo of Marion, referred to in her letter.

I'm enclosing the last cheap photo I got taken for officials. I've had to give away 12 from April to June! So I'm ordering 20 to see if that will do me for a few months! I was told by the last Japanese that as I usually wore specs I should be photographed in them. So here I am, looking wise and owlish.

Fakumen
19th July 1938

To Dad and Mother

I had several interesting days last week in Moukden. On Tuesday, as soon as the morning session of Assembly was over Miss Wang Ssu Wen (our Evangelist) had asked us round to her home to see the presents which had arrived for her younger brother's wedding on the Wednesday. We saw all manner of marvellous things – awful modern Chinese style, worst suburban English. Presses with pink glass doors and all flowered ones; large clocks under glass cases – imitation marble, with pillars and 'gold' ornamentation. Writing desk, chairs and tables, hat stand – dozens of small things for the house, all pretty gimcrack.

The bride's things arrived and they were the loveliest. Silk or satin embroidered bedspreads and pillows and mattresses, enough for a large family for a lifetime. There were a lot of guests to see the presents and watch one of the older women of the bride's family with one of the bridegroom's *[family]* arrange everything. They had a parcel of coins, probably copper, with which they sprinkled the bottom of each chest and drawer before they put anything into it. I thought how nice it would be for the bride to go on finding a little money all the 1st year!

Then, when the scarlet k'ang curtains were hung, lovely soft satin, everyone went round bowing to everyone else saying, "Great Happiness." That being the end of the ceremony for the day, we went off to a restaurant to eat – about 50 guests, all invited by the bridegroom's family.

Then, in the evening I was asked to an engagement feast. It was much nicer than the morning one – Wang Huei Chün's (headmistress) younger sister, Yin Yin, was being engaged to a young doctor, the son of a well-known elder in our Church. The difference in two things (1) Huei Chün's family have taste and (2) the young couple have known each other for 2 or 3 years. The other pair, Eu Te (Miss Wang's [evangelist's] brother) and Miss Lan, had met once before, but had probably never spoken to each other – imagine marrying a man whom you had bowed to once! Eu Te as a matter of fact was friendly with another girl in his class in the dispensary at the Nau Mau hospital, but the Chinese take things most philosophically – the Lans are rich business people, elders in the North Church, Moukden, and everything very suitable, including the ages – the boy 18, the girl 20! He is a big lad, good looking with a sweet good humoured mouth – he looked more like 24.

The engaged couple [sister of the headmistress and her fiancé] are both medicals, he graduated 2 years ago and has a good position. Yin Yin is due to graduate in the spring. We were a very happy, free and easy party at the engagement feast. About 20 people, elders and pastor, and a doctor or two. Mamie and I the only foreigners.

There was a lot of laughter and teasing ... They put the young couple side by side (very modern!) and Yin Yin was so shy she wouldn't eat at first – they teased her and said it wasn't time to refuse food yet. At the wedding feast the bride is supposed to refuse all food, and for a few weeks in her new home is supposed to eat very little – this covered her with confusion of course! but she started to eat, and after about 5 minutes the two of them were chatting away quite naturally. It was so nice to see a couple who knew each other, in China.

I came in for my share of the teasing too. I was sitting beside old Mrs Wang and she leant over to ask when I would be having a feast like this – I said, "Well she would be the first to know, because I would ask her to 'arrange affairs'." – i.e. find the man, or rather as the

Chinese put it 'find my mother-in-law'!! She immediately retorted, "No," she couldn't do that, Mrs Chuang (who acted sponsor that day for Yin Yin and Dr Ching) was clever at that business. And then to my confusion she called down the long table (men and women were at the one table), "Mrs Chuang, Miss Young is too shy to ask you herself, but she wants you to find her a mother-in-law, she is so pleased with today's feast." Whoops! The whole table nearly fell into the soup, and they started arranging it all for me. I retired behind my fan until they had finished, as all modest Chinese maidens should – which amused them still more. I enjoyed it thoroughly – I felt I was being received properly! There are not many of the foreigners they can be so free and easy with. Mamie and Wiggie Faulkner get teased and give as good as they get sometimes, but they stand off rather from some of the others.

15 Eastcliff
Pei Tei Ho
5th August 1938

Marion and Mary were staying with the MacNaughtans in PTH.

I told you that Mary Hamill, Mrs Mac and the servants went on a day before us, and Mrs Mac, had the house open for us when we arrived. Flora and I followed the day after, and Mr Mac, because he had to wait over the weekend for an ordination, came on Monday. It was good to get to church on Sunday amongst a big group of English speaking people. Sometimes it isn't so easy yet to worship in Chinese.

Photo of the house at 15 Eastcliff, where Marion stayed with the MacNaughtans. She wrote on the back of the photograph, 'The right side and ½ the curve was ours. Grand verandah.'

Our house here is a lovely one. I must see if I can get a get a good snap sometime, it is like a big castle. Two Scotch doctors built it years ago on the slope of a hill, but foreseeing building being done later on in front of them, they built it very high and the kitchen apartments are all underneath, while we live very high up with a glorious view and a lovely verandah. We are so high we are looking down on tree tops, the mimosa is out now like soft pink power puffs, and a green cool carpet of leaves leads right down to the sand and the sea. Beyond are the Shan Kai Kuan hills, glorious just now in the evening sunshine, ragged peaks and deep blue shadows.

One little bit of excitement about the journey happened to Mr Mac – and it might have been unpleasant – an attempt was made to derail the train he was in. Nothing serious happened, but each carriage went over the obstacle with a terrific bump. It was only the last carriage slipped off the line and was pulled along the sleepers a bit – it didn't overturn. Mrs Mac remarked, if he had been on the job he could have made a better thing of it!

A few trouble makers are supposed to be slipping up to Manchuria just now to help keep the authorities busy – but it is horrid to think they are willing to risk Chinese lives just to make a spot of trouble for the Japanese – as they did of course over the flooding of the Yellow River country. *[In June 1938, Chiang Kai-shek had ordered the blasting of the Yellow River dykes to stop the advance of Japanese forces. As a result over 500,000 people died from drowning, disease and starvation.]*

The envelope for Marion's letter of 5th August, with a stamp showing Sun Yat-sen, founding father and first President of the Chinese Republic.

Pei Tei Ho
30th August 1938

To Mother

Marion has received news of her grandmother's death:

Your cable came on Sunday afternoon and you have not been out of my thoughts long since then. I'm feeling as I am sure you all are, loneliness for dear Grandma, but thankfulness she was spared long pain. Your last few letters have prepared me for this news – I have almost been longing for it – she has never been ill since I remember her and these days of dependence on other people must have irked her. I do hope she did not have a lot of pain this month – I won't get your letters now for a week I'm afraid. I'm glad you sent the cable. I've been waiting – and fearing – the news this last fortnight. I'm afraid it was rather expensive for you.

I'm not fretting Mother dear, so don't worry about me – I can only imagine the loneliness of Millvale. I can't feel it as you all will. Poor Auntie and Uncle Frank will have lonely days until they get used to the house without her dear presence.

I'm glad I was old enough to know all my grandparents – each one whom we could love and respect so much. Grandma was always so young and alive – I like to remember her a year or two before I left home, getting up one night at a party with Uncle James to lead us in a barn dance.

There can only be pride and love for her in our hearts for her happy useful life, for the God fearing example that her own spiritual life has left for us – and the pride and love we have can help in part to wipe away the sorrow.

15 Eastcliff
Pei Te Ho
29th August 1938

From Mrs O'Neill to Mrs Young

Annie O'Neill wrote to express her sympathy on the death of Marion's grandmother. The O'Neills were also staying with the MacNaughtans. She continued: We have had a very very happy week here. Mrs MacNaughtan is the soul of kindness. When I tell you Marion feels that there is the same atmosphere of friendliness and hospitality as in her own home in Clones Manse, you will know why we all are at home in 'the MacNaughtans'!

... Suffice it to say we are a very happy wee family up there *[in Faku]* and Marion is awfully good to me. We hope we won't be disturbed by some other station stealing Marion from us. I don't see how they can, now that Mamie is in her new job.

If Mamie had stayed in Faku as the Senior Woman Missionary, Marion would probably have been allocated to a new station. She could still leave Faku if Mamie returned from Peichen. Throughout much of her time in Manchuria, Marion thinks there is a possibility of her being moved elsewhere, with Kirin being a possibility in 1938.

Moukden
4th September 1938

To Mother

Marion was staying in Moukden on her way back from Pei Tai Ho to Faku.

Mary and I hope to put our luggage in the morning bus at Tiehling tomorrow *[after arriving there by train from Moukden]* and then cycle home to Faku. The roads are good and there has been no trouble in our part of the country for 3 years – so we aren't expecting bandits by the way! If there is any trouble in any part of the country they put armed guards on the bus and I haven't seen any since I went to Faku 2 years ago. In the Peichen district, where it is mountainous, they have to be careful still, but our hills haven't cover for a grouse, so we've been pretty peaceful this year ...

The line south of Pei Ta Ho has had a bad time recently. Guerrillas have kept up the troubles, blowing up small bridges, wrecked a military train, burned railway stations and taken officials prisoner. Perhaps they preferred to be taken 'prisoner' than to be left behind to give an account to the Japanese authorities.

Our getaway from P.T.H. was most uncertain. There was no trouble at all on our line north, but the trains had to come through from Tientsin to take us on. The night before and the night after, people had horribly long journeys – the Stevensons with 3 small children sat for 7 hours at one station during the night, and there was no waiting room for them to sit in as far as I can hear. Or perhaps it was too odorous. We were a large party with the Fulton's small girls, and we had an excellent journey with only a 2 hour stop when we were comfortably in the train. We had berths at night, and hot coffee and omelettes from the restaurant car to supplement our breakfast, and arrived very comfortably in Moukden.

Elizabeth Fulton, 9 months old, is a darling. A very intelligent child and as good as gold. I took her over for most of the morning and she slept or played with me all the time. She never cried the whole 18 hours I think! The other two kiddies were very good and between books and drawing paper Mary Hamill managed to keep them occupied, so Flora *[Fulton]* got a rest from the family who gave us a great deal of pleasure.

Fakumen
8ᵗʰ September 1938

To Dad and Mother

Back again in Fakumen and enjoying the feeling of being 'at home' – looking back at it, the twelfth of the year seems a long time to give to holidays – but one needs it here. It is the getting amongst foreigners again that is the biggest break and rest of all. You don't realise it in the station – but just to be free of talking Chinese and trying to think 'Chinese' – is such a relief!

Flora and Marion at P.T.H. Marion wrote, 'Two Cheshire cats' on the back.

Flora did a war dance round the verandah the first morning at P.T.H., chanting, "I'm not giving lectures in Chinese for a month, all the difficult midder *[midwifery]* cases and abdominal operations in Acheng district can come to the hospital – and I don't care – Whoopee!! Whoopee!!!"

The freedom from responsibility is half the holiday. Now we've been lotus eaters long enough to get tired of it and are really glad to be back.

Mary and I had a great cycle ride from Tiehling here on Monday. Put our luggage on the morning bus and started off with the exclamations of the bus people to egg us on: "Could we really ride 90 li!? We'd be dead tired before we got to Faku; the road was especially bad just now (– it was!) and we'd have to use great strength to get there."

We'd planned for about 3½ hours for the 30 miles, knowing the road and that we'd have to walk about 2 miles on some especially steep hills – but it took us nearly 5½! About 10 miles of the road was <u>awful</u> and we walked most of it. You had a choice between deep ruts made in the soft clay surface during the rains, or the 4 – 6ins of dust to the sides of the road, where your wheels skidded as it does in soft sand. The rest of the road was something like the surface, as I remember it – of the side road to Miss Aford's *[in Clones]*, and 3 or 4 miles near Faku of good road, rock bottom and sand surface well rolled.

We were in no hurry and didn't worry. The country is glorious now with the harvest ripening, deep brown red heads on the gaoling *[probably sorghum]*and green yellow on the millet. The emerald green of young cabbage (harvested in November) and the yellow brown leaves on the drying soya beans. Everything grows so luxuriantly here, wild flowers, 4 different colours of convolvulus – purple, white, soft red, and mauve with red lines – a tall weed with a lovely aromatic scent, which they were cutting and drying for burning in the k'angs – long stretches of the road were scented with it.

We were a source of much interest of course! We are the first foreign girls to have cycled that road – and I am sure there are not many Chinese girls who have bikes about here. A few use them in the big towns. The roads were thick with forced labour – out mending roads when they should be preparing to harvest – poor souls, but we felt we had done our good deed for the day when we provided such a circus for them.

On one very steep hill we came on an old man pushing a hand cart. It was far too heavy and he was just puffing out his heart over it. I stopped and lifted the lead ropes and dropped them over my bike before he saw what I was doing – then his eyes nearly popped out of his head. That anyone should help him! and a girl moreover!! and a foreigner to boot!!! Boy o' boys were the heavens falling on his head? Chinese don't help each other much, I'd watched 2 young farmer lads pass him a minute before and it would never enter their heads to give a hand.

When the old lad had got his breath, we heaved the load to the top of the hill at a great rate – I had a stream of blessings poured on me all the way. "Ai! Ai! This girl has piled up merit, this honourable one has built well."! "Where would one find another like her? No Chinese girl would help an old man on the road." And so on, till I was all embarrassed. I told him I was a Christian (and he seemed to know the word) and that we followed our Lord in helping each other when we could.

I was pressed to stop at his village for a meal – well, then at least some tea. Well, what was my precious name? Would I come to their village when I passed through again? We stopped further along for a drink out of our thermos flask and spent so long taking some snaps that he caught up again. We were just at the foot of an especially long steep hill, so we hitched up again – and were nearly sorry! We were near his village and the road had a lot of people on it – so our merits and virtues were yelled at everyone as they passed!

Faku
14th September 1938

To Dad and Mother

Do you remember I told you we were making a tennis court on the foundations of Miss MacWilliam's house? It had turned out a great success. I hadn't imagined that it could have as good a surface with the little work that has been put into it. I got a couple of men for less than a week to rake up the stones and rubbish, they levelled it and rolled it. Then a couple of loads of sand finished it and we have a grand court.

We still have to keep it rolled, because the sand isn't quite rolled in and gets kicked up with a lot play. But we have a good court for less than £2, including the posts and winder for the net!

The tennis court. Marion wrote on the back of the photograph, 'Aren't our asters good!' Miss Chang, the drill teacher, is on the right.

Yesterday was the celebration of the recognition of Manchukuo by Japan, and the drill teachers (men) of the other schools all came visiting. The Boys' School teachers all came too, so we had more than a dozen men to entertain and kept them busy with tennis and tenniquoit. They aren't brilliant, but one or two can play a hard game. Li, the Korean, and I (foreigners), v. two of the Boys' School teachers (Manchuria), had a really good hard game in which we won – Li is a pretty hot player.

Mary doesn't play much, but she'll come on – Miss Chang, our drill teacher, shows real promise and I believe the Dr and head nurse have played before. I haven't seen them play yet.

In this group beside the moon gateway, which led into the women missionaries' house, are Wang Ssu Wen, Marion, Mr Li, Wang Huei Chün and Miss Chang. Mr Li and Miss Chang are mentioned as tennis players.

Fakumen
28ᵗʰ September 1938

To Dad and Mother

The Twins had started as boarders at Victoria College in Belfast.

Well, well – so your house is left unto you desolate, it is hard to picture. It is good to think that Hugh gets home at weekends at least – you'll be more glad than ever that he has the wee car. It is a great chance for the twins, they certainly need to get a good school, and to get a chance to get their Senior *[school certificate]* with good marks. I'm sure they will enjoy the new life they have, and regular hours and work will make them sprout like dockens. I hope they'll write home soon. I want their address, though I'm sure Victoria College, Belfast, would be enough. It is great news, I was very excited when your letter came.

But, and I says it firmly – you've got to get rid of another member of the family too. An old and tired friend, to wit Branny *[the manse cow]*. And whatever understudy she has at the moment. Come on boys and twins, tell Mother and Dad you can get on fine without your own milk and butter, Here I am thriving without it and you are all <u>big</u> boys and girls now and I think could keep up your strength without it during holidays. Besides think of what a grand time you'd have during the hols with no milking, churning or byres (<u>think</u> of it Jim!) and what is really the crux of the matter – Mother would have no more bother with milk ...

I'm writing this while waiting to be asked to a Chinese meal in the school – 7 o'clock in the evening. There seem to have been quite a number lately. Do you remember that I had asked the men teacher over to see our house after the last feast on Saturday – a rather amusing thing happened at that 'party', of which I heard a day later.

I had poured them out tea and then went out to the kitchen to brew a fresh pot (Fish had gone to the street) leaving Mary to hand round the sugar. The Chinese, whether drinking tea or hot water, count it a treat to put in several spoonfuls of sugar. She started by handing it to some of the men and they politely dipped the spoon in and took out about 2 grains each and then sat waiting to be pressed to more by Mary. Mary, thinking that in their taking the 2 grains they were pandering to our queer foreign tastes and thinking they preferred their tea without sugar, passed on and pressed no one! Then she came out to the kitchen to see if there were biscuits and (I heard this later) the minute she was out of the room one of the men in an agonised whisper to Huei Chün, "Pass the sugar quick, Headmistress – I <u>didn't</u> <u>take</u> <u>any</u>."! When I told Huei Chün that Mary was just being polite à la Anglaise as Shang was à la Chinoise, she laughed herself tired. From entertaining officials in my cabbage days I know to give them 3 heaped teaspoonfuls to a small cup and stir it before I hand it to them.

Marion took this photograph of the garden of the bungalow at Faku in September 1938. She wrote on the back, 'The green on the grass isn't very noticeable but our lawn is coming up nicely. The creeper on the sticks is a pretty thing with little scarlet flowers.'

8th October 1938
Peichen (Kwangning)

To Dad and Mother

Have a look at my address – you never know where I'll be writing from next, do you? I'm on a 2 day visit to Mamie at the moment. I was with the Wangs in Haicheng over the weekend and Mamie asked me to spend a couple of days with her and see Peichen, as Fedya *[her medical colleague]* was going to Moukden on business and she would be alone. I am writing a day or two early for the mail as I'll have a day travelling tomorrow, shopping in Moukden and then onto Faku (D.V.)

It was such a relief to hear the news in Moukden yesterday as to how things were settled in Europe *[the Munich Peace Agreement between Chamberlain and Hitler over Czechoslovakia]*, - and yet poor Benes *[Czechoslovakian President]*, the decision must have been a bitter one for him and his people to swallow. It seems hard to think that Hitler will be content – he wants his way clear to the Adriatic – perhaps Italy will not be content with that though, that is all one can hope. One could almost say like the old lady in Dublin, "Maybe the good Lord will put it into some decent man's heart to shoot him."!

On her way to Peichen, Marion had stopped at Haicheng to stay with the family of Wang Huei Chün, the headmistress and arrived there ... about dusk and I was hauled before the Japanese police and spent a very irate ½ hour with 4 of them, only one of whom could speak much Chinese. I don't mean they were irate – I was! Old Pastor Wang was there to meet me and he was perched outside on the platform on a chilly evening, waiting. I was perfectly willing to give my car, particulars of my journey and residence certificate, but they started through my bag, which was just blooming ill-mannered curiosity. They counted my money, examined receipts, looked at a book full of shopping lists and finally started into my bigger hand bag which had small parcels and a book in it. I knew that there was a large pair of woollen knickers in the bottom of it and I didn't relish the thought of him shaking them out in front of a room full of men! It was cold in the bus in the morning, so I'd donned an extra pair. When he started poking the parcels and asked what a bag of sweets was that I had for the small son on the house, I just snorted, "Sweets," at him, and then, "the rest are clothes." I think my tone of voice made him look up. I was simply glaring at him, so he said, "Excuse me," shut up the bag and handed it over. I was sorry I hadn't got my dander up a quarter of an hour earlier, but I was afraid to be too snooty for they could have kept me there for hours and would have done it quite happily if I had been rude to them.

The Wangs' orchard, photographed during Marion's stay with the family.

After staying with the Wangs, Marion went on to Peichen.

It is 10 o'clock and Mamie has gone to bed ... Peichen district has robbers, so there are guards on the city wall at night. The mission property is just beside the wall and from where I can hear the men calling to each other at the end of each turn of their beat. It is easy to hear it because they just give one 'Aiya' of a man in pain and keep it up constantly at about 2 minutes or less intervals! Different atmosphere to peaceful Faku.

Fakumen
11th October 1938

To Dad and Mother

Marion wrote about her journey from Haicheng to Peichen:

The country down there has a different atmosphere from here, and it's a-plenty, shooting season opens when the harvest is high. The stations had sand bag protections and plenty of soldiers about. There were soldiers in every compartment of the train and a few kept marching through the train from one end to another.

Ko Pang Tzu, the nearest railway station to Peichen, was a seething mass of people, the bus had already gone to Peichen and there was more than a bus load ready to leave. Harry Johnston had passed through the day before and had left his card and a message for me with an old bus office attendant. (I named him 'Caliban' to myself, but found Mamie and Fedya called him 'Bleery Bill'.) I think Harry imagined my Chinese at the stage it was when he left on furlough some 18 months ago! As it happened I am glad he did, as I hate shoving in a crowd and I'd never have got into the bus if Bleery Bill hadn't nabbed a seat for me,

I thought the Faku – Tiehling road could be bad in wet weather, but I didn't know nuthin. As we skidded out of Ko Pang Tzu, first of all dropping a case off the roof and then carrying away a low hanging electric wire, a man beside the driver said, "The road is not too good today." To which the driver grimly replied, "This bit is grand, you haven't seen anything yet." And we hadn't.

The scenery was lovely – we ran through small woods beside a river bank, always with the mountains south of Peichen before us in lovely changing colours. To a strong quiet minded person it might have been a delightful run – but I'll admit it – I was really scared. The bus was <u>packed</u> and the windows had 2 bars across them, you couldn't have got a child out – the back wheels skidded violently on the deep mud and we took our chance around trees and along the soft clay river bank. When we reached Peichen – and we did eventually without mishap (except that a small girl who had been sleeping peacefully on my knee suddenly opened her eyes and without any warning decided to be sick – and she was, very, though there was really no room to be sick, so to speak. I did juggling tricks with her gown and managed to save my coat. We undressed her and she went to sleep quite happily.)

Peichen was an old city and quite unlike Faku. Great city walls, 40 feet high and wide enough on top to drive a motor round with ease. Two pagodas rising up out of the mass of Chinese houses and the lovely carved roofs of temples. Along the streets you constantly pass the lovely old carved gates, sometimes with stone lions on guard, of rich old Chinese families, and the whole place has an old feeling of history about it. Faku is a colonists' town, settlers came from south of us, some from Shantung, and moving north in search of land settled here. There is no old aristocracy, I've only seen one old family home – and it is a beautiful place. I hope to get a snap of it some time.

I had a couple of days with Mamie, saw something of the work there and then came back to Moukden. Spent a night there and shopped, and then came back to Faku with Colin Corkey. Mrs O'Neill asked him down this weekend – came Friday left Monday – and the girls in compound were greatly excited to know whether he was coming to 'settle the engagement' with Mary or me!

Marion and Mary, photographed by Colin Corkey outside the Taoist Temple in Faku.

This weekend was the 8th Moon Feast and we had jollifications here and ate a lot of Chinese food. I had some of the teachers out of both Boys' and Girls' Schools in for a party on Saturday night, those who couldn't go home for the holiday. Usually they leave about 9.20, but it was after 11 before they departed, so I gathered they had enjoyed themselves. I just had a light supper – sweets and jellies, cake, tea and sweets and fruit – then we played games. A beetle drive – not racing beetles, but drawing them! and all sorts of the old games we used to play at home. The Chinese are so tickled at the idea of grown-ups playing games that they find every one of our old parlour games very interesting – even hide the thimble! The men laughed themselves tired out over that. When one spotted it, he sat down and teased the others unmercifully, the sort of impotent feeling at not being able to do such a simple thing as spot a thimble gave them quite a kick!

You asked if we had a wireless in Faku. No – not that is any use to us. There are Chinese who have them, but they are only allowed to get Hsinking and Moukden *[radio stations]*. The French priest had one when I came here, but those were the 'bad days' and things were made so unpleasant for him – his cook was put in prison and tortured – that he finally had to get rid of it. Our house was searched on the pretence of looking for a wireless, you know – although the gent doing it knew well that we hadn't got it.

Now the authorities and we are on the best of terms, we have very wise officials here now, and our school positively welcomes inspectors for we are one of the shining lights in the whole Faku district and rather a credit to the local Ed*[ucation]* Board. Recently, in a big handwork display held in Moukden for all Moukden district (probably as big as Ireland), our Girls' School got 3 credits and the Boys' School got one, while in the whole of Faku district there were only 2 other credits given.

On Tuesday 18th we go into Moukden for meetings, I'm on Locations and Language Committees and there is to be a meeting of Irish Council over a piece of special business. This is the October Exec. to prepare for the January big meetings when the year's work is settled as far as it can be. I'm looking forward to Locations. There is a lot to be done there – I hope I'll still be in Faku next year, I think it is pretty sure, but after last year when I was ready to pack almost before I went in to the meetings, I don't dare say where I might be next year – Moukden perhaps!

This is for your own ear and is to go no further. Several people who have a good deal to say on Committees, talk of me taking on Miss Hudson's place in West Moukden. It is a huge job and I quaver at the thought – also I prefer country to town life, but if it is offered me I won't refuse. I do hope it won't be till my 5th year, I don't feel ready for it yet. Mrs MacNaughtan in the meantime is holding it down well.

[Rosa Hudson had retired in 1936, so for two years Isobel MacNaughtan had been carrying on the work in West Moukden, although not listed as a missionary as she had been until her marriage.]

Fakumen
1st November 1938

Mother

Marion was sending birthday greetings to her mother.

I am writing this a day or two earlier than I mean to post it, but I am getting ready for a country tour and I was afraid that it might get skimped the last day or so. I'm looking forward to this one *[tour]*, last time I couldn't help at all – this time I've work planned, whether it comes off or not – and I'm very happy doing this sort of touring. I hope later on I'll be able to do more of it – that is why I'd hate to get into any of the big town places, I'm sure you can't help getting yourself tied up in all the dozen and one things in a town Church.

However, I'm also sure I will be put where I can do most work, whether town or county.

I'm so thankful for one thing that is part of me – hereditary, and that is the gift of being able to make friends with people. I've never felt 'strange' out here. I can always find folk to talk to me - or to listen to me! amongst the Chinese I mean, and in Faku especially, I feel very much at home.

T'ung Chiang K'ou
50 miles (Chinese) from Faku
5th November 1938

To Dad and Mother

I'm just going to scribble a little before we go to sleep. Mary and I are sitting on our mattresses on a k'ang with a light between us on a small case. Miss Wang is busy heating water for us to have a wash before we go to bed – and we are ready for both wash and bed!

When Marion sent this photograph taken by Mary, of Wang Ssu Wen and herself, to her parents, she wrote that 'it will give you some idea of what a k'ang looks like. It is 6 or 7 feet deep – this looks rather deceptive. The bedding is rolled to the back during the day. The chests at the side hold everything ... In the foreground is a stove with a kettle on it – that isn't proper Chinese, but a great many houses use them just for heat and to boil water. It was on a stove like this that we made most of our food on.'

We sent our luggage in the bus this morning and started out cycling about 10.30. It took us 4 hours to do the 18 miles! but we stopped on the road and took our time. Miss Wang can't manage very fast and the road was very hilly indeed. It was a glorious day and the hills looked lovely with the last red leaves on the trees.

This place is quite a big town on a river bank, we crossed in a ferry coming here – bikes and all. The streets are wide and clean and there are several big shops, we can buy fruit, sweets and sugar here without any trouble. The Church is a very warm hearted one, a clean bright room was opened by themselves just last year, the money being locally raised, and everything looks well kept. We have a nice quiet room at the back of it, very private and comfortable. The young evangelist, his wife and child, have another room at the other side of our common kitchen.

Sunday Afternoon

There have not often been foreigners here judging by the excitement we cause all along the streets; people shoot out of doors to watch us and children follow in crowds. Yesterday a schoolboy (I expect, we didn't look back!) startled and amused us by saying, "English girl" just behind us in clear English. The sight of us on bikes amuses everyone, because women in the smaller places never ride bikes, and the sight of Mary's fair, fuzzy hair just crowns it – the kids eyes light up and they yell at each other, "Blimey, look what's coming!"

We went out last night to get a couple of things in town and stopped at one shop where what looked like most of the apprentices were watching our progress down the street, asked if they had white paper. "No but so and so has," and he yelled down the street, "The ministers are coming to buy paper from you." Then as we walked on, a regular chorus from everyone on the street, "They want white paper, they are going to so and sos for white paper."

**T'ung Chiang K'ou
13th November 1938**

To Mother and Dad

It is Sunday evening and the 3 of us are sitting on the k'ang with a small lamp and a candle giving rather inadequate light.

The church at Tung Chiang K'ou, which Marion wrote had been opened in 1937, the congregation having raised the money themselves.

The snow has come and winter really is here. Yesterday was bitter. The deacons have been very concerned for us and insisted on putting up a small stove in the room. They had to make a hole in their nice freshly papered window to let the stove pipe through and we were very reluctant to let them, but now the heat is very pleasant and we couldn't be more comfortable.

There is a very nice deacon, Han, and his wife who have been very good to us. Mrs Han never learnt to read, so she is a pupil at our [Bible] School [here] and Han comes every day to bring us vegetables and eggs, to see if our k'ang is hot enough, and if it isn't up to his standard he burns some millet stalk in it for us.

Today after we had our meal with the Hans, Mary and I went down to the river to see how the ice was getting on. It was well frozen a couple of days ago, but when it snowed yesterday the weather got warmer and the ice has melted a bit. The ferry went across a couple of times at midday today, but it isn't running from 9 to 5 daily as it was when we came.

Two big sailing boats came up the river against the current as we came down, and their big sails were lovely. There was no wind so each was being towed by 4 men. I asked them where they had come from – Tiehling, and they told me they had been pulling all day. I felt my Chinese must be getting on when they understood me at once and answered me without a blink! Sometimes the Chinese don't expect a foreigner to be able to speak Chinese at all and just don't pay any heed to what we say – just gape!

These were picturesque looking, big toughies, in their winter clothes, with caps with fur linings pulled down around their faces. The towing rope strangely enough was fastened to the top of the mast – at least 20 feet high – a very strong thick one. The rope was very long and the boat was able to keep well out in the centre of the river – with a man steering it of course.

Today we should have gone to another small church for the morning service, but it is 20 li away across the river and there was no ferry either at the time we were going or at the time we should be coming back, on account of the ice. It was only yesterday that we knew and we had no way of sending them a message, because there is no telephone between here and there. Fortunately, Miss Wang in her letter said 'if nothing happened to keep us back, or if the snow wasn't too deep' we would go. So let's hope they had more snow there than here or they'll think we are weak kneed creatures!

The *[Bible]* School goes on happily. We've only lost one pupil, which is good work – sometimes a few people come just from curiosity and when they find they have to work, they depart for home. The pupils are all very keen and we have great fun, none of the classes are dull. My *[class on the Gospel of]* Mark has 8 pupils, all working hard and seeming from the way they reply, to take in what I tell them!

Chin chia Tiu (The village of the family of Chin)
19th November 1938

To Dad and Mother

The journey yesterday was a cold one. We were cycling straight into a north wind and the temperature was lower than it has been. Miss Wang's bike wasn't functioning properly. I think the ball bearings must be going; but walking was easier than cycling and we kept warmer. It was only 18 or 20 miles so it didn't take us long. A man carried our luggage on a long pole over his shoulder – about 80 lbs – no small weight for that distance – I'll send you a snap of how it is done later, if it comes out. Mary brought her camera along and had got a lot of snaps.

Marion and Wang Ssu Wen, with the man carrying their luggage, en route for Chin chia Tiu.

We have a nice room here, sunny with a stove in it, and are waited on hand and foot by Miss Kuan and Elder Ho. If we had longer here I would object, but as it is only 2 days there is no use making a fuss. We aren't allowed to tidy the room or do a thing, and Mary and I liked the chance of moving round a bit, because we have to sit so much otherwise!

Yesterday evening we had lit a candle just for 10 minutes to make our beds and tidy our room for bed. The compound is well hidden and we thought no one would notice anything for 5 minutes or so. We had hardly lit it, when there was a clump, clump and the clang of a sword and there was a Japanese officer at the door of our room. Miss Wang was kneeling on the k'ang and her shoes were on the floor just where he was standing, so she couldn't get down. I was my politest to him and got him seated on the k'ang – still beside Miss Wang's shoes! which I hadn't noticed in the dark.

He wasn't seated until another officer, Chinese this time, his interpreter, came in and then at intervals 3 more came in. The room is small and I was wondering if they had turned the whole force out to arrest us for having the candle lit. However, the Japanese was most jovial, bit of a lad I'd say – and they only stayed to gossip for half an hour and left without asking anything about our light or making any fuss. Miss Wang was so overcome by being shoeless on the k'ang that she just sat on her heels and did not budge until they spoke to her. They addressed all their questions to me and I managed to acquit myself better than usual – the Japanese officer loaded me with compliments, which I couldn't return as his Chinese was atrocious. At one time the interpreter asked me how we liked sleeping on k'angs and the J.O. understood, for he suddenly said "Bed" to me – fortunately, I caught it and asked if he spoke English, so he said, "Aaah!" and with an expression of beatific content said, "Double bed" and bounced on the k'ang, moving his hands to show he was on springs – then he gave a dissertation in Japanese to the interpreter on beds – I gathered, while I heaved inside.

Here are some of the things I answered.

"Coming here how did I come?" (It is a great hit to have landed in Japan.)

"How much money for the trip? Would $3000 be enough for a round trip?"

"Were we not allowed to marry?"

"How much money did we get a month?" (To which I said we kept enough to eat and dress ourselves and left the rest at home – it was in English money.)

"Were our crops like theirs?"

"What food did we eat here?!

"What food did we eat at home?" and it was here that interpreter was told by the J.O. that it was because the English drank so much milk that their skins were so white and soft and never wrinkled when they got old!

"Weren't we lonely here? How often did we get home? Where were our homes and how many members of the family were there?"

I thought they were never going – that isn't half of what they asked, but I was so thankful that they were so polite that I would have entertained them for another hour.

This place is our problem Church. It used to be a big place, with its own pastor, Boys' School, Kindergarten and Girls' Primary – that was in the old days. Property acquired through money taken as Boxer Indemnity gradually undermined the Church, rows started up, everyone sat back on their heels and took no responsibility for the running of the place – and apart from all that, the town has a bad name and drug taking in general everywhere.

Now there is a congregation of perhaps 20 on a Sunday, no schools and no pastor. The man in charge now is one of our Faku elders with a lot of experience, and he and a woman evangelist are working hard, but it must be heart-breaking work. There is no family feeling in the Church, such as there was in the last place, and the deacons don't rally round. I'll be quite glad to move on Monday, I'm only sorry for the folk who have to work here – they need inexhaustible patience and love.

Fakumen
26th November 1939

To Dad and Mother

I closed my last letter in Chin chia Tiu I think, and posted it in Tiehling on our way home. Did I tell you that I spoke for a minute or two in church that Sunday? We were introduced and Ho asked me beforehand to say something. I was getting on fine, when the police came marching in with swords clanking and everyone swung round to see who was setting up an ironmongery shop at the back. It was a trifle disturbing!

We had a good run the day we left Chin chia Tiu. We had engaged a droskey – and paid for all the seats – so that our bedding, Miss Wang and the like, all could go on it. She decided to cycle first and just when we were leaving the town we suddenly discovered to our wrath that the driver had picked up 2 men passengers. We couldn't do anything by this time, droskeys are not easy to get – however Miss Wang said plenty!

A young boy, one of the passengers, said if she got tired he'd cycle – so we had to leave it at that. The road was very hilly and she soon handed it over to the laddie, who joined us. Mary and I fairly enjoyed ourselves going at our own rate instead of waiting for Miss W. and swooping down hills without having her shout that she was walking. It was a glorious day, crisp and sunny, we never noticed the 23 odd miles.

The lad with us got talking and told me amongst other things that he had been engaged at 7, married at 13 and had a son at 16 – he is now 21, his wife 20, and he is still a student, living on the old folks. He said the foreign way of getting married when you were earning your own money, was the best! Perhaps he doesn't get much to spend!

That day, when we got to the railway station the droskey driver stopped at an inn about 100 or 150 yards from the station, Miss Wang went to see about the luggage and came back wrathfully to say that he wouldn't bring it to the station – he said the porters would beat him up. We couldn't see any porters to take it for us, so I went down to interview the gent, I picked up the bedding bundle, about 40 lbs, and swung it on my shoulder – I just said, "I can't manage that other one, it is too heavy – I won't let the porter touch you!" And he picked it up like a lamb and followed. Women don't carry bundles on their shoulders here, so I'd gathered quite a crowd by the time I'd got there – however, I didn't mind when we had the baggage.

We got to Tiehling that evening, had a nice time with the Cummings, Browns' successors, and started out for Faku the next day. 30 miles was too much for Miss Wang – she was dead beat when she looked at the Faku hills. However, by much persuading we got her up them, and the long slopes down to Faku were easy – we made her stay

220

on the bike and crawled slowly down with our brakes on. Mary and I felt grand, a bath and early to bed was all we needed. If we could have come back the way we planned, it would not have been so long a run for Miss Wang – but I think I told you the river hadn't frozen over.

Faku
1ˢᵗ December 1938

To Dad

The envelopes for this and the following separate letter for Marion's mother were marked 'to be opened on 25ᵗʰ December'.

Here's to wish you a very happy Christmas day and all of the best in 1939. It should be a rowdy house with everyone at home. I'm only sorry I'm not there to add to it – but it won't be so long until I am – whoopee!

We are busy these days with all the 101 things that have to be done before the end of the year. I haven't got into all the routine yet so it keeps me on the jump – but I'm enjoying it, especially this last half year when I have got over my fear of talking to people (except from the platform! I'll never be easy there!). It is all interesting work whatever you do – and you are never dull – at our stage anyway, when you don't quite know when the Chinese mind works.

The only things that beat me to a frazzle are rows. We've had a glorious one these last 2 days, a woman deacon with a bitter tongue. I don't know why she was ever elected. She is squashed now I think, but lies and filth are harder to stand than any bodily fatigue you could face. Poor Mrs O'Neill had to face the brunt of it – I felt the woman had to be faced with it without delay or muddling, and I am afraid my Chinese wouldn't get round all I wanted to say. I was sorry for Mrs O'Neill – she had the hardest part of the burden to bear. She is always being sent on nasty errands by someone. Lately the pastor deputed her to tell a woman she was being put on probation of 3 months before being put out of the Church for opium smoking. She gets so much of the exhorting of sinners to do, and she does it well – but it takes it out of her. Dr O'Neill always says she is <u>Pastor</u> O' Neill, not he.

Well that doesn't seem a cheery subject for you to be reading of on Christmas Day!

Faku
1ˢᵗ December 1938

To Mother

I hope you are reading this on Christmas morning, because I will be especially thinking of you then. We'll be back from church about the time you are getting up – and we'll be feeling Christmas day is ours then, and the O'Neills and ourselves will be preparing to forget that we are in Manchuria.

Once this Christmas is over I'll be able to say – "One more Christmas and I'll be home." It doesn't seem possible, I only feel as if I'm getting my feet under me now – and I'm not very steady on them yet! This year in charge of Faku has just fled by and I feel there is so little to show for it, but I've been glad to be here and working with the Faku folk. "I'm in charge of Faku, forsooth! What would the bishop say?"

The twins will enjoy their Christmas holidays especially, I am sure – coming home *[from boarding school]* will add a new flavour to them. I have already sent you 10/- *[ten shillings]* in my home letter this week, I hope you will get it in time to get someone in for a couple of days to help with the Christmas rush, the family will always be willing to do a lot I know, but it is nice to have someone in the scullery.

We are having 'company' for the weekend – Tom Blakely. Dr O'Neill wants to see him on business and Mrs O'Neill seems to believe that it is the married woman's duty to see that any girls on her station have a chance to meet a young man or two! She never says much, but I think she'd be a proper matchmaker if her sister wasn't on the W.A. Committee! *[The Women's Association Committee in Belfast did not approve of 'their' missionaries marrying soon after going to work abroad.]* She got Colin here, partly I'm sure because she had heard some Moukden folk link our names together. I could have fallen off my seat one day when she began to poke sly fun at me! I think she has given up any hope of him, so she is getting Tom along to see if he is any higher up in my affections!

I'll be thinking of you when you are reading this Mother O' Mine – all happiness today and every blessing in 1939.

With my love.

Fakumen
15th December 1938

To Dad and Mother

It was strange to hear of your fixing flower beds, Mother, in November – we were busy taking things out instead of putting them in – but all the bulbs *[sent out from Ireland]* both in Mrs O'Neill's and our house are coming on nicely – we are having a race to see whose is open first! The trouble is there will be several opening when we are in Moukden I'm sure!

Meetings *[of the Irish Council and the Missionary Conference]* run from 10th – about 20th January. They will be busy this year. Wish I'd belonged to simpler days when there were no government complications with Mission work. The unfortunate men, like T.C. Fulton, Harry Johnston, Dr O'N. and like brains on the Scotch side, are being overworked these days deciding Mission policy and trying to look ahead to days which none of us can picture. Will the native Church have to stand alone, or will we be here to help?

I go to Moukden on Monday, shop Tuesday, Irish Locations *[Committee]* 9-2 Wed – Joint *[Irish and Scottish]* Locations 4-5, Irish 5-7 o'clock. Come back Thursday, D.V. School has Concert for 2 days, Friday and Saturday, properties and stage are mostly in my hands, Kindergarten Christmas tree, carols for Service on Christmas Day – and then blessed Sunday afternoon when it will all be over and we can have our private Christmas Day!

Moukden
20th December 1938

To Mother and Dad

There is a proper Christmas atmosphere about now – I've been out today doing Christmas shopping. Sitting back in my rickshaw in a fur coat, collecting large parcels as I went, I felt like a millionaire's wife or daughter or sumpthink.

This was one of the designs on some sheets of notepaper which Marion used in 1938. On her visit to Moukden in December the hood on her rickshaw would certainly have been pulled up.

223

There has been quite heavy snow and although it has been swept into piles beside the footpath, all the clear spaces, plots of grass and squares round monuments, are still covered deep. The Russian and French stores are all gaily decorated for Christmas and have Christmas tree or Christmas tree decoration in the window – and there is mistletoe on sale in lots of flower shops! The Chinese use it as decoration because of the white – or red – berries, not for other purposes!

... I've been reappointed to Faku – still to pass Irish Council of course – and I'm sure you'll be as glad as I am. I felt I was just getting to know the personnel in the district and to have some idea of what work I would do next year here, so I had hope that I might be left here. On the other hand, Faku is an easy station to work in, for although there is plenty of work there are no problems amongst the Chinese staff, and I thought some of the young 'uns might be put in to see what they could do, while I might be sent to Kirin or West Moukden. Indeed at one point I was approached about how I'd feel about taking over W.M. and I was afraid it was all settled, but it was decided to let the new folk finish their exams and to ask Mrs MacNaughtan to continue in W.M. until the end of the year.

I'm afraid they have me up their sleeve for W.M. *[West Moukden]* and I dislike the thought of it. Moukden is a filthy place, I hate living in a town – but Moukden strikes me as being as bad as anything you could get in the manufacturing area in England. I feel filthy all the time I'm in at meetings and you'd honestly need to change your clothes every day. The only thing I would hope that if I was sent there that I should be able for the work in the town to go on under Chinese workers and that I might be able to get out a good deal into the district. But all that is in the future and perhaps after all I'll get staying in a country station.

Dr Fulton, just past his 83rd birthday, has withdrawn his resignation at our request and is taking another appointment at Peichen (or Kwangning). He really is a marvellous old man and wonderfully healthy, his hearing is the only thing that worries him, and younger in spirit than several of the men 20 years younger than himself, who are thinking of retiring soon.

I'm enclosing ... a Christmas card which one of the school girls did for me, copied off one someone must have sent to the school last year. I thought it was quite a good effort for a child.

224

*The Christmas card,
which Yü Fang sent to
Marion in 1938.*

*The greeting reads,
'Congratulations on the
Feast of His Holy
Birthday, respectfully
sent to Yang Chiaoshih.
Her student, Yü Fang,
drew this with her own
hand as a sign of
happiness.'*

**Fakumen
30th December 1938**

To Mother and Dad

Your letter of the 13th came today – and the twins' Christmas letters, thanks to them both. They seem to be well looked after by relatives and friends in Belfast! They don't have many lonely weekends I think.

I am glad the boys were at home for the McWhirters' visit – I like folk to meet my family! *[the Rev and Mrs McWhirter were in Ireland on furlough from Manchuria]* and I know the boys would be interested in both of them – there is plenty of fun and life in them both! They add considerably to the gaiety of any group they are in.

I have my accounts all done and passed by our local Board, whoopee! It is such a relief to have that off – now I've got to prepare a report on the Station's work to be delivered in Irish Council and don't like that any better – I don't like writing for an audience. The immediate future has worse in store though. I have to lead tomorrow's (Sat.) prayer meeting with pastor, elders, evangelists – and O'Neills! at it, and what is more, probably some of the representatives of the district stations who are coming in for the District Board meeting next week. I prepared it roughly and I thought I'd soothe the shattered nerves by writing to you before I go to bed.

Then next week we have 2 days District Board meeting and 6 days meetings for deacons – Bible Study and telling 'em what a good deacon should do and be. After which I hie me off to Moukden on the 9th Jan for a committee meeting, and on the 10th our Conference meetings properly start.

Did I or did I not tell you that Flora and I are planning to go off to Peking for a week and work off steam after the meetings? I have no money to spend, but I'll scrape up enough for board and travel and watch Flora buy things. She has had a pretty heavy year and we both decided a month or two ago that if we did not have a chance to relax for a while, we'd burst into tears. I'm not feeling so bad now. I took Monday off and read a detective story and ate a box of chocolates – a Christmas present and just said, "Let the accounts go hang," with a careless wave of the hand. It had a wonderfully refreshing effect.

The last few days seem to have been spent in an atmosphere impregnated with the Question of Money (which seems a mixed metaphor). I've been doing accounts as I may have mentioned before, been refusing small girls and their more importunate parents the honour of paying for their schooling, been hearing hard-luck cases, no money, no work – won't the chiaoshih [i.e. Marion] think of a plan for us? The obvious one being to put my hand in my pocket. [I have] been refusing to pay for the 'flitting' [using a 'flit-gun' to spray with insecticide] of Mary's Chinese teacher's home and also refusing his afterthought that I give him 2 months' pay in advance. His pa can lend him the money quite easily, only they think I have dollars to fling round me for the asking, and just today have been refusing to buy the millet stalks for our Boy. When he came, I gave him $2 extra a month on the condition that I was responsible neither for his firing or his rent, so I was fair boiling when the cook came as the go-between and pressed it rather on me. I told him to git and keep going, I wanted to deal with the Boy-o, and begorra I did.

But it isn't easy to go on refusing, it is rather wearing in fact. If anyone asked me tomorrow, I think I' nearly have to give in I feel so brutal after all these refusals!

Well it is 10.30 and I have to be up betimes, besides the fire is going out and I don't want to go to the kitchen for more coal. The temperature doesn't rise much above 20 degrees *[Fahrenheit]* these days, even at midday. How's that? They boys would enjoy skating.

Marion still added a P.S.

I heard of a novel punishment the other day – a laddie in a village near here who is a 'small thief' pinches people's clothes off the lines and their vegetable out of the yard and so on, was caught with another man stealing someone's firing. Normally I think the police would just beat them up, but I suppose they had sinned once too often, and they decided to punish them. The order was that the man should kill a pig and provide grain and vegetables for a feast. Then the town crier went out beating a gong and announced that each family in the village was to send one member of the family to the house for a meal! How's that for an original punishment?

CHAPTER 6
1939

Fakumen
5th January 1939

To Dad and Mother

Boys o! I'll be home in '40.

I don't know where the temperature is this morning – but it is cold! I've been at the bus station for more than an hour seeing some people off, and although I was wearing layer upon layer of clothes, I felt like a block of ice before I got back. I've had some tea and am trying to thaw out in front of a roaring fire.

The School has holidays now. Miss Wang and Miss Chang were leaving this morning and with them were going –

1) two would-be nurses, whom I am sending to Flora

2) a small girl with a TB sore, who is going to Tiehling for an X-ray. She 'graduated' from our school last year and went to Dor's *[Dorothy Crawford's]* Middle School in Hsinmin ... She got 2nd place in exams in a class of 40 (our other girls got 3rd, 4th and 6th places in Hsinmin, so up Faku!!) and came back for hols with this bad sore. The rib may or may not be affected, but I want the kid to get every chance of getting better quickly, so with her people's permission I'm sending her to hospital. Her father earns about 24/- a month, enough to feed the family, but nothing left for extras, so I'll be paying for her. I now have two students in hospital, two going to Hsinmin next year for whom I am to pay half of the fees, one in the Bible School and one at our Primary School. My family is growing, isn't it?!

3) To go back to the bus station! There was also another Hsinmin student of ours who is a protégée of Mamie's – her mother is a lady of not too good repute and I was very worried to think of her going home for hols. However, an aunt, a Christian, has invited her there and I was seeing that she got off safely.

6th

We have had splendid Deacons' Meetings this week. Chuang is very good on the constitution of our Church Synod, District Board, and various rules connected with Baptism and Marriage and the meaning of Communion. But the hour I like the best is Professor Ma of the Moukden Theological College on 'The Church'. He is so practical and simple and yet so spiritual – he has a quiet 'good' face and a delightful sudden smile. I felt uplifted today that 50 or 60 years of Christian work in Manchuria could produce a man like that. He isn't 40 I should think and his family were not Christians when he was a boy, but they must have been religious people. Our best and most spiritually minded Christians are from warm Buddhist families.

K'un Kuang Girls' School
Moukden
17th January 1939

To Mother and Dad

Marion is attending the Annual Conference of the missionaries, in Moukden.

My appointment to Faku has been passed for this year, so you can rejoice with me! I was afraid Kirin or West Moukden would push again, and as Mary could take over Faku accounts and so on now, I couldn't have refused. I have a very good evangelistic staff in Faku this year who could carry on with Mrs O'Neill to advise them. We have 2 junior Theological graduates as well as Miss Wang *[Ssu Wen]*, and both are very fine workers indeed. These 2 are doing their 2 years practice and I had not thought I would be able to keep both.

We've had a topping good time together here – 13 girls in one dorm, and rowdy isn't the word for it. Lilias Dodds, Dor Crawford, Flora, Mamie, Margaret McCombe, Mary, Hessie, Joey, 5 Scotch girls and myself. At night and in the morning there is a continuous row, practical jokes and reprisals all the time. The 3 new girls are the Juniors and are badly sat upon for their good. Flora and I concocted quite a good set of rules for Junior Missys, which we wrote on the blackboard over their beds. This was in return for them having sewn up the legs of our pyjamas – and sewn neatly and firmly they were. It took me ages to get mine undone!

Two nights ago a Scotch doctor nearly laid us out. She is a red headed lassie with a pep that seems to go with that colour of hair. She was undressing in an absent minded way one night and reached her vest and knickers before she remembered that she had still on her big fur lined boots. I looked up and saw the picture and demanded a Cossack dance. Her vest was green, her knickers red, and to complete the picture she put on a lacey hat that had been brought over for dress ups, and then proceeded to give us the most gorgeous dance. She has been near Harbin all her life out here and has seen Russian dancing often – she could make a great burlesque of it and had us all in fits.

The rest of the household all demanded to share in the joke next morning, but we thought Annie's costume hardly up to the standard required for public performances. Another night, the men all came and serenaded. There are 6 or 7, some grass-widowers and some with their wives here. They made a most melodious noise and we gave them coppers in the end, which they scrummed for on the floor. Sech goings on! If the Home Committee could get a glimpse of us – (without being able to join in with us in spirit!) they'd want to recall us all.

In the next few paragraphs Marion described the entertainment the missionaries organised for each other at their 'party night'. This included Colin Corkey and James Stobie, a Scottish missionary, appearing as Greek maidens.

In case you think this meeting is all play and no work, let me assure you it isn't. It is really one of the most difficult conferences there has ever been and every day seems to bring more and more trouble. If we hadn't this way of letting off steam, we'd get all up in the air and nerves would begin to rub raw. Every now and then I realise how good it is to be in a mission which can frivol.

We had a day of retreat before the Conference opened, a day of prayer and praise led by Austin *[Fulton]*. Each year Austin takes more and more a leading part in Conference and Council matters, and he does everything so quietly and thoroughly that there is no sense of him bossing things. He must have spent much time in prayer and preparation for this day, and it was a wonderful strength to us all in the busy days we have had since.

These are the most critical days there have ever been in Mission history, except the Boxer days. We may have to close our education down and it is going to be a terrible blow to the whole Church. Where are our pastors, evangelists, doctors and nurses coming from? and what are our Christian children going to do, thrown into the evil that there is in Government Schools?

You know something of the history behind this trouble, after the McWhirters' visit I expect, but things seem to have reached a crisis now. All we can hold onto is that if it is God's will that we close down, that he will open another door. This next year may bring terrific changes in our Mission policy. The Govt is taking more and more charge of things and a new Religious Law they have passed is giving everyone much cause for thought ...

After the close of the Missionaries' Conference, Marion went with Flora to spend a week's holiday in Peking, where they stayed at the Language School.

Language School
Peking
23rd January 1939

To Mother and Dad

I'm having the grandest holiday here – wish you were here to see Peking along with me, I feel like a resident now! We came down on Friday 20th night, arriving here Saturday morning – Lilias Dodds and an English friend of hers, who is out on a world trip, were with us, so we had a cheery journey – 2 meals on the train and sleeping berths for the night. We travelled 3rd, and the berths, 3 tiers of them, were just provided with a sawdust pillow. You don't need bedclothes – the train is very hot. A half curtain just going down to cover your face, but nothing more.

The Japs are most indelicate in the matter of dressing and undressing in company and I suddenly realised that in the berth opposite a gentleman was divesting himself of his trousers. Flora was in the berth below him and I saw her eyes widen and her mouth open when a pair of bare legs came dangling over the edge of the berth. It doesn't worry them tho' – so why should it worry us?

Since Marion's last visit the city had been occupied by the Japanese:

Peking is still Peking, but there are a good many changes in the inhabitants. One would say that there could be no overpopulation programme in Japan at the moment. I've heard it said that there are 50,000 Japanese in Peking at the moment – counting a large garrison of course – and it looks like it, one positively trips over them. The place is lousy with 'em.

The city is lovely – I'm sure there is no place quite like it in the world. Colour, history, romance – and the ageless Chinese, whose philosophy I admire more and more. I often feel how young we are, and the Japanese still younger, when we come up against the Chinese as a nation.

A corner of the Language School Hostel, where Marion stayed when she was visiting Peking.

Fakumen
4th February 1939

To Dad and Mother

Our week in Peking finished all too soon on Saturday 28th, but we felt it had been a great week and we packed plenty into it! 4 pictures, one Chinese theatre, one Chinese feast, 2 invitations to supper, a 'Manchurian' supper in College, plus games and chat after it, 2 days sightseeing – one at the Temple of Heaven and the other at the Summer Palace and Yeuching, <u>and</u> shopping galore both for ourselves, our houses and other friends up here.

But the holiday didn't finish on Saturday, by any means, we had an unexpected extension granted by a benevolent government. We were told by someone that we had to get police and military passes to get out of Peking on our way back and were given two addresses in Chinese. One had 'Police' on it and we decided the other was the Military one – without deciphering it! The office in College said they got the Military Pass for their guests, so we started off on Friday and got our Police Pass.

Armed with both these, our British passport and our Manchurian Residence Certificate, we thought we were ready to go anywhere, but we had not reckoned with a government which revels and rollicks in red tape. Most countries, if you are resident in them do not require a transit visa to allow you to cross their borders on your way home – but Manchuria does, and we hadn't one. The un-deciphered address was the one we <u>should</u> have gone to! At Shanhaikwan *[on the border between China and Manchukuo]* on a cold dark morning, we knew it, and out we were on a station platform to wait for a train back to Peking. We were lucky really, it wasn't nice going back, but it was really our own fault and we could blame no one.

It was the might-have-beens that is a worse picture. The passport man came round first and finding we had no visas, took our passports off with him – to prevent us going on in the train! Then we had to wait for the customs man to come and examine our many cases and parcels. He came to us just before the train was due to start and went through everything – Flora had cups and bowls for a friend and each had to be unwrapped, every packet opened, and our cases looking like hay. Just then the whistle tooted and if we hadn't had Lilias Dodds on the train I don't know what would have happened to us. Our luggage all to be packed and our passports were on the platform. Lilias, the angel *[who had obviously obtained the correct visa]*, undertook the awful job of repacking and delivering our luggage in Moukden, and we, grabbing our purses and coats, leaped off the train as it was moving. The passport man was very decent and took us to his office for 2½ hours before train time ...

We travelled all Sunday until 4 o'clock back to Peking, and were the college people surprised to see us! It was just tea time and we walked in arm and arm to the dining room with a nonchalant air, which we couldn't keep up when the whole crowd rose to their feet with their jaws dropping! We had no clothes back and felt filthy, but we had a bath, borrowed clean blouses and got round to the Legation Chapel in time for Evensong at 6. We felt we needed something to soothe our savage breasts.

On Monday, we got the visas, bought a few more things, saw a picture! And got the evening train back, and funnily enough the very same berths. This time we sailed through confidently and got to the MacNaughtans' without any further mishap.

Fakumen
10th February 1939

To Mother and Dad

Thanks to Helen for a note that was in the last letter. Her writing and Clara's have changed such a lot in 3 years, and since Clara went to Vic *[toria College]* there has been a big improvement. I notice it especially since Christmas somehow.

Mamie was in the night I got your last letter and she enjoyed Dad's description of the Orange Concert. It sounded the sort of programme we would put on at Conference for a skit on a County soiree.

We are having quite an exciting time for Faku. Dor *[Crawford]* is here with us, Mamie is in O'Neills' and a Scotch girl, Isabel Mackenzie, is coming on Tuesday. These two weeks before Chinese New Year (18th Feb this year) are very slack. Schools not open yet and no one wants to see the evangelist, the women are all busy preparing new food and clothes. It is busier than Christmas at home I think!

Weddings come off round the New Year too, holidays are on and the men are home from school or business. Quite often they get married and then the husband goes off in a week or two, leaving the wife at home with the mother-in-law and family, and only comes home off and on during the year. It's a peculiar system. Younger China is breaking away from it, in educated circles at least.

Fakumen
15th February 1939

To Mother and Dad

I'm starting this letter a bit early this week as I may not have time to write on Friday or Sat. Chinese New Year is on then and visits or invitations to eat are the rule of the day. At present too we have a guest, Isabel Mackenzie, a Scottish second-generation missionary, very nice lass, came out the same time as Mary. I sent her out with Mary for a walk this morning on the plea that I had business with Miss Wang Ssu Wen, but she *[Ssu Wen]* has gone visiting and I hope she comes back soon and 'saves my face'!

234

We have to settle details about the evangelistic week next week and about our country trip in the spring. Also, she has to write letters for me. This letter writing is a business in China. A foreigner who is very friendly with the Chinese can write her a letter and know she will understand the writing and mistakes. But letters to Churches, business letters, or letters to people you don't know, have to be written for you, because the howlers the best of the missionaries would make are awful. One or two can manage it – Isabel's mother, Mrs Mackenzie (M.B.), can write beautiful Chinese. Dr Miskelly, possibly Dr Fulton. Dr O'Neill certainly <u>can't</u>, Mamie can't and she is one of the best linguists we have. It is a strange thing that Chinese writing and language seem to belong to two different worlds! I'm taking it up again – I hate the look of a page when I finish writing to Huei Chün or Ssu Wen that I feel I have to do something about it! I've been doing an hour a day with Huei Chün, who writes well, and now I'm getting a slate and copy book like the ones they start small Chinese children with! and I'm to do my copy every day – even if it's only for 10 minutes!

We are having lovely weather just now. The temperature doesn't go above 32 degrees at midday yet – but there is great heat in the sun and when you get a quiet hollow in the woods down out of the wind the sun is lovely and warm. We plan to have a picnic tomorrow and spend most of the day out walking, then we are having the O'Neills in for supper and games.

The picnic with, from left to right, Ssu Wen, Huei Chün, Marion and Isabel Mackenzie. Marion wrote on the back of the print, 'We didn't sit long!'

**Fakumen
24th February 1939**

To Dad and Mother

Marion was accompanying seven girls from the School at Faku who had passed the exam for the Girls' Middle School at Hsinmin, which provided higher academic courses than the school at Faku. The party had been held up at Tiehling, awaiting the girls' luggage which arrived five hours after the bus from Faku had. As they had missed their train connection, Marion arranged for the girls to stay in a ward in the Tiehling Mission Hospital, which was empty as all the patients had gone home for the Chinese New Year.

When Marion was in Tiehling: ... I was held up by a Japanese policeman and requested to come to the Police Headquarters. Fortunately, I had remembered to put my Residence Cert. and some cards in my purse – a card goes a long way in this country towards proving one is a respectable citizen, so I went quite happily with him. Much more happily than my rickshaw man, who took one frightened skelly *[glance]* at me, wondering what he had picked up and whether he'd get his fare, I expect.

When we went into the office, a Japanese policeman who could only speak very broken Chinese, asked me if I "understandy Chinese", so I assured him "understandy" and he got a Chinese lad over to interpret, and lo and behold on my saying that I was from Faku he beamed on me and said, "I'm a graduate of the Christian Boys' School there." Thereat ensued a great chat about where he lived and all the Faku folk whom he knew, and the Police Officer, thawing, provided an approving chorus of "(Chinese – No) Manchukuoan language too good, too good."

He asked to see my Residency Cert. and looking at the photo (quite a good one) about it remarked (in Chinese), "Ah! Pretty!" Then he called another man over, and then looking at me (who by this time looked as if I had been pulled through a whin bush backwards, wot with not having washed or done my hair all day, and a splitting headache, having had no food) with beautiful candour and complete disregard of Oriental courtesy, "Much prettier than you are."

My Chinese friend gulped heavily and swinging round buried his head in a cupboard where I could see his shoulders heave – I remarked demurely, "Probably the photo was just well taken, it was done in Moukden." To which he said, "Ah Chinese language too good," and handed me back the certificate, after which he let me leave without a stain on my character, but with a bad fit of the giggles.

The next morning, I got the girls to Moukden and having 3 hours to wait for the Hsinking train, got droskeys and drove them round a bit.

236

Their eyes nearly popped when they saw shops of 5 or 6 storeys and all the rush of motors, rickshaws and people! I got the girls off on a 2 o'clock train, did some shopping and went back to Tiehling that night, getting back to Faku on the 3rd day after a journey which was 36 hours longer than it should have been.

School has started and the pupils are pouring in, 20 more than last year. So the headmistress is very pleased. Evangelistic meetings are on in 3 places in town. I only managed to get to one yesterday, but they are being very well attended and 10 or 12 women have put their names down as enquirers ...

Marion's father subsequently wrote to ask what the role of the missionaries was in running the Girls' Schools in China. Marion replied in her letter of 10th May that neither she in Faku nor Dorothy Faulkner in Hsinmin were the Heads as: ... the authorities are not keen on us foreigners pushing in our noses there and most of our schools have Chinese heads. Dor is, as I am too, called the school's 'hsiao chien', or director, actually the position above the Head, but we are not supposed to do much of the negotiating between the school and authorities – there the Head is the school's rep.

Flying kites in Faku Schools. (Above) Dr O'Neill in the Boys' School. (Right above) Marion wrote, 'Up she goes like a fairy' on this photograph of playtime in the Girls' School in March 1939. (Right) Ssu Wen and children from the Women Missionaries' compound.

Fakumen
13th March 1939

To Dad

I arranged last night with Dr O'Neill that he is to take me for part of my 3rd year *[Chinese language]* exam work on this coming Friday 17th – I should have done it long ago, but with being out with my tour in the autumn I didn't get down to it, and now that I realise I'm into my 4th year *[in China]* I feel I <u>must</u> get it done!

The 3rd exam you can take any time. It is really only set to give some reading to do outside the preparation which you must do for classes and addresses. It is not a very long course, but you spend so much time in preparation for every day's work that there really *[is not]* much time for *[the]* extra reading.

1) 56 chapters of ordinary conversational Chinese

2) Selections from Confucius and Mencius

3) Modern journalistic Chinese – awfully hard!

4) Bible: Isaiah, Jeremiah and Ezekiel – 20 chapters

　　Job, Proverbs – 10 chapters

　　1 Corinthians

5) 1,000 characters for writing, of which we are already supposed to know 800 having done 400 each year in the first 2 years – but I <u>don't,</u> having not touched them since then. Also, got to learn 214 radicals and 200 odd phonetics which are used in building up the Chinese characters most used.

That is about all I think. It is really only the newspaper Chinese that worries me – the rest I know I can do if I work hard enough.

I have a date with Mensius this morning, wish he'd been a bit more chatty and less compressed in his conversations with his disciples. This ignorant barbarian from the West finds great difficulty in following his more profound thoughts.

Chungchia T'un
North of Ssupingkai
South west of Hsinking
4th April 1939

To Dad and Mother

The above address is just to give you an idea of where I am – roughly: if you haven't a fairly new atlas, Ssupingkai wouldn't be on the map. It is a new town made out of little villages through which the railway passed. 20 years ago there wasn't anything there, now it is a big modern city with wide streets, parks and a zoo of a sort!

I stayed there for 2 days with the Johnstons, Ted and Kitty, who were at Language School with me – Canadians. They are a most interesting pair, and Kitty, who taught in a Nursery School, has a great way with her children. They are brought up on all the new methods and seem to thrive on it. Ann, who will be 3 at the end of this month, tidies up her bedroom each morning, hanging up her dressing gown, nightie and any other clothes left lying around, on a small clothes stand specially made for her, and puts her shoes into a shoe box! It is all a game to her and she enjoys it thoroughly, then she calls the amah to make her bed. She is a very self-reliant and intelligent wee scrap for her age. Peter is not quite a year old and is at the stage when he crawls all over the place.

We have a pleasant little room here, Miss Wang and I have it to ourselves, the local woman evangelist has a smaller room on the other side of the church. The other people in the compound, 4 or 5 houses, are all either Christians or enquirers, so it is a comfortable sort of compound to live in.

Wednesday

The *[Bible]* school is going well. It is very easy to run because quite a number of the pupils are of 2 to 4 years standing and they understand the rules of the school and the way to work. They take the new ones under their wings and help to explain things to them. We have 38 or 40 *[girls and women aged between 12 and 67]* now, and as this is the 3rd day, we don't receive any more after this.

Today we had the special police, one Jap and one Manchurian, both very courteous. It happened to be repetition time and they came into my class of 3 or 4 illiterate old wifies. They 'gave me face' because they knew all we had done to date and one old lady took it on herself to explain, "God is a spirit and we must worship him in spirit and in truth' – to the Japanese!

At Chungchia T'un
10th April 1939
Easter Monday

To Mother and Dad

Today is real spring weather and I stepped out of my winter clouts with much gusto. I put away my padded gown and got out a thin one, but when we go another 200 miles north at the end of the week it might have to come out again.

We have had a lot of dusty days and if I thought I knew what dust was like in Faku I was mistaken! Here the roads are all beaten earth and after 6 months without rain there is 6 inches to a foot deep of dust on all the roads. It is really like walking on soft sand in some places. Your feet are <u>filthy</u> every day. You can imagine the storm one puff of wind raises, and when a howling gale blows it is nearly impossible to go out. Dust comes in through every crack in the window frame and you can't see a foot from the door outside. Fortunately, we have only had one really bad day, but we've had dust 4 days out of the 6 the school has been running. The pupils don't seem to mind it and one of our older women, over 60, with small feet walks over a mile here every day without fail.

The water is our other trial! Full of soda and hard as can be. A drink of it boiled is just like the aftermath in your mouth of globan salts. I have prepared juice of yu tzu – a fruit, a cross between a grapefruit and an orange, and we add a little to the boiled water – it helps to kill the taste. Washing clothes is quite a feat. I've just finished washing a few things and by dint of using a lot of washing soda and soap got up a lather.

The people here are mostly colonists from China who came up in search of land, they live a rougher life than the people who have been longer settled in the country. Mongols and Koreans are here too, the latter to grow rice near the river. They follow water and settle there. When you go to the streets to buy something, you'll hear all sorts of accents, some high and singing, some the broad Shantung with the same good humour behind it that comes from Lancashire and their parts.

12th   There is a very small girl disporting herself outside my window.

She has got two plaits done up with 4 or 5 different coloured wools, they look very gay and neat and stick out at about an angle of 45 degrees from her head. She is called 'Hsiao T'so', or 'Small Mistake' because her parents have a girl or two already and don't want any more. This is a notice to the gods that they are to make no mistake about sending them a son next time.

Marion and Miss Wang then travelled north west by train to a place close to the border with Inner Mongolia to take another Bible School for women.

Tao Nan
15ᵗʰ April 1939

To Dad and Mother

We arrived here yesterday and really it is the funniest spot I've hit yet! Every other place prepares for us and has made obvious preparations – even if they aren't all perfect. But they are casual here to the last degree, yet very kindly in an offhand sort of way. Usually there is a meal on the way when we get to a station. Yesterday, we arrived having had nothing to eat from 8 o'clock till 7 except some oranges and a very Chinesey bun or two. We were put into a cold room, some water produced in about half an hour for washing, and then we discovered that the family was all feeding in their own room before they came to see about us!

We saw the dog being fed and I gave Miss Wang a fit of the giggles by saying morosely, "They feed the dogs before the chiaoshihs here," which was in the nature of a curse in this language. Anyway, about 7.30 the pastor and his wife arrived with the materials to make a meal, and put them in our kitchen. The lady stood and chatted to us for a while before she started to make the meal, and when we <u>politely</u> offered to do it and let her get back to her own duties, she protested and then just vaguely wandered off.

We got the meal between fits of the giggles and about 9 o'clock went round to visit. We found several children asleep on the k'ang, the youngest stark naked, being fed. Several men visitors were in, and a fug in the room that would have knocked you down.

241

Yet you can't help liking them all! They just like going their own way – and really [it] suits us best too. They have no idea of time here either, and I foresee we will have fun getting the classes started in any sort of time in the morning. We had our breakfasts eaten and the room tidied before there was any movement in the other houses in the compound, but they were still drinking tea and cracking away at 11 last night – which is very late for country places.

Coming yesterday from Chungchia T'un to here, we passed through the most sparsely populated country I've seen yet. We were 5½ hours in the train and only stopped at 5 or 6 stations, all of them tiny villages. The country was bare, hardly a tree to be seen, just sandy country with brown coarse desert grass on it. Here and there were small hills, but mostly you could see for miles and miles into the distance into a blue mist which looked just like the sea.

Every now and then you saw the gay feathers of a cock pheasant in the grass near the line. Miss Wang saw several hen pheasants, she was looking out for them. They are not so easy to spot, and I was working at my Mark for the class here. There are deer and what sound like jackals (Miss Wang said they were 'neither wolves nor wild dogs'), but we didn't spot any.

The 3rd class going north these days is simply <u>packed</u>, every day the same. You'd wonder where the people come from. They are the very poorest and dirtiest Chinese I've seen outside the beggar class. They are all moving north in the spring now to open up new land. They have friends or relatives there who have found them work or places – or sometimes the father goes first and sends for the family when he has got work to do. Yesterday it was old folk, women and children mostly, who were travelling. Small girls of 10 to 15 carrying the baby, while the mother staggered under a big bundle of their bedding and belongings. One woman I saw carrying a baby that didn't look more than 2 months old, a huge bundle on her back, a child or two clinging to her gown and an old man who was just dottering along. Poor souls, they don't know much of comfort. They just packed into the carriages until there was no room to stand and we were thankful we had taken warning from the view of the station and travelled 2nd. It wasn't much either – about 7/6 [7 shillings and sixpence] for 200 miles and very comfortable carriages.

Tao Nan
23rd April 1939

To Dad and Mother

Did I tell you that we were having special meetings here in the middle of our school in spite of all our rearranging of dates? Kao ('Gow' is the pronunciation) is a special secretary appointed for travelling round the churches leading Bible classes, Retreats and Special Meetings, all directed towards the education of the Christians both in Scripture and in Church matters. This time he is taking 3 days, 2 meetings per day, in our 3 biggest outstations in the Faku district. He has been doing the 5th 6th and 7th chapters of Matthew here and is a splendid speaker and teacher.

He gets quite a lot out of his audience. He was at New College, Edinburgh, for 2 years and speaks excellent English – he and I quite often talk in it and it is quite a relief to get a chance of using one's own tongue now!

He goes tonight, we have two days more school, Wed is exam day, Thurs graduation and we hope to get the right train to Tiehling which will get us back to Faku before our Friend (D.V.). He is one of the folks who has 'done time' *[being imprisoned by the Japanese]* and had enough time of it. All of our biggest men have been through the mill and they have all the more witness to make for it.

The meetings have been well attended – the Canadian Mission and a Japanese Mission to the Chinese join in with us for all the special meetings, and the church, which is as long as ours in Clones, but not so wide, has been packed to the door.

Marion and Ssu Wen in T'ao Nan, with Miss Shi and Miss Ning, junior theological graduates, behind. Marion wrote that 'Miss Ning especially is a very fine girl.' The two graduates would have come to the special meeting led by Pastor Kao.

One very interesting man who has come, is a Chinese missionary to the Mongols, who lives in Tu'chuan, our furthest away station, – Li Ta Ku To – he took a Mongol name. He looks a bit like some of the French priests here, soft pointed black beard and a very high forehead, tall and well built, with bigger feet than most Chinese men, on which he wears foreign brown boots with huge thick soles. He walks like a foreigner too, with long springing strides – probably used to walking a lot on his mission work. His salary is raised by private subs and his own friends.

The first day I saw him, he and I studied each other for quite a while – each wondering what the other was! I thought he might be Korean and he probably thought I was the daughter of a Russian-Chinese union! It is amusing to hear people on the street say in puzzled tones – "she is like us – no she's not, look at her eyes, what is she?" I'll have to wear dark glasses then they won't know. The train policeman passed me umpteen times coming north and never spotted me until once I looked up and our eyes met. I saw him start with surprise and then he asked for my passport – very polite this time – I expected he would be mad at not spotting me, because he is responsible for checking up on all foreigners, and the policeman at the barrier saw me on the way out and would report.

T'ao Nan
26th April 1939

To Dad and Mother

This is exam morning. I've just finished my class and they all did quite well. Miss Wang is busy taking the hygiene exam in the same room – and I can't get on with my writing for listening to her. One of the old wifies has listened with half an ear and she has got a smattering of the material. She was telling Miss Wang what daily habits you should have – wash well, brush hair, brush teeth and so on, then she ended triumphantly, "sit on the k'ang and spit spittle." Miss Wang had told them that they <u>shouldn't</u> sit toasting on the k'ang spitting round them when they had finished their work, that they should go out and get some fresh air – and that is what she *[the old wifie]* had remembered!

Faku
1st May

We had a good finish up to our school in T'ao Nan and got away on Thursday after the 'graduation' ceremony. Did I tell you about the Chinese missionary to the Mongols – Li Ta Ku To? He came to the graduation ceremony and made a speech, after which he sang 'Jesus Loves Me' in Mongolian. That night, just before we left for the train, a big parcel of fruit came round for us with his card inscribed in Chinese, 'The Lord bestows this little parcel of fruit upon His handmaidens through his servant Li Ta Ku To.'

We had fun trying to catch that train too. It left at 10.45 at night and was ½ hour by droskeys from the church. At 10 o'clock there was no sign of the messenger we had sent for the carriage, and at last he came tearing back to say that he couldn't get one. The night before, an unfortunate droskey driver had been strangled for the sake of what money he had on him and his horse, on a lonely part of the road to the station, so no driver could be got out after dark for love or money. The station is outside the city walls and there is a lonely bad piece of road to it, I don't know why they don't fix the surface up. There was a bus to the station, but it does not usually take luggage – however, the elder, deacons and pastor shouldered our bundles and ran to the bus station, where we found very few people and managed to get the luggage on.

We got to the station with little time to spare and I was held up by a policeman who wrote all particulars of my murky past down slowly and laboriously. We wanted 3rd sleepers, but when we got on they had all been taken, and then when we reached the ordinary 3rds, we found everyone had got stretched on the seats and we were left with a narrow little seat beside the train guard. Each compartment has a soldier on guard at night to prevent robberies, presumably. He was a decent laddie and wanted to turn 2 farmers out of their seats so we could lie down, and was surprised when we wouldn't let him! During the night he let one of us sit by him, while the other took turn about to lie down. We didn't get much sleep though, I was cold and was wearing my coat and was easily spotted, and was favoured with the attention of seven men – Special Police, ordinary police and military – all separately, between 11 0'clock and 4 in the morning. They all had to copy out my past history from my residency certificate, and all had to get a card – my stock was getting low by the time I got home.

The train was delayed and we got in *[to Tiehling]* just in time to get round for the 9.30 bus *[to Faku]*. I saw the Special Policeman at the gate of the station and me heart sank because 5 minutes would make the difference about the bus and might mean a 3 hours wait. However I kept my head down, got to the other side of the crowd, and he never spotted me. I hope he didn't get a wigging for not reporting me when all my 7 friends' reports would go in.

Fakumen
12ᵗʰ May 1939

To Mother and Dad

I have a class in the Kindergarten now, Arithmetic with about 6 or 8 wee 6 year olds – we do it mostly with marbles and slates. The smallest in the class is a bright wee girl of 4, and she is easily the quickest and best, she wrote from 1-5 for me yesterday as quickly as I could nearly, but funny wee squiggly writing – which she laughed at herself! They use our figures for all arithmetic in schools now, and shops and business places generally use them too, they are much simpler than their own ...

I've had a great time these past two days putting winter things away and cleaning out a few old things for poor Russians. There is a centre in Moukden for helping out White Russians, to which we send clothes that are still wearable. The clothes that are too torn or worn for much use, Chinese can use for making cotton shoes, they stick layers together with paste and make very neat, warm shoes. It is good to get things aired and put away – a pleasant feeling of spring in the air.

Have you heard of a book by Edgar Snow, *Red Star over China* – it is a book about Communism in China and is an epic. I've been thrilled by it these last few days. It is one of the few things that has pulled the Chinese together and made them fight for an ideal and not only fight for it, but live it out. It is worth reading if you can get hold of it.

'Red Star Over China' *by the American journalist, Edgar Snow, was the first full account of the Chinese Communist Party. Snow had journeyed to meet Mao Zedong in the area which the Red Army controlled and had written a very favourable account of this, contrasting it with the parts of the country still controlled by the Kuomintang government under Chang Kai Shek. It is therefore not surprising that Marion appears to be endorsing the rule of Communists.*

Fakumen
27th May 1939

To Mother and Dad

It is funny to see you referring to our T'ao Nan doings in your last letter, I have nearly forgotten that I was in the country! This month has been full enough for three. We have the school medical inspection on at present and there is more filling of forms for government here than ever our red-tape experts thought of at home. The headmistress is lying up with a poisoned toe and I have had to see a good deal in the school, not teaching, other small things which take time. The teachers are all good workers, but they need someone behind them, they have not much initiative.

I measured the chest expansion of 60 odd wriggling little girls and boys, all under 10, the other day, and took the height of more than 100 for the medical inspection. The big children were easy to do, but those 60 were the funniest little articles. One small boy nearly lost his trousers in the fray, the belt had come undone and he hadn't noticed it! Whoops of glee from the other small ruffians.

Last night I was at the saddest baptism service I have ever seen. A girl of 16 from our school, a very gentle little thing who is dying of rapid consumption. She wanted to get baptised last year, but we thought that as she was to be at the school for another year she could wait a little longer till she had time to read and think some more. She has been in hospital these last few weeks, she was at school until quite a short time ago. She had a very bad turn last night and did not seem to be likely to be long alive. Her family are Christian, her sister is our fine little evangelist, Miss Man, and they asked if the pastor would baptise her. She was able to sit up, and looked so happy, her breathless wee voice trying to sing nearly did for me, but I was standing opposite her and she looked up at me with such a happy smile every now and then, that I did not dare to cry. She is still alive, but the doctor does not hold out much hope for another week. It would be a mercy for the family, they are heartbroken watching her waste away.

I have just finished my S.S. *[Sunday School]* training class, and have to go to the Kindergarten in a minute or two, for a class on character recognition. Me! teacher of characters. I love the class. Yesterday, I was taking them for sums and it was the first time I had been over for three days. I was busy one day and gave it to a small assistant, it rained another and there was no school. When I went in, a small boy looked up at me earnestly and said, "Yang Chiao shih, why have you been away so long? Don't stay away so long again." I felt quite touched!

I forgot to tell you F.W.S.'s last feat. He has been in the district and the day he was due back it rained so heavily that there was no bus. The rain was over, so when he saw the bus could not go he started walking. He did 90 li – i.e. 30 miles – in 9½ hours, which included ½ hour stop to eat a couple of apples. He is 68 or 9 and except that he was a trifle stiff about the knees, he was all right. He had one day's rest and started out to the west Churches! Some going, wasn't it – a steady over 3 miles per hour.

Fakumen
2nd June 1939

To Dad and Mother

Marion had been told in a letter from her parents that the father of Mrs McWhirter, a missionary colleague, had died in Ireland.

... Mrs Mac told me last year that he said he hoped he could reach his 100th birthday, it is a tremendous age isn't it? Few of the Chinese reach it. Most of them consider 80 just tremendous. The old Bible woman, retired, is 82 and everyone talks about her with baited breath. I must get a snap of her sometime soon, for she is not retired really! She goes every day to the hospital and gives out tracts and hymn sheets, which she first explains to the people, also there are a few houses on the street nearby that she still goes to for preaching. She is a great old soul, and full of life and a wee joke about her still.

Did I tell you how things are going up here? Everything, food, clothes, imported articles are all over double the price. We usually give

248

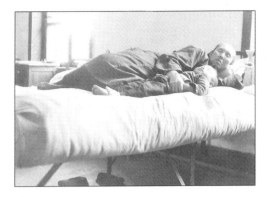

Marion wrote on the back of this photograph that it showed an old woman and her grandson in hospital, although it is not clear whether this was in Faku.

Fish money for a fortnight and do accounts with him at the end of that time. Well, the money we used to give him for a fortnight does on an average <u>6</u> days now. I do not know how the poor people are managing to live, cotton for their gowns is 3 times the price now and white flour is nearly unprocurable. Fortunately we laid in some, but I know most of the stations are out of it and can only buy in 5 and 6lb bags as they need it. We can still get the wheat meal, so we are not really stuck for bread, but the Chinese miss it badly.

I heard a good way to get flour, we are chortling still. There is a station where the letters get the go over by Robert *[the Japanese authorities]* still, we think ours don't! So Lilias and Tom Blakely in every letter wrote of the shortage of flour and how it could not be got for love or money. This touched Robert's *[Japanese]* pride, he does not like it to leak out that all is not well in the state of Denmark. One day he came, profusely polite, to say that possible flour was a bit difficult to buy, the merchants were hoarding it for a better price (there is a fixed government price, and we know it goes to feed the Tommies in the S. *[Japanese soldiers in the South]* but if they could be of any assistance ... why, they might be able to persuade the merchants to unload a little ... they would be delighted to do anything they could to help ...? and so on. AND the result was 10 blooming bags, when the rest of us buy it in 5lbs! We are still laughing. Who thought we would ever be glad of Robert's inquisitiveness!? It is a wonderful world.

I think the last time I wrote I forgot to tell you about a wedding feast we were at a couple of weeks ago. It was a Mohammedan household, the nephew of the doctor who looks after the Boy's School. *[Marion then explained how Dr Yang provided free medical services to the school, because a great friend of his had been educated there.]* He is a very decent little man and comes to anything that the Schools have in the way of special meetings, but he is one of the most influential Mohammedans in the town and shows no sign of wanting to study Christianity. That is unity among the religions for you, isn't it!

He asked us to help at the wedding, and one of our teachers went to instruct the bridesmaids what to do, they were having a 'modern' wedding. I was busy and did not get to the wedding, so I thought, although they had sent to invite Mary and myself three times (to eat), that it was only their courtesy and they would not miss us if we did not go. Miss Wang kept on pressing me to go and said that they would count it a real favour if we would go. The more important guests were there, the more 'face' he got in the eyes of his neighbours.

Well, in the end we went, I not thinking they would make any special fuss of us. I did not really believe Miss Wang, but bless you, I have never had so much courtesy shown to me in my life. We were taken to the most honourable room, his father and mother came to be presented to us, two clever-faced, handsome-faced old people, and the old lady stayed to talk to us for a while. Then his Great wife and his second wife were presented, and each took it in turn to stay and talk, although there had already been <u>500</u> guests that day, and all had been fed and were leaving in sections, we always had a member of the immediate family with us to entertain us.

We were led through the big tent where the poor bride was on show and as we went Yang sailed ahead clearing the way shouting, "Honourable guests have come, lend us your light," to clear the way. The place was still full of the various big bugs of their Church, officials of the government offices in the town and all sorts of important people, so they naturally took a look to see what females were worthy of all this honour from the head of the house, instead of being left to the women. I felt like giving a little wave of the hand the way the Queen does to acknowledge folk!

The special food was prepared for us and very good it was too, and to our horror we were led to the highest table by Yang himself and I was put in the top seat. I demurred for a long time, but was put there in the end and Yang stayed to eat with us, which he would not have done if we had been his own country-women. Then the greatest honour of all was when his old mother wished to come to give us food off the central dishes with her own fair hands, an honour paid to few people. We did not allow it of course, but the last courtesy possible had been paid when she offered to do it. Wot a day! I managed not too badly in the matter of being courteous, but the free and easy atmosphere of this compound is not the best training ground for these old-fashioned courtesies.

Fakumen
15th June 1939

To Dad and Mother

I do not know what phobia the Japanese have about ages, but every form of any sort you fill up you have to tell your age. Even when we go to Moukden or leave the town, in fact, we have to announce our coming and going, and each time down goes your honourable age. Just this minute the boy is in to say the police are here to say that the Special Affairs Bureau has rung up about my age – in Japanese!!! It makes me mad at times and then I can't help laughing. I have already filled up umpteen forms about myself this year, Special Police, ordinary cops, for the Magistrates, for the Church, forms that are to be sent to Hsinking, giving the official census of our foreign Church workers. And then as I say, each time I leave the place it all has to go down again. The house to house census, I forgot to add, and every time

The cook and headmistress (Chang Te Eu) of the Bible School.

either the Head of the Special Police, the ordinary police or the officer in charge of the Police box in our area changes, why then they come to make our acquaintance and get all the facts again. I have even had to fill up a form with 'all your name', ages, and what each is doing, which made me giggle, partly in wrath and partly in joy at the sheer foolishness of it!

Now our boy is going to be half the morning in that bally police box when he should be here putting straw under the ripe strawberries. It is going to rain and they get beaten into the ground. I do not know what the police do with all the forms they have, I think every time a man is changed he makes a bonfire

251

and the new man starts fresh. That may be an explanation of why the heads of departments change so often.

The Short Term Bible School is getting near the end. The last classes are being taken today and the exam is tomorrow. The weather has been very kind to us, it has only got slightly hottish these last two days, and today is cool again. It is a great relief, a room with nearly 100 women in it can be a hot place without the temperature assisting too much! They have all worked hard though and we should be able to give most of them their certificates. I have just finished hearing their repetition.

Also I must get my accounts for the half year done up at the end of the month and get my estimates for next year done in time to take to Synod in July. Synod is from the 5th to the 14th or thereabouts. I come back here and Mary goes on to P.T.H. There are evangelistic meetings for the last 10 days of the month and then glorious, glorious P.T.H., my bones are aching for it already – just to be floating in the sea and not feel sticky any more.

I see that at the beginning of the letter I said that today was cool. Well it changed its mind and it is a real roaster, we had to shut the windows to keep the house bearably cool. It is lovely to come in out of the glare and the hot air to the coolness of the house, if you shut the windows before the air gets too heated up.

Fakumen
24th June 1939

To Dad and Mother

By the way, did you know what country you belonged, Dad? I suppose you always thought you were British, didn't you? Well you are not – you are a Kuang Tung man, but Mother is English, thanks be. What's this all about? Well, hist and listen. One day recently three officials, one from the Municipal Office and two from the Education Board were in the School on a friendly visit. The headmistress in the conversation mentioned me a couple of times and one of the men who did not know me, asked who this 'Yang chiaoshih' was. One of the men, not waiting for Huei Chün to reply, piped up, "She has a Kuang Tung father and an English mother – but she works for the English – haven't you seen her? She is very like our people – not like an English person at all."

Huei Chün, when she got her breath, asked, "But how do you know this?" and he said the man in the office where my records were kept said I was partly Chinese (I'll admit the photo I gave them does look so) and anyway he had seen me several times and I looked like a southern Chinese. So there! I said I wanted Huei Chün to introduce me on the first opportunity and the minute he heard my accent he would know I was a foreigner! But did we laugh! The teacher though it was a grand joke. Don't you like your new nationality, Dad? Anyway Kuang Tung are reputedly very clever and quick, so you might be worse!

Fakumen
28th June 1939

To Dad and Mother

Yes, little Hsiang Ling died a few days after being baptised *[referred to in letter of 27th May]*. She was very happy and died exactly the time she wanted to. Towards the end of the week she did not want to die on either Saturday or Sunday as we were all busy and "it would be a bother". If she could die on Monday morning then she could be buried on Monday evening, and so it was.

When her breathing became laboured on Monday morning, she still was conscious and could look at them all and pat their hands. Her father is not a Christian but has been influenced a lot, especially by his daughter, and he was heartbroken over her dying. He could not bear her labouring in her breathing and at last he said to her, "The angel has come for you – why do you not go with him daughter," and with that Hsiang Ling closed her eyes. The school girls made wreaths and went to the grave. She had told her mother and father not to cry and they kept it up all day. It was one of the most peaceful and beautiful funerals I've been to here, almost happy, one would say.

Fakumen
16th July 1939

To Mother and Dad

Marion usually started her letter by referring to news of her family and of people in Clones, which had been included in letters which she had

253

received from her parents. Here she is referring to a cutting from The Northern Whig *newspaper, which had a photograph of her sister, Clara, who was part of the Victoria College team which had won the Schools' Perpetual Tennis Cup in Belfast.*

That was a very good photo of Clara in the Whig – good work, she seems to have beaten her opponent well too. I won't be up to their style at all when I get back – wouldn't it be awful to be beaten by my young sisters? I'll have to refuse firmly or I'll lose face completely.

I had a hottish but pleasant journey home yesterday. When I got to the station in Moukden, I found the place crowded with officers and soldiers down to meet a big pot in the Army and I was wondering where I was going to find a seat, when Jim Stobie, a Scottish newcomer, stepped off the train. He got me a nice corner with a breeze and fixed all my luggage within easy reach so I had no trouble when the short stop at Tiehling came – if you have a lot of stuff it is a nuisance getting off the train in a hurry, for there are not many porters at Tiehling.

When I got to the bus station there was a great crush and I again just stood back and let them pile in. I'd rather sit on the luggage nearer the door than be squashed in the back of a bus on a hot summer day! The driver was a man I knew and he spotted me surrounded by luggage – stuff for our own house and the O'Neills – so he sat me on a seat just beside him and sent the ticket collector to help me with the bundles – so I had a grand airy ride, all for a smile and thanks! The country was lovely and the shades of blue and mauve on the mountains made me think of Donegal – a bit of gorse would just have completed the picture!

We had a most interesting Synod this year. The Moderator Chin (Jean) is a very fine man and a good business man. He is over 6 foot tall, fine physique and a beautiful round powerful voice which he never has to strain to fill the church. He has a fine strong face and a very sweet tempered mouth. One of the men I wish could go home to let our Church see what 70 years of Christianity in this country can produce. He has been through it too in Crumlin Road *[this was a prison in Belfast and is a coded reference to Chin having being imprisoned by the Japanese]*, as with the others, it has made him all the more inspiring a leader.

Do you know that the Chinese Church has its own Home Mission to a place in the North, supported by local funds and men only? This time a young man was set apart by Synod for work there – it is no easy job, conditions are pretty rough and winter is bitterly cold. Also there were 8 licentiates at Synod and the 2 who belong to our Presbytery have been called already to Churches where they will become 'Pastor' in the autumn.

Fakumen
20th July 1939

To Mother and Dad

It is 'ot – 'orrid 'ot and it is most unfairly blowing hot winds – not done in July – and adding dust to the general discomfort. If you 'glow' a lot and are outside for any length of time, you come back feeling a good imitation of a mud pie! However, the thought of P.T.H. in another 10 days is helping us to bear up, and I'm having a slack time this week before the evangelistic meetings start on Tuesday.

One thing I am thankful for is something I must have inherited from my Kuang Tung father! a top knot that seems impervious to the sun. I would not guarantee if for the 2 midday hours all at once, but a short time does not worry me in the slightest, and some of the men have to wear a toupee here in the summer months. The Chinese women rarely wear anything on their heads – the men wear a big straw hat to protect their head and shoulders when they are working in the fields all day – but I imagine, I can't say for some of course, that no Chinese would take sunstroke. The kids run about naked in the worst heat and flourish in it.

The son of Kuei I, the houseboy, 'in sun suit'.

I can't remember if I told you anything about the anti-British meetings, when I wrote last. The two ports,

255

Darien and Newchang (Ying K'ou) had them on the 7th July (date of outbreak of war between Japan and China) but no other places. The Japanese grudge is, of course, that England has helped China, so they innocently ups and gives that as the reason why the folks of this part should hate England. I don't understand them – they honestly know nothing of the people they are ruling. I wish I could tell you something of the remarks I've heard!

Last night Dr O'Neill had a bright idea – says he, "We are Irish – down with the Oppressor England. Let's go and offer ourselves as speakers in the anti-British campaign which may start at the end of the month here!" The local friends who were in, thought this was the best joke they had heard for a long time and fair whooped. They were worried that <u>we</u> would be worried at first – but honestly it is a farce and even the officials who don't know us well send us messages assuring us that there a'int nothing to it.

I think at the moment the *[Japanese]* authorities are too busy wondering what is going to happen up north to have time to hate us. The Russians are busy biting their tails and the over population that has worried them for the last ten years has been settled in this one. There have been visitors from Japan over who say it is pathetic to see the houses with anything from 2-6 wooden slips hanging outside their doors with the name of their men folk who are fighting. The Japanese losses that I saw were nearly 1,000,000 killed and wounded already, but it is hard to get statistics now I'm sure. Japan certainly will not publish them. And all because of the madness of the military rulers.

Fakumen
27th July 1939

To Dad and Mother

Does W.A. (her brother William who was a medical student) know of any cure for blisters on the behind? I've been sitting on a hot hard seat from 9 to 12.30 and from 4 to 7.30 for the last two days. The Chinese are wonderful listeners, I think there must be some affinity between them and Scots of the last century. If I was not doing 'my duty', I don't think, however interesting the speakers, that of my own free will I would sit through 7 hours of meetings in this weather! The speakers are especially good, and the audience most attentive and interested.

We have, I'd say, 200-250 every day for most of the meetings and an unexpected crowd of young men and women. One man who is responsible for bringing a good many non-Christians, is Chao, a teacher in a government school and an earnest Christian. He brings officials and teachers every Sunday with him to church, and one Sunday recently he brought over 20 young people, all coming for the first time. He has brought a keen Buddhist official from the government offices to the evening meetings each day this week. He is 'salt' in the group among whom he works all right.

As I write there are 4 children, all under 10, standing round my knee to see me write. They think they are the most amusing marks to be making on a sheet. I've just offered to write one's name on his bare little tummy – he has only on trousers and shoes. The others thought that was a grand idea and they are off chasing him round the compound to bring him back to me. There will be a row. He objects!

**The Oriental Hotel
Shanhaikwan
1st August 1939**

To Dad and Mother

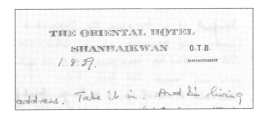

Just look at my address. Take it in. And I'm living in real Oriental luxury too. A small boy has just fetched me this paper, sold me the photos, filled my pen with ink and this minute came along to see if I had stamps. Now he is hovering in the background to see if he can think of some other possible want. Flora and I have 3 bottles of fizz and a large ice cream inside us.

Well, we are not really staying here – I'll admit that at once. We left Moukden last night at 11.30 and got here this morning at 7. We should have been at P.T.H. 2 hours later, but when we got to the Customs here, we found our bicycles and bedding bundle had not been put in the van at Moukden – so Flora and I had to stop off and wait for them. We were rather fed up and didn't know what sort of a place this was, but we are thoroughly enjoying this interlude. We toddled off to find a hotel and came on this place near the station.

(Hurrah! the ministering angel has thought of another thing – would we take some "whis-key"? Flora objects to my blaming her sunburnt nose as being the cause of his offer Really, I expect it is because the Japanese drink a lot of light beer all known under the generic name of 'whis-key' and he may have thought we looked hot. Now he has presented us with a fan each. If he'd just wave it over my head I'd feel like Mrs Nero or Cleopatra.)

We had a wash up and a large breakfast including really well made flake porridge and cow's milk, and then we got our friendly waiter to call ricks *[rickshaws]*, arrange the price – and tell them where we wanted to go to. We saw the sights and ended up with an hour daundering along part of the Great Wall. I've said that it is 20-40 feet high because someone once told me so, but I am sure there are places where it is 80 – I got quite dizzy this morning looking over one precipice of a place. Look at those rugged mountains and think of the work that went into the building of some 2 or 3 thousand miles of wall. It is a colossal thing.

Commercial photos of the Great Wall at Shanhaikwan which Marion bought from 'the ministering angel'. She wrote that it was 'wide enough for a carriage to drive along the top with room to spare'.

(Cheers! the lad has thought of something else – blotting paper – although it is so hot that the ink dries before I have finished a word.)

We hope to have lunch soon and then go back to meet a train that comes in at 3, which should have our luggage. If it has we go on to P.T.H. at once. If it hasn't, we'll just have to find the Japan Tourist

Bureau and give the key to him to see it through the Customs and send it on tomorrow. If it only comes, everything will be lovely in the garden and we'll have had a profitable and amusing day.

15 Tung Po' Lee
Eastcliff
Pei Tai Ho
13th August 1939

To Mother and Dad

Marion, who is staying with the MacNaughtans, refers to the death of a friend in Ireland:

You know I can't imagine Sadie is dead, she was such an alive person. Some people would make you believe in a life after even if you were not a Christian at all, you could not imagine that the spirit in them would die and just vanish leaving no trace. What a hope we Christians have been given in Christ. These days when things are so uncertain and so much on top of us, are the days when we have moments of deepest and most real peace of heart.

I do not remember what I told you about things in Manchuria *[the outbreak of hostilities there between Russian and Japan]* before I left. We have no trouble at all so far south as Faku and not much chance of it, but there is certainly bombing going on in the north. How much, it is hard to know from the papers. The Japanese and Russian accounts contradict each other so completely. I can't imagine the Rs *[Russians]* are doing anything more than biting this *[Manchukuoan]* government's tail. With things as they are in Europe, the Russians are not going to start a war in the East. Her borders are too far apart. And Japan has her hands more than full just now.

Things are urgent enough here, but we are safe and quiet in P.T.H. There have been rumours of anti-British processions here, but each time they have been put off. In other places inland the local toughs have looted missionary houses and made them clear out, but that was in places where there were only a few people. It is a different picture here where there are several thousand and twenty odd nationalities. It is curious to be here in this quiet and beauty and to hear of war and trouble. It doesn't seem real here.

Take in this weather note. We are having the first heavy rain that there has been in P.T.H. and district since last September. There is no snow in the winter here and the farmers depend on that for dampening the ground for the spring sowing. Sometime in the spring there were a few light showers, then in July there was one night's rain and one shower this month. You can imagine the ground is dry as a board and all the crops are brown withered things. The millet is a hardy plant and some has grown several feet – how it is hard to imagine. The men say that if this rain is heavy enough they can have grain this autumn after all. It looked horribly like famine until this week.

I think even the birds are enjoying the rain, the air is full of swifts swooping about high up, although it is just pelting heavily. We have a nice deep verandah and can sit safely out of the rain outside. We have our meals outside too and possibly because it has been so dry, we rarely see a fly.

George Taylor and I were put out of the *[tennis]* tournament yesterday – after a good game against 2 English Baptist folk. It was a very cheery game and they were nice opponents – so we didn't mind losing to them!

Bathing is perfect, we usually spend 11-1 on the beach and have a dip after tennis and before supper in the evening. I'm very brown, proper sunburnt shade. I can imagine Hugh will look like a Chinese farmer in the summer, if he comes out here!

It is lunch time and I've been reading your letters and writing to you most of the morning! We have Sunday service at 5 in the afternoon here. It is too hot in the morning usually! Must stop.

On the way to Peking
23rd August 1939

To Mother and Dad

'Scuse the scribbles but I'm writing in the train and though it is going pretty slowly it is not too steady. Mrs Mac*[Naughtan]*, Flora and I are on our way to Peking to get visas for returning to Manchuria. Everyone has to go, but a wife or husband can fill the forms for the other one. It is fortunate *[currency]* exchange is in our favour this year or this would be an expensive trip, for we have to pay $16 each way for travel and spend at least 2 days in Peking! Then they say they give visas <u>free</u> to residents in Manchuria!!

Travelling isn't done for the pleasure of it these days either – there are terrible floods between Tiensin and P.T.H. and the railway lines are sometimes impassable. There has been a bad drought affecting most of N. China this year, and now floods have come. As far as I could see from the railway, there was nothing but water. Here and there villages and single farm houses were stuck up out of the water or their mud walls were crumbling away under the force of the floods.

The people are in a terrible state. All along the line we came on groups who had come to camp on small bits of ground on either side of the line – wet mud under foot, a grass matting roof above them spread over walls made of heaps of any of their household things they had managed to save. Where they get food or firing I don't know. Each biggish station had groups of refugees camping out, using the wooden sleeper of planks, which were there for transportation, as flooring.

There are schemes for relief being started already and funds being called for, but there will be a far bigger problem this year even than last year's war refugees. They say it looks as if it will be worse than 1917, which was the peak year. A great many of our Manchurian missionaries went down to China to help distribute food and funds at that time.

Here and there through the floods you saw boats or rafts with a family's belongings on it trying to make for a town or village. I saw one pathetic Korean group with a heavily laden raft. There was so much stuff on it that the people could not get on, so they had all to walk in the water. Three men and a woman were hauling it strongly, and a woman walking behind it carrying a bundle. An old man with a long white beard was behind and all were up to their waists in water. It was grey and pouring – the water muddy – what a picture of desolation – I can't get it out of my mind. Mothers with small children must be in the worst plight of all.

The rains cleared up in P.T.H. after about 4 day's typhoon and it seems to be settled and dry again. The crops are growing quickly and the people hope to be able to harvest them this year.

Language School
23rd evening

We have heard the wireless news about the non-aggression pact
*[between Germany and Russia to agree those country's spheres of
influence in Eastern Europe and divide up Poland]* and the Polish
situation – things look black. Pray God, Hitler may be kept back from
plunging Europe into war. It is too awful to think of – and the sight of
this poor country's refugees makes the horror very real.

College of Chinese Studies
Peking
27th August 1939

To Mother and Dad

*This letter was only posted some days after Marion had travelled back
in Fakumen, as it was in her luggage which arrived back after her.*

You may not realise that the floods in the Tiensin area are having
anything to do with your daughter – but they are! And with a good
many more Manchurians. *[Marion lists eight missionaries]* and myself
are all here ... getting visas to go back to Manchuria, and the line has
been broken since we came down, so here we are marooned. There
must be several hundreds of foreigners here who are waiting either to
go to Tiensin, Pei Tai Ho, Tangku or the port of Tiensin en route for
Shanghai. We are not affected otherwise, the floods don't come
anywhere near here, but we hear bad news through the wireless of the
continued rise of the water and the plight of the Treiutsin people. This
is a good place to be stuck in, and we are very comfortable here,
though thinking regretfully of our last week in Pei Tai Ho slipping
through without bathing or tennis.

These are anxious days too as we wait for the European news. We
get it the same time as you do by wireless. Your 9 o'clock news at
night is our 5.30 in the morning and there is usually a group of
Britishers up to listen in – the Americans feel they can wait till
breakfast to hear the news.

These talks and discussions *[with Germany over Poland]* seem
the only ray of hope. Three days ago when we heard that German
soldiers had their marching orders, it seemed that nothing could avert

war, but the delay since then makes us hope that things may clear up.

The German – Soviet pact has been the most tremendous smack to Japan. One can't help but feel sorry for her. Here she is fighting Communism for all she can and Germany is her only powerful 'friend' – and now she has let her down slap. The Japanese papers are very very bitter on the subject, and who'd blame them. Even in these few days it has given a new turn to the anti-British feeling – it has not been pressed with the same bitterness that it was.

Dr O'Neill preaches that the world is getting worse – a theory I dare to differ with, and I think this is another time when we can say that it seems to have progressed. There was no thought of peace talks before the Great War – even Hitler, bloodthirsty warrior as we picture him, is ready to get together and discuss things rather than fight. He believes in the right of his demands and he is ready to fight for them, but I don't think he wants war any more than the rest of us or surely he would have marched this week. Well, things will have happened before you read this – war or peace – even if only temporary, what is it to be? God grant our prayers for peace.

Moukden
5th September 1939

Marion, whose journey from Peking had been delayed by the floods, wrote this postcard to her parents after hearing that Britain had declared war on Germany following Hitler's invasion of Poland.

Doesn't it all seem unreal? Like a nightmare you can't wake up from. We'd hoped till the last moment that peace could be kept, but there was no hope for it as things are – we can't keep out. We get wireless news and have heard everything as soon as you do – Chamberlain's speech was heard here too. I am longing for letters, but must wait now.

Fakumen
13th September 1939

To Dad and Mother

I see I didn't tell you about our trip back from Peking – or did I? I'll be brief in case I did?! We waited over one day, when we heard there was a train through and were glad we did for Austin *[Fulton]*, Ruth Dickson and Janie Henderson (Scot) all came back – *[as they]* were not allowed on, too many. That night, 30th, we celebrated by going to a picture, a Chinese meal and then to the 'North Sea' (a big lake) to see the ceremony for the Festival of the Dragon King. Children carry lanterns, coloured and shaped like lotus flowers, and ones of the actual lotus leaves which float off lighted on the lake – full moon – lake looked beautiful and lanterns just like real lotus.

Got to bed at 12 – up at 4, had breakfast and got to train at 5. Stood in queue till 6, literally into the thousands of people waiting. Saw British and American Legation people go round by side door and slipped after them – Found Japanese were going in that way too and our tickets were taken and no comment made. We could hardly believe ourselves when we got on train. Left at 7 and got to Tiensin at 11.30. I'd forgotten my cholera certificate and saw us all being held up until I found someone to jab me! Didn't ask me for some reason – tho' they asked several others of our party and I was fair in the jitters when I heard them. Took river steamer from Tiensin to Tangku, as the line was still broken there. 5½ hours, mostly standing, but it was a lovely day and the river was very interesting if you forgot the plight of the poor refugees of the flooded land.

Got to Tang Ku parched with thirst – at 5.30 and found we had to wait till 11.30 for the train. Rickshaw man took us up to "English Club" which turned out to be a private one belonging to Kai Ling Mining Association, but they kindly gave us tea and fizz, and we had a picnic basket or two with us. By this time our party numbered 14, Americans, Canadians, Scots and Irish! At 11.30 we got our train – another scrum and long waiting in queues. Sat up all night, got to P.T.H. 5.30, <u>pouring</u> rain and cold. Got to Eastcliff eventually and we just rolled into bed, clothes and all, and slept till breakfast was ready. For 72 hours it never stopped pouring and blowing big guns. There was a typhoon and tho' we got warning from the gun boat, it didn't hit us directly. The minute the rain stopped we packed and came up to Moukden, arriving on the 4th ...

I had to do some shopping and then get a girl out of the Moukden hospital and take her up to Tiehling. She is one of our girls who got T.B. and I sent her to Liu, a very fine T.B. doctor in Moukden Medical College. She is much better after 2 months, so I have taken her up to

Tiehling to convalesce and feed up. Moukden is so busy there is a waiting list for the beds.

I got up to Tiehling on the 6th to find there was no bus – roads too bad. Stayed with Mary Cummings two nights and then went to Moukden to do some shopping for Mary and self. I meant to get back to Tiehling that night, but the engine of the evening express gave up the ghost about a mile from the station or less. Sat there 2 hours and then were pulled back to the station. Too late to go that night, so went back to Macs *[MacNaughtens']* and there the O'Neills persuaded me to stay over Sunday and come back here with them on Monday. Did that and the bus broke down ½ way! We were 3 hours on the road longer than we should have been.

What travels I've had this summer! Held up a day at Shanaikwan on the way down. Delayed 8 days in Peking, 3 days in P.T.H., a week in Moukden, a broken engine in both train and bus, I think I'll 'stay put' here!

Fakumen
20th September 1939

To Jim

Marion wrote of problems at the Schools' Sports Meeting:

... a rival of the Boys' Middle School, which always runs us close, got really nasty the day of the races three days ago. There were several of them wearing those spike running shoes and they deliberately set themselves out to damage some of our boys, especially the best runner. Two of them marked him all the time and managed to knock him badly in the ribs with their elbows, ending up with tearing his leg badly with the spikes on their shoes. Bad feeling was up all day and the head of the school could do nothing with them. Our boys kept fairly quiet, thanks be, but finally the other head had to take all his boys off the field, they were getting so wild.

Yesterday, during the ball games one of the other boys threw a vicious ball at one of our men teachers who was applauding on the touch line, and missed him – but got one of his own masters on the face, he was all puffy eyed and bruised today. It was a terrific loss of face of course, for the masters of that school, all they are not allowed to the Meeting today – the boys had all to go to class. I was sorry for the teachers!

The trouble here is that half of the boys in a school are married, from 16 up, and have children of their own. They have full charge of their homes too, if their father is dead, so they do not take kindly to discipline. There are several boys expelled every year from each school, till they learn to shake down to it. Even our school, which has a rather good reputation, had to expel three this year, one for gambling, one for being drunk and for climbing out of school and spending the night out on the razzle. Not Campbell standard, what, what? *[Campbell College in Belfast was the boarding school attended by Jim and, also formerly, three of his brothers.]*

Fakumen
23rd September 1939

To Dad and Mother

I hope you are not anxious about us out here, since the German-Soviet Pact and now the Japanese-Soviet Pact, things are moving quite smoothly here. What a daft sort of game this pact making is – here is Nazism and Japan making friends with their enemy, Communism. And Wang Ching Wei's Japanese-sponsored government in Shanghai is to be based on the 'Three Principles' of Sun Yat Sen – the which to have in your house in print means death here or in North China. It's wunnerful. The I.R.A.s will be offering themselves to fight for King and Country soon.

Fakumen
25th September 1939

To Mother

Marion had begun referring to her parents' recent holiday:
Donegal is a lovely spot, there is no place quite comes up to it, the air has a special tang to it – even better than the Mournes, Mother?! I get something of the same feeling of spaciousness about Pei Tai Ho. You can always get on the top of a hill and see the country and sea spread

miles around till the Shanhaiknaw mountains tower up with their rugged edges – unlike the flat topped hills round here.

We had a good holiday this year despite the fact that storms, floods and war rather took the flavour off the last 10 days for us. I enjoyed the tennis and bathing thoroughly and we had some good parties.

I also had an attentive young man who floated around a lot – a doctor in the Scottish Mission, but from Manchester. Small, dark and dapper, a good lad – but I didn't encourage him Mother dear! Still, as you know yourself, it adds an interest to the holiday! And makes a girl thinks she isn't on the shelf after all. Flora thinks it is my duty to provide a home for her in Moukden now that Mr and Mrs Mac are leaving after New Year! *[i.e. if Marion married the 'young man' she would be living in Moukden.]*

He is in the Moukden Medical College, but I wonder if he won't go home now that doctors are so much needed, if men are called up from here. The Ambassador sent out a notice that Britons were to stay put till notice was sent them and not be dashing off home at once. Put in more ambassadorial language of course.

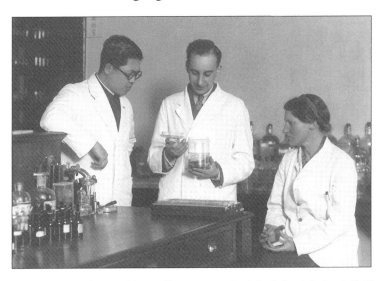

Rymer Cayton and two of his colleagues in the Moukden Medical College.

The 'young man' was (Henry) Rymer Cayton, who had been at Edinburgh University. Marion had in fact seen him from a distance

267

then when she was a student at St Colm's and Rymer was on the platform at a Student Christian Movement meeting which had been addressed by Albert Schweitzer.

In view of later developments it is tempting to speculate whether Marion was being entirely honest about Rymer. However, a study of the book in which she recorded all the letters she received and wrote, suggests she was at this stage. For the next few months there is no mention of letters between Marion and Rymer.

Fakumen
29th September 1939

To Mother

We are going to have a hard winter here. Cold seems to be coming earlier than usual and there is no coal to be bought. Mary and I have enough to do us for a while and we can use wood in the dining room till after Christmas, but the schools and hospitals are going to be in a bad way. The classrooms have to have coal stoves from the middle of October onwards and the cooking pots couldn't be kept in millet stalk, it burns away too quickly.

Miss Shang Te En, Ssu Wen, Marion and Miss Liu (left to right) among the gaoling or big millet. There was a shortage of millet in September 1939. Miss Shang and Miss Liu were junior graduates of the Moukden Theological College who were doing two years practical work in Faku.

The Chinese are really worried about things. Flour is getting scarcer and scarcer. Rice is being sent to Japan, they have had no time to grow their own apparently. The gaoliang (big millet) is very dear, though it is hard to see why it should be scarce. Cotton wool, with which they pad their gowns, is four times the price it was and cotton is only being sold when you say what you want it for and give strict measurements. They say that the shops have been searched and an inventory made of the materials and until they are sold they will get no new stock, and that will be limited.

It really looks pretty serious, isn't it ridiculous that in the country which has the biggest coal seam in the world, there should be such a coal shortage? The working conditions are appalling apparently, and the work is forced, for no one wants to do it. One of the hospitals near a mine has a daily 400 outpatients and over 100 in-patients, all sick or injured in the mines. Shortage of rolling stock and carts is another thing. There has been a constant stream of men and carts going up north to build trenches and defences against the Russians. It is still going on – they don't trust Russia, and the men are still up there working, although the pact is signed. Trains are too busy running men and stores, both up north and into north China, to have time for goods.

It is nearly impossible to get anything in the goods train from Moukden to Tiehling, about 40 miles, in less than 3 weeks. I have had that experience twice this summer. We foreigners are moderately comfortable, we can still get what we want, within limits, for we have a little money, but I do not know how the Chinese who are living on the edge of things are going to do. All the world over this is going to be a bitter hard winter. And we cannot but say that man has brought all this misery on himself. Aren't we poor miserable half-baked creatures after all?

Marion then refers to a photograph she is sending of the Faku pastor and his family:

The foreign clothes have been brought in by the Japanese. All men in official positions have to wear western suits when at work, it is horrible expensive for them. The pastor does not wear them often and always wears his nice Chinese ceremonial gown for church, but I suppose this time he wanted to dickey up! It was a Chinese boy with a good camera who took this, the pastor made me a present of a copy. It seems to be the thing to do to give your photo to people. My evangelists write and ask me for copies of mine – so I suppose I'm hung on the wall to keep any eye on their doings. One wrote not long ago and said that the Bible said, 'Ask and ye shall receive' – so what could I do after that but send one, and not do any damage to a faith like that. They have a most disconcerting, to us, habit of quoting the scriptures, positively dragging it in by the scruff of the neck, in the most incongruous places.

Fakumen
5th October 1939

To Mother

Mrs MacNaughtan left for home on Monday morning and I dashed in for a day to see her off. I was glad I had gone, she has made a real home for me and I hated to think of her leaving without my seeing her again. It was not so bad seeing her go away with Mr Mac, as it would have been if she had gone alone. He was appointed Conference Delegate to the Japanese Synod and was able to go and see her off at Yokohama before he went to the meetings.

She has done a great work out here – there are few married women out here who have been able to hold down both the work of a mother and that of a full time evangelist. She did a piece of work it will be hard to find anyone to take on, the prison work – and it is not like prison work at home, it is really a very hard, heart rending place to go to, and she has kept her health and her youthful spirits through it all. We young evangelists found her a great person to go to if there are any problems to discuss, for she was a single evangelist to understand the problems before she got married! Now she has both the wisdom of a married woman and a single 'chiaoshih' to offer us!

After seeing Mrs Mac off, I went to a Chinese wedding. And it was SOME wedding. It was the sister of our headmistress who was getting married, Wang Yin Yin. These are the Wangs whom I have visited, the pastor's family. They have not much money, but the boy she was marrying has and the family of the boy has to provide the feast and fixments, the opposite of our ideas. I was to go and help her dress, and fix her flowers as they were wearing foreign clothes. The boy is a clever lad, a doctor, who has a research scholarship in the big Japanese hospital and medical college in Moukden.

It was the wish of the young people this time, they have been good friends for about 4 years, so this is a modern Chinese wedding! She wore a very pretty white frock and veil, borrowed from a friend who got married earlier in the year, and he was all dickied up in tails and black bow *[tie]*.

In this photo of a 'modern Chinese wedding' of two doctors in Xi'an, from Marion's album. The groom is wearing tails and black bow tie, as at the wedding Marion attended in October 1939.

The wedding was held in a big restaurant, where a room had been taken. There were nearly 300 guests, including the principal of his medical college, and a number of the professors, all Japanese, then all their classmates, both school and college as far as they could be gathered up. A number of the elders of both their churches, and also the elders belonging to the old church in which her brother was minister. The families of both and their close friends made the numbers soar …

Front of the programme for the wedding of Wang Yin Yin and Ching Tsung Te.

The service was held first by one of the Moukden pastors and I thought it was a good idea having it there, as the outside folk would probably not have come to a church service. It was a very reverent and well conducted service, there was no exchanging of rings as they had already done that at the engagement service, but the older minister in the Church here pronounced the benediction over them, as the sealing of their marriage in the eyes of the Church.

The programme for the wedding of Wang Yin Yin and Ching Tsung Te.

I am waiting at the minute to go and see Faku's Uncle Charley Rafter *[a great uncle who had been Chief Constable of Birmingham]*, a Japanese. Now, what do you think I have been doing to be up before the police. I am going to ask a favour of the gentleman, and I'm hoping that he will grant it. We foreigners can buy flour in Moukden now, as much as we need to use, but the sale to Chinese is restricted as it is a luxury. We can only get a few lbs here at a time and our store will soon be finished. I am afraid if I go into Moukden next week (we have Conference) and bring back a stone or two, that I may have trouble with the police at the city gate. They are searching luggage for flour and cotton wool, and if they have orders to let none through, foreigner or no foreigner, I might be detained until the matter is settled. I want to get a step ahead if I can, and get a note from the Head of Police to permit me to carry this through. Unfortunately, our old friend is gone and I do not know the man I am going to see. However, it is not a great matter to ask for, there should be no difficulty I think.

Friday

Well, the interview I mentioned took a different turning to what I had expected – and a pleasant one. The gentleman came round here with his interpreter, instead of asking me to go to him. When I explained the difficulty, he asked if the flour sold here would not do for our bread. I said I understood that there was none. He said that it had to be rationed for ordinary consumers, but that it would be possible to get me some. Then he gave me his card with a word or two on it and let our boy go to the shop to get a few lbs to try out in baking. If it does, then he will let us have as much as we need. If not, we can bring it from Moukden and no questions asked.

He stayed for more than an hour chatting of this and that, very polite and kindly, were we worried about war in Europe?, letters?, any of my folk involved? and so on, going away with this parting message, "We special police are here to protect you, so any time you have any difficulty or problems you would like to discuss with me just ring me up, and the moment I hear your message I will be at your house." So there you are. It is wonderful how politeness oils the wheels, if within their power, I've found.

Mary and I went out with the Bible School for their autumn picnic today, and are just back now, the students left on the hill – they do not want to come back for another hour or two, but Mary and I have both Training Classes to prepare for tomorrow morning. The weather was perfect, crisp and sunny, and the wild flowers are amazing just now. It is like a second spring. There was a long drought in July and the heavy rain, after a few weeks very cold it has turned sunny again, and some of the spring flowers have bloomed again. Even the grain which was cut earlier is putting up little new sprouts beside the old one, and the wild pear has bloomed a second time. The ground is a mass of flowers, and the leaves on the trees are changing colour, so it was glorious to be out and to see all the colours. We are quite sunburnt and this when we thought all the warmth had gone.

This photograph of the students picking flowers (and their dog) with the harvest fields in the background appeared in the January 1940 issue of Woman's Work. *The article recorded that the students were wondering if the wild flowers, coloured leaves and berries would last another week until Harvest Thanksgiving Sunday. It mentioned that some of the most beautiful berries did keep and decorated the pulpit, along with marigolds, dahlias and larkspur from Marion and Mary's garden.*

Fakumen
21st October 1939

To Mother

Yesterday we had a visitor who interested me very much. The local Catholic Priest. What would some of our good friends in the North of Ireland say? He has been at O'Neills' on a visit and they were very struck with his friendly, kindly ways. We got a vine from Mrs Mac and I had brought the root back after the meetings. I had no idea how to put it in and the Mac's gardener had only given me a few hazy directions, so I sent Kuei I round to the priest with a note to him to ask him to allow Kuei to have a talk with the man who looks after his vines. He sent a note to say that he would come himself as the vine might be spoiled if not planted carefully.

274

We all had tea in the O'Neills' and then he came over here with Dr O'Neill to act chaperone. He got the boy to do some of the digging, and then as he was not doing it just the right way in he leapt into the hole, long skirts and all, and dug away vigorously himself. Then when he had the root in the ground, he picked up his skirts and started dancing down the earth round it. I was longing to go away and have a good laugh to myself at the thought of what a fierce little White Ribbonner and Orange Woman *[references total abstinence and Protestant organisations]* who writes to me from Derry would say if I could send her the picture. He took no end of trouble over it and gave us careful instructions about its future. He is going to give me another kind next year and said that he would come in the spring when it was time to take it up. All of which I thought very neighbourly of him. He is French Canadian and speaks quite good English, when he is stuck for a word, if we do not know the French we can always fall back on Chinese, our conversations are full of surprises.

Tung Chiang K'ou
4th November 1939

To Mother and Dad

Marion and Wang Ssu Wen had arrived at the start of one of their country visits to run Bible Schools for Women. The start had been delayed as the people in one of the places they were visiting had not finished winnowing their harvest – separating the grain from the chaff.

Marion wrote that these photographs showed how chaff was removed from grain in Manchuria. Mules pulled heavy rollers over the crop (left) before it was thrown up in the air with winnowing shovels (right) so that the wind blew away the lighter chaff and the heavier grain fell back down on the ground.

We have just spread our bedding on the k'ang to toast up before we get into bed – and as Miss Wang is preparing tomorrow (Sunday's service) I thought I'd start my letter to you. We have got here safely without any adventures. Left Faku by bus at 10 and got to the river bank about 11.30. Young Yu, the evangelist, who is a junior theological graduate out on his 2 year's practice work, and two deacons were on the Faku side of the river to meet us. They took charge of our luggage and put us into the ferry.

We were held up about 10 minutes while a countryman argued with the ferry man about his fare. He said he'd pay it on the way back and the ferryman wasn't having any. Country people are very funny when they come up against anything with a fixed price – they don't understand it and feel cheated of the fun of arguing I think. Often on the Tiehling bus some country folk will get on between villages and try to beat the conductor down. They always look as if they thought he wasn't playing the game fairly when he announces that prices are fixed.

We crossed in a small boat which had about 20 people, 2 small hand carts and a lot of luggage, including a small haystack! The current on the Liao is very quick and the water is pure brown mud – it is never clear – I'd hate to fall into it. The boats sidle across like crabs and we went quickly this time because we were going partly with the stream. Deacon Han and his wife asked us for a meal before we went to the church.

8th November

This is the 3rd day of our School and we are getting along famously. Last year we had about 22 pupils, this year there are 34 daily and nearly 40 put down their names. The weather has suddenly changed and some have not been able to come. About 10 or so of last year's pupils are back – it isn't easy for them to get yearly, so we are very glad to have so many. Yesterday a proper rain storm blew up, very cold and lashing rain, strange weather for November here. Expected snow – not rain – however it came during the night and we woke up to a Christmas scene. It is a raw bitter day, but the sun is out now and we are quite warm inside the house.

T'sui Yao Ting *[who also attended the Bible School here last year]* ... is a young wife of 19 married to a boy of 15. Her family had engaged her to the boy before they became Christians and there was no going back on the bargain. The old folk and her husband treat her quite well apparently – but there are several women in the family, wives of her father-in-law's brothers (they are a big undivided family) and they have their knife in her for being a Christian. She is a most attractive girl. Plenty of character about her face and handsome. She got away to the School last year with difficulty and this year appeared a day late. She had got her mother to invite her home and then came on here. A girl is allowed to go to her home if her parents invite her once a year or so. I hope she won't get into a row later on.

Tung Chiang K'ou
12th November 1939

To Dad and Mother

Two of your letters arrived just an hour ago and wasn't I glad to see them! I told Mrs O'Neill not to forward any, but she made up a packet of them and registered it so as to make sure she could get them back. One was a letter of August 29th – via Siberia! – from Dad, posted in Clones. The other was 23rd September, from both of you posted in Enniskillen – censored *[examined in Ireland]* – with enclosure from twins and Willie to you. I thought when I saw such a fat one that I'd get a note requesting me to tell my friend to write more shortly! However, I suppose there is not a big foreign mail from Enniskillen, so it would not bother them. I'm so sorry to see that you had no letters from me on the 23rd September, but I'd hoped that the ones I'd posted at the end of August would reach you soon after that.

I was very interested in the twins' letters to you, written when you were on holiday. Every now and then I get a new shock when I realise they are bigger than when I left home! Their being able to take over the housekeeping – bake, wash and churn as well as entertain their young brothers' friends, was what brought me up short this afternoon! I sometimes wish my furlough was this year to get home and see you all – but on the other hand I have a sort of feeling that I should get a better grip of the language before I go home! I feel ashamed of the amount of preparation I have to give the slightest thing still. I sometimes wish my father was that Kuang Tung man you heard about earlier this year!

The boys have all been keeping very busy with their preaching – 4 services for Hugh on one Sunday sounds good going! The Young family can cover a lot of ground on a Sunday when they all get going.

At the moment I have 3 pairs of solemn little eyes looking at me. They spotted me through the window so they came in. They are rowed up in front of me where I am writing and the red cork of my ink bottle is interesting the biggest boy at the moment. He is a bright looking kid, rosy cheeked, brown healthy skin. There is a wee girl exuding a grand smell of garlic.

Tung Chiang K'ou
Sorry Chiu Chia T'un
19th November 1939

To Mother and Dad

I'd just been talking about Tung Chiang K'ou, so I wrote it by mistake. This is Sunday morning, we have just had breakfast and Miss Wang is busy preparing her sermon and service. It is a foggy morning – a thing we rarely have here, and I've been out sniffing it and imagining that I was standing on the Manse steps in Clones. The smell of pigs is rather more prevalent here than it might be at home – unless that pig still lives down the avenue of course. Pigs is pigs the world over and smells much the same whether they are black or pink.

We came on here on Friday 17th and leave tomorrow Monday 20th. We hope to get back in the same day, but the bus at this end has broken down and the man has gone to Moukden to buy spare parts. So it won't be running for a day or two!

Our School finished off well, with 26 students. They got a photo taken after the 'graduation'. If it is good I'll send it to you!

I enjoy Tung Chiang K'ou – the students who live in add to the fun and we get to know them so much better. We were mutually sorry to say goodbye when it came to the last day. We had planned to come here by bus but, as I say, it had broken down. There were no droskeys so we hired a push cart for our bedding. It was about 3 feet wide by 4 long, low down between 2 wheels with pneumatic tyres, swung about a foot off the ground. The handle is just like a big heavy pushcart – pram handle. The man who took our stuff is used to pushing 500 lbs of stuff

The graduation ceremony at Tung Chiang K'ou with Yu, the evangelist, Marion and Ssu Wen in the centre of the front row.

on it 70 li (23 miles) in a day, so he put our 80lb bundle of stuff at the back and made us sit on the front on a small mattress.

I had planned to walk it – it is about 15 miles and I was looking forward to a good tramp. He, however, insisted that it wasn't easy to push unless the cart was heavy in front, so we had to sit on. I think he was afraid a woman would keep him back, because after a while when my feet got very cold and I insisted on walking for a bit, he saw that I could walk and didn't push for me to get back again! I probably got walking about 10 miles and felt all the better for it. He kept up a good steady pace with Miss Wang and the baggage for we got from church to church in 4½ hours. It was a crisp sunny day and a good road – if you don't think of tarmacadam!

I enjoy the chance of a long walk, we don't often have it in Faku unless we go to one of the villages on foot. The pastor has a bike and he prefers us to use ours – we can get back early before dark comes if we cycle.

We had a rather amusing interview with the police yesterday. The moment we arrived *[the day before]* there was one on the door to take down particulars, but he was polite and businesslike and soon departed. The one species of official that raises my ire and to whom I long to give a swift kick on the pants is the small official who is too, too big for his boots. Yesterday was one of that species. He is a nasty little wart anyway, chases any girl whom he sees on the street into their home and makes himself objectionable there. Some of the Christian families have been bothered by him. I had heard of him, so when he came in yesterday I wasn't over polite. Answered what he asked me and sat there silently when finished. He found the conversation heavy going for he had no errand to us – all information was already in. He told me he spoke English and tried to say, "This is a book". I fortunately made out 'book' or he'd have lost face completely – but I made no comment on his English! Then he asked me if I knew English pretty well and Miss Wang started to giggle on the k'ang behind me. I said, "Yes, pretty well." – and then I think he realised what he'd said and after silence he pushed off abruptly. He is the sort of nasty specimen who throws his weight around amongst the ordinary householders and shopkeepers till he has them scared stiff!

The likes of him in other places has been known to take evidence in his pocket into a house, 'find' it and accuse the person of not being a loyal citizen. The unfortunate man might not have the money to buy him off – if he has, he does – if he hasn't he goes into prison. The Japanese judges are fair enough, but when they are working through interpreters the truth doesn't always reach them and there are lots of cases of bad miscarriages of justice in this country.

Elder Liu and his wife, photographed during one of Marion's tours of country churches, showing them in their winter clothes.

Fakumen
21ˢᵗ November

We had an eventful journey yesterday. Chiu Chia T'un to Tung Chiang K'ou we did by droskey, and it was a cold ride – there was a bitter wind and although we were bundles of clothes and wraps, we couldn't keep warm. We got tea in Tung Chiang K'ou church, and then started off with our friend of the push cart, who was to see us across the river to the Faku bound bus. He took us to the top of a lane leading down to the morass which stretches for the best part of a mile on the Tung Chiang K'ou side of the river bank. He went to look for the best road to cross it and left us with the luggage. It wasn't long till we were the centre of an interested crowd and some of the kids knew me from the time I was at the Short Term Bible Study, so I played with them till he appeared.

The going was too soft, so he had had to get a pole and carried our luggage slung from each end of it across his shoulder. The river had overflowed with the heavy rains this autumn and the frosts came too quickly for it to dry up. This was noon and although the wind was cold there was a hot sun so the top coating of ice was all melted. We ploughed through it, standing one to waggle the 'clobber' off the other – hoping our shoes wouldn't get lost with it! – every minute or two, and wondering what would happen if the next step proved really soft and one fell flat. We got to the river to find it white with floating ice cakes – I should think it won't take more than another week to begin to 'seam' *[freeze]* up as the Chinese say. Our boat went crunch, crash, through it, and the man in the prow pushed us off the bigger pieces with an iron pointed pole.

Our man dumped us on the road where the bus would pass and went back to Tung Chiang K'ou. We were nearly an hour early, we had heard such tales of the river crossing that we'd left plenty of time. We got there at 2 and the bus was due at 3. 3 came and no bus. It was cold on the road and our feet were frozen with wet mud, so we had to keep moving to keep warm – at last we found a firing pile – beanstalk, and got on the sunny side of it away from the wind where we were moderately warm. 4 o'clock and no bus. The people in the houses round did their best to persuade us to go in – but we were afraid of the bus coming and also we were not keen on leaving our luggage dumped on the road. To take into the house would have been a slur on the village honesty! The sun was beginning to look like setting and our problem was that the boat ferry stopped at sunset so if we did not go soon we would have to camp in a village house for the night.

We had settled at 4.30 that if the bus had not come that we would get a farmer's boy to take our luggage and start back to Tung Chiang K'ou. On the dot of 4.30 the bus hove into sight. Were we glad! It had to go to another village first, but we knew it was there so we waited till 5 thankfully and then got ourselves and luggage aboard. The reason of the 2 hour delay was that the driver – a Japanese need I say? – had taken the bus guard's gun and gone shooting pheasant on the way. He got none I'm glad to say (said she nastily). I have to laugh when I think of it now, but I felt so cold and hungry at the time – we'd had nothing from 8 in the morning except Chinese tea, thinking we'd be home about 4 – that I nearly told the driver I'd report him. However, I suppose – fortunately – I refrained. I discovered afterwards he spoke no Chinese. There is a bus guard of one valiant well-armed soldier on the bus for that run – to shoot bandits, Mother dear. There ain't any really, but they still keep up a guard in autumn which is bandit shooting season ...

When we got to the end of our lane, here were two of the boys' schoolteachers waiting with Kuei to receive us. That was true courtesy for you now – 2 hours in a cold wind and then they were enquiring tenderly if we were cold. Today one of them came round to ask about me and hoped I was not too fatigued after my journey. The Chinese do know how to be polite, it makes me feel as if I was living in Cranford sometimes.

Fakumen
24th November 1939

To All-of-yous

I suppose this is my Christmas letter, though I'm just wondering if there is a chance of it being home in time now. Anyway you'll know that I will be thinking of you all on Christmas day and wondering if I will be with you next year. I hope you will have a happy time, though it won't be possible to get the thought of the war out of your minds, I know you have it in you all to make your own happiness together. May the peace of the Prince of Peace be in all your hearts this Christmas day and in the year ahead. Now that it will soon be possible for me to say 'this year', I can hardly believe that it is true, I almost want to put it off for another while to savour the flavour longer!

If I could let you see the scene outside at the moment, you would feel proper Christmassy. There was a heavy fall of snow last night and there is more in the sky to come. I am going to Moukden tomorrow, or so I plan. I hope it will not come down heavily enough to stop the bus. I always seem to strike 'weather' in my travels. I expect to be back before the end of the month, but Mary insisted today that I prepare the salaries and leave them for her, as she says, "If the bus does not break down, then we will have heavy snow – when you go away I never know when I will see you."!

We are having great times trying to get coal these days. The government has taken over the distribution and sale of coal here and we are to be on strict rations. We got several small bags of coal – about 100 lbs each – some time ago, and then even these dribbles stopped. We enquired and found out that the coal office had no ticket for us and refused to recognise us. The Catholic Mission, our church (we need a stove for Sunday services) the hospital, the Bible School and the O'Neills and selves, are all without. It looked at first as if our friend in charge of that office, who is an ardent anti-Britisher and who does not move with the times, had done us a dirty one in the eye. However, the blame was apportioned elsewhere. In the meanwhile all the requirements for Faku have been reported to central authorities and there is no provision for us. With much trotting back and forward and interviewing of authorities we have been led to hope we may get some soon. The forms have gone in today. We have enough to last till Christmas with careful use, and we are burning wood mostly in our dining-sitting room. We are not putting up stoves in our bedrooms, we did not have them for more than a fortnight last year and really have done without them. We are not too cold blooded fortunately.

It was our Japanese head of Special Police who helped again – the one who got us rice and flour. The last time the boy went to get some he got a whole bag, enough to do us into the new year, and cheaply too. The villages and smaller places have neither flour nor rice now and here it is only in small rations monthly.

When we were in the country I heard a good crack from a farmer – "You people in the towns can still eat rice and flour. You always get luxuries like that before us – but when the bombs come, you will get them served out first too." That is the grim form of humour that the Chinese like!

In Moukden
At Mamie Johnston's
26th November 1939

And as that wouldn't come up to Censorship Rules – suppose this <u>were</u> opened … <u>Sender</u> Miss M.C. Young, Fakumen, Manchuria. Via Canada.

[This reference to censorship rules probably refers to the fact that several of Marion's letters had been opened by the Irish Censor.]

I'm writing here in Mamie's – I'm in Moukden for the weekend, and I can't go to church this morning because I haven't a hat. Isn't it a tragedy? Mamie only has things that make me look like a pie on a plate. A rather undercooked one.

Later

I have 2 hats – one I wear in Faku when I take the notion, which isn't often, and the other I leave in Moukden to wear on my visits there when I feel I need one *[but which Marion had just discovered she had forgotten she had taken back to Faku]*. The Chinese women don't wear hats, except those who are trying to ape the West, so a lot of us don't either – even to church. The church I wanted to go to this morning was Anglican and they are strict on the subject, so I missed the service.

All of which is beside the subject and really is unimportant. What I was going to say is that it is cold. Someone says it was 51 degrees of frost this morning at 10 o'clock on his front steps, which I suppose is 9 degrees below zero and nasty and nippy for the end of November, considering as February is the coldest month.

I took a rickshaw boy this afternoon, a big toughie about 20 odd – he had on a padded gown and took that off soon to run in his one thin little cotton jacket which he opened from neck to waist and left himself bare from shoulders to the top of trousers. He was sweating a bit and when he stopped for a moment to let some traffic pass, the down on his face and neck froze into little white bristles in less than a minute, which may prove my former remark that it is cold these days.

It isn't so cold yet, though it may come, but if you spit the result hits the ground in a nice little ice ball. Yesterday, the train I travelled in had white whiskers all along the engine. Later, after Christmas, the icicles form all along the roof. I often think it would be a horrid sore bump you'd get if one fell off point down on your head!

Did I tell you before that there is a new bicycle rickshaw here in use in Moukden now. I believe it originated in Hong Kong and has reached here. There are not many in general use yet, but I've had a ride in one several times ... They travel fast on the broad tarmacadam roads in the new part of Moukden – there are no hills, so there is no strain. You have all the comfort of a rickshaw and the men can sit back and peddle comfortably.

Fakumen
14th December 1939

To Mother and Dad

This letter has been resealed with a gummed strip, showing that it was examined by the German authorities, which suggests that the ship carrying the letter from Canada might have fallen into enemy hands. It still reached Marion's parents, probably because Eire was a neutral country (and Marion had not made any derogatory comments about Hitler in it!). It appears that other letters Marion wrote in December may not have been so fortunate and did not reach Clones.

I'm watching an exam at the moment, invigilating I suppose is the proper word – graduation exam for Senior and Junior Primary. Tomorrow is graduation day and then the students will have to put their hearts into preparing for the Christmas entertainment. They are having 3 days of it – their own wish – and each night will probably have over 200, as many as the room will hold. 1st night, elders, deacons, leading Christians, hospital, Bible School and our own students. 2nd night, representatives from 5 other schools in the town and the West (government) Hospital. 3rd night, headmasters, teachers and government officials from Municipal Office, Special Police, ordinary police, Education Offices, Taxes Office, the O'Neills, Pastor and the Boys' School teachers to help look after all these important guests. Some show – what?! The 3rd night especially is a great opportunity particularly to do some preaching of Christianity in an unobtrusive way. We have a short service – 15 minutes to begin with and an explanation of Christmas and of Christ's birth from Dr O'Neill.

[Marion then lists the tableaux telling the Christmas story accompanied by a small choir singing carols.] Then the 'entertainment' starts. Kindergarten have an item and the Chinese <u>love</u> to see the Kindergarten turn out to do anything. The sight of 5 year olds dancing or singing seems to be something utterly new and delightful to them ...

We are hoping to have 2 guests for Christmas, Mamie and my new colleague, Mabel Dalgleish. It will be great fun having 4 of us in the house – I do hope Mamie will be able to come, she is very rushed, but she always feels Faku is a restful place and I pressed her to come if she can.

Marion and her new colleague, Mabel Dalgleish.

Fakumen
26th December 1939

To Mother and Dad

We had 3 very busy days over the School entertainment and had great crowds – 200, 300 each night. Then on Christmas afternoon the girls did it again – just the play 'Love' this time – for Mamie, and somehow the word leaked out and the hall was crowded again. Christmas Eve was Sunday and we had the Baptism Service then – 10 girls out of our graduation class were among the 26 baptised, and Kuan and P'eng, the two Boys' School teachers of whom I've spoken before, were also baptised.

Christmas afternoon, the 4 of us went for a walk and then after the play was over we had the O'Neills over for supper – including a Christmas pudding with meths burning round it – candles on the table, a small Christmas tree, all of us in our best frocks, very festive.

I hope all goes well with you. Much love to you each one, and thanks for your telegram and letters.

CHAPTER 7
1940

At MacNaughtans'
I Ching Lu
Moukden
7th January 1940

To Mother and Dad

Sunday afternoon – a white world outside and a bright fire inside, not to speak of a dish of very good sweets at my elbow. We have a service in an hour or two, so while Flora has a snooze I thought I'd write a line to you. We are having Retreat for these three days and start business meetings tomorrow, Monday. Devotions Committee has arranged a very fine programme for Retreat ... You get starved for beauty and order in the *[normal Chinese]* service, for no matter how good the Chinese are, they have to cope with a different congregation from ours at home – as Tom Barker said this morning, we got the "parlour type of worship, as opposed to the Cathedral type." I always plan my visits to Moukden for a weekend when I can, so that I can get to the Anglican service in the morning and our own missionary one in the afternoon.

Just before I left Faku, two of your missing letters came in, and a postcard, all of the middle of October. You told me more about the boys' exams and Mr Clarke's death.

A funny thing too – You sent me a great pile of the boys' home letters and inside <u>Jim's</u> was a printed notice from the *[Irish]* Censor that if letters were not short or <u>legible</u> they would be sent back. I don't blame him! For Jim in his letter said, 'I've just been looking back over what I wrote yesterday and I couldn't make out my own writing, I hope you'll be able to.' I think you shouldn't send too many letters together. If there is special news – or special crack! – send them on or tell me of the news in your own letters.

c/o MacNaughtans
I Ching Lu
Moukden
14th January 1940

To Dad and Mother

I think I'll begin by breaking the news to you – gently of course. Prepared? Get the smelling salts. You won't be seeing me till this time next year, 1941, I expect. You know that I landed here on Christmas Eve 1935 – so although I sailed in October, my furlough doesn't really date until the end of December. If Mary Hammill had been left in Faku, I would have put in a special request to get home before Christmas. Our mission is not sticky about a few months here or there – but the end of the year is the very busiest time and I could not hand over to Mabel Dalgleish, for she won't be out long then and things are complicated for a newcomer. Mabel is to be my new companion, I told you, didn't I? ...

You don't mind too much, do you? – I'll be looking forward to seeing spring at home. If it were not for the war I'd be making my plans more joyfully, who knows what 1940 will bring forth, either here or at home?

Another thing which complicates matters is this school business. I've never told you much about it, but I think you know we were having to prepare a Juridical Body i.e. Board of Trustees out here for our school property for the government. It was to be a body with whom the government could deal <u>here</u> and all the property was nominally to belong to them. We were insisting on getting a Christian clause put into the constitution, otherwise the government could run our schools as they liked, change staff and so on, and force us to produce funds for what was in reality a non-Christian school.

Some folk have been working on it for three years with the help of an English trained Japanese lawyer, but now it has been turned down – 'Education and religion must be separate in Manchukuo', so our schools must go. The govt. have made us a very fair offer – sell or close down. If we close, we are to have the 3 years necessary to graduate the students in our schools by not taking in new classes each year. I can't tell you what we have planned this Conference, as our representative has not gone up to Hsinking to see the government reps yet, but it is the end of our educational work. It is a sore blow, especially for those who have been interested in educational work for long years ...

I don't blame the government. Christianity is subversive to the totalitarian state. I often wonder that they are so patient with us. Christianity claims a higher loyalty than any state and from their point of view we are weak spots – and yet, if they only knew it, the Christians are their best citizens. They know it in a way – our Christian schools give the best education, and our hospitals the best medical work in the country, but I suppose that is a sore point, not one for rejoicing.

The next few years won't be easy for our schools, with fewer pupils, we have to find work for our teachers and the spirit of the schools can't be the same. It will be hard to hold our staff together. Who'd blame them for looking round for a job which is more secure? So for this reason, amongst others, I feel I should stay over the turn of the year.

After the meeting, Marion and Flora went to Peking for a week, mainly spent in shopping, and stayed at the Chinese Language College, as they had in previous years.

Peking
21st January 1940

To Mother and Dad

We've been having a grand time – if busy. We both had a lot of commissions for other people which have kept us busy, but we've managed to spend some money ourselves too. We are both buying presents to take home – and hope they will reach there. Flora will, or

Flora and Marion photographed in 1940, probably in Peking.

should be, home by August, but mine will have to lie by for another year.

One thing I'm very pleased with Mother, is a new costume! I have nothing to go home in, the Donegal tweed I got is no shape at all, although the material is still good. So I had been planning to get some home material here in Moylen & Powell's and have it made up by a very good tailor in Harbin ... *[Marion then found the material was very expensive, but later]* was in a very 'swank' place called 'Josephine's' and here was a very nice navy costume priced $150 – home wool. Tried it on and swithered, and immediately she ran it down to the old price (all home things have gone up about once again since the war broke out) and offered it to me for $85, about 35/-. It is a winter weight and she does not want to leave it over summer, so I landed on my feet in going in there! Now I'll feel ready to face anyone if I can pick up a hat before I go home – I haven't bought one since I came out ...

There are a big crowd of Britishers here *[in the College]* compared with Americans. Usually the American students are about 2/3 to the English 1/3, but the war in China has scared them off I think. I was speaking to one girl yesterday, whose boat was sunk in Chinese seas on the way out – you may have seen it in the paper – hit a mine laid for defence purposes in Hong Kong harbour. The boat, 400-500 aboard, sank in 20 minutes, it was daylight, so the loss of life was small, but imagine the suddenness of it – this lass was very fortunate in that all her heavy luggage was in another boat, but nothing was saved at all and it was all they could do to get into the boats.

Funny, uneven life this out here – before Christmas I was eating Chinese food, sleeping on a k'ang and only washing partially and seldom – here we have servants to do every turn, sail round in rickshaws, wear furs, see good pictures, lovely buildings, interesting people, buy pretty things, eat chocolate peppermint creams! and have two baths a day and a shower if I want it – positive luxury that only a few people could touch at home. It is well for only a week at a time or we'd be softened!

We plan to go back on Wednesday and I've some business to see about in Moukden before I go on to Faku. I hope there will be a very large pile of home letters. I feel starved this week or so.

I.P. Mission
Fakumen
2nd February 1940

To Mother and Dad

It is so long since I got down to writing you a decent letter that I should have plenty of news for this one. I hope the fact that I have not been getting your letters this last month does not mean that mine are not reaching you either. *[Marion's letters were in fact now taking six to eight weeks to reach Ireland, as opposed to three weeks at the beginning of 1939.]*

The results of our discussions *[about the Mission's proposals for their schools, which were mentioned in the letter of 14th January]* was that (1) We could not sell schools in the same compound as other Mission work *[these schools would have to close]* (2) We were willing to sell some – names given (3) Some staff might wish to take up Church work or might have other plans for the future, so we could not answer for them.

The schools to be sold are nearly all Boys' Middle Schools – the Girls' Schools are all in compounds with Ladies' Mission Houses or Bible Schools. *[Marion then listed the schools to be sold.]*

We can't realise yet what it is going to mean. It is like a death in the family and we haven't got over the shock yet. The govt. has received our reply favourably and made no trouble so far about not selling all.

I spent 2 days in Moukden on my way back, buying groceries and doing several bits of business anent schools and sich. Got back here on Saturday 27th and found Mary and Mabel in the midst of packing and unpacking respectively. Mary got away on Tuesday and we were all very sorry to see her go. The Chinese gave her a great send off too, hospital, evangelists, what school teachers were not away on holiday, some of the deaconesses came first to the house and then went to the bus to see her off. She was a great lass and a good colleague. She has lots of good sense and is very friendly, she'll get on well here.

I like Mabel too – they are two very different people. Mabel is 'artistic' – what a horrid word. I mean she likes colour – in clothes and in her belongings. Is tall and graceful. St Andrews graduate, was a Church Sister for 2 years. Is a few months older than myself (<u>another</u>

Junior Colleague older than me! very trying on my dignity!) strikes one as belonging to a nice family …

During her two days in Moukden as well, 'buying groceries and doing several bits of business anent schools and sich', *Marion had found time to meet up with Rymer Cayton the* 'dapper young man' *of the* 'holiday romance' *in Pei Tai Ho. We can judge that this is when their real romance began by the fact that Marion now began to keep all his letters.*

Mabel Dalgleish and children in Faku.

In the first of these on 28th January, Rymer, who had received a note from Marion, wrote:

'Situated as we are between the upper mill-stone of mission gossip and the lower of Chinese etiquette there is not much room for finesse. I'd like very much to see you whenever there is a chance so please let me know when you come again to Moukden. I know this seems a bit crude but otherwise as you know it seems it would take about ten years to get beyond a nodding acquaintance.'

The letter finished: 'Regards sounds a bit formal! I will be affectionately yours Rymer Cayton.'

Fakumen
16th February 1940

To Mother and Dad

Things are looking up – I've had quite a number of letters in the last few days, although they are all ones written in early December ...

Now that the Macs *[MacNaughtans]* have gone, another family has adopted me! Dr and Mrs Pedersen, she a Scot, he a Dane, and both dears. Their daughter Jennie is out too, an evangelist in the Scottish

Mission. They were the people who lived in the next house, on the same verandah as us at P.T.H. last year. They asked me to join them and go to Korea this year, which I accepted with pleasure – I'd like to see some place else now that I won't have Flora to play round with at P.T.H.

They have a small house of their own at a place near Sornai on the inner side of the Korean peninsula. The place where we holiday is pronounced Sor-nay (a long 'o' in sorry!) and looks lovely in photos. Later we revised our plans and 6 of us are taking a house just behind Pedersens, still to live and eat with the Ps, but to sleep there ... Sounds like good fun!

I plan to go on there straight after Synod, which is first week in July, and that will bring me back here about 12th August, in time to let the O'Neills off a bit earlier this year – they prefer to go late in the summer, but the weather was really getting cool in September when they went last year.

I told you about our coal ration 'ticket' didn't I! and how we have to send Kuei I 5 days each month to draw our share – wastes a lot of time standing round. Still we get it, which is the main thing. This month for some unknown reason they were not selling any here, but there was coal to be got in Tiehling. The man here made a ticket out for 5 tons for us and Kuei I went on Tuesday, only getting back today. It is to be divided up between Schools, Hospital and we 2.

You need not worry about our being short of flour either – the Head of Special Police, an official in the ordinary Police (both Japanese) and the Magistrate have sent us word that they will see we get flour when we need it. We have enough in the house for a month's use, so we feel in easy circumstances again.

I'm sending you some snaps – tell me if you get them safely. The one of me all dressed up is daft, but I send it to you for the sake of the gown. This is the lovely gown that Yin Yin, Miss Wang's *[Huei Chün's]* sister, had for her wedding day. I'm sure I told you about it. It is deep blue, with embroidery in all the colours of the rainbow. She is not as tall as I am, so it looks short on me. You can see the phoenix in the embroidery and the sweep of its tail feathers, the collar is embroidered too. Headmistress Wang is dressed in a suit she had borrowed from a friend for the Christmas play!

Photo of Marion in Yin Yin's wedding gown and Huei Chün in the suit borrowed for the Christmas Play.

At Ta Wa
22nd March 1940

To Dad and Mother

You don't know the above address, I bet. It is the first time I've been here myself. Got here yesterday – we are spending Easter weekend here and going on to T'ung Liao on Monday ...

Sat 23rd

We have just finished our morning meeting and are waiting now for the evening meal. We had a good crowd this morning, very attentive, though the children make rather a distraction when they raise their voice in protest, or the bigger ones yell, "Ma! I want to go outside," and Ma audibly replies, "Well, get out quickly and don't wet your trousers." I spoke this morning, but I don't flatter myself that the attention I got was all for my material – a good many of them had not seen a foreign woman before. Mamie only came here once or twice, as it is off the railway and you have to spend two days on the way from Faku here.

I went up to Tiehling on Wednesday and spent a pleasant afternoon with the Cummings – Wilfred the Second is a dear wee article, now 7 or 8 months old and very lively ... On Thursday morning I joined Miss Wang's *[Ssu Wen's]* train – she had gone to Moukden to her home for the night – and we travelled for 5 or 6 hours, with one change to a place called Pa Mien Chang – We got in after 2 and thought we would have to wait for a 4.30 bus, but as we drove up to the bus station we saw the 2.30 draw out of the station yard. The droskey man said to us, "Yell," and we all lifted up our voices and yelled with a will. The bus obligingly drew up and off we bumped for 14 or 15 miles along a road that would be marked 'Not motor road' on a road map at home.

294

We are living in a room across the kitchen from the evangelist and his family. There are just a boy and a girl, nice kids, 17 and 15 years old. The evangelist and family are old friends of ours, they used to be in Faku. Elder Hu was there helping Pastor Shang when he was too busy with both Boys' School and Church on his hands. They make the food for us – very good food too, but we enjoy the fun of making our own.

We have 2 meetings a day, the morning one in the church and the afternoon one in the home of a Christian. Yesterday, the one we were in could produce 50 of its own family members – so we had not far to go for a congregation. Of all that family there is only one a baptised Christian and a great many of them are opium smokers.

Tomorrow is Easter Sunday and we have 2 services on Sunday, and on Monday we move onto T'ung Liao for our Short Term Bible School.

Call to eat has come – dumplings stuffed with meat and vegetables, also fried onion and pork and fried flower leaves. The flower petals of a huge yellow flower they grow and the seeds of which they dry and eat. I've been told of the progress of the meal by Miss Wang, who is watching it.

T'ung Liao
27th March 1940

To Mother and Dad

Here is a new address for you too – this the first time I've been here. It is an interesting place, unlike anything I've seen before. It is north-west of Faku, I don't know whether it is on a map – it is north west of Ssu ping kai where we branch off the Moukden – Harbin line. All these northern towns are comparatively newly built and the streets are very wide, mostly beaten clay that lies ankle deep in dust all winter and spring. There always seems to be a wind here and even on the calmest day there is a terrific dust kicked up by passing carts and droskeys.

There are all sorts of folk here, Japanese in plenty of course, but also Mongolian whom I've never seen in any numbers before. The soldiery is Mongolian and they have a flatter face and squatter figure than most Chinese. The ordinary Mongolians about here mostly wear

Chinese clothes as far as I can see, but many wear their own hat – I've seen gay purple ones, round, like Mandarin hats with a button on top, and theirs are ornamented with gold edging and the button is gold.

One picturesque figure went past this morning on horseback, I hadn't time to take in anything more than a red-figured short coat with a fur collar and a red hat before he flashed past. I think he was just sitting on an embroidered mat strapped onto the horse.

There are a great many Koreans here, they follow the rivers to grow rice. So with myself added it is quite a cosmopolitan place!

The Church here is a very warm hearted group and there are many of the Christians who live at the other end of town 2 miles away, but they think nothing of coming over <u>every</u> morning before 7 o'clock for a prayer meeting, winter and summer. I don't mean they all come, but there are quite a number who come from a distance and their prayer meeting always has at least in the teens of people at it.

Thursday 28th

There is an attractive girl here of 7 years old with a game leg and has to use a crutch. I don't know what is wrong with it, she had been at Moukden Hospital and a Japanese one too and both *[hospitals]* say they can do nothing for her ... She is a nice wee thing and very bright, I must send her mother some books I have in Faku, children's books of stories about Jesus with a picture a page.

Fortunately, her people have money, but a crippled child in this country is a problem. A well-to-do family don't want a wife like that for their son and a poor family, who would take her because she would be 'cheap', wouldn't treat her well. Her folk seem nice people and very fond of the child, but I'm sure they often wonder about her future.

The other child who comes about here a lot is the pastor's son, 'Heaven's Grace'. They were married quite a while before he was born – they only have the one, hence the name. He is just 4 and an attractive child. I'm sorry I haven't my camera here to get some snaps. I have not been able to get a reel the proper size in Moukden and they are heavily dutiable posted from Peking.

T'ung Liao
31st March 1940

To Mother and Dad

This is Sunday afternoon, you are just about finished breakfast I expect
– and I'm about ready for my evening meal. We have just come back
from the Easter Service at the Christian graveyard and a lovely spring
day for our walk out to it. This is the week after Easter, but last Sunday
there was a special request from the Korean Christian Church in T'ung
Liao for the leaders of our Church to go to an ordination of elders on
Sunday afternoon, so they had to put this service off for a week.

I expect this service is taken over in part from the Chinese
practice of tidying up the graves in the spring and burning incense to
the forefathers, but it makes Easter a very real thing to our Chinese
Christians. The road was through one willow clump after another, the
catkins are well out and the farmers are preparing the ground in
preparation for the spring sowing.

There was a man practising a couple of young horses in a field
nearby and he was thoroughly enjoying himself. The Chinese and
Japanese are not good horsemen as a rule, but here they look part of
the horse, it must be the Mongolian influence. I've seen a number of
Mongolian soldiers riding through the streets here, and they look well,
very much at their ease. There are always men on horseback in the
streets here, shaggy beasts about the size of a well grown pony, they
have few as tall as our riding horses, unless they are crossed with a
Russian strain and then they are magnificent beasts.

Liao Yuan or Cheng Chia T'ung
7th Sunday

Morning Church is just over and we are thinking about preparing our
afternoon meal. We got here yesterday afternoon quite comfortably,
after our graduation service was over. A lot of the students came down
to see us off and we left with big bundles of fruit and sweet cakes to
add to our luggage – the usual present one gets here.

There are a couple of the station officials who are Christians there
and they got us our tickets, saw our luggage through and put us into
the train. I'd been talking to one of our pupils and she asked me if my
large bedding bundle was all bedding. I said, "No there are a lot of
books and leaflets in it." Just as I said that a nasty looking specimen of
the Secret Bobbies passed – one knows the look after short residence

here, and looked me up and down for a long time, listening into the group. Finally he moved off and consulted with another, Alexander [*policeman*] this time. I thought I was going to have the trouble of opening up my bundles – books are not approved of in this country unless thoroughly inspected – but evidently the presence of officialdom saved us at the time.

The two laddos were not content with that however. They got into the train and when we were unprotected, so to speak, bore down on me – but I was all prepared. Not only had I my residence certificate and the magistrate's permit to preach (he is nominally the biggest man in the district) but a friend in the police in Faku had made me out a special permit for this trip with dates and place given so that there was no mistake about it. They just looked at this array of documents and departed without any comment. They got off at the next station and I saw them get into a little motor-train that was going back to T'ung Liao and thought 'a blessing go with them' for they had their little trip for nothing.

I'm going to get a police permit every time after this. I never bothered about it before, but this works like magic. I've had manners from everyone the moment I produced it – 5 interviews in 7 days! We are well 'protected' in this country.

Liao Yuan
13th April

To Mother and Dad

This is not as interesting a place as T'ung Liao. It is getting nearer civilisation and is more respectable! Did I tell you I saw a camel loping off into the desert on our way here? Two men aboard the camel – a huge hairy beast, moving at speed. They come in trains to T'ung Liao with skins and things from Mongolia, but I hadn't the luck to see one. I was quite excited over the one solitary one – it looked so much part of the picture.

The country we were passing through at the time was sandy hillocks with little scrubby bushes and the only life visible were little conies and pheasants. Once in a while we saw flocks of sheep, but always near a village.

Fakumen
24th April 1940

To Mother and Dad

On her way back to Faku, Marion had stayed two nights with her Canadian missionary friends, the Johnsons, and their children. She had hoped to go back to Faku from Ssu ping kai on the same Saturday, but on arriving at Tiehling:

I went to the bus station, found there had already been 3 buses that day and there were about 60 odd people waiting for this one. They said they'd run 2 buses at once, but late – 4ish. I hear someone say that they wouldn't take luggage, so I went and saw the Japanese manager (him and me's very pally) to see if it was true. He said he'd slip me a ticket – out of my turn (nothing like being a furriner sometimes!) but with all these folk it would be impossible to take baggage. It was after 3 by this time and I didn't want to leave my bedding behind with no one responsible, so I thought 'nothing for it but to bother the Cummings over the weekend.

Went to the hospital – no Cummings. Wilfred was off to buy medicines and had taken Mary to Peking for the trip. So I legged it for the station to go on to Moukden. Got there 6ish, went to Mamie's – no Mamie, she was off on a lecture tour. Thought I'd go to Flora Fulton, but asked Mamie's woman first and she told me Fultons had 2 guests. By this time I felt like Noah's dove and contemplated sitting in the middle of the path howling, till a policeman would take me to a lockup for the night.

I went to Mrs Davidson's in the end – I don't like bothering her, because she is never free of guests and though she often invites me to go there, I don't feel as free to bother her as I would an Irish person! After that, the weekend couldn't have been nicer. Went over to East Moukden on Sunday morning – perfectly gorgeous warm spring day, and found all the doctors, their wives and children in their gardens, or wandering about chatting in the big general compound that belongs to the Scots. I saw a lot of folk I had not seen for some time and was delighted to see Jim Brown back from home. Emily has stayed on in Scotland to look after the 3 children, but is in very good health ...

Rachel *[Irwin]* invited me for lunch and Mrs Pedersen for tea as soon as I appeared, and after lunch Rachel and I lay in her lawn and sunbathed (properly clothed of course) for a couple of hours. The English Service at 5 was very fine, taken by Mr Finlay head of the Theo College, and then I went back with the Davidsons for supper. It was a lovely day – I think I enjoyed it all the better for being in the district for so long! Everyone was so kindly, all seemingly pleased to see me! – and the spring weather alone, with grass up, trees bursting into leaf, and yellow forsythia out in all the gardens was enough to want you to burst into song.

I got back here safely on Monday morning, found a large mail – so all was lovely in the garden.

One person who would have been particularly pleased to see Marion on her unexpected visit to Moukden was Rymer who had written to her on 16ᵗʰ April c/o the Johnsons at Ssu ping kai, in response to a letter from Marion, agreeing that his proposed trip to Tiehling or Fakumen to see Marion would need to be postponed, but was hoping she might be able to come to Moukden on business in May. It seems certain that Marion visited East Moukden to see Rymer (who lived there). This probably increased the gossip among the missionaries about their friendship. A letter from Rymer on 4ᵗʰ March said that he was 'Sorry to hear that you have been the subject of conversation on my behalf'.

Her meeting with Rymer might well have been another reason for Marion's high spirits.

Fakumen
29ᵗʰ April 1940

To Mother and Dad

I've been getting swelled head this week – correcting a Chinese manuscript for Dr O'Neill! He has been preparing a book for printing in connection with a Literature Committee of the Church on the Sacraments.

He did not get it finished in rough till last week, and he was due to leave Faku on Saturday morning. He got the headmistress, whose education is of high quality, to correct it – grammar and phrasing, and then it had to be recopied – 8,000 characters! On Thursday Huei Chün *[the headmistress]* was busy all day and only got a couple of hundred characters written, so at 8.30pm we started and worked until 3.45am, got to bed at 4 and Huei Chün was up at 6 to put the finishing touches. My job was to go over the two scripts comparing it character for character after she finished writing each page.

Dr O'Neill was all apologetic – he never dreamed it would take so long – but we were pleased to do it, there is nothing like having new experiences!

On the 20th April, in a letter to Dr O'Neill, the Catholic priest who lived in Faku, Edward Gilbert, sent Marion instructions on how to tend the vine that he had planted for her the previous October:

'I would have liked to go to Miss Young's place for the plant of vine, but I must wait a few days as I am too busy now. However, it is time to uncover it. First, remove the earth and the "shoukai"; after, have a little horse manure covered the foot of the plant and that will be enough for the moment.

If Miss Young intends to plant the small plants (cut off from her vine last fall) she may proceed this way:

Plant a vine every 6 inches

And keep only two eyes out of the soil:

Next fall all these small plants (thus bearing roots) will be unearthed and kept in a cool place during winter. Next spring, it may be planted in a permanent place –

I hope she will have success –

With best regards

Yours sincerely

Edward Gilbert

We are getting the garden put in this week – the new vine that the priest put in for us has been dug out of its winter pit and looks quite flourishing. We'll miss the home seeds this year, especially for vegetables. The flower seeds from Japan do all right, and produce quite a splash of colour in the garden, but I never think their vegs are up to ours. We can get pretty nearly all the same sorts as we get at home, except peas, beans and turnips – No, I think they are selling peas now. You can buy tinned ones and dried ones in Moukden. Their tomato seeds are all right the first year, but turn very bitter the second year, they go in more for a very sweet kind of tomato than we do.

You were asking about wells in a letter, Mother. They are very deep – by '<u>very</u>' generally 10 to 20 feet to the surface of the water, with the result that in winter the water almost feels warm when drawn up and in summer frosts a glass if you drink it at once. In summer, if we buy fizz to drink we put it in a basket down the well till it is icy cold – and my! It is good!

The paper, printed out here provides us with a few good laughs – especially in its headings, where they go in for terseness ... I give you an example. Here is a beauty I got this week.

'Dutch decline to sell bottoms to Great Britain.' Who wouldn't, I thought to myself? but when did England turn such a Shylock? And then, reading further on I found all she wanted was cargo space.

The next letter arrived in Ireland later than subsequent ones, with the envelope stamped 'SAVED FROM THE SEA'.

Fakumen
1ˢᵗ May 1940

To Dad and Mother

We have had a week of wind and dust – everything grates to the touch. I expect you could find a good deal of Faku dust on this paper if you looked hard. It is tiring weather, fuggy inside – you only dare open windows for short intervals, and horrid outside – ordinary wind can be tiring enough, but when it is hot and thick with dust it is temper-making.

To cheer us up this morning we had an unexpected visit from the magistrate. This is the 1ˢᵗ time he has been to our school, though we have asked him several times. He is an inaccessible being and it is rather like receiving a visit from royalty. He usually has an escort of soldiers. This time he just rode round in a droskey with one of the heads of department in the Education Office.

They came at a time when most schools would be in rather a mess, the place not cleaned up and the children not into class. He found them as neat as a new pin and all hard at work doing morning preparation. The place really looked very nice and from all he said he got a really good impression. One of his remarks was – "Religion gives a strength and a togetherness. Faith in God makes the teacher put her best into her work, gives her a personal interest in her pupils." "Our government schoolteachers are not up to your standards, because each is out for himself." All of which was very interesting, coming from a non-Christian. There are a great many like that – thoroughly approve in an academic way, but are afraid of getting involved themselves.

Fakumen
10th May 1940

To Mother and Dad

The newspapers make bad reading *[about the war in Europe]* these days. I'm longing to get into Moukden to hear what the wireless news is – our paper is a bit one sided. I have to go into Moukden on the 15th to get a tooth seen to. I'd hoped to have taken it home – it is the wisdom tooth – isn't it a pity to think what little wit I have is going? – but it is getting fractious so I'd better have Mr Horei's opinion upon it. He is an extremely fine Japanese dentist who has worked in Moukden for 20 or more years.

When I go, I'm to have the good wife of our worthy pastor and two of his youngest bratlings put in my charge. I'm to deliver the party all complete and correct, at the Moukden Hospital where she has a relative who can take charge. Mrs Tai has to get her eyes seen to and the baby is to have an overhaul. No. 2 bratling is a spoilt 'un and cannot leave his Ma! – I'd sort him if she'd let me! I wanted her to just leave him to yell – he'd soon stop it – he is 4 and is at the K.G. *[kindergarten]*. I'm sure he'd soon stop yelling, but she is afraid of him crying himself sick, so he has to tag along, and what she is going to do with one in her arms and another by the hand I don't know. Still, that's her worry and doubtless she loves 'em both. Mothers are like that.

c/o Mrs Fulton
Moukden West
21ˢᵗ May 1940

To Dad and Mother

Summer has started here with a vengeance. I'm fair dripping all over this letter! I think we feel it most the first few days, in a week or two this will seem cool. I've been staying with Austin and Flora for a week, getting teeth done. I only intended staying a long weekend when I came, but the dentist found more wrong than I'd expected and he believes in moving smoothly, so I won't get home in much under 10 days. In the meantime I'm enjoying the holiday, and though I know I should be in Faku working, there's nothing to be done about it! Poor F.W.S. is busy with my classes as well as his own work, that is all I'm sorry for.

We've had the wireless news this last few weeks and you can imagine how everyone here hung round the set. It has been more heartening these last few days, but German losses make heartbreak for other women too. It is terrible to think of the eagerness with which we hear of enemy losses.

I've had a great time here and have seen a lot of the Moukden folk. I was at Pedersens' for tea on Wednesday; and for lunch and tea on Friday. To Rachael's for tea and supper on Saturday; to Pedersens' for lunch on Sunday and to Stewarts' (Scottish Mission) for supper. Yesterday I had a dinner engagement and the flicks, and tomorrow I have a picnic and then dinner with the same person (no questions answered). Life has been full of interest these few days! I had 2 other dinner invitations I had to refuse as well as those I've mentioned.

The person about whom Marion was answering 'no questions' was, of course, Rymer. He had sent her the following letter from Mukden on 13ᵗʰ May.

'Your last and exciting message arrived today after I had posted my letter.

304

So you have decided to dare the eyes and talk of Mukden again. I am afraid that I am not sufficiently hard boiled to walk into the West Compound and ask if you can come out to play, unless it is really necessary. I suggest we meet at the Yamato Grill for tea as soon after four pm as you can. If you for any reason cannot turn up, I shall after 5pm make for Fultons' and braving all terrors enquire your where abouts.'

The letter was signed 'Love again, Rymer'. *It reflected the deepening romance between the two. Another was that Marion had ceased to correspond in April with her friend Jack, to whom her letter book shows she used to send letters twice a month. We know little about Jack apart from the fact that her parents disapproved of him.*

'Grandmother's Temple'
On the Faku Road
24th May 1940

To Dad and Mother

I'm sitting outside an inn on the way back to Faku while my charioteer has something to eat – I've a lunch with me that I'll eat further along the road. There are a great crowd of kids round me, so I'm not getting on very fast with the letter. A mother has just come along with a baby who has malaria and she wants some medicine from me. The baby has a string round her neck and Chinese coins on it, it has a tiny lock on it. I asked the woman what it meant. "She is locked safely." – I said I didn't understand so she said, "The baby won't be fed to the dogs." i.e. it won't die and the body be thrown out to the dogs.

There are seven wee boys perched on the side of the droskeys watching me with great interest – they say English is all squiggles, which I suppose it must look to them after their neat characters. I like the kids better than the school teacher who came along and asked impudent questions about my age and salary. He didn't get much change, so he has gone now.

There is a very brown faced wee article has his nose nearly pressed on the page and every second he says again in surprised tones, "I can't understand a bit of it." One of them has said, "Let's go for a bathe in the pond," but another – and it seems the general opinion,

"Let's wait till she goes." – they can bathe any day, I suppose, an English woman isn't a daily occurrence.

I had a lot of luggage, including a good many breakable *things [Marion had been shopping for Mrs O'Neill as well as herself]* and I decided a droskey was the most comfortable way of doing things. It has been a glorious day and perfect way for daundering along the road, and no feeling of hurry about it. I'm hoping in an hour or two I'll be seeing some letters from you – there should be some gathered inside a week's absence.

Fakumen
1st June 1940

To Mother and Dad

In a country like this where you are not often bothered with rainy days it is funny to have the same uncertain feeling that you have at home the day of a picnic or a S.S. *[Sunday School]* excursion. It is black and cloudy today – the day of the big Sports Meeting for all Faku schools. We have had a lot of belated spring rain this week – the crops badly needed it, so we can't grumble.

Later in the same day,

It has rained, the worst I've ever seen. We've had a really exciting day! The morning passed off all right – the K.G. *[kindergarten]* item was over and the infants all handed over to their mothers, thank goodness, before lunch. Mabel, Mrs O'Neill and I had a picnic lunch and we had a lovely hour on the hill behind the sports ground where we had a great view of all the county round about. Then it clouded up and just when our girls were well started their rhythmic drill, the rain came down. The judges called them to come in – they were going on happily in it! Then it just poured – you couldn't see 20 or 30 yards away, it was so thick! The students all got into the dormitories of the school in whose grounds the sports were held, but Miss Wang and I had to collect the hand organ and some of the things that the students had been using. We were soaked through in a minute and then had the pleasant feeling that it didn't matter, so we salvaged several mothers and babies who were stuck in a grass tent and couldn't run with the small children.

306

It was still coming down straight, so Mabel and I made for home – 1½ miles away, got out of our good clothes and shoes into things that didn't matter, and then went to the end of our road. The centre of the town is higher and it was all right, but our end was flooded and the road was one swirl of dirty water above my knees every place and almost to my waist in some places. Our girls are some of them 9-10ish and it would have been above their waists – and coming at the rate it was might well have swept them off their feet. The big girls formed chains and they got through all right, but Fish, Mabel, a Boys' School boy and I carried the wee ones in relays for about 300 yards or more – it took us the best part of an hour and it was beastly cold! The teachers were getting the stragglers rounded up and seeing that there were no possessions left at the *[sports]* ground, so they had no idea it was so dangerous at our end. Finally, two of the smallest seemed to be lost, but the head-mistress found one and I the other after a search.

There has been mighty little rain for 6 months so you can imagine the dirt there was in the water! I had a grand old scrub when I got back and feel fine now. I haven't had so much exercise for a long time.

It is very feeding *[frustrating?]* to think that there are probably letters of yours in town and can't get them for 2 days. There has been no bus all week with rain off and on, but that did not give the roads time to dry. There was one bus got through yesterday, Friday, that brought mails. The postman had already taken all the mail off this morning at 8'o'clock. I sent Kuei I round to inquire at P.O. and at 7 at night he has not turned up yet – held up on his round with the rain, I suppose. So I doubt if he'll reach here tonight, we are about the end of his beat. Tomorrow is a holiday, Sunday – so it looks as if we'd have no mail till Monday. Which means no papers for a full week – and things are happening horrible quickly in Europe these days. I couldn't do anything if I was at home I know, but I just dread the sight of a newspaper now – one feels so helpless.

Fakumen
5th June 1940

To Mother and Dad

No letters for a fortnight, but we have hopes now – English mail has arrived in Tientsin as announced in the paper and the Moukden mail comes about the same time, so any of these days there should be some along. 'Hope springs eternal'; on this late date my last from you was March 30th.

Dr O'Neill is out in the district again for 10 days, he must be having damp travelling. It suits very well that he prefers the heat to travel, because we don't clash and he can be at home to take my English classes when I am away. I'm enjoying the English now. I know a lot of the boys by name now and all their faces – 58 takes some knowing!

Members of Marion's Boy's School English class photographed with her in December 1940 just before she left Faku.

We are preparing for exams now and when I started to pick out the lessons we intended taking for the exam, after I'd mentioned two a voice pipes up, "This will be enough Miss Young, if we spend 3 weeks preparing these two, we might manage to pass." So I thought, 'We are getting on, a month ago they would not have dared to be so familiar.'

Fakumen
23rd June 1940

To Mother and Dad

I'd love to have had a letter from you this week – the news of France has left us all wondering where the pits of our stomachs are, and a letter would have been a touch with you all ...

What a week we've had with one thing and another – poor Mamie *[who had come on a week's visit]* has been left to herself, bed and books very much. Any free time I've had seems to have been taken up with the authorities. We've 114 on the role for our Short Term Bible School, but just round 100 come daily. Prayers are at 8.30 – I've a class of 13 on St John at 9-10. The next 2 periods I'm not in charge, but have to be round to keep order – then before noon I have a period for Devotions, which is not particularly easy to lead as there are a great many of the women who have not been at church and have no idea of what worship means. 12-2 is a break, lunch and rest – roasting hot just now, so we are ready for it. 2-3 I've a class on repetition, back for a cup of tea and off to English in the Boys' School, back at 5 and some time during the evening I have to put in at least 3 hours preparation for the next day.

In addition we've had (1) a visit from the French Canadian priest (2) from an Education Department official on the S.T.B.S. *[Short Term Bible School]* – religion here is under the above department – note! (3) a high official in the Special Police – polite but lengthy (4) the head of the Education Board – a real honour! – who gave our S.T.B.S. 15 minutes talk on (a) the need for faith in these days (b) if they did nothing but <u>listen</u> to our good teaching then they might as well not have come (c) "Sin is any want of conformity unto or transgression of the law of God" – that was his point, but of course he doesn't know his Catechism! He is a Buddhist by the way. (5) A visit to the French priest to see his grapes, his roses and have tea with him – he is going away this week and will not be back till after we go on holiday, so he made rather a point of inviting us and we couldn't refuse. He had a great tea for us, with strawberries and iced cakes.

Acheng *[Ashiho]*
2nd July 1940

To Mother and Dad

Marion was staying with Flora and helping her pack before she set off for Scotland on her furlough.

... I hope Flora will be posting this to you from Edinburgh in another 6 weeks or so. I felt it has more certainty of reaching you than ones posted here, unless as Flora says, she and it goes to see what the bottom of the Atlantic looks like. I told her I hope she wouldn't as it would be such a bore to think I was wasting all this time writing to you.

We finished off our Short Term Bible School last week, end of June, and about 80 took their exams – not a bad percentage of the 114 who enrolled. Then some business about our land deeds turned up and I had to dash into Moukden a day early to get them. These were with the Conference Secretary, but one was round with the Consul to be registered and I sallied round there in roasting heat at 2 o'clock to get it. "No deed," said the lad in charge of deeds and he and I went through all he said he had. *[Marion then returned to the Conference Secretary to see if she could find it there as all deeds had soon to be handed to the theological student who was taking them to Faku early the next morning. She discovered the deed had been sent separately to the Consulate, so went back there.]*

... – was there ever such a discomforted young man! He had put it in a despatch case where it shouldn't have been, and my mentioning the date recalled it. Did he apologise or did he apologise? I was very gracious and said even the British Consulate was permitted to slip up once in a while in weather like this.

I'd arranged to take the night express to Harbin and me young man *[Rymer]* was to get me a berth ticket a few days before – all the express trains are booked up at least 3 days ahead – I don't know where everyone is going to these days. We'd arranged dinner on the roof garden of a hotel here – pretty lanterns, a fountain and a Russian band dispensing music. Gloriously cool in the summer and here I only met a servant with a note to say, 'Here was the ticket and please he was in bed with a temperature,' too, too distressing. I hope he hasn't got anything serious, there is a lot of illness in Moukden – diphtheria, cholera and typhus. The hospital has been extra busy and 2 doctors off with typhus.

Letters written by Rymer (top) saying he will get the sleeper ticket from Moukden to Harbin, and by Colin Simpson (bottom), one of his colleagues, explaining that Rymer was ill and could not meet Marion and enclosing the ticket.

I want to tell you about my doings in Harbin – Flora moves in high circles and I move with her. The day we came away *[the letter was finished in Moukden where Marion was attending the Synod]* we were to go to the Consulate for dinner. We arrived early to get washed up and were asked if we would like a bath. Kimonos, bath towels, powder, all provided and we did revel in it after a hot day shopping. The Davises were very friendly interesting people not at all 'high hat'. There were two other guests, Allans from Edinburgh, Insurance people.

We had iced drinks on the verandah looking out to the sunset, served by a servant who moved as quietly as any Jeeves and spoke perfect English, not pidgin. The dinner was good and the conversation amusing ...

Then the 4 of them came down to the station to see us off and as the train moved out the Consul blew us kisses with gay abandon – and we did the same back! It was a huge station with Russians saying emotional farewells all over the place – men kissing men, kissing the ladies' hands, not once but often, so no one would notice a mere kiss thrown. The Chinese think it disgusting of course, but in Harbin I loved to see old poorly dressed men and women greet each other and the man would bend so gracefully over the old woman's hand and kiss it.

5 Sorai Beach
Kumipo
Korea
15th July 1940

To Dad and Mother

Here's a new address for you – but it is one you'll hardly ever have a chance of writing to – I'll be back to Faku (D.V.) before you see this. I'm sitting on a cool verandah in a house on the edge of a cliff overlooking the sea – there are islands in the bay below us, and the hills of the mainland rise up behind them, blue and wooded right to the skyline.

There are 6 of us in the house, 3 Irish – Mary Hamill, Joey McCausland and myself, one Scot, Jean Kent, one Dane-Scot, Jenny Pedersen, and one Dane, Dalgman Petersen. Jenny and I live here, but feed with her father and mother in a house nearby. We are having a great time to ourselves and with the 6 girls in the house we are as free as the wind to come and go as we like – dressing or undressing is not done behind closed doors either! and we take meals in our kimonos when we don't feel inclined to dress.

Just where I am sitting on the verandah I can see 10 square sailed junks slipping across the bay about 100 yards from the foot of our cliff. I wish I could send you a photo of them. They are interesting looking craft and not at all like our home fishing boats.

We are having fun about taking photos here. The Japanese police have sealed up our cameras and whenever we want a photo we have to trot down to the police office and fetch a policeman along to see a photo being taken. No scenery and nothing 20 metres above sea level is to be taken, so that is going to cramp our style.

A photograph that Marion was able to take in Korea.

There are so many snaps you want to take in passing, no one has time to run for a policeman to get a photo of an old Korean wifie passing with a bundle on her head or these boats passing in the bay!

Synod finished on Wednesday 10th and there were some locations fixed which are going to affect me. Mabel is to leave me, I'm sorry to say, and go to Acheng as companion to the girl that Flora has left alone. I'm very sorry to lose her, she was a good colleague to have. Joey McCausland is coming to me, she is to take over for my furlough and they want her to have a few months with me before taking over. I'm going to suggest that the change does not take place until October. We have a good language teacher and Mabel might as well have her as long as she can. If Joey has 3 months with me it should be plenty.

My furlough has been granted from when I can get a sailing in Jan. '41, so here's hoping.

On the 11th the 4 of us and Fish started off from Moukden and had a not uneventful journey down here. We had customs on the Korean border, which are rather a trial for you never know what is dutiable and they have no list – so it means they make hay of your case and you can say nothing or all you have might have duty charged on it!

We got to a junction in Korea at 4.30am, pouring rain and we and our luggage were decanted into a pitch black platform. Fish was very puzzled at the fact that no matter how hard you spoke Chinese to the porters, they didn't understand a word! We got our tickets after some trouble and got into the little narrow-gauge train that was waiting there, and then waited 2 hours past the railway guide time before it started off on its leisurely way.

Fortunately, at this point an American woman, Mrs Millar, a Korean missionary, joined us, and she took us under her wing or I don't know when we'd have got here. We had 5 hours on that train and then got to a place where we had to take a bus. Pelting rain, no bus, and the clay roads like mud seas. If we hadn't had Mrs Millar we might have stayed put on that platform for our holidays. No one understood Chinese and we'd have been completely at sea as to where to go next. Mrs M. sallied off to the bus station and chartered a whole 25 seater bus for us and our luggage! And landed us on our own doorstep, decent woman, before she left us.

Envelope from a letter sent by Marion from Korea, which has been opened by the Irish censor.

5 Sorai Beach
Kumipo
Korea
21st July 1940

To Dad and Mother

We are just back from church on a wet Sunday morning and it reminds me of August in Donegal – 1924 wasn't it?! We've had 5 days rain out of the 8 since we came down, but we have not been dull. Even if it rains you can always put on your bathing togs and go for a walk – or a bathe. With 6 of us in the house too, we can always get up games when we get tired reading and sleeping.

Marion then refers to her Sunday School class in Sorai Beach: ... We've been enjoying it – American S.S. isn't run on the same lines as ours and one thing I like about it is that the children take more part in the service. They read, lift collection, one plays the organ and there was a band today of 3 German girls with wooden flutes, a pipe, 3 bugle affairs, 2 violins, the latter played by 2 very small girls. It was very tuneful and those performing evidently enjoyed it as much as the audience.

Our Sunday evening service and a Thursday P.M. *[prayer meeting]* are held on the point of a cliff where the hill conveniently slopes slowly down and then broadens out a little on a platform before becoming cliff proper. The congregation sits on steps cut out of the hill in the shape of a section of an amphitheatre, and the speaker is slightly below them, but at an easy angle for speaking.

The evening services have been on dry days this week as it happened, and it was glorious sitting there looking out over the sea as the sun set and the moon rose. We always think of you folks at home when we are especially enjoying the beauty and quiet here and wondering how you are all are and how things are going with England. These few days are anxious days, we wish now we were near a wireless to know how things really are.

This place is built on a promontory, a narrow strip of land on both sides, and where our house is high on the hill we can see sea on both sides. Both bays are beautiful, for the hills of the mainland run right out almost enclosing the bay and there are about 6 or 8 quite large islands in sight, all with high hills on them; Mysterious Island, Star Fish, Clam Island, Deep Blue, Sarcophagus Island ... these are some of the names I've heard.

Although there had been some suggestion in his letters that Rymer also might go to Korea at the same time, this did not happen, partly because it would not have been considered proper for Rymer, as a single man, to take a house there, and partly because he had to take his holidays later than Marion. He did write to Marion at least twice when she was in Korea. He also wrote several times when he was on holiday in Pei Tai Ho in August and September. This was at the same time as the O'Neills, with whom he stayed for part of the holiday, and it is clear from his letters that they were aware of the situation between Marion and Rymer. In fact Rymer said it was like staying with the 'in-laws'.

Fakumen
31ˢᵗ August 1940

To Dad

Marion was sending birthday greetings to her father:

It isn't fair that we 'ministers' should never have a feeling of weekend freedom that other folk have! Before Mamie left, when I was still at Chinese *[language study]*, Friday night had a grand feeling – Saturday was the day that you could do all the things that had accumulated during the week, things that with a free conscience you couldn't cut your study to do. Now Saturday is the busiest day of the week. Friday night, Beginners S.S. Training Class, Saturday morning, Beginners Sunday School Training Class, 10.30, Evangelists' weekly meeting to discuss the women's work. This week or two I also have an English Class in the morning, afternoon preparation for S.S. Service – a proper service too ... The weekly P.M. *[Prayer Meeting]* 6 p.m. Saturday is led by all of us in turn, teachers, nurses, evangelists all alike, there is no division of the Church work and secular amongst Christians in this country. Sunday is like: home ... Sunday School, morning service and evening Bible Class. Then at 8 or so, we foreigners have an English Service.

Monday morning begins with a P.M. at 6.30 in the compound for the women workers in this compound, about 10 or 12 of us. Then at 8 I have a Scripture Class. And so the rest of the week begins. I'm feeling as if I'd got all caught up in a routine of classes and general business and have done little evangelistic work.

Just this week I said to Mabel, "Oh dear, Bible Classes and Training Classes take so much time in preparation and that's about all I seem to do in the way of religious teaching – what's to show for it?" To which she solemnly replied, "A Training Class is one of the atoms in the link of the chain of teaching that is helping build up the Manchurian Church." Which made me feel better, for the moment!

I'm scribbling this between Sunday School and Church, and judging by the silence in the compound the school has gone off to Church so I should be gone too.

[Later] Today's service was taken by a woman – and very well too. She is a language teacher and my writer. She was an evangelist, but married a school teacher and since then has done some teaching

herself to help educate the children. She speaks well, and always vividly.

Fakumen
2nd September 1940

To Dad and Mother

Being a missionary is sometimes very like being in a manse at home, the folk have the same kindly way of bringing in presents. A girl came in yesterday on her way back to theological college from her home in a village. Her father is the leading deacon there, a friendly good soul and he never comes into Faku on business without coming in to see me. Just like a big inarticulate farmer at home – I have to go on thinking hard for questions to ask him, or the conversation lags sadly. This lass arrived with a big basket of grapes, pears and apples – what pears! big, yellow and sweet – from her father as a present to the 'Lady Teacher'.

Then this morning the O'Neills' cook's wife came over with two fresh fish as a present. "The ladies were so good to her children, always giving them presents – that she wanted to make us a small offering. It wasn't worth anything but she hoped we would eat it." Not an hour later another huge fish arrived – a present from the headmaster. His wife had been in town and found a few fresh fish had come in – (we don't often get fresh fish here, the Japanese get a little sometimes, but we are too far from the railroad and there are no rivers near here.) So she hoped we could eat this. Sometimes people drop in with a few eggs tied up in a hanky, "I know the lady teacher likes fresh eggs, these were laid yesterday," or Chinese cakes. The cook's children like to see cakes arrive – they know they will be called upon to help put them away.

You'll think I don't stay long in Faku! I'm planning a weekend in Peking 7th-10th (a missionary weekend is Thursday to Wednesday, but it is business calls first and pleasure follows rapidly behind. I've got to go this week, because September and October are going to be busy months and if I don't go at once I wouldn't have the chance again.

September is a lovely month in Peking – I wish I could persuade myself it was my duty to stay longer! but I've too many classes here. I'll be cutting 3 as it is and have to cram 4 more into this week. I'll probably go down *[to Peking]* with the new Mrs Barker, she wants chair cover and curtains, material cannot be bought up here which is worth using. *[Tom Barker, who was a widower, had recently married Annie Allan, a Scottish missionary doctor.]*

Fakumen
14th September 1940

To Dad and Mother

We are watching the news these days and feeling very sick at heart. The next 3 weeks are going to try out England's strength and one wonders all the time where Ireland comes in in Germany's plans. All we can do is to remember you hourly before the Father and to try to forget our own fears and trust you all to a love and care infinitely greater than ours. Poor London – it is hard to think how much that is old and lovely is being destroyed, not to speak of all the families being broken up.

I've been longing for letters this week, with all this bad news even a 6 weeks old letter would seem a warm touch with you! The last I had were of the 9th July and I got them nearly a month ago. I hope you have not had a long blank without letters from me ...

I've had a trip to Peking since I wrote to you last – a most interesting one and a full one. Left here on Friday 6th. Called in on Wilfred Cumming in Tiehling and found he was completely out of chloroform and could take on no bad midder *[midwifery]* cases in the country – chloroform can't be bought in Manchuria for love or money just now. I think most of our hospitals use a spinal injection for ops. I don't know much about it, though. So I promised to get him some *[chloroform]*, then on to Moukden where I got some more commissions in – in all I had things to buy for 9 people, not including myself, before I go off! I didn't promise to get them all, but I did get the important things.

I had 2 young Americans put in my charge, who could speak no Chinese and who were going to Peking for the first time. They were business people, out only a few months. I travelled 1st class for the first time in my life. 2nd was crowded out, I couldn't get a berth and as they were travelling 1st I thought I might as well splash a few shillings more and be comfortable. They were an amusing pair to travel with, full of comments on everything they saw, and the girl especially had plenty of quick come-backs ...

I had Saturday afternoon to Tuesday in Peking and travelled fast and hard all the time. Peking in September is glorious, warm days and cool evenings, flowers still lovely and the fruit trees – apple, pomegranate, pears, still covered with fruit. I had 2 lunch and 3 dinner 'dates', a picture and some sightseeing – as well as my shopping!

Marion and Rymer in the Forbidden City, in Peking.

One night me and a young man *[Rymer]* went to the flicks and then on for dinner at the roof garden of the Grand Hotel de Peking – a band, a table at a corner where we could look down on the lights of Peking, the sunset just dying out behind the Western Hills, a moon coming up – who could ask for more!

I got my business done – the job that took me there – and now since I got back I've been busy trying to catch up on arrears of work. I

319

had 9 business letters to answer, got the last of them off today – I often wish I had a typewriter. Perhaps all being well I'll get one when I get home.

People continue to encourage me about the possibilities of furlough. Tom Barker says he thinks the rule about no women and children crossing the Atlantic only applies to the Canadian wives who wanted to follow their husbands to England. Flora was 'advised' not to go home – she wasn't forbidden, so perhaps there is a hope after all. So in the meantime I'm still not setting my heart on it, but I'll go on preparing in the chance of a dream coming true.

The trip to Peking was indeed an 'interesting one' as Marion and Rymer had arranged to meet there. It was then they decided to become engaged, although not communicating this information to anyone. In a letter of 15th September, Rymer wrote to Marion that he had been on the receiving end of several pointed enquiries about this visit to Peking by those who knew Marion was also there:

'... However I'm glad you are not anxious for an official announcement yet. I suppose I ought to stir up courage to write to your august and reverend father before we took so grave a step. Peking was a happy time, but it didn't contain any arm chair conferences did it? Gradually one will become less speechless, I suppose. I am much touched by your exalted opinion of your humble servant and should hate to disillusion you, the feeling is reciprocated.'

Fakumen
16th September 1940

To Frank B.A.

Marion opened her letter by congratulating Frank on being awarded his recent university degree and then commenting on the ages of her brothers:

... Isn't it awful the way you are all growing up when I am not at home. Here I'll be, an old woman of almost 30 when I get back to you, and the most trying part of it is I don't feel like 30 and can't remember to act like it.

Something nearer 22-3ish is my permanent mark and the Chinese still call me the 'wee girl' behind my back, because when an official asked who was in charge of the women's work here a couple of years ago and heard it was me, he said, "What! that wee girl! I thought she was here as handmaid to the lady missionary." So 'wee girl' I am still to the people I work amongst, it is very trying.

Today is the 8th Moon Feast. It is the biggest autumn festival the Chinese have. There is great feasting today and a holiday for everyone. Tonight they eat Moon Cakes – sweet stuffed cakes and made in the shape of the moon – and let off crackers in the evening when the moon comes up. It is full tonight and should be glorious in about an hour. Mabel and I will go out for a walk, nearly everyone stays outside to see it rise – it is like the harvest moon at home, and I suppose this is a sort of harvest festival.

You'll see in my home letter this week that I was in Peking for a visit last weekend. It is about the length of England away from us – takes a day and night to reach it from Faku, so we don't often go. I just love it, it has something of the same feeling to me that Edinburgh has. A capital city, with dignity and history. Every time I go there I like it better, I just sat in my rickshaw and hugged myself as I was pulled along the wide road running between the Forbidden City and the Legation Quarters. It passed under great arches, painted and carved in

gold and red, blue, black and green – beautifully proportioned and so gay in the September sunshine.

One of the tinted photographs which Marion refers to in her letter.

I've bought a lot of pictures this time, photos enlarged and painted by a woman I know there, which gives you an idea of the loveliness of Peking – I'm longing to get them home to show them to you all. The longer I am in this country the more I fall in love with it. I'd break my heart if I thought I couldn't get home to see Ireland again, but my work is here and the fascination of the place holds you – so that you have a home in two countries, a sad state to be in!

I've eaten too much today, I had a Chinese feast and am feeling positively comatose – must stop. See home letters for my news.

Fakumen
19th September 1940

To Mother and Dad

Mabel and I had a glorious walk on Monday, the day of the 8th Moon Feast ... *[We]* walked about 15 miles that day – the harvest is just ready for cutting, the brick red of the big millet, golden brown of barley, small millet and wheat, emerald green of winter cabbage and dark green of the pines on the hillsides was a picture I won't forget. Warm sunshine, soft blue hill and just enough breeze to make walking a pure joy.

Mabel goes in a week's time and she wanted to see the Snake Mountain before she left Faku. It is the one rugged hill near us – all the rest are soft rounded tops – more like the Featherbed *[one of the Dublin Mountains]* than anything else I know in Ireland. We took some snaps, if they come out you should get them in another couple of weeks.

Fakumen
10th October 1940

To Dad and Mother

Today we are celebrating Dr O'Neill's 70th birthday, Chinese fashion. He had it when he was in P.T.H. as a matter of fact, but like the King, he is permitted to change the date!

A 70th birthday is a very big day in a Chinese family, so we, two schools, hospital, evangelists and pastor, are to be his family and act the thing out. There are 23 of us altogether. Sons and daughter, granddaughters and number of great granddaughters.

We are all wearing Chinese clothes. Joey and I are going as twins

– his granddaughters. Dressed in deep red gowns. We are having our photo taken surrounding our 'head of the home' in about an hour's time and then this evening are to have a meeting.

Dr O'Neill's '70ᵗʰ birthday celebrations'. Frederick and Annie O'Neill sit in the centre under the banner. Pastors Shang and T'ai is to the right of Fredrick. Huei Chün stands behind Annie next to Ssu Wen. Marion is fifth and Joey McCausland seventh from the left. All those in photograph, apart from the missionaries and Mr Li, the Korean, the teacher of Japanese, second from the right, were Chinese, a reminder that they were the majority of those involved with the work of the Christian institutions in Faku were Chinese.

Fakumen
10ᵗʰ October 1940

To Mother and Dad

I wrote you a scribble this morning, which I hope will fill in the gap till I get this off to you. I've had a busy day and won't finish this tonight. I told you all was set for Dr O'Neill's birthday celebrations this morning, but within an hour of our starting someone suddenly remembered that this was the day of the celebrating of the Chinese Republic's foundation and that a meeting that day would look funny to some folk, so in a great rush everything had to be called off until tomorrow.

Then I had an hour with a policeman, we see a lot of them these days – I fancy they are interested to know our reaction to the treaty between Germany, Italy and Japan. So far no repercussions here, so I hope you have not been worrying about it.

I had an exhausting two hours trying to soothe down someone in the most terrific rage, *[the worst]* hysterics I've ever seen. One of our best Christians, a sane fine girl, but the old heathendom is not far below the surface, and oh dear! It all spewed out. Such language I never hope to hear again from a member of the Church. She was sorely injured by another person – she had right on her side, but if she had gone to have it out with the other person, as she wanted to, it would have led to a terrific row in the Church. The pastor and I were there to talk her into going on 'eating bitterness' as the Chinese say, and in the end she promised to take no revenge and to let things pass. It was a real victory for her, but the three of us were pretty tired out when it was all over.

Then I had an interview with both our servants, who had resigned, just as a tit bit to finish off the day. Ticked off the cook firmly – and he bowed and thanked me for having "wasted my heart in instructing him" and praised up the boy who is having to suffer a lot from the other gent without there being any real row. I've told the cook he is on appro till the end of the year and the boy has promised to stay till then and after that we'll see how things go.

Now having poured out my woes to you, it is time I went and entertained Joey who has not seen much of my illustrious presence since she came.

22nd   The letter continued in pencil:

This is terrible! I've never let so long go before without writing to you – but the last 10 days have been hectic. I am writing this in the train, so please excuse the scribble.

I have not been in Faku for nearly a week so I hope when I get back there, there will be some mail from you.

You will be worried about us out here just now, I'm afraid – but I hope the telegram I hope to send tomorrow will reassure you. Things are not too secure, but no one feels there is any urgent necessity to leave the country. The Americans are leaving, but they get the scare up easily.

I won't tell you much about what we have been doing this last week. I want to get this letter off to you tomorrow and when I get to Faku I will write to you in more detail.

Mary Cumming, Tiehling, is an American and she is supposed to leave, still being under the protection of the US consul. She has 2 small children, 1½ *[years]* and 2 months old, so I have offered to see her home to Pennsylvania before I go home. The men are not leaving. It is not much out of the way and I can see Uncle Charlie without too much trouble, I think, from Mary's home. *[Her father's brother lived in Corning, New York State.]*

We sail about 20th January from Japan and should be in Pennsylvania about 15th February roughly, so I'll hope to be home in early March, God willing. It is great to have some plans made, at least. I've been so undecided about things these last 2 months and did not know where to begin planning.

Fakumen
24th October 1940

To Dad and Mother

Marion wrote about the details of her plans to return home via the United States: ... It isn't so long now – I can hardly believe it!

The Scots Mission Committee advise their missionaries not to go home and small children are forbidden a crossing, but thank goodness R.H. *[Boyd, Irish Foreign Mission Convenor]* has not sent us any orders – long may his shadow last.

I forget what I told you in my last letter. The American women and children are all evacuating, a few of ours are going because their husband's furlough is due in the next year, but otherwise the British stand where they stood. I'm half sorry to be leaving at a time like this – I'd like to see it out with my colleagues if there is trouble coming.

Another thing you may have seen in the paper is that we have the bubonic plague in Manchuria, but the authorities are doing wonders and it is not spreading. It got to Hsinking a month ago and does not seem to have spread anywhere since then.

I was in Hsinking this week getting my visa for leaving the country and had to get a jab before I went and a certificate to say I had it. I could not get my ticket without it and at Hsinking I could not get off or onto the platform without producing it. Everyone in Hsinking wears masks over nose and mouth – it was funny to see nothing but 2 eyes visible wherever you looked,

In 1911 the plague wiped out 60,000 or so, including Dr Jackson *[an Irish Presbyterian medical missionary]* who was just out 6 months. So far, in Hsinking only 40 deaths are reported and many who were ill have recovered. As soon as it reaches an area that part is all cordoned off with soldiers, the case is isolated and everyone in that area has to stay put till the fear of infection is over. It must be awful for the folk cooped up, but it has proved most effective.

Fakumen
1ˢᵗ November 1940

To Dad and Mother

Things look like hotting up here, now that Japanese citizens are being evacuated from England, but no one expects anything to happen immediately – and we hope nothing will. The thought of having to leave the Church here – strong though it is – fills us with dismay. But God over rules all and it may be for the strengthening of his people here if they have to stand alone.

It is a difficult time for our leaders and we do not want to suggest to our local leaders yet that we may have to leave – they have enough to think about without that, till it comes nearer the time.

I was out in a home visiting yesterday where there is a woman I have often longed to draw. She is a broad faced, 'decent' kindly soul with bright twinkling eyes and always interested. She is a good Christian and her daughters-in-law are a good advertisement for her. In China the mother-in-law is usually past a joke. She is a real autocrat in her home – Hitler could take lessons from most of the old ladies here. One day Mrs O'Neill was in when Mrs Ai was away visiting relatives, and both the daughters-in-law spoke in the same strain, "I wish she were back. The house is empty without her. There is no interest in working when she isn't round to talk to us. There is always something doing when she is about." She is one of the women I hate leaving – now that it is near furlough, I'm half sorry to go! Whole sorry sometimes – the Church here is a good place to work in. There is many a problem, but a lot of joy in it too.

Fakumen
18ᵗʰ November 1940

326

To Dad and Mother

In your letter you told me young Jim had gone for an interview for the R.A.F. Uncle told me he had been accepted as a flight mechanic. It is hard to imagine 'wee Jim' in the Air Force, but I am sure it is hard for the boys to stay out of it when our country is up against it. War is so horrible, but Nazidom is worse, it is getting harder and harder for the younger men to stay out here at their jobs while other men do their fighting for them. It is hard to see one's way – Pacifism or War? – these days, there are few of us are out and out Christians when it comes to that question.

I got a letter from Uncle Charlie this week. A very warm and kindly invitation to the U.S. He says there are still boats to England, but not to Ireland, so I may be landed in Liverpool or some other port. If I am, it may be a nuisance getting across – I was thinking I might get Dennis O'Neill's [one of the O'Neills' sons] address before I leave, he is in a high position in the Ministry of Transport and might help if it is difficult getting a pass.

Mamie is holding a week's meetings on the Religious Education of the Young, and is entertaining us during her spare time – She is a most amusing talker. She was telling us about plague prevention measures in Hsinking. A prize was offered for the greatest number of fleas caught by any one person in a set time. One woman caught 2,300 and had a special paragraph in the paper all about her feat. Another caught 500 in one night and got a certificate to hang on her wall.

You can only get your rations tickets if you produce a rat and, as one might expect from the Chinese, a flourishing business has now been created. They are breeding rats and one is known to have been sold for as much as $15 (5/-). They will be bringing them in from other places to sell when the stock gets really low I'm sure! What a country!

I've had a great time trying to get my forms filled up for the U.S. visa – you might as well as be an ex-convict as a missionary when it comes to getting into God's Own Country. I have not even been given a form to fill up yet, but I have been asked (1) for a letter from our Missionary Secretary that I am still in Active Mission Service. (2) to produce evidence, i.e. a letter that I have relatives in America. (3) To have at least $100 gold in my hand when I land there. Then I believe there is a form with most searching questions to fill up and even my finger prints are taken! Again, wot a country! However if they let me go through it to go home, that's all I want.

Fakumen
28th November 1940

To Dad and Mother

It is just about bed time, but I thought I'd start this at least before I crawl off to my downy couch. Joey is off to the country, so I'm alone in my glory. This is her first real country trip and it is the roughest part of our district, so I wonder how she will stand up to it. She has to eat Chinese food, and pretty simple fare at that, for 10 days. So it should be a fair test.

The travelling is easier than when I started it – part of the journey can be done by bus, which in fact I regret. It was the one part of our district in which I felt really like a pioneer missionary – now it is getting too civilised! Still there are lice and you live in the same room as the evangelist – so perhaps Joey won't feel things too too easy yet.

It was on that trip that I first met Finn McCoul – do you remember telling you about him? and how he told the wife how to cook our meals for the day, starting before daylight to go over the forthcoming menu. It was also he who almost made me blush once! I, having decided to slip outside in the early dawn on my lawful occasions, he heard me and started shouting, "Teacher Young, teacher Young where are you are going to? It's too cold and dark. Don't be going outside! Here's the wee pot, wait till I reach it to you!" Never a word from me – but I fairly legged it for the yard, scared still he might chase me with it in his hand. And as I went I could hear smothered snorts from Mamie and Miss Wang. I'm sure he thought me a queer stiff foreigner, much too modest for this job.

I warned Joey she would have to dispense with washing, except for face and hands while there – the old gent is usually round the room all the time and curiously enough, in spite of the above incident would be greatly shocked if Joey showed off bare shoulders and arms.

[Marion and Mamie (who was visiting for a week to take meetings) were invited to a meal by the teachers at the Boys' School] ... and what a feast. It was scrummy and the crack was good.

We sat at that table, eating the greater part of the time for 2 hours!! There were 18 dishes brought on one by one, several soups and rice. I feel bloated.

Yesterday I had a holiday from eating, but today again I was asked to a Chinese meal in the Hospital. It was in honour of our headmistress's mother, who is paying a visit here, so I could not do other than go. I'm going to fast tomorrow I think. It is worse than Christmas week at home.

At Pai Chia Kon
6th December 1940

To Dad and Mother

I've got out to the country at last and am sitting on a k'ang at the moment, thinking long – no, not for you – for my breakfast. It is now 10 o'clock and our last meal was at 4 o'clock yesterday afternoon. They must be making something special for us!

This is an interesting wee Church. It has only been in existence for 6 years and some of the most warm-hearted deacons have joined the Church within the past 2 years. They take the Church as the centre of their life and any spare time they have they drop in for a 'crack'.

Later

At that point I went for a large breakfast of fried potatoes, onions, flat heavy fried cakes and soup made of cabbage and vermicelli. Like it? It's wonderful what one can eat out here.

There has been a lot of snow, the winter 'founding' passed 3 weeks ago. The Chinese have a date for all changes in the weather and they seem to hit it every time. The day we came, the country was glorious, covered with snow. Miss Man *[the graduate of the Moukden Theological College, who was travelling with Marion in place of Miss Wang]*, a man evangelist who was going to another village, and myself were in a droskey and we sang hymns most of the way – to the scandalisation of any of the folk we passed. They probably thought we were mourning as we came towards them! The relations mourn ahead going to a funeral – but we didn't look much like a funeral.

There's an old wifie in the room at the moment who has us in fits. She is sure I am a Korean and keeps on asking me about Korean customs. Don't we eat dogs? Don't we carry babies on our backs? Don't we carry the water pots on our heads? She is certain I'm not a girl – my eyebrows are very thick, my hands are strong like a man's. She asked me a few things and then turned round to announce triumphantly that I understood her – that she thought Korean was different from Chinese – this after Miss Man had told her half a dozen times that I was English. She has seen Japanese and Koreans – these are the only foreigners she knows.

I'm going to post this in the little local P.O. *[Post Office]*. A deacon is in charge of it and he sells sweeties and biscuits, school books, washing soda, oranges and nuts, just like any wee village shop at home. We had our evening meal in the shop yesterday and were of great interest to all the customers.

The envelope from the letter posted by Marion in Pai Chia Kon. It has been refranked when passing through Moukden.

Fakumen
18th December 1940

To Dad and Mother

I'm glad to have had a week in the district to finish up – the work there is always so full of interest and seems so worthwhile. Their faith sometimes seems a bit crude and their conduct far from perfect, but there is a spark there and we have an ideal to aim for, very different from the old non-Christian days. I'll enjoy telling you about these country Churches when I get home, Dad – they are like a bit out of Paul's Epistles sometimes. Something we see little of at home.

It had been snowing very lightly every day for a week – just an hour or so daily, but every place looks lovely. This morning early, the compound was like fairy land. I was out just as the sun was getting up. The moon was still bright in the west and the east beginning to glow, the hills were steel blue and the sky soft green blue, the trees all heavy with hoar frost – it was like another world. Then when the sun got up a bit, the snow was soft pink with silver sparkles – I longed to have some way of preserving it for you to see.

What has made me especially busy was that I took a week off when I shouldn't, and went to Tiehling on a visit to meet Rymer. The time for parting is horribly near and we decided we <u>must</u> have a few days before Christmas. The O'Neills aided and abetted me, so I didn't feel too conscious stricken!

We had a glorious time – the Tiehling hills are laid out as a big park by the Japanese, and there were several groups out skiing Saturday and Sunday. Rymer and I went off through snowy paths, with fir trees covered with snow on every side, for about three or four hours on Saturday – and had another long walk on Sunday afternoon. The weather was perfect for walking, sunny and no wind.

There was another guest there, a Mr Littlewood, he came unexpectedly. Tiehling has no resident foreign minister and he is charge from a place called Kai yuan. He, poor man, had a bad weekend, feeling apologetic all the time and dodging us as if we had the plague. We didn't know whether to be more annoyed or amused with him – I remembered a bit out of *Three Men in a Boat* as I watched

him, 'Disadvantages of living in the same house with pair of Lovers'. But I swear we behaved ourselves with all due propriety – in company – it must have all been in the thoughts of the beholder – but I <u>was</u> sorry for him, poor man. *[It is amusing to recall Marion's letter of 7ᵗʰ April 1937, when she was then the uncomfortable third guest in the same house with a pair of lovers and had to take refuge in her bedroom from them!]*

Faku is going to make sure I go. They have already begun giving me farewell presents. I have a <u>beautiful</u> gown from the headmistress's family. You can't see it in the

Marion wearing the gown referred to in the letter, photographed with Mrs Wang and her two daughters.

enclosed photo – black satin, with a conventional design – peacock, lotus flowers and clouds done in soft coloured beads, I'll have it home with me D.V. This photo was taken when Mrs Wang came to pay her daughter a visit last month. The other photos explain themselves.

My sleeves are short – and fashionable – though chilly. It makes me look awfully fat in the photo, not so bad in reality I think.

The Church is getting up something – one part of the performance is that the whole congregation is to have their photo taken with me after Church next Sunday. But the thing that amuses me and is rather touching – is an expression of esteem from a group of officials I've got to know pretty well within the past three years. A Police officer, head of his department, a young Education Board official and a Head of Department in the Municipal offices, all non-Christians – the others in the group are a woman teacher, non-Christian, a boy in an office in town, who is engaged to one of our teachers, and a woman who taught in our school as a sub once. It is all pure friendliness – none of them have any reason to give me anything – and I've certainly never done anything for them except to be polite to them! So I value this presentation all the more.

Marion's farewell photo taken with the congregation of Faku Church.

Fakumen
27th December 1940

To Dad and Mother

A pause in the feasts and farewells to write a line or two before I am totally incapacitated by too much kindness. Today's feast is my own fault – I thought I'd like to get all my women co-workers together and give them one slap meal in a restaurant. There are 17 of us in all, not counting the hospital nurses. I couldn't start on them!

The worst rush is over now, I have accounts closed for the year and am beginning to show Joey a list of the things she has to see to during the year in both school and evangelistic work. The District Board will be my last 4 days here and I'll be busy then between attending meetings and seeing my friends.

I must tell you all the groups that have asked for the honour of being photographed with me. It is wonderful to be loved ... *[Marion then listed 14 groups.]*

Three of the many farewell photographs taken just before Marion left Faku.

I hope to leave here on the 6th, have 4 days in Moukden and then we

333

leave on the 10th, 11th from Darien, 20th from Kobe, 5th of February to San Francisco, and 14th D.V. to Uncle's. Thereafter I'd like a week with them and if there is a boat anyway soon I'd be home at least in the 1st few days of March. It will depend on how much time I will have to spend in England with my stuff and in getting a pass. *[to go to Northern Ireland]* I must get a note to Dennis O'Neill – what is the use of knowing the private secretary to the Minister of Transport if you can't get a travelling pass out of him!?

CHAPTER 8

1941

On Board *Oryoku Maru*.
O.S.K. Line
13th January 1941

To Dad and Mother

Perhaps this letter will reach home before I do – perhaps not – but I'll start the tale of the beginning of my journey to you now. I'll probably have forgotten it all by the time I get across the Atlantic!

I had a wonderful send off from Faku, folks are kindly. It was added to by the fact that the District board had met and all the representatives were in. I got my photo taken with them and then when I thought they had finished their share they unexpectedly sent me a presentation banner with my 'good qualities' inscribed on it in gold characters. I have it packed in my trunk – I hope it will reach the Manse Clones safely.

I had to speak in church on Sunday – that was hard. And the sight of two of the pastors wiping their eyes almost laid me out – I got finished – but only in time. The sort of kindness that was hardest to bear was people like the Bible School cook, or an old sewing woman bringing me presents. I also got things from people in the districts, folks I had no idea even knew I was leaving, and several very friendly letters.

I had 4 or 5 days in Moukden before I left. Grace Leggate, her husband is a young Scots doctor, put herself out to make things pleasant. She had asked me to stay there and when Mrs Pedersen wanted me she still insisted on having me – because she had 2 sitting rooms and the Pedersens haven't. So Rymer and I had a room to ourselves every evening and did not vacate it too early! On Monday he was in Leggates' for supper, on Tues I was out all day with Chinese friends, but I when I got home at 9, I found him there waiting for me. On Wednesday we spent most of the day in town – had lunch, saw a film of the Olympic Games in Berlin 1936. Marvellously well done – we were thrilled to the boots to see the English winning some items and to hear 'God Save the King' played in Moukden – Japanese soil – in a German film.

Then we were asked to supper in McNairs', also young Scots doctor. On Thursday another old pal, Dr Hugh Taylor, asked me to lunch and the Pedersens *[asked us]* to supper. No getting away from it now – even if we have not made any announcement people take it *[their engagement]* as an accepted fact!

Receipt for the inventory of the property which Marion was leaving in Manchuria.

On Friday there was a big crowd down to see me off – about 25 – in spite of a snow storm and an inconvenient hour. Folks <u>are</u> kind! All the Faku folk were there. Wand Ssu Wen, Wang Huei Chün, the O'Neills, Mamie, Joey, Mabel, Mary – my colleagues in these 5 years. It warmed my heart to see them all together.

Rymer came down to Darien to see me off. He would have come to Japan, but Jim McNair's wife is leaving this week and he has to come over to see her off, so Rymer has to take on his work. She has 2 small children – so her need is greater than mine! It was horrible saying goodbye with things so uncertain at both ends – and no possibility of making plans. However, I have a letter for Dad and another for his own folk. I may go and see them first if I land in England ... They live in Manchester.

In the meantime I'm hoping you'll have had my letter in time to write to America and tell me what you think of it *[the engagement]*! Your blessing is still awaited, even if I am 29 and my own mistress, parents o' mine.

I'm continuing this in the Yamato Hotel Kobe. We landed this morning 14th and will be here till the 21st morning. The reason for the length of time here is that any business in this country has so much red tape round it that a large margin is needed and we don't want to miss our boat. We have money, vaccination and passports all to see to – and each item takes thought and time ...

As I've said, Rymer came down to Darien with us before he went

336

back to Moukden. Wilfred Cumming has come with us to Japan, thanks be. Mary *[Cumming]* and I would have had our hands full with

all the business to see to, as well as the two infants *[the Cummings' son aged 16 months and daughter aged 3 months]* and all our luggage.

Marion's luggage label from the Yamato Hotel.

The Inland Sea was a dream – I'd love to see it in autumn. You are sailing all day close to wooded islands, some with high pine covered hills and others with towns which are a spangle of lights after dark. One island rose sheer out of the sea and as we passed it at night it was like a long sprawling triangle with the slope outlined clearly, right to the top of the hill. There was a wonderful moon last night – it was like fairyland.

Kobe is a beautifully laid out city. Right squashed up against a hill and along the coast. It is clean and has wide streets from all of which you can see the sea and the pine covered mountains. The Japanese love trees and flowering shrubs – everywhere there are fruit and flower shops, a mass of colour, and the little wooden houses look so picturesque and fragile after Manchuria's mud wall. Still – I know where my heart is!

On Board the Kamakura Maru
Yokahama Harbour
22nd January 1941

To Dad and Mother

Marion had travelled from Kobe to Yokahama to stay with an American friend, Mary Ballantyne.

After breakfast we started off to the seaside resort for which this boat is named *Kamakura*. A lovely spot beside a bay, which is surrounded by

Postcard of the Buddha at Yokahama

high pine covered hills. There is a huge Buddha here, find him enclosed – 44 feet

high. There was a temple over him once, but it was burnt, then an earthquake and latterly a tidal wave have left their mark on him, see the cracks, but he looks very peaceful.

This photograph shows Marion (third from the left in the left back table) in the dining area of one of the two Japanese ships she travelled on in January 1941.

Marion then visited Tokyo with her friend, before returning to Kobe where: On Sunday morning a big contingent arrived at the Yamato from Manchuria – 5 families. One Scot and Austin Fulton are taking furlough in Canada, Mamie Johnston is going home via Canada, and Molly McCreery is taking her baby to Australia. Mrs Stevenson and her family are going to Canada and a young Scots doctor's wife and two children are going there too. It is an awful breakup for all these families and a good many tears were shed by the young wives *[presumably as their husbands returned to Manchuria]*. It is quite a responsibility for them to start off on their own, most of them have no friends in the countries to which they are going and they have to start off with couple or three children and no one to help them.

We left Kobe yesterday and have had a quiet night. The boat is a big one and very comfortable ...

Label pasted on Marion's luggage.

Unfortunately the boat soon ceased to be comfortable. In her letter of 29th January, posted in Honolulu, Marion recounted how it ran into a storm and 'wallows like an old sow settling down into a mud hole.' She and all the passengers suffered from sea-sickness.

Fort Dearborn Hotel
Chicago
9th February 1941

To Mother and Dad

I'm still living in a dream. I hardly believe I'm in Chicago at the moment. Being on the move all the time doesn't make it easy to sit back and think out your impressions and I've seen and done so much this trip that it's hard to remember it all.

The new Japanese Ambassador to U.S. was on board *[our ship]* so we got a great welcome and send off from the first American port we touched. Two destroyers came out from Honolulu, 12 hours, and escorted us in. Were the Japanese on board pleased!! You could feel them all growing about 2 inches in height and chest measurements. It was a good move at the time. He is pro-American and was not a popular appointment with the army. We heard that they had tried to assassinate him before he got off.

Landing in San Francisco was a thrill – me foot was on the U.S., and it is a different country from England. Such free and easy friendliness and such back-chat. We spent 3 hours in the Customs shed. Mary took Wilfred off to the 'C's *[for Cummings, the queues being in alphabetical order]* and I kept the baby at the 'Y's. My landed trunks were the last taken out of the hold I think, that is what held us up.

The officer in charge of the desk beside the 'Y's started chatting to me and immediately said, "You'll be Irish, Ma'am." I was 'Ma'am' till I disowned the baby. So when I said, "Yes," he said, "My father came from Cork way and I'll introduce you to some countrymen," so in turn I met Inspectors Murphy, Fahy and McNamara!

Another man from the distance, as he passed, shouted out, "Hello Miss Young, welcome to U.S." He came up later and when I asked him how he knew my name, he said, "Sure everyone knows there's an

Irish colleen arrived in San Francisco, your name's billed already," then, "I can't claim to be Irish, worse luck, but my mother came from Scotland."

It was a joke how many people claimed Irish connections the moment they knew where I came from. Both the men at my table on the boat, 2 missionaries, a woman on the train, both the Immigration Bureau men a Honolulu and San Francisco ... I half expected the negro porter on the Challenger Express (San Francisco – Chicago) to tell me that his "grand poppy came from Belfast way".

**188 Wall Street
Corning. N.Y.
15th February 1941**

To Dad and Mother

I wrote in Chicago to you, so the rest of my story is to be told still. We got a comfortable run to Mary's home and she got a great welcome. The father is a miner and is losing his sight, poor man, but can still work. They are kindly, decent folk – good – you just feel the same honest goodness and uprightness in the atmosphere that there was round Grandpa Cromie – erring on the strict side, if that is any fault!

I spent 24 hours there and left, travelling by Baltimore, Washington, Philadelphia and so on north to Corning ... It was good to look out of the train window and spot Uncle Charlie on the platform. Ruth and Chucks *[two of Uncle Charlie's children]* were there too, and Auntie was in the car ...

I got a great welcome – everyone is so kind – a neighbour woman sent in a great bunch of red roses to welcome me – a newspaper man rang Uncle up and got the facts about this 'Interesting Visitor to Corning' and had it on the front of the paper that night. Then he asked for an interview and has given our work a good write up today. I'll bring you home a copy. *[See opposite page.]*

Uncle has been enquiring about the Clipper, and it is booked up 6 weeks ahead and Imperial Airways to June ... *[Pan American Airways was still operating a Clipper flying boat service to Foynes in Ireland and Lisbon in Portugal, and Imperial Airways a service to Lisbon; both Ireland and Portugal were neutral. In view of the timescale*

Manchuria Missionary Greeted Here

Miss Marion Young, En Route to Ireland, Directs Grade School Education and Supervises Women's Work in Fakumen; Has Chinese Companion in Mission Field

From far-off Manchuria, land of millet and soybean, of paper windows and bandit-infested countrysides, of close-knit families run by the mother-in-law, of friendly Chinese farmers and colorful Mongol tribesmen—Corning welcomes a visitor. She is Miss Marion C. Young, one of that earnest little group of whites who are doing the Lord's work in strange lands of the East.

Miss Young arrived here this week for a visit with her uncle, Charles H. R. Young of 188 Wall street, and Mrs. Young. She is on a delayed furlough after more than five years at one of the farthest inland mission points of the Irish Presbyterian Church in the north of Asia.

A missionary to India years ago inspired Miss Young to spend her life in the mission field. Her father, a clergyman of the Irish Presbyterian Church, had always wanted a post in China, and it was to that land that his daughter sought an appointment. Since the long journey that took her past Suez and Malay to Mukden and then overland to her post at Fakumen, she has not seen her family in Eire. Meanwhile four of her five brothers are training for the clergy.

Miss Young now has a year' leave — and her goal is home, in Ireland. She is remaining here until she can arrange transportation. Reservations on the "Clippers" to Lisbon are filled for months ahead, so that she is now investigating the possibility of shipping via Montreal.

In Fakumen — which means "gateway to Mongolia," because it is on the old border of Manchuria and Mongolia — the Irish Presbyterian Church has one of its oldest missions. There Miss Young is one of four whites, the others being an elderly clergyman and his wife, and a girl in training for the mission field. Over a territory some 250 miles in the latitude of New York State, she superintends grade school education and supervises women's work in all the outlying mission points.

Her work requires her to be in the field for weeks at a time, accompanied only by a Chinese woman companion, traveling antique railroad lines and open country. Such an assignment would appall even an adventuresome man, but Miss Young tells of her work in most matter-of-fact way possible. She mentions casually that one point in the north of her territory she has never yet been able to reach as it means a 60 mile bus ride from the end of the railroad over roadless prairie through bandit-infested country.

"I like my work in the country field," Miss Young says. "Chinese farmers are like country folk anywhere, friendly and hospitable. And the work is worthwhile. Shortly before I left I was in a wee church, where all the community was gathered together, talking cheerily, stopping for an informal prayer meeting. The church has become the center of community life."

Ethical codes of Buddhism and Confucianism give the Christian teacher an entry to the moral codes of Christ, Miss Young points out. Mohammedans are much more difficult to work with. In her field work, Miss Young will stop at the guest-room usually attached to the local mission and conduct a Bible school (in Chinese of course). From girl to grandmother, the women are eager to learn, she says, and she speaks of the pride of the Chinese peasant woman when she masters even a few characters and is on the path to learning to read.

The Non-Conformist Churches in China use a name which, translated, means "Jesus Christ Church," Miss Young says. The only other missions in her territory are those of the Catholic Church, principally French Catholics. Their name, in Chinese, means "Heavenly Lord Church." The two groups work in harmony and Miss Young says that somehow doctrinal conflict does not seem so sharp as at home.

Missions now have a new direction, she points out — to make the local churches self-supporting and self-governing, so they will stand if white should some day be forced out of the country.

Miss Young has one formula for smoothing things over with premptory native police or officials who sometimes become sharp with whites. She points out that the Chinese consider white persons barbarians in the matter of manners; therefore, if you are just as polite as can be to an angry or officious Chinese, he instinctively feels that he must show his racial superiority by being more polite than you are —so the meeting ends in a competition of compliments.

Though anxious to see her home and family again, Miss Young knows that she will be glad to go back to Fakumen when her furlough ends. "There is something about the Orient, its color, its challenge, that draws you once you have lived there," she says.

341

involved with these Marion had] written and asked for information *[about returning home by a Canadian Pacific boat from Montreal].* I've no idea how long it will take, but don't expect me before the 2nd week in March anyway, then you won't be disappointed.

Uncle gets worked up over the danger and feels everyone would blame him if he let me go and anything happened. I'm of age I tell him and will make my own plans so he doesn't have any decisions for me! But he is willing to help every way he can, so I hope I'll get home sometime – I'll be wiring before this reaches you I expect.

What the Customs man said to me, "Well, Ireland must be heaven if you'll go through hell to get there," and I said, "Sure it is." Love to all the angels, Marion.

188 Wall Street
Corning. N.Y.
11th March 1941

To Mother and Dad

I had two letters from Rymer a few days ago, after a famine, and work goes on as usual there. With all the wives gone, the English classes in the medical college are thrown on the men and they are kept terribly busy. A job is waiting for me if I go back before September – so I hear from the principal of the college, Dr Petersen! *[Marion was increasingly frustrated at not being able to return home and was considering returning to Manchuria and joining Rymer there.]*

Marion sometimes wrote letters to her mother which were not intended to be circulated round her brothers and sisters. Such was the one below, whose envelope was marked 'Personal':

188 Wall Street
Corning. N.Y.
19th March 1941

To Mother o' mine

You know things are pretty tense in our part of the world just now. We are wondering what Matsuoka's *[the Japanese Foreign Minister's]* visit to Berlin will bring out. If Japan is to start trouble in the Pacific, either our folk will have to leave at once – if there are boats to take them out, or go into internment camps for the duration. And neither way will it be fun. If we once leave the country it will be very very hard to get in again – Japan doesn't want us there, but so far has had no good excuse to shove us out.

If Rymer is interned there I'm not going to be happy – so here's to hoping Matsuoka is not going to be too pliable in Herr Hitler's hands. He thought once of coming home to join up, but the staff is short now and he has more work than he can manage easily so he has decided to stay put for the present till a call comes. In the meantime his name is still on the list for doctors for Malay R.A.M.C. *[Royal Army Medical Corps]* – we wouldn't be any the nearer meeting if he were sent there to join the army!

Oh well, let's meet our troubles as they come – they seem very small when I think of Europe. There are few people in this old world whose lives are not being touched by the war and we've been pretty easily treated so far.

Has Mrs O'Neil written to you yet? She said she would, but I don't know whether she would wait till I got home first. She has quite a high opinion of Rymer and as he stayed with her for part of the holidays at P.T.H. this summer, she feels she knows him. She has been very sympathetic! and would have asked him to Faku any time I said the word. I was afraid of the Chinese spotting something and didn't dare say yes to that. She would even have backed up our getting married before I started for home! I was surprised when she spoke to me about it one day – but apart from anything else it would have been far worse saying goodbye if we had been married and I didn't even consider it. Rymer mentioned it too, but didn't press it when I said no – so how would you have liked Mrs Cayton arriving on your door step, Mother!!

188 Wall Street
Corning. N.Y.
27th March 1941

To Dad and Mother

I had never expected that you would cable Rymer *[after he had written*

343

to her father about marrying Marion] so when I got a very nice cable from him the other day it was a real surprise. A million thanks for doing that. I am sure he would be surprised too, for my letter telling him that the momentous document *[Rymer's letter to her father]* had gone would not have reached him yet ... I hadn't felt really engaged till his wire came, see how much I depended on your approval!

I was away for the weekend and Uncle opened Rymer's cable to see if it was important ... so the cat was out of the bag! Its head had

already been out for I have his photo on my dressing table, but being polite they had not said too much. Uncle fixed a quizzical eye on me and just laughed as I read the telegram ... wasn't it mean of him?!

I have no further news of when I may be home ...

St Patrick's Day card sent by Marion on which she had written, 'It's a pity this whale wasn't the only thing between the U.S. and Ireland.'

188 Wall Street
Corning. N.Y.
14th April 1941

To Dad and Mother

I have not been doing very much this week, knitting *[socks for British troops]*, reading and visiting a few folks ... and longing I was working again. I have had more than enough holiday now, and I wish I had something regular to do. There is still no hope of getting away for some time. I wrote to the Clipper offices and they tell me I might not be able to get away from Lisbon if I did get there, as the Imperial Airways is only taking govt. officials and the like at the moment *[from Lisbon to Britain]*. I still hate the thought of spending all that anyway. If I were to be earning some money next year I wouldn't mind ... that is the worst of getting married, when you have been an independent woman, isn't it Mother!

188 Wall Street
Corning. N.Y.
7th May 1941

To Dad and Mother

Mary Hamill, Joey, Hessie and a lot of folk you wouldn't know are arriving in Canada any day soon, they will be very fed up when they find they can't get home. I am waiting to hear what they plan to do, and whether they can find any work to do in Canada. The Y.*[W.C.A.]* wants workers, but I do not know what they would need in the way of qualification.

I hope the G.A. will write to me soon, I sent a note to the Secretary a while back, and I suppose the Mission Committee will send us some sort of orders, soon. The Scots got very firm ones ... no coming home for anyone, two of them, including Mabel, have gone to India. They may just stay there eventually, as they have only been out two years ... but imagine having just got a working knowledge of Chinese to have to start into an Indian dialect. American is bad enough for me. I will be coming home with the most peculiar 'a's, I hear myself wavering between the two and I am beginning to pronounce tomato, aluminium, vitamins in the proper Amurrican way ... otherwise they don't know what I mean, and I haven't time to correct the whole nation.

188 Wall Street
Corning. N.Y.
13th May 1941

To Dad and Mother

Rymer writes that things seem tenser in Moukden, the Japs are throwing their weight round a bit more than usual. They are in and out of the missionary houses asking what they think is going to happen in the Pacific, and explaining all about what Japan is ready to do in case of war. There is word among the Chinese of an internment camp being built near Hsinking for the foreigners, which is no pleasant hearing. Amongst the girls you know who are left there, are Wiggie Faulkner, Dor Crawford and Maggie McCombe, three of the stalwarts ... all the younger girls were ordered out and given no choice in the matter.

Thanks for the information that we are to have full salaries for furlough – that will cheer up the hearts of a good many folk! Furloughs come harder on the pocket than living in Manchuria, said she feelingly.

188 Wall Street
Corning. N.Y.
18th June 1941

To Mother and Dad

I've something to discuss with you – pity it can't be by word of mouth! It is looking more and more as is I'm not going to get out of this country for some time and as you know I've written to the Canadian Immigration Bureau to see if I would be allowed to work if I went there. I have not had an answer, but if I'm given permission I think I'll go before the end of July.

I had a letter from Rymer a day or two ago and he tells me that Dr James McNair is coming over to Canada for a holiday this summer, instead of taking furlough next year. He is due to go back to Manchuria about the end of October or thereabouts, and Rymer suggests if things are no worse in the Pacific that I might travel back with James.

The thing is this. I want to get home to see you all and if there is any chance I meant to take it, but if I should decide to go *[back to Manchuria]* in October, I'll have to start getting my papers and making reservations at the beginning of September. Once I do that, even if a chance to get home should turn up, I don't think I should take it. Once I make plans to go, Rymer will start having to start getting a house and making arrangements with the consul for the wedding – and it wouldn't be fair to go back on him at the last minute. It is all so beastly uncertain.

I just want your reaction to the idea, I know you can't advise me much at this distance. It makes me heartsick to think I got this length and may get no further. Rymer's furlough is due early 1943 – another year and a half. It is horrid far away – and who knows what Japan will have done before that? But tho' I know both you and Rymer would prefer to have me 'safe' in the U.S. – put yourself in my place for a moment – if you couldn't get home, wouldn't you go back to

346

Manchuria given half a chance – ?! ...

When I think Rymer and I might be married by the end of the year I'm floating on rosy clouds – till I realise that would mean not seeing you folks, then I want to throw my head back, tuck my head under me and howl.

188 Wall Street
Corning. N.Y.
14th July 1941

To Dad and Mother

As you say in the last letter *[travelling by Clipper sea plane to]* Foynes seems off the map for me – I hate, hate, hate to think that I may not see you this year, but the more I think of it the more I want to get back to Manchuria if the going is still possible in October. If we were interned, we wouldn't suffer too much I'd think – the Japs don't treat any of the foreigners they imprisoned at intervals these last few years too badly and I'd be in a much worse state if I were here unable to get home and Rymer were interned for the duration.

There is nothing definite at all yet – James McNair has landed *[from Manchuria]* this past week and if Rymer wrote [a letter to be posted] by him I should have it any day soon. I'm going to write to James tonight or tomorrow and ask him what he thinks are my chances of being allowed back. You don't think I'm crazy wanting to go back – do you?!

188 Wall Street
Corning. N.Y.
4th August 1941

To Dad and Mother

First – my big news – I've got my papers for Canada and hope to be off there by the 17th at the latest. I'm feeling sorry already to be leaving Corning, but if I can get up there and do some work, I'll feel a lot happier independent.

I was afraid your reaction to my proposal to go back to Manchuria would be what it was! but as far as 'safety' goes I think I'd be as 'safe' there as in Ireland. The problem may not come up at all, it will just depend on how the Russo-German war goes, whether Japan is going to step into trouble in the South Pacific or not. I think she has enough sense to be cautious, but this war plus the Anglo American embargo, has cut off her markets both ways and a scared beast is the most vicious.

If both *[Church Mission]* Council and *[British]* Consul say nothing against going back you wouldn't say I was foolhardy, now would you? and I'd be travelling back with Dr James McNair so you'd know I had company. If war does come in the Pacific, it is most unlikely that anyone would get out of Manchuria. We are served by Japanese boats only ,... However, I'm just living a day at a time now and I'll take note on your feeling on the matter.

64 Duggan Avenue
Toronto
17th August 1941

To Mother and Dad

Here I am in another new world and I hardly know where to start telling you about it. Manchuria – America, now Canada – it seems quite a jump in 8 months.

As Hugh Young, one of Marion's American cousins, was going by car to Canada, he offered to take Marion to Toronto.

Hugh, son Bob (18) and I started out for Toronto at 5.30 on Thursday morning. It was a beautiful morning and we had a good road to travel on. Bob was driving and we were rarely under 50, sometimes over 70 most of the way! With these good cars and concrete or tarmac roads, you never feel it – until you hit something, and then I fancy you wouldn't feel much else in this world.

We got to Niagara Falls about 9.30 and I had no trouble with my papers *[on passing through the Canadian border]*. I've now been allowed into Canada 'for the duration' – that gives me leeway enough!

We got to Toronto, travelling on the beautiful 4 lane Queen Elizabeth Highway, recently completed, round 10 o'clock, and I was dropped at this door. Ella Gordon, Judy Grieve (CofS) and Marjorie

Ryland (L.M.S.) *[London Missionary Society]* have rented this house until the end of August, much cheaper than rooms. And Ella and Judy hope to sail for home about the 26th! They have had their passage postponed about 4 or 5 times this last month and are rather fed up living in suit cases. In the meantime I'm glad they are here and I'm enjoying Toronto.

I've been offered a job already – mother's help to a lady with 3 children *[Mrs McClelland. the owner of 64 Duggan Avenue which the missionaries were renting]*. I'll tell you details later if I take it (- or she me!). I'm meeting her today. It would probably mean bed and board + about £5 a month. If I were able to say I would be permanent for some months, I could look for something with higher pay – but being so uncertain of plans I can't be too 'choosey'.

These last few days news about Manchuria were not cheering. The report is that the Manchukuo border is closing today. Anyone wanting out had to git immediately, the lines by Shanhaikwan to be closed for troop movements only.

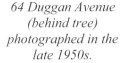

64 Duggan Avenue (behind tree) photographed in the late 1950s.

64 Duggan Avenue
Toronto
20th August 1941

To Mother and Dad

[Marion first wrote she no longer felt it was possible to get from America to Ireland by Foynes Clipper flying boat, so it was] the sea for me and it is about that I'm writing.

Mamie and Dr F*[ulton]* are home. These girls *[staying in Duggan Avenue]* are probably getting away. Colin has a passage and I'm getting more and more fed up. I was down with the C.P.R. *[Canadian Pacific Railway, who operated trans-Atlantic ships]* man this morning and he suggested I write to you and the Mission Secretary and ask you to pay my passage Tourist at the C.P.R. office in Belfast (cheque enclosed) and ask you to cable confirmation here. The C.P.R. would do that perhaps and the office here would ring me up. Then I have to get in touch with the Office of External Affairs, or some such in Ottawa, and get permission to sail. I will call you then the day before I sail – no sooner, for there seems no certainty judging by the experience these girls have had.

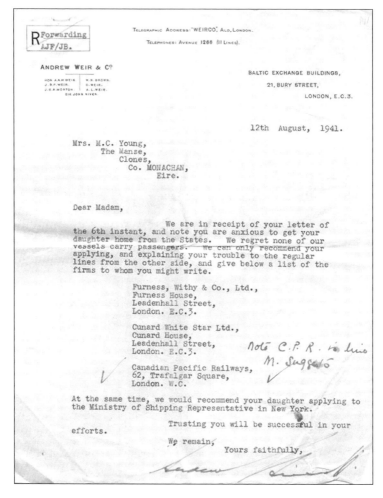

Letter to Marion's mother showing how her parents were trying to find a steamship line which would bring her back from Canada.

I don't see any sense now in the chance of a Foynes air line – it is too uncertain, and you may be sure if conditions don't look moderate to fair there will be no sailing from this end. So <u>please</u> – I hate this hanging on and if you or the Committee don't give me permission to go home by boat, I'll resign and look for a war job here I think. I feel neither fish, flesh, fowl nor good red herring at the moment, so many Canadian girls are over in England and here I am waiting to be wafted safely over the Atlantic.

Perhaps I'll feel better when I get into this job next month, but at the moment I'm not fit to be lived with ...

64 Duggan Avenue
Toronto
24th August 1941

To Mother and Dad

Your last of the 26th was very welcome about 6 days ago, but I was sorry to think how much trouble you had gone to re Clipper passage. You'll have my last re sailing and I'm hoping that I'll have some word from you before September is out. When I re-read the letter I noticed that my remarks re resigning looked more like a threat than I meant it to be – but I hadn't time to rewrite it, so I let it go. What I meant was that my furlough year is up at Christmas and my salary should stop then as I have not been able to do anything for the Mission all this year. So I <u>must</u> resign from here, if I don't get home, in time to stop them paying in my salary cheque for Jan – March quarter. When we were in Manchuria it was paid in early in November, so that we got acknowledgement of it by Christmas time. A pleasant practice, we thought!

One day last week I was taken to tea in the house of some of some Canadian missionaries, Mackenzie. A daughter, Flo, is the wife of one of your heroes, Mother – Eric Liddell. The Mackenzies are a large and pleasant family, mother and 7 children about out our ages, and I've a feeling I'm going to have friends in it. Why do nice things happen to me? Flo has two adorable small daughters and is expecting another child soon, that is why she came home before Eric. One of the sons of the house told us that there was a Welsh concert on that night, proceeds for war victims, so we ups and off to it.

I start work as from next Monday – Mr and Mrs McClelland have been over to see me and also invited us out to a picnic tea on an island in the lake *[one of the Toronto Islands in Lake Ontario]* where they have rented a summer cottage. They are pleasant folk. She isn't 40 yet, lean, red headed and full of 'go'. He has a clever, sensitive face – and has some very nice books in his library! I'm going to have a good month in the reading line. I'll tell you more of what the house and work is like after I've started, but it won't be too hard judging by what I've seen of it.

I can't remember if I told you that we are in the house now? Mrs Mackenzie, a retired Scots missionary, is living next door with her sister, Mrs Brydon, and her daughter, Isabel, who had to leave with the other girls when Council ordered them out of Manchuria. She heard Mrs McClelland say she would like to rent her house for the summer, and suggested to Ella Gordon and Judy Grieve that they take it. They have had transients all summer who shared in rent and housekeeping so they have had a much cheaper summer than if they had been in digs ...

Mary Hamill, Joey and Agnes Gardner have all got teaching jobs this month, Hessie Stewart is doing something like me in Toronto, and Mabel Dalgleish, my ex colleague, has reached India. We are well scattered!

Now if I only knew what is happening in Manchuria, I'd feel happier. Having no letters for a month now makes Rymer feel even further away than ever.

64 Duggan Avenue
Toronto
28th August 1941

To Mother and Dad

This house is in another splutter again, the girls have had their sailing postponed, this time indefinitely. They were fit to blow a fuse for all of one day. Crossing the Atlantic needs some little facing up to these days, not to mention the details of having trunks all packed and ready for over a month while they live from day to day in a small suitcase. Now the cold weather is coming and they have to unpack and repack for a possible journey next month. The boat that they are booked for hasn't sailed – 'waiting for special cargo' – we wonder if it has been bombed on the way over and has been laid up for repairs. Anyway, it and Ella and Judy have not gone. They went out the next day to look for my jobs and my new boss knew of two who would be glad of temporary help.

So the three of us have something to keep us from going off our beam end this next month – we have all had the fidgets this past week and we are as jumpy as cats.

64 Duggan Avenue
Toronto
9th September 1941

To Dad and Mother

I don't know where to start with my news. One good piece is a letter 1st August, which reached Corning 6th September, from Rymer in P.T.H. Probably the fact that he was out of Manchuria accounts for it reaching me. The trouble was just starting then and they were going to have to get military passes to get back, which he said were not being granted very freely. It seemed such a very fragile link across all the Pacific, it almost made me feel worse than if I'd got none – ungrateful aren't I?

I don't really mean that, but no one knows what has been happening to our folk this last month, or what they are deciding to do if the worst comes to the worst – and we are afraid of cabling in case they are not allowed to reply. Even in Shanghai, American mail has been held up.

I'll be having that cable *[confirming Marion's passage from Canada had been paid to the C.P.R. in Belfast]* from you next week – I hope? If it doesn't come soon I'll explode. But there is one thing I warn you – don't think that because you've paid the passage, that I'll get a boat soon. Mamie got a lucky chance. Ella and Judy have been put off this week again, having thrown up their jobs and packed for the 6th time!!! since the end of July. I'll send you a cable the day I am leaving and don't begin to get excited for a couple of weeks after that. The Leggates took 26 days I think, so you had better take that as a minimum and stay calm until then.

Now, as to my doings – this job is proving pleasant but uncommon active. I've had as hard a week's physical labour as any 4 since 1935 I think, and my creaking bones do not take kindly to it. I started Saturday week last 30th August and I've had very little free time since. We were at the Island both weekends, and that means a break in the house routine and added work, although I have not much to do up

there, but simple house cleaning and cooking. Here I get up at 6.45, am steadily at it till 1.30 – free till 3 – and work straight on until about 8.15 ...

I think I've told you that the children are John 11, Jane 7 and Bobby 2½. They are not near enough to be companionable and all the harder to manage for that ...

Jane, Bobby and John McClelland in front of the porch at 64 Duggan Avenue.

Marion had made contact with her great aunt Mary, her grandfather Cromie's sister, who had emigrated with her husband to Canada years before:

I've left a piece of news to the end which will interest you – my visit to Aunt Mary's. It was a great fun and I'm looking forward to seeing them again soon. I went last Thursday, about 40 minutes by train from here and a couple of blocks to walk at the two ends. Aunt Mary, Mrs Creery and Arleen (22) live together with a couple of young folk who board there. Aunt M. is a bright as a button, sight and hearing about perfect – she heard even my quietest asides to Mrs C. – very full of fun and bright eyed – a tiny, long chinned slip of a woman. She nearly wept over me, she was so glad to see me, and she told me that I'd be as welcome there as in my own home any time I wanted to go. Mrs Creery is a friendly soul – pure County Down still – she gave me the best cup of tea I think I've had since I left home ...

64 Duggan Avenue
Toronto
18th September 1941

354

To Mother and Dad

I'm sleepy and too too full of Chinese food (burp) *[after a meal at a Chinese restaurant with five friends]* but I feel I must at least begin this letter or another week will have gone with not a scrap from the McClelands' skivvy. I'm getting into training nicely for home – nothing will come amiss to little Maria – washing porridge pots is even a common place. Ah for my nice Fish! With all his faults he would look so dearly familiar at the sink. Today is my half day and I now know the vivid pleasure it can be in the life of a maid.

I've had one piece of good news since I wrote last, which hasn't cheered me up any. Rymer cabled to say he wasn't leaving Manchuria. I'm glad and sorry. Ours isn't a job we took up to lay down on the first cry of wolf and I'm glad he feels enough to want to stay there. But I had been hoping more than I realized that he would get away – now I'm cold afraid our separation may be for the duration.

Friday

No letter from you this week. I hope the cable *[about Marion's passage home]* will arrive soon too! I cabled you today for your anniversary – hope it arrives in good time – I only wish I could have been home for it. Perhaps I'll be on the high seas by October – when we were in London 6 years ago celebrating.

I didn't tell you that the girls got away and Marjorie Ryland, who had just put her name in a week before, got passage with them and 4 days' notice. She had some scurry to get her papers through. Happy landings to them.

64 Duggan Avenue
Toronto
28th September 1941

To Mother and Dad

The long awaited cable has come too *[as well a letter from home]* – the P.O. phoned it to me last night, as they do when a cable comes after hours, and then I got the text this morning, 'Family and Committee consent you coming home Stockman' *[Jean Stockman was the General Secretary of the Women's Missionary Association]*. I can hardly believe my chance has come at last, this year has been so long – I'll ring up Mr Baker in the C.P. steamship offices tomorrow and see what my next move is. Don't expect me too soon – the girls are not away yet – been stuck 17 days in Halifax now – They'll need the patience of Job – it is very wearing to be kept keyed up for so long – starting off to China was nothing compared to the Atlantic crossing now-a-days.

I've a lot to do now I have a hope of getting home – clothes to buy. I suppose it would be silly starting off without a winter coat, I haven't had one since I left home – and shoes must be bought. I only got the one good pair in America, as I didn't want to spend Uncle's money on my personal wants. Letters to write and accounts to do and my own affairs to straighten up – it is all quite a thought.

Tomorrow – Squeak, squeak, squeak – that's me squeaking with excitement over the news your letter brought – to think that brother William is to be married on Wednesday, Bless his wee heart ... I bear the brat a grudge that he has got in before me – but at least Rymer and I had announced our engagement first. Great excitement for our family anyway. I'm only sorry I can't be there to help celebrate – our first wedding and not me, too, too annoying.

Another piece of good news is that Mary Cumming's husband is on the high seas, Japan – Singapore – San Francisco. He, Scott Morton (C. of S.) and a Jim Stobie, 2nd generation missionary, are all on their way now. That only leaves Tom Blakely and Rymer amongst the young folk.

64 Duggan Avenue
Toronto
7th October 1941

To Mother and Dad

I've had one windfall this week – three letters from Rymer all in one day. Nothing could hurt me that day! Two of the missing July ones and one of 16th August written just before he went back to the Northern Paradise. He had a grand holiday, and an interesting one – a few of the men took a three day trip to a famous mountain near the Great Wall where there is a temple in an almost inaccessible spot which tempts the adventurous. He was in Peking a day or two also, where we had 4 glorious days in early September last year. Alack! the times that we do be in, it have scattered the hopes of us being in Peking together for some time to come.

Mrs O'Neill also wrote a long letter – I often think of them, he over, she almost 70 – faced with the chances of another war. 1900, 1904, 1911, 1914, 1924, 1931, 1933 – all wars, plague or trouble. The Boxer Rebellion, the Russo Japanese War, the Plague – 60,000 died in Manchuria. He served in France 2 *years [with the Chinese Labour Corps, for which Dr O'Neill was awarded the Chinese Order of the Striped Tiger]*, the Student trouble and the Shanghai Incident, Manchuria taken over. The Persecution of the Church – they have seen a lot in their lives in Faku, and lost two dearly loved sons there. And they have not been soured on China by it all – I think it means home to them much more than any place in Ireland.

I also had a long letter in Chinese from the head mistress – I've only written her one, but it took me 4 days at intervals. I must try to get down to another sometime before I leave Canada.

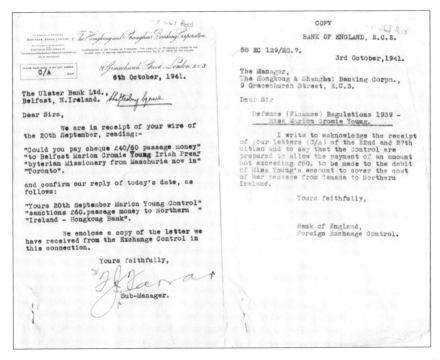

Letters allowing the transfer of money to cover Marion's passage from Canada which had been requested by Marion's Uncle Hugh who was the Manager of the Shaftesbury Square, Belfast, branch of the Ulster Bank.

357

My permit will be forthcoming soon – I've had a letter from the Under Secretary of State for External Affairs, no less, to that effect. Hessie Stewart may be travelling with me – it will be pleasant to have company.

64 Duggan Avenue
Toronto
19th October 1941

To Mother and Dad

I had great excitement on Friday afternoon – got a telegram saying that Uncle, Auntie and the Ketchums *[from Corning]* would be up yesterday if it suited. If not to <u>phone</u> them.

As it happened it was impossible. Mrs McC*[lelland]* had a big dinner arranged for a friend who was visiting Toronto and we were tied up with that all afternoon and evening. Then today they had to go away and wouldn't have had a free moment. So I phoned long distance. It was fun – 350 miles at least and clear as a bell!

I spoke to Auntie and they arranged to come next weekend. Mrs McC says I can have my half day on Sat and be free all Sunday, so we will have plenty of time to see the sights. If I leave in the meantime, I'll have to phone them, but the C.P.R. man didn't sound as if he expected any more this week. He doesn't know very long beforehand himself. It will be grand to see something of the country around Toronto, now that the autumn has come the leaves are very lovely.

On Monday I was invited for the day to the 'Chinese' Mackenzies – Eric Liddell's in-laws. Flo Liddell is tied to the house by her month old Maureen, so I went to spend the day with her, but most of her very pleasant brothers and sisters were at home, so we had a great household, The oldest, Flo, is 32ish, and the youngest, Agnes Louise, is 15, so they range round our own ages. Norman, a theological student, is the only one not at home. 4 girls and 3 boys – Findlay and Kenneth are 22 and 18 – nice lads. Do the dishes and rag each other and their sisters in a cheery atmosphere like to what I remember in the Manse of yore.

I've had letters from Rymer up to 16th August, they have been very irregular – the last I got this last week were dated 23rd – 7th July!

Where they have been lying I don't know. Things in the Pacific look worse than ever – I hate to hear the news these days. If war comes with Russia, Manchuria is for it and I only hope some of our men won't try to escape into Russia. Rymer hints that way, and his colleague was through the early part of the Great War in Russia, so he might support the idea. I do hope he will stay put – tho' I know he will long to be up and doing and the thought of an internment camp would be no cheery future. Troubled days we live in – Russia is taking a hard knock – the loss in life must be appalling.

Three days after Marion wrote this letter her plans for the week changed dramatically as address of the next letter shows.

The Manse
Clones
Co Monaghan
12th November 1941

To J.D. *[Jim]*

I'm sorry I haven't got a letter off to you long ago – but you can imagine how full the days have been. I am just beginning to draw a breath and settle down a bit after 10 days dashing round like a hen on a hot griddle and making a lot more noise than the said hen ever would. While we are on the subject of the farmyard, I want to tell you that you nearly caused hysterics in this house with the final remark in your last letter – 'Best news I've heard since Branny calved'. You didn't need to bother any more about your telegram of greetings – if you had just sent that, it would have been enough. It was nice to get it anyway. Thanks.

I think Dad has given you some details of my journey – forgive me if I repeat. The call to go gave me as big a surprise as my arrival gave the family. I had been speaking to the C.P.R. man a few days previously and he gave me no hope of leaving for some time. The work had kept me busy that week and I hadn't been in town, so I had a long list of shopping, I wanted shoes and stockings and a lot of odds and ends, including more groceries, before I left for home.

On a Tuesday evening, 22nd, at 6 o'clock he rang up and asked if I could leave on the 11 train that night!!! I had 30 cents in my pocket, I planned to go to the bank the next day, the McClellands were out, I had to feed the kids, bath and get them to bed, then make the McC's supper and I had a lot of letters to write and arrangements to make in case I didn't reach this side – so I just gasped weakly and said, "Not a hope," feeling ready to weep into the telephone. He got quite worried, he's a nice bloke, and said that that he'd look up other connections and see if I could make it in the morning.

When it came, I didn't know whether I was asleep or awake. The next few hours were a dream. Isabel Mackenzie, a Scots lass who was in Moukden and lived next door to my boss in Toronto, came in to help, and honestly I'd never have got away without her. I finally got to bed about 2 – wakened at 3.30 and stayed awake till 6 when I got up and finished packing! Got off 8.30ish with lots of kindly help. C.P.R. man came to the station to see I'd everything right. Mrs Creery (Agnes' mother) and Jim Ross were there to see me off.

When I got into the train, here in the seat opposite me was a woman I knew in Toronto. She insisted on inviting me for lunch and wanted to take me out for dinner in Montreal. There were other friends there to meet me however, and they entertained me royally and put me back on the train a couple of hours later. A nice young Canadian couple *[Ted and Kitty Johnston]* who were in Ssupingkai, one of the junctions for Faku district, and with whom I often stayed when I was touring round. I seemed to have friends wherever I moved.

We were to be in the port *[Halifax]* from which we sailed the following evening, but a freight train was wrecked ahead of us and from 4am to 6 or 7pm we sat outside a French Canadian village, Mont Joli. I had an interesting day of it and rather enjoyed that day, plucked out of space as it were. Life in China prepares one for things like that. I met a lot people who later were on the boat with me, including, funnily enough, my 3 other cabin mates. One Canadian businessman was very friendly and interesting. He lent me a book, very amusing, which I read that afternoon, and we yarned a lot. I also met several American boys. There were over 100 on board, later on the same boat, radio engineering – coming over in the Civilian Technical Corps – a cheery if somewhat fresh lot. When I say 'met' I mean they picked me up or I picked them up – or something – our misfortunes made everyone very pally!

We didn't get in until early next forenoon, got our business all through, into the boat and off we went. Our convoy was small, hence the speed – only 10 days in the water. I've never spent a more pleasant or happy 10 days on all my journeyings around the world. We had a very congenial table and cabin ... We had the cheeriest table in the dining room – our steward, a cheerful Jeeves, "Well Miss, I've been on this job for 28 years and I may say I've never had a more humorous table." I'll tell you all the crack when you get home. Come along quick!

Dad told you I got over to Belfast the night I arrived in Scotland, there's a tale in that too. *[Marion had arrived without a permit for Northern Ireland. To gain access to the boat from Glasgow to Belfast without being stopped at the control point, she 'chatted up' a soldier who was driving a lorry through and who told her to duck down out of view until she reached the quayside. Marion had just enough money to pay for her fare to Belfast. Here she took a taxi to her uncle's house, hoping he was at home. Fortunately he was.]*

My pleasure in getting home was greatly added to by Uncle Hugh's "Holy Moses! Is it you?!" as he stared pop-eyed over his porridge spoon, and by Hugh's and Frank's yells when I phoned. I gave the parents 6 hours' notice before arriving, I thought the shock would be too much if I walked in. It is good to be here.

I sent you a card from Canada! Perhaps it has already arrived? My letters – air mail! – are still arriving here at home saying not to expect me before Christmas.

I'm longing to see you and W.A. *[Jim, who was serving with the RAF in Wales and Willie (Bill) was a doctor in Wolverhampton].* I've spoken to Bill on the phone – Hugh came home with me the first night – the twins were here for 4 or 5 days to the great envy of their schoolmates and Cyril and Frank were here for the weekend ...

Frank said in disgust, "We sent a big sister away – and look at what we've got back!."... If you are as big as the rest, I'll fade out. I'm suffering from a rapidly developing inferiority complex.

Marion's joy at being home was tempered by her concern for Rymer in China. The first letter she wrote from Clones was to him.

The Manse
Clones
Co Monaghan
8th November 1941

To Rymer Beloved

Yes, I'm really here, and only beginning to believe it myself. I do hope you got my cable alright, I'm rather hoping you may acknowledge it so I'll be sure you know. I've tried all week to get down to writing, but I haven't had a moment, with friends and relatives coming and going, but if thoughts would have written letters, you would have had a thousand these last few days. I'm feeling more lonesome for you than ever, now that the Atlantic has added itself to the Pacific as a barrier between us. Your photo, which I sent home, is on the sitting room mantelpiece and my own is on my dressing table, so I don't get far away from you.

Marion then described her journey from Toronto in a similar way to that in her letter to Jim, but a note of exasperation crept in:

If I can't get any more time to myself than I have today I see no future in letter writing to you! I'm getting just about ready to tear this up. I've been interrupted about 6 times and it must seem stiff and stilted – I'll tell you no more about the voyage now. Suffice it that ... I had very congenial companions and all I lacked was a certain lecturer in M.M.C. *[Manchuria Medical College i.e. Rymer]* to make my joy complete.

The homecoming was added to by the fact I didn't let them know I had sailed, so I had a lot of fun ringing up two brothers and the twins and hearing them yell. I gave Dad and Mother 6 hours' notice before I descended on Clones, and all has been joy unconfined since then. This weekend I've had no quiet, but a lot of fun. Two brothers (another came down from Belfast with me the day I arrived), the twins, an uncle and cousin have all been here. Tomorrow we go to Belfast for 2 days and after that I promise you I'll write to you to my heart's content.

I wish, I wish, I could hear from you – your last was of August 16th – a miserably long time ago – when you were in Peking for your pass to get back to Moukden. Nothing but your cable since then.

Ever my love, sweetheart.

Yours (more than-ever) Marion

Rymer never received this letter, which was sent back to Clones marked 'NO SERVICE RETURN TO SENDER'. Two other of Marion's letters posted after this were not returned and she only received one further letter (of 23rd August) from Rymer in China.

Marion's concern deepened with Japan's declaration of war on the Allies and its attack on the United States fleet in Pearl Harbour on 7th December 1941. She had already expressed her fear that Rymer would be interned by the Japanese. This was indeed what happened to him and the other missionaries in Moukden immediately after Pearl Harbour.

CHAPTER 9
After China

On Deputation in Ireland

Marion was not given much time to recover after she arrived back in Ireland, as from January 1942 she was sent out by the Irish Presbyterian Church 'on deputation'. Missionaries returning on furlough, or as in Marion's case, unable to return to the country where they had been based, were expected to travel around to speak to meetings about their mission work.

Some weeks Marion had to speak to as many as five evening meetings, often to the Women's Missionary Association and the Girls' Auxiliary in different places, as well as being involved in a service on the Sunday. When she heard that Wiggie Faulkner had been given freedom from deputation work because she was a doctor, Marion wrote that Wiggie was a 'lucky beggar'.

In the next fifteen months Marion visited every Presbytery of the Church in Ireland. While visits were mainly in the northern part, she frequently went to meetings in Dublin. She travelled by train and bus, noting some of the Great Northern Railway carriages compared unfavourably with those of the South Manchurian Railway.

When she was not on her travels, Marion was based in a flat in Belfast, which she shared with her friend, Honor Brown, who was the Presbyterian Church's Secretary for Missionary Education in Sunday Schools. This gave her opportunities to meet up with some of her brothers and sisters, and with colleagues who had also been able to return from Manchuria. These included Mamie, who had been placed in charge of a hostel in Ballymoney for 'unbilletable children, mainly wee boys' – evacuees from Belfast whom nobody was willing to take in, but whom Mamie felt she would be well able to deal with in view of her experience with children in China.

But while Marion had family and friends close by, this could not compensate for her concerns about Rymer, from whom she had heard nothing since his letter of 23rd August 1941. On 30th August 1942, however, a telegram redirected from her parents' home in Clones arrived in Rostrevor, where Marion was about to address a meeting as part of her deputation work. Rymer was on his way back to Britain! The telegram had been sent from Lourenco Marques, in Mozambique,

which was colony of Portugal, a neutral country, and where British and Japanese citizens were exchanged.

Telegram sent by Rymer from Mozambique.
'El Nil' was the name of the boat Rymer was travelling to Britain on.

In a letter sent by Rymer to Marion after he returned to Britain, Rymer outlined the 'bare bones' of what had happened to him after Japan had declared war in December 1941. He and other missionaries had been interned in the Moukden Club, which became the Moukden Camp.

Photograph of the internees in the Moukden Camp in 1942.
Rymer is in the back row seventh from the left.

On 4th June 1942, the missionaries were shipped to Kobe, in Japan, where they stayed until the 30th July when they were transferred to Yokahama via Tokyo and boarded the ship which took them to Lourenco Marques, where they arrived on 28th August and boarded the ship which was to take them home. Rymer's happiness was, however,

365

tempered by the fact that several of the Manchurian missionaries had been told there was no room for them on the boat from Yokahama and had been left behind in Japan, although he hoped they would be able to leave on the next exchange sailing.

Rymer's pass from the Tatuta Maru, the Japanese boat which took him from Yokhama to Lourenco Marques.

Marion's joy on hearing from Rymer can be imagined. She immediately sent him a telegram and then a letter, which reached him on the boat from Lourenco Marques which sailed on 8th September. Rymer was greatly relieved to learn from the letter that Marion had not enlisted in the forces, as he had found out that in this case she would not have been allowed to resign on marriage and might only get a fortnight's leave for the ceremony.

Rymer arrived back in Liverpool on 9th October, and then took the train home the next day to Manchester. His sister, Margaret, had suggested that Marion obtain a permit to travel from Northern Ireland to Liverpool to meet him off the boat. Marion was to be in Dublin that week where she had a full series of meetings, although she would have scrapped them 'like a flash' if she had not decided that Rymer's family had first claim on him. She also felt that they should meet when they had 'time to talk our heads off'. They were, however, soon to speak on the phone, as Rymer rang Marion's flat in Belfast, fortunately catching Marion between two committee meetings. She wrote, 'I won't sleep tonight after hearing your voice,' and Rymer in his letter wrote, 'It was bliss to hear your voice again after nearly two years.'

Immediately after arriving in Manchester, Rymer obtained the forms which would allow him to travel to Northern Ireland, which was a restricted area for those in the mainland. Thomas Cook 'didn't hold out much hope, but on compassionate grounds thought I might be permitted to visit you.' Rymer filled in the forms and put 2nd November as his hoped for date of departure for Ulster.

The permit was fortunately granted and Rymer arrived in Belfast by boat on 3rd November. Marion wrote that after his internment, Rymer was 'thinner and very white – a bit brain fagged now and then, as if he felt it an effort to talk. He has a great story of their experiences, but I'm sure it was a long strain too, that will take some time to get over.'

Rymer was able to stay near Marion's flat in Belfast until 26th November. They visited her relatives in the area, as well as travelling to Clones. He had suggested that they could get married during his visit, but they had eventually decided to leave the wedding to the spring, which would be the next time they would be able to meet.

In the middle of Rymer's visit, the Central Conference of the Girls' Auxiliary took place in Belfast, at which Marion received the President's Gold Badge. This meant that she now had additional duties in visiting GA branches as well as her deputation work. Her letters record constant travels. In early December she was speaking in Drogheda, along with Dr O'Neill and Tom Blakely. Tom Blakely had been interned with Rymer before being taken with him to Yokohama where Frederick and Annie O'Neill, who had been under house in arrest in Faku, joined them before returning to Britain via Lourenco Marques. Like Marion, Tom and Frederick had been given very little time after their return to Ireland before being sent out on deputation, in spite of their treatment by the Japanese.

Marion during and after the Easter School at Clough. Over the previous fifteen months she had carried her suitcase on many journeys throughout Ireland.

Marion's travel throughout Ireland continued. In her letters to Rymer she told of the people she met, including a member of the Cromie family whose sister was the wife of Sir John Jordan, who had been the British Ambassador to China from 1905 to 1910. Miss Cromie had inherited some of her sister's Chinese possessions. These included 'great pots given by the Dowager Empress to Lady Jordan who had led a deputation of British ladies to meet the old lady'. On the same day she had visited three 'dear old ladies' who were the cousins of her grandma Young and who turned out to be sisters-in-law of Dr O'Neill.

At the same time as she was recounting who she had met on her travels, Marion was suggesting in letters to Rymer possible furnishings for the house he had found to rent in Manchester. She also detailed the presents which were beginning to come in during March 1943 for their wedding at the end of April.

Marion continued her church work until only a couple of days before her wedding on 30th April 1943, as she was chairman of the Girls Auxiliary Easter School in Clough County Down from 25th to 27th April 1943. Members of the GA formed a choir at the wedding service, which took place in Knock Presbyterian Church, close to the home of her Aunt Meg where the reception was held.

Marion and Rymer on their wedding day.

The marriage ceremony was conducted by Marion's father, assisted by Dr O'Neill, with Marion's cousin, Billy Young, playing the organ.

Helen and Clara were the bridesmaids and Tom Blakely was the best man; a few days earlier he had been the best man at Colin Corkey's wedding. Because of the travel restrictions to Northern Ireland, none of Rymer's family were able to attend, nor were Flora and other of Marion's friends who lived in Scotland or England.

Four of the most important people in Marion's life photographed after the wedding. From left to right are her parents and the O'Neills.

Life in England

After their honeymoon in Dublin, Marion and Rymer travelled to Manchester to begin their life together. Rymer had been appointed Assistant Bacteriologist at Manchester University, a position to which he was well suited. He had been the lecturer in pathology and also, for a time, been in charge of the bacteriology department at the Moukden Medical College. As well as lecturing, Rymer's post involved work at the Public Health Laboratory, which was part of the University.

For Marion, her marriage not only meant a move to England, but also the end of her official role as a missionary, because by marrying she was deemed to have resigned. As she and Rymer were intending to go back to China, it meant in fact that after any return she would be carrying out missionary work without designation or pay, as Annie O'Neill had done for many years.

The Young family in Belfast in November 1943. Marion had travelled back for a reunion with of all the family; Cyril and Jim had been unable to attend the wedding. From left to right are: Willie, Clara, Jim, Marion, Frank, Mrs Young, Cyril, Helen, the Rev. William Young, and Hugh.

Marion soon settled down in Manchester, making particular friends with Rymer's sister, Margaret. Marion and Rymer became very active members of St Aidan's Presbyterian Church of England and she became involved with the Presbyterian Church's Women's Missionary Society. Marion worked for a while at Moorholme, a home for girls. She gave this up after she suffered a period of ill health in 1945, but returned there in a voluntary capacity.

In November 1945, Marion and Rymer travelled to Liverpool to welcome home the unfortunate Presbyterian missionaries who had been left in Kobe when Rymer and others travelled on to board the ship in Yokohama. A passage on another ship to be exchanged in Mozambique never materialised in 1942. Instead the missionaries had been transferred to Nagasaki, where they were when an atomic bomb was dropped on the city; fortunately they were protected from the blast by a hill on the outskirts of the town. With the surrender of Japan they were at long last able to return home.

After the end of the war in the Far East, the Church of Scotland and the Irish Presbyterian Church sent out a Joint Commission to find out what was the situation of the Church in Manchuria. Among the Commission's findings was the important role that the Chinese evangelists had played after the European women missionaries had left. In Faku, Wang Ssu Wen had been placed in charge and remained listed as the Women's missionary there until October 1947. The Commission found that the women evangelists had suffered much for their work, being followed and kept under observation by the police. The Commission noted how ill and undernourished they looked. For Marion, the sad news came out that Wang Huei Chün had died.

A number of missionaries travelled to Manchuria in 1946. Among these was Tom Blakely, who wrote to Marion and Rymer from Moukden in January 1947, to say that '… all the work has suffered terribly, but the church has survived marvellously well. The hospitals and the college have perhaps maintained themselves best of all.' He was, however, extremely pessimistic about the future in view of the civil war between the Nationalists and the Communists; this was to result in the victory of the Communists who were in control of all Manchuria by 1948.

It was now obvious that there was no future for foreign missions in Manchuria; the final missionaries left Moukden in 1950. Before then it was clear to Marion and Rymer, and others, that they had no hope of returning to China. On 20th July 1949, Rymer submitted his resignation as a missionary of the Church of Scotland, 'because circumstances have made impossible my return to Moukden'. James McNair's resignation was accepted at the same meeting, with Tom Blakely and several of the Irish missionaries also resigning in 1949.

By the time of Rymer's resignation as a missionary, Marion and he already had two children – Joy, born on Christmas Day in 1947, and Helen, in April 1949. Harry was born in March 1950. The family moved to a bigger house in Manchester, and a further move, this time to Bristol, came in 1952 when Rymer was appointed to the post of Deputy Director of the Bristol University Bacteriology Laboratory which included the city's Public Health Laboratory.

The Rev William Young retired in 1952 and died in 1973, five years after Marion's mother, but four of his sons – Hugh, Frank, Cyril and Jim – carried on the Young ministerial tradition. Indeed it was only with the retirement of Cyril's son, Gilbert, in 2013, that there ended a period of over 130 years when there had always been one, and sometimes as many as five, members of the Young family who were ministers or missionaries. Of Marion's other siblings who did not go into the church, Willie was a doctor, and Clara and Helen both became physiotherapists.

Ireland was where Marion and Rymer and their children frequently spent holidays, as this was where the majority of the members of William Young's family lived in the 1950s and 1960s. The exceptions, in addition to Marion, were her brother, Cyril, and her sister, Clara. Cyril became a missionary in India, in which he had expressed interest in 1938; he later returned to Ireland to become Convenor of the Foreign Mission Committee. Cyril's daughter, Clara, came to stay with Marion in Bristol to complete her schooling. This was a reminder of the dilemma the O'Neills had faced during the time they were in China, in feeling that they could only provide a good education for their children by sending them thousands of miles away.

Marion and Rymer spent the remainder of their lives in Bristol. In 1958 Rymer was transferred from the staff of the University to the Public Health Laboratory Service as Director of the Bristol Laboratory. He oversaw the development of a new laboratory which opened in 1969, where he remained in charge until he retired in 1978. As well as his work in Bristol, Rymer's expertise gained in China was used elsewhere in the service. His family recall being vaccinated against typhoid before he travelled to Liverpool in connection with an outbreak among sailors there.

Both Marion and Rymer were much involved with Trinity Presbyterian (from 1972 United Reformed) Church. Marion also held office in wider Christian organisations, such as the Bible Society and the Shaftesbury Crusade, and was committed to causes of social justice. In 1963, she and Rymer took part in a protest march against the refusal of the Bristol Omnibus Company to employ black and Asian drivers.

Although much involved with her local community, Marion still valued the links with her earlier life in Ireland and in China. She was President of the Bristol Ulster Society. She gave talks about her time in China, and to raise funds for Trinity Church served Chinese meals at home (or as she called it 'The Pavilion for the Relishing of Indolence'), making use of the knowledge of cooking she had been able to glean from Fish (the cook in Faku).

372

Mamie Johnston in 1984.

Of her close colleagues in Faku, Fredrick O'Neill died in 1952 and Annie in 1956. Marion remained in touch with Mamie Johnston, who had become a Deaconess in Belfast, until Mamie's death in 1985. In their letters they reminisced about their life in China. In 1981 Mamie sent Marion a copy of *I Remember it Well*, her memoir of her life in China. Other former missionaries visited the Cayton home in Bristol, including Flora who had gone to live in South Africa.

Mr Sung from Singapore with Helen, Harry and Joy at Berkeley Castle in 1956. He was one of many people from abroad who were staying temporarily in Bristol and whom Marion and Rymer invited to their house.

One of Marion's regrets was the loss of contact with friends in China. But she and Rymer were able to welcome into their home people from the Chinese communities in Hong Kong, Taiwan and Singapore, as they did others from different parts of the world, particularly Africa.

In her later years Marion was greatly encouraged by the news that the Church in Manchuria had not only survived the Cultural Revolution, but was also now growing. In 1987 she even received a letter and photographs from Tai Ying, whose family lived in Faku.

Rymer and Marion shortly before Rymer's death in 1989.

Rymer died in 1989 after a long illness. Marion was increasingly affected by severe arthritis, but continued to show the same positive attitude that had always characterised her life. She was sustained by her gentle, quiet, but strong Christian faith until her death in February 1999 at the age of 87.

In a letter for her family to be read after her death Marion wrote:

'I have had a long, interesting and happy life, married to a man made for me. There is never a day passes that I do not remember him and wish I could discuss something with him.

What lies on the other side I do not know, but I am sure that God who created us to love will continue that love in Heaven. So many who have gone before are as real to me as you are here on earth. 'And now abideth faith, hope and love, and the greatest of these is love.''

CHAPTER 10
Conclusion

Marion's letters reflect the views of a young Irish woman who was working thousands of miles from home in a very different society, but who came to regard China as her second home. Marion certainly felt an empathy with the Chinese people. As she wrote on 1st November 1938, 'I've never felt 'strange' out here. I can always find folk to talk to me - or to listen to me! amongst the Chinese I mean, and in Faku especially I feel very much at home.' Coming from Clones, a market town situated in an agricultural area in Ireland, and with her mother being from a farming family, she saw similarities with the lives of people in Faku and its hinterland.

The times she particularly wished she was back in Ireland were when she compared the green countryside with the arid surroundings in Manchuria. 'I like China, and never feel particularly 'strange' in it – as far as the country goes, but it hasn't many half tones like Ireland – every season comes loudly – no wee green sprouts slowly coming out on hedges – they pop and burst at once, no first snowdrops, no wee pink rose buds, they are born roses I think!' This was a comment in her letter of 31st January 1937, and then on 11th April of the same year – 'Can you image a country completely without green? and what a joy it is to see the first blades of grass?'

Marion was from a Presbyterian background, like her fellow Irish and Scottish missionaries, but in China they had wider contacts with other Christian denominations also in China. She mentions enjoying going to the Anglican services in Moukden. The good relations of the Roman Catholic priest and nuns with the Irish missionaries are recorded. Mamie indeed continued to keep in touch with one of her

Photograph by Colin Corkey of the incense burner in the Taoist Temple on the hills near Faku, where Marion recorded that the old priest was 'rather a friend of Mamie's'.

French-Canadian Catholic friends from Faku to the end of her life. Similarly, the missionaries had friendly contacts with leaders of other faiths in the town. There is no mention of conflict with other faiths, until the Japanese attempted to impose elements of their Shinto state religion.

In reading the letters it is necessary to remember that they were subject to Japanese censorship and do not tell all the details of life in Faku, although Marion managed to convey information by using terms such as the 'Sassenachs' as a code for the Japanese. After the Second World War broke out, letters were also censored at the receiving end and some show that they were examined by both British and Irish officials. Indeed the only example we have found of censors apparently deleting information is that Marion's comments about De Valera's attitude to Britain in the Second World War seem to have been cut out!

One must also remember that Marion would not have told her parents about events that she thought might worry them greatly and that she probably underplayed some of the situations she had found herself in. In her letter about the rescue of Gow's wife from the well on Christmas Day 1936, for instance, she does not mention the frozen blood from cut and scratched arms, hands and feet, which Mamie Johnston records in *I Remember it Well*.

The letters are presented in date order, but certain themes emerge over the entire time Marion spent in China, which are worth highlighting in this chapter.

The Japanese

As the letters make clear, and as the League of Nations Lytton Commission had established, the existence of Manchukuo as an independent state was a fiction. It was a run as a colony of Japan, and having Pui Yi as a puppet emperor, whose head could appear on stamps, was a convenient means of covering this up.

Japanese control of Manchuria was ever-present in Marion's time in Manchuria. The authorities were suspicious of the missionaries, whom they associated with European colonialism, and of the Christian religion. They felt all religions should be subservient to the State and that Christianity might encourage the Chinese population to question their (Japanese) right to rule the area. Marion's letters show a degree of

INFORMATION BULLETIN

— Bulletin No. 211 —

INSTRUCTIONS BY PREMIER
AND DIRECTOR OF THE
GENERAL AFFAIRS BOARD
AT PROVINCIAL GOVERNORS'
CONFERENCE

FOREIGN OFFICE
MANCHOUKUO

Jan. 1, 1940   HSINKING

harassment, particularly in searching luggage and the long time taken in examining passports and papers.

The myth of an independent Manchukuo was perpetuated in documents such as this Bulletin from its 'Foreign Office' in 1940. In the text it is noticeable that it states that 'All the necessary facilities should be provided concerning the garrisoning of Japanese troops in this country; police systems perfected; seditious thoughts suppressed and anti-espionage campaign pursued vigorously.'

It is clear that any problems caused by the Japanese varied greatly according to the individuals involved and some behaved in a courteous, as opposed to an arrogant, way. After 'Pig Lips' left Faku, matters improved greatly.

The situation of Marion and other missionaries in the 'country' stations was different to those missionaries who lived in Moukden. Probably the concentration of missionaries in the compounds in Moukden and having the British Consulate in the city discouraged any harassment. As a result Marion's colleagues in Moukden had access to radios which could receive the BBC World Service relayed from Hong Kong, telling them of happenings in the wider world, which she did not.

As Marion wrote, her life was never in danger from the Japanese during her time there. The Japanese would have faced retaliation from harming citizens of the Western powers. The situation was very different for the Chinese, whom as the letters show, the Japanese felt that they could torture or kill at will. This was to pose a moral dilemma for the missionaries as, though the Japanese could not harm them, they could take out their displeasure on their servants and colleagues. The Catholic priest in Faku gave up his radio after his cook was put in prison and tortured by the Japanese. One reason for the torture of Pastor Liu in 1935 was because he was known to have been close to Dr O'Neill who had given evidence to the Lytton Commission.

Mamie Johnston suggests in *I Remember it Well* that another reason for Pastor Liu's torture was because some innocent remarks made the Japanese suspect him and that he could be described as 'harmless as a dove' but certainly not 'wise as a serpent'. The latter term sums up Mamie's and Marion's approach of being polite and conciliatory and 'using a bit of Irish Blarney' which avoided conflict with the Japanese on many occasions.

Marion left Manchuria before the Japanese war with the West broke out. After this, life became much more difficult for the Westerners, and particularly so for the Chinese, until the defeat of Japan in 1945.

The Bandits

The Japanese were not the only dangerous group. Because of the lack of government control in the past, bandits or brigands existed in Manchuria and Mongolia and even attacked Japanese outposts. Marion's first letter from Faku has a plan showing where the bandits were in the hills above the town.

In her book, Mamie Johnston relates the terror they could bring. Mamie and Ssu Wen were travelling to the outlying Christian communities and were told that there were Mongol bandits in the area. When they arrived in the town they were aiming for, they found smouldering buildings and dead bodies on the streets; arson, looting, murder and torture to reveal where wealth was hidden had taken place. Mamie thought if she and Ssu Wen had met the bandits on the road they would have been killed too.

Mamie also recounted how, before Marion's time, the bandits had set on fire the home of Elder Feng ('Father William II' of Marion's letter of 11th December 1937), and how he had been threatened with death for not worshipping the Chinese gods. Fortunately, the bandit leader had intervened to save him.

The bandits posed a threat to railway travellers, even in Eastern Manchuria. Marion tells of how the train between Moukden and

Peking had been held up by bandits and how the vegetation on either side was cut back to prevent ambush, and also of the soldiers that travelled on trains to protect the passengers.

The notes on the back of this picture of Kitty Cherry on skis on the frozen river at Kirin in February 1937, mention that the small round tower at the right hand side of the railway bridge is an outlook and guard post against bandits.

Missionary Life

Working in a country station like Faku, as opposed Moukden, meant Marion living for most of the year with one, two or three missionary colleagues, among Chinese people who, with a very few exceptions, only spoke Mandarin. In view of this and the stress of dealing with the Japanese, it is hardly surprising that missionaries valued the social events, such as charades where 'they could let their hair down' at the

meetings at Moukden and also their annual holidays at Pei Tai Ho. The climate in PTH must also have been a relief from the heat and the sand storms in the country, one of the extremes of temperature in Manchuria.

Although no photographs exist of the charades which the missionaries took part in, another example of their sense of humour is shown in this spoof photograph where Flora, complete with a splendid hat, plays the part of the official visitor whom the missionaries must have sometimes found rather patronising. Marion's caption on the back reads 'Mrs McDingwall of the Home Board visits the dear missionaries in Liaoyang, Manchuria. A happy snapshot.'

379

The area of Pei Tai Ho where the missionaries gathered was purely for Europeans, apart from the Chinese servants. Eighty years on, the accepted divisions of the 1930s between the missionaries and the Chinese Christians, is notable. There is no talk in Marion's letters about any romance between members of the two groups. In 1898, Anna Jacobson who served with China Inland Mission, scandalised her colleagues by marrying a Chinese Christian who was a lay preacher, Cheng Hsiao-yu. She was sent away from her mission station; this in fact saved her life, as her colleagues were massacred in the Boxer rebellion.

Marion, like Mamie, made friends with the Chinese easily and went, for instance, to stay with Huei Chün's family, something which seems unusual for a missionary. Marion's empathy with the Chinese certainly proved invaluable when she went out into the outlying areas which stretched 250 miles north and south and 60 miles east and west of Faku. She and Ssu Wen shared a k'ang in a room at the other end of which could be the local pastor and his wife. The only washing facilities for up to six weeks were the 'wash-face' enamel basins, and of course washing and dressing had to be undertaken without offending their Chinese hosts.

The Chinese Church

As Marion's letters make clear, it is major mistake to think that the history of the Presbyterian Mission in Manchuria is the same as that of the Church and of schools and hospitals there. There were far more Chinese ministers and evangelists than there were missionaries. In the Faku district in 1937, the missionaries were Frederick and Annie O'Neil, and Mamie and Marion. The Chinese involved were Pastor Shang (later Pastor T'ai), Ssu Wen and two other women evangelists, the Bible Woman, the three heads and the staff of the Boys', Girls', and Kindergarten schools. When the hospital opened in 1938, it was entirely staffed by the Chinese. In addition, all the pastors and elders in the outlying churches were Chinese.

The Chinese Church existed as a separate institution from the Manchurian Mission; its congregations financed their own ministers and church buildings. The Church held its governing Synod Meeting, which Marion attended and said she preferred to the Missionary

Conferences. *Through Earthquake, Wind & Fire*, Austin Fulton's history of the Presbyterian Mission, implies a degree of influence of the Chinese Church, such as on the placement of the different missionaries, which is not borne out by Marion's letters. One feels that this is not just because the Synod decisions were constrained by the knowledge that the Japanese were sending their Chinese agents in to report back on the meeting.

Marion wrote on the back of this photograph, 'Some of my friends here – nurses, Girls' and Boys' School teachers and our Pastor T'ai in foreign clothes to the right (wearing hat). Sitting in front is a Korean Christian boy who teaches Japanese [Mr Li]'. The photograph is a reminder that the majority of those working in the Christian institutions in Faku were Chinese.

It is clear that in the 1930s the Chinese involved in the churches, schools and hospitals were regarded as being junior to the missionaries, and if there were problems the missionaries would decide how they were going to be resolved. Whatever the rights and wrongs of the breakaway church in Faku, it is noticeable that there was a reunion after Frederick left.

There were a few exceptions to the predominant role of the missionaries. Ssu Wen seems to have been regarded as an equal to Marion and Mamie, especially when they were on their tours of the outlying churches.

Developing the Chinese Church was undoubtedly one of the most important achievements of the missionaries. After Marion, in August 1940, complained about how much of her time was being taken up in preparation for the Bible Classes and Training Classes, Mabel Dalgleish rightly pointed out that these were helping, in a small way, to build up the Manchurian Church. Marion did realise the future lay with her Chinese colleagues, writing in December 1937 that: 'If ever we foreigners had to leave the country, the Church could never die with men like him.'

The Role of Women in Mission and Church

The journeys to the districts, where the women missionaries and Chinese evangelists would lead Bible Schools and lead services, were an example of the far greater responsibilities given in China to women than would have been the case in churches in Ireland and Britain. This arose from the nature of Chinese society, where it would have been considered inappropriate for male missionaries to have close contact with women.

There were significantly more women than men in the mission in Manchuria. This reflected a general pattern for the Protestant missions in China and India, which is shown in Rosemary Seton's book, *Western Daughters in Eastern Lands.*

In spite of their greater numbers, attitudes to female missionaries reflected those towards women generally of their time. The ordained male minister was always senior in all the missions, although it is noticeable that in Frederick O'Neill's second year of absence from Faku, he was not replaced by a male missionary, as previously, and that Mamie Johnston was in charge of the Station for the year.

It is also a reflection of the times that once a female missionary married she was deemed to have resigned, even though married women were carrying out missionary work and running hospitals, but without designation or pay. The number of women listed in the history of missions in China which have been compiled from official records, should be increased significantly if a true picture were to be given. One record which includes missionaries' wives, as well as those regarded officially as missionaries, is a list of names of those in Manchuria in *Earthquake, Wind and Fire*, which shows that there were almost twice as many women as men in the Irish, Scottish and Danish mission in 1941.

The more significant role give to women as missionaries in China must have been frustrating when they returned home and could only act as deaconesses in the Presbyterian churches. It is perhaps significant that one of Marion's colleagues in China, Ella Gordon, after taking a theological degree, became the first woman minister in the Presbyterian Church of England in 1956.

Rev Wu Mingfeng, with Mark O'Neill and Helen and Neil in the offices at the West Church, in Shenyang in 2013.

The role of women in the Chinese Church was even wider than that of the women missionaries. Marion wrote that they had the same theological training as ministers and could carry out all the same duties, except to administer communion. In the chapter about China in *Into All the World*, Jack Weir wrote that reason the ordination of women as ministers was deferred was 'in deference to the mother churches in Ireland and Scotland'. The legacy of the important role of women in the Church can probably be seen today. During our visit in 2013, the Rev Wu Mingfeng, the senior minister in Shenyang, told us that the majority of ministers in the area were women.

Eighty Years On

It is notable that the contribution of the missionaries to Chinese life is now being recognised. In 2013 a statue of Dugald Christie was unveiled at Shenjing No.1 Hospital, recognising the role the missionary had played in founding the institution. Two years later Liaoning Television broadcast a programme which showed the role

Dr O'Neill had played in presenting the case of the Chinese people to the Lytton Commission, which concluded Manchukuo was merely a puppet state of the Japanese. It used one of Marion's letters in this and also showed her photograph.

Eighty years on, one can look back positively on the contribution made by Frederick and Annie O'Neill, Mamie, Marion and the other missionaries in Faku. Marion's letters show that equally important was the work of Pastors Shang and T'ai, and of Ssu Wen and Huei Chün to the Church and to education. They and their successors have ensured that there is now a growing Christian movement in China.

Statue of Dugald Christie outside the present site of the hospital (now the Shengjing Hospital) at Moukden, which he founded. This photograph was taken during a visit by the Scottish Churches China Group in October 2013, just after the statue had been unveiled.

The Women

Annie bore a brood in Manchuria and buried half of them.
Mamie spoke the best Mandarin of all the missionaries
And scared bandits off, playing the organ and flute.
Dot held fort in HsinMin,
Was buried in Belfast with flowers.
Marion hand-delivered an important letter.

Single women, obedient or heartsick wives,
They were nurses, teachers:
Hester, Joey, Margaret, Agnes, Ruth, Lillie, May, Janie, Sara,
Alice and more,
and doctors: Agatha, Elizabeth Eileen, Rachel, Fedya, Emma,
Ethel, Ann Sara the consultant surgeon,
Dorothy known as Wiggy,
and Isabel known as Ida who finally got her hospital
where she operated, instructed, died at thirty-seven.
Only grass grows there now.

By Frances Corkey Thompson
from *Wild Gooseberries of Hailung*

APPENDIX
Working in Partnership with China Today

There are two ecumenical groups which do valuable work in partnership with several organisations in China, particularly the Amity Foundation. Amity, which was established by the initiative of Christians in China in 1985, is one of the earliest, and one of the leading, Non-Governmental Organisations there.

Friends of the Church in China

The Friends of the Church in China has built up close links with the country's Protestant and Catholic communities. Its activities include study visits and the chance of participating in other China opportunities, such as the Amity Summer English Teaching Programme. The FCC also sponsors Amity members of staff to come to Britain to improve their knowledge of English.

The FCC supports a wide variety of educational, social welfare and development projects. One of these is the Amity's Orphans Programme in China. The children chosen have been orphaned for many reasons, including parents having died from contracting HIV/Aids. On an FCC visit, Helen and I saw the positive work being done by this programme in Henan. It is especially in view of the assistance that Marion and other missionaries gave to support orphans in the 1930s, that we are contributing the royalties from this book towards the Amity Orphans Programme.

Further information can be found on the website www.thefcc.org.

The Scottish Churches' China Group

The Scottish Churches' China Group (SCCG) works in partnership with both Christian and secular organisations in China, focussing on health, general and religious education. It also aims to increase understanding, in Scotland, of poorly reported dimensions of Chinese society.

The SCCG particularly supports work in Shenyang, formerly Moukden, which was the centre of the Scottish and Irish Presbyterian missions. Among its projects are supporting the development of spiritual care services for the terminally ill in Shengjiing Hospital and through the Roman Catholic Caritas Centre. Shengjing Hospital is the successor to the missionary hospital. The SCCG also assists the Amity Development Centre for Children, in Nanjing, and Amity's Care of the Elderly programme.

The SCCG has both arranged for Chinese staff involved in these programmes to travel to Scotland to see examples of good practice, and for Scottish specialists to visit China to undertake training there.

More information can be found on the website: www.sccg.org.uk.

BIBLIOGRAPHY

Colin Corkey, *Letters from China: Letters Home from Manchuria to Culnady*, privately published (2005).

Frances Corkey Thompson, *Wild Gooseberries of Hailung,* Indigo Dreams Publishing (2015).

Peter Crush, *Imperial Railways of North China*, Xinhau Publishing House (2013).

Austin Fulton, *Through Earthquake, Wind and Fire*, The St Andrew Press (1967).

Mamie Johnston, *I Remember it Well*, Presbyterian Church in Ireland (1981)

Laurence Kirkpatrick, *Presbyterians in Ireland*, Booklink (2006).

Laurence Kirkpatrick, *Made in China*, Manleys (2008).

Michael Meyer, *In Manchuria*, Bloomsbury Press (2015).

Rana Mitter, *China's War with Japan 1937-1945*, Allen Lane (2013).

Frances Moffett, *I Also Am of Ireland*, Aerial Books/BBC (1985).

T. Ralph Morton, *Today in Manchuria: The Young Church in Crisis*, Student Christian Movement Press (1939).

T. Ralph Morton, *China the Teacher*, privately published (2000).

F.W. S. O'Neill, *Dr Isabel Mitchell of Manchuria*, James Clarke & Co (1918).

F.W. S. O'Neill, *The Quest for God in China*, George Allen & Unwin (1925).

Mark O'Neill, *Frederick: The Life of my Missionary Grandfather,* Joint Publishing Co. (2012).

Audrey Salters, *Bound with Love: Letters Home from China*, Agequod Publications (2007).

Rosemary Seton, *Western Daughters in Eastern Lands: British Women Missionaries in India*, Praeger (2013).

Edgar Snow, *Red Star Over China*, Left Book Club/Victor Gollanz (1937).

William S. Upchurch, *A Prevailing Wind*, privately published (2007).

Jack Weir, 'China' in *Into All the World*, (Ed. Jack Thompson) Presbyterian Church of Ireland (1990).

Woman's Work (the magazine of the Irish Presbyterian Church Women's Association for Foreign Missions), 1936 -1949.

INDEX

The topics included within the index all relate to China, Japan and Korea. Pages with relevant illustrations are in italics.

Manchukuo:

    Establishment by Japanese, 25, *97*

    'Foreign Office', *377*

    Lytton Commission, 41, 376

    New Capital, 60

    Pui Yi, Emperor, *25*, 60, 120

    Residency Certificate, *69*

Mongolians, 26, 240, 295-296-297

Mukden Incident (1931) 25

Muslims (Mohammadens), 30, 250

New Year and Other Festivals, 99, 106, 168, 212

People:

For those people Marion met in Faku, on the Bible School journeys and elsewhere in Manchuria, the references are to when they are first recorded and then to certain other mentions, as well as to the illustrations they appear in.

In Faku:

    Chang, Miss, 118-*119*, 207

    Ch'ang, Dr, 166, *196*

    Cha'ng, Miss, *196*

    Chang Te Eu, *167*, *271*

    Dalgleish, Mabel, *286*, 291-*292*, 313, 345

    Fang, Elder, 103-105

    Gilbert Edouard, 274-275, 301,309

    Gow and wife, 86-87

    Hammill, Mary, 137, *140*, 173, *212*, 291